Hobbes on Justice

THE HISTORY AND THEORY OF INTERNATIONAL LAW

General Editors

NEHAL BHUTA
Chair in International Law, University of Edinburgh

FRANCESCA IURLARO
Max Planck Institute for Comparative and International Private Law Hamburg

ANTHONY PAGDEN
Distinguished Professor, University of California Los Angeles

BENJAMIN STRAUMANN
ERC Professor of History, University of Zurich

In the past few decades, the understanding of the relationship between nations has undergone a radical transformation. The role of the traditional nation-state is diminishing, along with many of the traditional vocabularies that were once used to describe what has been called, ever since Jeremy Bentham coined the phrase in 1780, 'international law'. The older boundaries between states are growing ever more fluid. New conceptions and new languages have emerged that are slowly coming to replace the image of a world of sovereign independent nation states that has dominated the study of international relations since the early nineteenth century. This redefinition of the international arena demands a new understanding of classical and contemporary questions in international and legal theory. It is the editors' conviction that the best way to achieve this is by bridging the traditional divide between international legal theory, intellectual history, and legal and political history. The aim of the series, therefore, is to provide a forum for historical studies, from classical antiquity to the twenty-first century, that are theoretically informed and for philosophical work that is historically conscious, in the hope that a new vision of the rapidly evolving international world, its past and its possible future, may emerge.

PREVIOUSLY PUBLISHED IN THIS SERIES

A Century of Anarchy?
War, Normativity, and the Birth of Modern International Order
Hendrik Simon

The Individual in International Law
Anne Peters, Tom Sparks

Pufendorf's International Political and Legal Thought
Peter Schröder

Victims
Perceptions of Harm in Modern European War and Violence
Svenja Goltermann

Sovereignty, International Law, and the Princely States of Colonial South Asia
Priyasha Saksena

Sepúlveda on the Spanish Invasion of the Americas
Defending Empire, Debating Las Casas
Luke Glanville, David Lupher, Maya Feile Tomes

Hobbes on Justice

JOHAN OLSTHOORN

*Associate Professor of Political Theory, Department of Politics,
University of Amsterdam, the Netherlands*

OXFORD
UNIVERSITY PRESS

Great Clarendon Street, Oxford, OX2 6DP,
United Kingdom

Oxford University Press is a department of the University of Oxford.
It furthers the University's objective of excellence in research, scholarship,
and education by publishing worldwide. Oxford is a registered trade mark of
Oxford University Press in the UK and in certain other countries

© Johan Olsthoorn 2024

The moral rights of the author have been asserted

All rights reserved. No part of this publication may be reproduced, stored in a retrieval system, transmitted, used for text and data mining, or used for training artificial intelligence, in any form or by any means, without the prior permission in writing of Oxford University Press, or as expressly permitted by law, by licence or under terms agreed with the appropriate reprographics rights organization. Enquiries concerning reproduction outside the scope of the above should be sent to the Rights Department, Oxford University Press, at the address above.

You must not circulate this work in any other form
and you must impose this same condition on any acquirer

Public sector information reproduced under Open Government Licence v3.0
(https://www.nationalarchives.gov.uk/doc/open-government-licence)

Published in the United States of America by Oxford University Press
198 Madison Avenue, New York, NY 10016, United States of America

British Library Cataloguing in Publication Data

Data available

Library of Congress Control Number: 2024943015

ISBN 9780198867982

DOI: 10.1093/9780191904585.001.0001

Printed and bound by
CPI Group (UK) Ltd, Croydon, CR0 4YY

Series Editor's Preface

Thomas Hobbes is famous for his theory of sovereignty. It is well known that Hobbes defended a doctrine where the huge gulf between a very unpleasant and violent state of nature and peaceful political order could only be bridged by submission to an absolute sovereign, a sovereign not subject to any other human power. Sovereignty on this view provided the only possible exit from the violence of the state of nature, the only entry ticket to a realm of order and peace to be had. This realm of order and peace was the state and its distinguishing feature was sovereignty: the authority to establish peace within the state and a common defence against other states. The nature of this authority is tantalizingly difficult to grasp, and its oscillations have led to an incredible amount of scholarship.

The oscillations begin with the important fact that sovereignty for Hobbes is a kind of authority, not mere power; sovereignty must be absolute in the sense of not being subject to any higher human authority, yet its foundation, according to Hobbes, lies in consent, and necessarily so: only consent can create and give legitimacy to the political order, but what precisely it is we can be assumed to have consented to has been debated by scholars for a very long time. Suffice it to say that Hobbes's theory of sovereignty has been both interpreted as a precursor to totalitarianism and celebrated as the progenitor of liberalism.[1]

Given the nastiness of the state of nature, Hobbes believed that it would be irrational for its inhabitants not to give up almost all of their natural liberty in order to gain peace and 'commodious living' and thus to bestow a very far-reaching authority on the sovereign—but at the same time, the fact that this authority was thought to be based ultimately on the consent of subjects, who were conceived as equals, opened the door to a liberal interpretation of Hobbes where he is seen as introducing that most liberal criterion for legitimate rule, the consent of the governed. In addition, scholars more recently have pointed out that Hobbes, on pain of undermining the very purpose of his political theory, namely peace and material prosperity, was pushed to devise a sovereign authority which had to act through law: given the sovereign's *raison d'être*, namely the impartial adjudication of disputes and the making and enforcement of civil law, the state made possible by

---

[1] See Noel Malcolm, 'Thomas Hobbes: Liberal illiberal', *Journal of the British Academy* 4 (2016): 113–136.

vi SERIES EDITOR'S PREFACE

sovereign authority is a legal system, one that at times even starts resembling a proper *Rechtsstaat*.[2]

Johan Olsthoorn in the present monograph proposes to shift focus from sovereignty, which has been discussed very extensively, to Hobbes's theory of justice, which has not received anywhere near the same amount of scholarly attention. The shift from sovereignty to justice, it turns out, is consequential and manages to clarify a great many aspects of Hobbes's political theory that were hitherto hidden from view. Olsthoorn shows that Hobbes's concept of justice serves as the foundation on which Hobbes erects his political theory, for without this conception of justice, which serves as a demarcation criterion for what lies within the political realm and what lies beyond, Hobbes could not have developed his account of sovereignty in the first place.

Hobbes has been generally portrayed as a conventionalist about justice: justice is whatever we agree or the sovereign decides it is. Olsthoorn believes that this take on Hobbes's justice is true as far as it goes, but that Hobbes had provided a complex argument in favour of the conventionalist view, an argument that has not received the attention it deserves. Many commentators have noticed the Epicurean flavour of Hobbes's account of justice.[3] For Hobbes, as for Epicurus, justice is instrumental: a means to the end of peace. Everyone, Hobbes writes in *On the Citizen*, 'is assumed to be naturally after his own good; he seeks *Justice* only incidentally, for the sake of *peace*' (DCv 3.21). In Hobbes's *Leviathan*, this yields a definition of justice as consisting in the performance of contracts: 'the definition of INJUSTICE, is no other than *the not Performance of Covenant*. And whatsoever is not Unjust, is *Just*' (L 15.2). Epicurus similarly thought that 'nature's justice is a guarantee of utility with a view to not harming one another and not being harmed. Nothing is just or unjust in relation to those creatures which were unable to make contracts over not harming one another and not being harmed'.[4] But note that for both Epicurus and Hobbes, this conventionalism about justice required an account of why justice manages to create obligations via contract in the first place; of the extent to which contracts could create obligations; and of the conditions under which contracts could be said to be valid.

Olsthoorn demonstrates that once we put justice front and centre, there are new insights to be gained into Hobbes's political theory. Discussing Hobbes's developing views about justice from the early works to the mature edifice of the *Leviathan*, Olsthoorn gives us an overarching view of Hobbes's ideas driven by his reformulation of available theories of justice. This yields important new interpretations along the way: we learn that Hobbes entirely redefined distributive justice as equity, turning it into a non-enforceable virtue of the sovereign, albeit a virtue that

---

[2] David Dyzenhaus, *The Long Arc of Legality: Hobbes, Kelsen, Hart* (Cambridge, 2022), ch. 2.

[3] E.g. Bernd Ludwig, *Die Wiederentdeckung des Epikureischen Naturrechts* (Frankfurt a.M., 1998).

[4] A.A. Long and D.N. Sedley, *The Hellenistic Philosophers*, vol. 1 (Cambridge, 1987) 125.

places important procedural constraints on the sovereign and 'orders the sovereign to treat citizens impartially, as equals, when apportioning goods'. The impartiality of distributive justice, we learn, is necessitated by Hobbes's agnosticism about differential worth of human beings. Turning the Aristotelian notion of distributive justice on its head, Hobbes declares merit to be the outcome, not the yardstick, of distributive justice: one merits whatever it is one gets.

This has important consequences for the concept of private property, which can now in the *Leviathan* be conceptualized as created entirely by the sovereign and thus constituted by distributive justice. Thus created out of nothing, property serves as the yardstick for another, more central, kind of justice: commutative justice, the justice of contracts, which creates rights and corresponding duties among citizens. Commutative justice is enforced within the state and thus demarcates the realm of peace and enforcement from the state of nature. Olsthoorn reminds us that this conceptual matrix ensures that the sovereign cannot be accused of injustice, only of iniquity, which is not justiciable. Still, some natural rights are retained in the state, those 'without which a man cannot live, or not live well', such as the 'right to governe their owne bodies' and Hobbes's inalienable right par excellence: self-preservation (L 15.22).

We learn, further, that a focus on justice can shed new light on the old debate as to whether Hobbes was a natural lawyer or a legal positivist. Olsthoorn argues that 'Hobbes's conception of civil law is moralized in two ways' and hence non-positivist. This is because Hobbes does not think that law depends on social facts alone, but rather believes that 'moral analysis is needed to establish whether a particular command by the sovereign is binding law to some citizen'. In addition, Olsthoorn argues that Hobbes posited an 'ineliminable connection between law and injustice', thus violating the positivist stricture that there be no necessary connection between law and morality. This brings to the fore an interesting tension in Hobbes's thought: whereas civil laws can never be unjust, it may well turn out, on moral reflection, that a particular command by the sovereign—decreeing something I could not have rationally promised to do or undergo—is no law to me and cannot therefore oblige me.

Finally, we learn that Hobbes's theory of justice, driven by concerns of domestic peace and political order, had important implications for the international realm. Hobbes clearly believed that covenants in the state of nature were fragile but under certain conditions possible and obviously beneficial. However, since justice presupposes civil law for epistemic no less than enforcement reasons, the very possibility of injustices committed by sovereigns vis-à-vis other sovereigns in the international state of nature is excluded. This leaves room, Olsthoorn suggests, for a theory of just defensive war for the sake of self-preservation. Since the criteria for what counts as self-protection are up to each sovereign, this subjectivizes these criteria and even 'objectively disastrous actions are performed rightfully if done for the sake of self-protection', Olsthoorn writes.

viii SERIES EDITOR'S PREFACE

But what if the sovereign is not entitled to its judgement call, what if objectively disastrous actions are imprudent and tend to self-destruction? Hobbes would have to say that such a sovereign falls afoul of natural law, while insisting that this constitutes no injustice.[5] Still, we might think that sovereigns, qua artificial persons and lawmakers, might be in a better epistemic position than individuals are in the state of nature, precisely because they have already established legal order domestically—sovereigns, that is, might harbour the resources to hew more closely to the prudential demands of natural law than individuals ever could, by Hobbes's own lights.[6] Olsthoorn might or might not deny this, but in any case insists that when it comes to *rights* in the state of nature, Hobbes's '*international* rights of war' can be constrained no better than individual ones: sovereigns can simply not be accused of waging unjust wars because the law of nations, which is the law of nature, binds sovereigns in conscience only. This does not turn Hobbes into a reason-of-state thinker, however: 'Hobbes's principles of international ethics exclusively concern defence against external enemies, rather than pursuit of national interest generally.'

This book, with great ambition, learnedness, and precision, succeeds in giving us a new view of Hobbes via his theory of justice. This theory determines when natural law binds and when it doesn't and we are now in a position to see more clearly the relationship between justice and natural law, a relationship driven by the two radical axiomatic assumptions Hobbes puts forward: that human beings are naturally equal; and that we should seek peace. Justice is 'a precondition for peace and self-preservation' and therefore can only create obligations that stick once natural rights of private judgement give way to the legal order of sovereignty. To find out how Hobbes reached his conclusions about justice by arguing from plausible and widely endorsed premises, we now can turn to Johan Olsthoorn's great book.

Benjamin Straumann
Zurich, 18 June, 2024

---

[5] For the required understanding of the laws of nature as causal laws, see Jean Hampton, 'Hobbes and Ethical Naturalism', *Philosophical Perspectives* 6 (1992): 333–353.

[6] Benjamin Straumann, 'Thucydides, Hobbes, and the Melian Dialogue' in Mark Somos and Anne Peters (eds), *The State of Nature: Histories of an Idea* (Leiden, 2021) 6–27.

Acknowledgements

In his autobiographical *Verse Life*, Hobbes remarked that composing *De Corpore* 'prov'd a constant War' to him (VL 260). I felt much the same when working on this book. Countless times I felt overwhelmed by the task I had set myself: reconstructing in full the conceptual and argumentative foundations of Hobbes's theory of justice. The challenge of producing a coherent and original reading, amidst a daunting and ever-growing library of secondary literature, at times paralysed me. More than once I set aside the project, for long stretches on end, to work on more rewarding academic projects. Articles on Hobbes I can handle and finish. A monograph the size of ten articles, I learned to my dismay, makes for unending toil and frustration. Sorting out one philosophical puzzle often revealed as untenable the very interpretive assumptions upon which all earlier chapters were based. Parts of this monograph rework previously published material. Quite a few interpretive claims advanced in those publications I now consider to be at least partially mistaken. Not vain enough to imagine readers will care about how exactly my current reading relates to earlier published ones, I have left my interpretive turnarounds unflagged.

This book was written in three stages. Though little of it has survived the various rounds of rewriting, the foundations were laid during my PhD, funded by research grants from the KU Leuven (2009–2010) and the FWO-Research Foundation Flanders (2010–2014). During the second stage, funded by an FWO postdoctoral research fellowship (2016–2018), I turned to just war and interstate morality and secured a book contract with OUP. The third and seemingly interminable stage was interrupted by breakdowns of various kinds (global, academic, motivational) (2021–2024). I am grateful to Kim Vollrodt and her team at OUP as well as to the editors of this series (especially Benjamin Straumann) for their patience and support—and do apologize for having missed so many deadlines.

Numerous debts were incurred during each writing stage. Thanks goes out to my PhD supervisors (Helder De Schutter, Eric Schliesser) and external examiner (Stephen Darwall) for their encouragement, guidance, and mentorship. My PhD and postdoctoral research were conducted at the Institute of Philosophy, KU Leuven. Its centre for political philosophy (RIPPLE) provided me with a hospitable and stimulating research environment for over a decade. My current institutional home—the University of Amsterdam, Department of Politics—has proven equally welcoming. Research on this monograph has further benefited from a teaching spell at the LSE, Department of Government (2014–2015), as well as from several shorter visiting research stays at Yale (2011); Queen Mary University of

London (2012); King's College London (2014); UC Berkeley (2016); and Boston University (2016). Many thanks to Stephen Darwall; Quentin Skinner; Adrian Blau; Kinch Hoekstra; and Susanne Sreedhar for hosting me and for enlightening conversations.

My deepest intellectual debts are to Robin Douglass and Laurens van Apeldoorn. They have commented on the entire manuscript—and numerous earlier drafts— with astonishing precision, care, and erudition. Many thanks as well to other members of the *European Hobbes Society*, past and present, with whom I have spent so many days and nights discussing Hobbes: Adrian Blau; Dirk Brantl; Mónica Brito Vieira; Gonzalo Bustamante Kuschel; Elad Carmel; Alexandra Chadwick; Hrvoje Cvijanović; Daniel Eggers; Mauro Farnesi Camellone; Signy Gutnick Allen; Ryan Harding; Elliott Karstadt; Eva Odzuck; Joanne Paul; Francesca Rebasti; Luka Ribarević; Dietrich Schotte; Gabriella Slomp; and Luciano Venezia.

Over the years, many other academics have been kind enough to provide feedback and pushback on my ongoing struggle with Hobbes. To name only those that come to mind: Arash Abizadeh; Marcus Adams; Deborah Baumgold; Donald Bello Hutt; Rudmer Bijlsma; Allan Cardoso dos Santos; Alan Cromartie; Eleanor Curran; Hannah Dawson; David Dyzenhaus; Ioannis Evrigenis; Luc Foisneau; Thomas Fossen; Aaron Garrett; Ursula Goldenbaum; Michael J. Green; Heikki Haara; Kinch Hoekstra; Ben Holland; Matthew Hoye; Max Jaede; Susan James; David Johnston; Sungho Kimlee; Michael LeBuffe; Daniel Lee; Juhana Lemetti; Sharon Lloyd; Michael Lobban; Jan Machielsen; Alissa MacMillan; Al Martinich; Lodi Nauta; Eric Nelson; Thomas Pink; Thomas Poole; Laetitia Ramelet; Katherine Robiadek; Enzo Rossi; David Runciman; Kari Saastamoinen; Paul Sagar; Peter Schröder; Quentin Skinner; Max Skjönsberg; Johann Sommerville; Patricia Springborg; Susanne Sreedhar; Benjamin Straumann; Tim Stuart-Buttle; Mikko Tolonen; Jo Van Cauter; Guus van Nifterik; Rosemarie Wagner; Matthijs Wibier; Robert Jan Witpaard; and George Wright.

A book manuscript workshop at the University of Amsterdam, funded by the Research School in Philosophy (OZSW), provided plenty of useful feedback. I am deeply grateful to all invited commentators: Arash Abizadeh; Robin Douglass; Daniel Eggers; Signy Gutnick Allen; James Harris; Rebecca Ploof; Meghan Robison; and Laurens van Apeldoorn. Earlier versions of chapters included in this monograph have been presented at academic events at the following universities: Amsterdam (2011, 2019); Athens (2012); Belo Horizonte (2013); Bucharest (2010); Dubrovnik (2021); Erlangen-Nürnberg (2016); Groningen (2022); Harvard (2013); King's College London (2012, 2014); LSE (2014, 2015); Manchester (2010, 2011); Marburg (2011); Princeton (2014); Queen Mary (2012, 2017); Rome (2021); Rotterdam (2013); and St Andrews (2018). In addition, I have presented stand-alone papers on Hobbes at several other academic venues, enhancing my general understanding of his thought: Berkeley (2016); Boston (2016); EUI (2017); Ghent (2015); Grenoble (2013); Jilin (2019); Mainz

(2013); Manchester (2009); Nijmegen (2014); San Diego (2011); Santiago (2019); and York (2018). Many thanks to the organizers and attendees of all these seminars, workshops, conferences, and roundtables for constructive comments and searching critiques. I am grateful to Allan Cardoso dos Santos for providing meticulous research assistance during copy-editing.

Lastly, I thank my loving wife, friends, and family for reminding me that, in some ways, a finished book is better than a flawless one.

Contents

Abbreviations   xvii

PART I. INTRODUCTION

1. VINDICATING THE 'MORTALL GOD'   3
   INTRODUCTION   3
   1.1 THE CONVENTIONALIST INTERPRETATION   5
   1.2 A CIVIL THEODICY   8
   1.3 THE PLACE OF JUSTICE IN HOBBES'S PHILOSOPHY   15
   1.4 A WORD ON METHOD   17

PART II. BASIC MORAL CONCEPTS

2. JUSTICE, RIGHTS, AND INJURY   29
   INTRODUCTION   29
   2.1 INJURY AS AN ACTION WITHOUT RIGHT   32
   2.2 JUSTICE, INJUSTICE, AND INJURY   36
   2.3 TURNING INJURY AND INJUSTICE INTO DIRECTED
        CONCEPTS   39
   2.4 INJURY AND LOSS   44
   2.5 ABSOLUTE NATURAL FREEDOM   49
   CONCLUSION   54

3. JUSTICE AND NATURAL LAW   56
   INTRODUCTION   56
   3.1 ARE NATURAL LAW DUTIES MERELY PRUDENTIAL?   58
   3.2 SINNING WITH RIGHT   63
   3.3 UNTRACEABLE INTENTIONS   65
   3.4 NO ACCUSATION WITHOUT LAW   71
   3.5 NATURAL LAW, DIVINE LAW, AND CIVIL LAW   74
   3.6 NATURAL LAW DUTIES OF CITIZENS   78
   3.7 THE VIRTUE OF JUSTICE   83
   CONCLUSION   86

PART III. JUSTICE WITHIN THE STATE

4. DISTRIBUTIVE JUSTICE AND EQUITY   89
   INTRODUCTION   89
   4.1 COMMUTATIVE AND DISTRIBUTIVE JUSTICE   90

xiv CONTENTS

4.2 EQUITY 94
4.3 EQUALITY 99
4.4 VINDICATING SOVEREIGN MALDISTRIBUTIONS 101
4.5 MERIT 104
4.6 EQUITY AS PROCEDURAL JUSTICE 110
CONCLUSION 115

5. JUSTICE AND PROPERTY 116
INTRODUCTION 116
5.1 WHY *MINE* AND *THINE* PRESUPPOSE THE STATE 118
5.2 ENFORCING THE JUSTICE OF CONTRACTORS 122
5.3 PRIVATE PROPERTY AS *PECULIUM* 126
5.4 FROM DISTRIBUTIVE LAWS TO DISTRIBUTIVE JUSTICE 131
5.5 THE CREATIVE JUSTICE OF ARBITRATORS 135
5.6 THE STATUS AND LIMITS OF PROPERTY IN ONESELF 139
CONCLUSION 143

6. JUSTICE AND CIVIL LAW 145
INTRODUCTION 145
6.1 LEGAL POSITIVISM 146
6.2 CIVIL LAW AND SOVEREIGN PREROGATIVE 149
6.3 CIVIL LAW AS THE PUBLIC MEASURE OF JUSTICE OF
ACTIONS 153
6.4 ARE ALL CIVIL LAWS JUST? 157
6.5 CAN CIVIL LAWS CONTRADICT NATURAL LAW? 161
6.6 WHY AND IN WHAT SENSE CIVIL LAW CANNOT
BE UNJUST 165
6.7 WHY HOBBES WAS NO LEGAL POSITIVIST 172
CONCLUSION 175

PART IV. JUSTICE OUTSIDE THE STATE

7. NO PEACE, NO JUSTICE 179
INTRODUCTION 179
7.1 THE (REVISED) COVENANT ARGUMENT 182
7.2 JUSTICE BEFORE *LEVIATHAN* 188
7.3 THE PROPRIETY ARGUMENT 191
CONCLUSION 196

8. RIGHTS OF WAR 198
INTRODUCTION 198
8.1 JUSTIFYING VIOLENCE 200
8.2 RADICALIZING RIGHTS OF SELF-DEFENCE 205
8.3 (BEYOND) PREVENTIVE WAR 210
8.4 CHARITY AND THE RIGHT-INTENTION REQUIREMENT 213
8.5 JUST FEAR, DISTRUST, AND NATURAL ENMITY 215
CONCLUSION 221

9. MORALITY AMONG STATES — 223

INTRODUCTION — 223
9.1 STATES OF WAR — 225
9.2 NATURALIZING THE LAW OF NATIONS — 227
9.3 THE ASSIMILATION ARGUMENT — 230
9.4 THE OFFICE OF THE SOVEREIGN — 233
9.5 INTERNALIZING THE LAW OF NATIONS — 236
CONCLUSION — 240

10. REBELS, TRAITORS, ENEMIES, AND FOOLS — 242

INTRODUCTION — 242
10.1 'THE HIGHEST CRIME OF ALL' — 244
10.2 REBELLIOUS SUBJECTS AND/OR ENEMIES? — 247
10.3 BEYOND THE LEGAL ORDER... — 252
10.4 ...YET WITHIN THE REALM OF JUSTICE — 256
10.5 THE FOOL CONSIDERS COMMITTING TREASON — 258
CONCLUSION — 261

PART V. A REVIEW AND CONCLUSION

11. THE 'MORTALL GOD' VINDICATED — 265

Bibliography — 271
Index — 289

Abbreviations

The following abbreviations are used for works by Hobbes:

AW   *Thomas White's De Mundo Examined* [c.1643], transl. Harold Whitmore Jones (London: Bradford University Press, 1976)

B   *Behemoth, or The Long Parliament* [1679], ed. Paul Seaward (Oxford: Clarendon Press, 2010)

DCv *On the Citizen* [1642, 1647], ed. Richard Tuck, transl. Michael Silverthorne (Cambridge: Cambridge University Press, 1998)

DH   'De Homine' [1658] in *Man and Citizen*, ed. Bernard Gert (Indianapolis: Hackett, 1991) 33–85

DPS 'A Dialogue between a Philosopher and a Student, of the Common Laws of England' [1681] in *Writings on Common Law and Hereditary Right*, ed. Alan Cromartie and Quentin Skinner (Oxford: Clarendon Press, 2005) 1–146

EL   *The Elements of Law, Natural and Politic: Part I, Human Nature, Part II, De Corpore Politico* [1640], ed. J.C.A. Gaskin (Oxford: Oxford University Press, 1994)

EW   *The English Works of Thomas Hobbes of Malmesbury*, 10 vols, ed. William Molesworth (London: John Bohn, 1839–1845)

HE   *Historia Ecclesiastica* [1688], ed. and transl. Patricia Springborg, Patricia Stablein, and Paul Wilson (Paris: Honoré Champion, 2008)

L   *Leviathan: The English and Latin Texts* [1651], 3 vols, ed. Noel Malcolm (Oxford: Clarendon Press, 2012)

LL   Latin *Leviathan* [1668] in *Leviathan*, ed. Malcolm

LLA 'Appendix to the Latin *Leviathan*' [1668] in *Leviathan*, ed. Malcolm, pp. 1142–1243

OL   *Opera Philosophica quae Latine Scripsit*, 5 vols, ed. William Molesworth (London: John Bohn, 1839–1845)

VL   'The Verse Life' in *The Elements of Law*, ed. Gaskin, pp. 254–264

References to L and LL are by chapter and paragraph number. This should allow readers to find the cited passage in any of the many available editions of *Leviathan*. References to AW, DCv, DH, and EL are by chapter and section numbers. References to B and DPS are by original page number (included in the Clarendon editions). References to EW and OL are by volume and page number. All other works by Hobbes are cited by page number of the edition used.

The following short titles are used for frequently cited works by other historical authors. Citation methods follow convention.

xviii ABBREVIATIONS

De Jure Belli	Alberico Gentili, *De Jure Belli Libri Tres* [1589], 2 vols, ed. John C. Rolfe (Oxford: Clarendon Press, 1933)
De Legibus	Francisco Suárez, 'De Legibus ac Deo Legislatore' [1612] in *Suárez: Selections from Three Works*, ed. Thomas Pink (Indianapolis: Liberty Fund, 2015)
Digest	*The Digest of Justinian*, 4 vols, ed. Alan Watson (Philadelphia: University of Pennsylvania Press, 1985)
Institutes	*Justinian's Institutes*, ed. Peter Birks and Grant McLeod (London: Duckworth, 1987)
Jus Gentium	Christian Wolff, *Jus Gentium Methodo Scientifica Pertractatum* [1749], 2 vols, ed. Joseph H. Drake (Oxford: Clarendon Press, 1934)
Law of Nations	Emer de Vattel, *The Law of Nations* [1758], ed. Béla Kapossy and Richard Whatmore (Indianapolis: Liberty Fund, 2008)
Nature and Nations	Samuel Pufendorf, *Of the Law of Nature and Nations* [1672], transl. B Kennett (London: J. Walthoe, 1729)
Nicomachean Ethics	Aristotle, *Nicomachean Ethics*, ed. Roger Crisp (Cambridge: Cambridge University Press, 2000)
On Duties	Cicero, *On Duties*, ed. M.T. Griffin and E.M. Atkins (Cambridge: Cambridge University Press, 1991)
Politics	Aristotle, 'The Politics' in *The Politics and the Constitution of Athens*, ed. Stephen Everson (Cambridge: Cambridge University Press, 1996) 11–207
Second Treatise	John Locke, 'Second Treatise of Government' [1690] in *Locke: Two Treatises of Government*, ed. Peter Laslett (Cambridge: Cambridge University Press, 1988) 265–428
Six Books	Jean Bodin, *The Six Bookes of a Commonweale* [1606], ed. Kenneth Douglas McRae (Cambridge, MA: Harvard University Press, 1962)
Summa Theologica	Thomas Aquinas, *Summa Theologica: Dominican Edition*, 22 vols, transl. Fathers of the English Dominican Province (London: Burns, Oates and Benziger, second and revised edition, 1912–1936)
The Peloponnesian War	Thucydides, *The Peloponnesian War*, ed. and transl. Steven Lattimore (Indianapolis: Hackett, 1998)
The Republic	Cicero, 'The Republic' in *The Republic and the Laws*, ed. Jonathan Powell, transl. Niall Rudd (Oxford: Oxford University Press, 1998) 1–94
Treatise	Richard Cumberland, *A Treatise of the Laws of Nature* [1672], ed. Jon Parkin (Indianapolis: Liberty Fund, 2005)
War and Peace	Hugo Grotius, *The Rights of War and Peace* [1625], 3 vols, ed. Richard Tuck (Indianapolis: Liberty Fund, 2005)

The following named doctrines and arguments are discussed in this book. The ones marked with an asterisk (*) scholars have wrongfully attributed to Hobbes. The ones marked with a dagger (†) Hobbes initially endorsed but later came to reject.

Doctrines:	Arguments:
*All Laws Just	Allotment
Citizenship Forfeiture	†Assimilation
†Collective Victimhood	Authorization
Mutual Containment Thesis	†Consent
No Law Unjust	*Covenant
*No Wicked Laws	Creation
*Separability Thesis	†Liberality
Sinning with Right	Merit-Grace
Sole Measure	No Accusation without Law
*Sources Thesis	No Pact
Statism about Justice	Precision
Statism about Property	Propriety
	Revised Covenant
	Security
	Untraceable Intentions

Spelling

Spelling, capitalization, and punctuation follow the conventions in the editions cited. Rounded and pointed forms of 'u' and 'v' have been modernized, however. In-text Latin spellings of *jus* and its cognates have been standardized as written with a 'j'. To retain continuity between Hobbes's quotations and my paraphrases, 'he' and 'him' are used throughout to refer to the sovereign. I trust readers will not forget that women and assemblies can hold sovereignty as well.

Emphasis

Any <u>underlining</u> in quotations has been added by me, to emphasize key clauses or phrases. Any *italics* in quotations is in the original.Internal cross-referencesInternal cross-references of the form '§[chapter].[section]' direct readers to other parts of this book for further discussion of the point in question.

PART I
INTRODUCTION

1

VINDICATING THE 'MORTALL GOD'

INTRODUCTION

And men, it seems, are more passionate for injustice, than for violence[1]

Legend has it that on a windy autumn day in 1532, a horse trader from Berlin was stopped on his way to Leipzig at a tollgate near Düben, Saxony. Servants of a local nobleman ordered the merchant to obtain a transit pass in faraway Dresden, keeping hold of his two horses in the meantime. Upon his return, the horse trader discovered to his horror that the nobleman had utterly ruined his horses through hard fieldwork and severely mutilated the protesting groom (left behind to attend to the animals). Refusing to bow to such blatant injustices, for two long years, the horse trader pursued every legal path to procure compensation. Finding legal justice thwarted at every turn by the corrupt local elite, he eventually initiated a private war against the abusive nobleman to recover his due by force. Leading an army of deprived peasants, the horse trader terrorized the countryside for years, burning villages and razing cloisters. His vendetta continued even after Martin Luther personally told him off. Apprehended at last by the authorities, the horse trader died at the rake in March 1540. Immortalized in Heinrich von Kleist's 1810 eponymous novella, Hans Kohlhase embodies personal justice pursued to excess.[2] His story also tells of the extremes to which unjust treatment can move people. The passion for justice can be powerful and politically destabilizing indeed.

The English philosopher Thomas Hobbes (1588–1679) was acutely aware of the threats religious and political ideologies can pose to civil peace. Many '*Diseases* of a Common-wealth', he observed, 'proceed from the poyson of seditious doctrines' (L 29.6).[3] His earliest political treatise lists three conditions that must obtain for subjects to be incited to rebel. Besides present discontent and hope of success, seditious dispositions require 'pretence of right; for though a man be discontented, yet if in his own opinion there be no just cause of stirring against, or resisting the government established, nor any pretence to justify his resistance, and to procure

---

[1] EW 8: 84 (= Thucydides, *The Peloponnesian War*, 1.77).

[2] Heinrich von Kleist, *Michael Kohlhaas*, ed. Axel Schmitt (Berlin, 2013). Just before the German peasant wars, Machiavelli warned princes not to commit injuries against citizens. 'Because if a man is greatly injured' by the state, 'he is never quiet until in some way he has avenged himself'—even if this means his own downfall or the republic's. Machiavelli, 'Discorsi' in *The Chief Works and Others*, vol. 1, ed. Allan Gilbert (Durham, 1989) 2.28.

[3] On the motivational power and political import of such 'transcendental interests', see S.A. Lloyd, *Ideals as Interests in Hobbes's Leviathan* (Cambridge, 1992).

Hobbes on Justice. Johan Olsthoorn, Oxford University Press. © Johan Olsthoorn 2024.
DOI: 10.1093/9780191904585.003.0001

4   VINDICATING THE 'MORTALL GOD'

aid, he will never show it' (EL 27.1; also EL 27.14; DCv 12.11).[4] To promote domestic peace, the government should suppress all ideological pretexts for revolt, including claims of mistreatment that could inflame disgruntled subjects.

Hobbes realized this irenic objective in a startlingly novel way. Contemporary thinkers denouncing rebellion generally conceded the obvious truth that political rulers can govern unjustly, while insisting that citizens should suffer rather than resist these injustices.[5] Martin Luther (1483–1546), for instance, presumably admonished Hans Kohlhase that 'superiors are not to be resisted by force'. Christian subjects should refuse to carry out any legal order to commit evil. Yet they are obliged to 'suffer injustice' from their divinely ordained rulers.[6] Even punishment imposed for refusing to comply with wicked commands must be patiently endured. Jean Bodin (c.1530–1596) concurred. Subjects are required to suffer whatever hardships legitimately instituted absolute rulers inflict upon them, 'yeah and death also'. They must 'patiently borne all his wickednesse and outrages'.[7] In the same vein, Samuel Pufendorf (1632–1694) decreed: 'If a King or a Senate ordain evil Laws, execute wrong Judgment, appoint unfit Magistrates, or undertake unjust Wars', then subjects must undergo 'these publick Crimes ... with the same Patience as we do extreme Drought, or immoderate Rain'.[8] Immanuel Kant (1724–1804) joined the chorus a century later: 'a people has a duty to put up with even what is held to be an unbearable abuse of supreme authority'.[9]

Hobbes chose a different path, more radical and ostensibly less promising. He boldly attempted to vindicate the sovereign from all stains of injustice. However heinous his commands, nothing the sovereign says or does can be unjust towards his citizens: 'whatsoever he doth, it can be no injury to any of his Subjects; nor ought he to be by any of them accused of Injustice' (L 18.6). Citizens cannot possibly have justified grievances against government. This stunning doctrine holds true not only for saintly rulers. It would have applied also to Nero and Caligula. Hobbes's blunt denial of the possibility of sovereign injustice has been called a 'major innovation', unprecedented among earlier political absolutists.[10] The boldness of this thesis is only reinforced by the sovereign's near total power, 'as great,

---

[4] S.A. Lloyd, *Morality in the Philosophy of Thomas Hobbes* (Cambridge, 2009) 88–94, 249–251, 314, takes this passage to be indicative of a more general human desire to justify oneself to others—an additional source of normativity in Hobbes's ethics.

[5] Johann Sommerville, 'Hobbes and Absolutism' in A.P. Martinich and Kinch Hoekstra (eds), *The Oxford Handbook of Hobbes* (Oxford, 2016) 390.

[6] Martin Luther, 'On Secular Authority' in *Luther and Calvin on Secular Authority*, ed. Harro Höpfl (Cambridge, 1991) 39, also 29. For discussion, see Quentin Skinner, *The Foundations of Modern Political Thought*, vol. 2 (Cambridge, 1978) 15–19.

[7] Bodin, *Six Books*, 224–225.

[8] Pufendorf, *Nature and Nations*, 7.2.14. Also Grotius, *War and Peace*, 1.4.1.

[9] Immanuel Kant, *Practical Philosophy*, ed. M.J. Gregor (Cambridge, 1996) 463. Also e.g. John Bramhall, 'The Catching of Leviathan, or the Great Whale' in G.A.J. Rogers (ed), *Leviathan: Contemporary Responses to the Political Theory of Thomas Hobbes* (Bristol, 1995) 136.

[10] Johann Sommerville, *Thomas Hobbes: Political Ideas in Historical Context* (London, 1992) 104.

as possibly men can be imagined to make it': absolute power provides unlimited scope for corruption (L 20.18). What were Hobbes's arguments for absolving an all-powerful sovereign from all taints of injustice? On which conceptions of 'justice' and 'injustice' were those arguments premised? And what normative and conceptual arguments did he advance to persuade his audience that he was speaking about justice proper, and not about something else?

1.1 THE CONVENTIONALIST INTERPRETATION

This book answers these questions by offering the most comprehensive analysis to date of the meaning and place of justice in Hobbes's moral, legal, political, and international thought. Hobbes is widely regarded as one of the most important political theorists in the western tradition. Justice is one of the main political concepts and values today. Yet systematic studies of Hobbes's ideas on justice remain scarce.[11] This is surprising, given that his notoriety rests in part on a series of bold claims he defends about justice. Norms of justice do not apply prior to and outside of the state (including in the international arena). All that justice requires is performing one's covenants—including foremost the original covenant that sets up government. For citizens, the civil law is the sole authoritative standard of justice and injustice of actions. Sovereign rulers cannot commit injustices; let alone be accused of injustice. On which conceptions of justice were these startling claims premised? And what reasons did Hobbes give for favouring those conceptions?

On a prominent line of interpretation, these questions do not require much parsing. Hobbes is simply a conventionalist about justice. To forestall internecine conflict arising from pervasive moral disagreement, citizens have agreed to let the sovereign define justice and injustice at will. As Waldron puts it:

> Hobbes was a conventionalist about justice (and right, good and evil, property, honesty, and honor). He did maintain that these terms have the meaning, and only the meaning, that the sovereign assigns to them in a well ordered society... Hobbes's subjects are to be told that 'just' has no inherent meaning apart from the sovereign's stipulations not only because that is convenient and peace-promoting, but also because it is true.[12]

---

[11] Dedicated studies include Michael J. Green, 'Justice and Law in Hobbes', *Oxford Studies in Early Modern Philosophy* 1 (2003) 111–138; Luc Foisneau, '*Leviathan*'s Theory of Justice' in Tom Sorell and Luc Foisneau (eds), *Leviathan after 350 Years* (Oxford, 2004) 105–122; Daniel Eggers, 'Injury, Injustice, Iniquity: The Evolution of Hobbes's Theory of Justice', *Intellectual History Review* (2014) no. 2: 167–184.

[12] Jeremy Waldron, 'Hobbes and the Principle of Publicity', *Pacific Philosophical Quarterly* 82 (2001) no. 3/4: 467, also 469.

6 VINDICATING THE 'MORTALL GOD'

Bobbio agrees. For Hobbes, 'there is no eternal or natural justice. "Just" is what human beings have agreed to call by this name'—and 'in the last instance, what the sovereign wills.' 'As a consequence, all that the sovereign commands is just merely because it has been commanded; and all that he prohibits is unjust merely because it has been prohibited.'[13] According to May, 'justice is completely based on what the sovereign says it is.'[14] Lamprecht seeks to save Hobbes from the 'Hobbist' claim that 'moral distinctions . . . are arbitrary conventions which rulers impose upon their subjects' by arguing that this applies only to 'justice and right', and not to 'morality'.[15] In Hampton's assessment, Hobbes ultimately fails to demonstrate the rationality of consensually instituting an absolute ruler. Yet not because justice permits or requires civic disobedience—for he 'defined injustice simply as disobedience to the sovereign's laws'.[16]

The conventionalist interpretation is of old pedigree. Hobbes was widely denounced by contemporary critics for reviving the Epicurean tenet that justice is a matter of convention.[17] Ralph Cudworth (1617–1688) already ranked Hobbes among those 'philosophers, that affirm justice and injustice to be only by law, and not by nature'.[18] The Cambridge divine John Edwards (1637–1716) accused Hobbes of holding that, by nature, 'nothing is virtuous or vitious, just or unjust; for he holds that these arise only from Compact and Society. The *Magistrate* is Mr. *Hobbes's God*, the *Prince* is the maker of Good and Evil, and he can unmake them what he pleases'.[19] Hobbes's long-time interlocutor John Bramhall (1594–1663) exclaimed aghast that 'he fancieth no reality of any natural justice or honesty, nor any relation to the Law of God or nature, but only to the Laws of the Common-wealth'.[20]

The conventionalist interpretation correctly identifies Hobbes's basic doctrine about what justice in practice demands. On Hobbes's mature account, injustice consists in breaking valid covenants; justice in keeping faith (L 15.2–3). Whether

---

[13] Norberto Bobbio, *Thomas Hobbes and the Natural Law Tradition*, trans. Daniela Gobetti (Chicago, 1993) 96–97. Also J.W.N. Watkins, *Hobbes's System of Ideas* (London, 1973) 110–111; M.M. Goldsmith, 'Hobbes on Law' in Tom Sorell (ed), *The Cambridge Companion to Hobbes* (Cambridge, 1996) 280–282; Sheldon Wolin, *Politics and Vision: Continuity and Innovation in Western Political Thought* (Princeton, 2004) 232; Philip Pettit, *Made with Words: Hobbes on Language, Mind, and Politics* (Princeton, 2008) 111, 115, 127; Allan Beever, *Forgotten Justice: The Forms of Justice in the History of Legal and Political Theory* (Oxford, 2013) 186, 192.

[14] Larry May, *Limiting Leviathan: Hobbes on Law and International Affairs* (Oxford, 2013) 40.

[15] S.P. Lamprecht, 'Hobbes and Hobbism', *American Political Science Review* 34 (1940) no. 1: 33, 43. Also A.E. Taylor, 'The Ethical Doctrine of Hobbes', *Philosophy* 13 (1938) no. 52: 413.

[16] Jean Hampton, *Hobbes and the Social Contract Tradition* (Cambridge, 1986) 199.

[17] Bernd Ludwig, *Die Wiederentdeckung des Epikureischen Naturrechts* (Frankfurt a.M., 1998) 401–424; Catherine Wilson, *Epicureanism at the Origins of Modernity* (Oxford, 2008) 178–199. For an overview of the Epicurean approach to justice, see John M. Armstrong, 'Epicurean Justice', *Phronesis* 42 (1997) no. 3: 324–334.

[18] Ralph Cudworth, *A Treatise Concerning Eternal and Immutable Morality*, ed. Sarah Hutton (Cambridge, 1996) 13–14.

[19] John Edwards, *The Eternal and Intrinsick Reasons of Good and Evil* (Cambridge, 1699) 23.

[20] Bramhall, 'The Catching of Leviathan', 154, also 178. Also Henry More, *The Immortality of the Soul*, ed. Alexander Jacob (Dordrecht, 1987) 49: 'That there is no Religion, no Piety nor Impiety, no Vertue nor Vice, Justice nor Injustice, but what it pleases him that has the longest Sword to call so'.

an action is just or unjust thus depends exclusively on whether or not it is something one has promised (not) to do. Which actions justice requires agents to perform is determined wholly by the agreements they have entered—above all by the original covenant, in which citizens promised to simply obey the sovereign. 'SIMPLE obedience' is a technical term, meaning 'the greatest obedience that can be given' (DCv 6.13). Citizens have promised to obey whatever the sovereign lawgiver shall decree, provided their obedience is non-futile and compatible with duties owed to God.[21] However, the conventionalist interpretation misconstrues the *grounds* of this doctrine. It states that the sovereign legislator can proclaim actions 'just' and 'unjust' by fiat because justice lacks fixed meaning and content. That is false: justice does not *mean* whatever the sovereign or anyone else decides it means. What justice requires of citizens is indeed in practice determined by civil law alone, but this is not true by definition. Rather, it is the upshot of a complex and multilayered argument, painstakingly developed over time.

This book unravels and scrutinizes that argument, and its conceptual presuppositions and theoretical implications. It thereby takes up the question—neglected by the conventionalist interpretation that has the sovereign stipulate what just and unjust mean—of how Hobbes modified received ideas of justice, rights, and morality in order to support his provocative doctrines about justice. My analysis reveals that he had to work hard to justify these doctrines, creatively revising numerous prevailing distinctions and definitions in order to draw arresting conclusions from commonplace suppositions. Hobbes was notorious for his semantic shenanigans:

> Mr *Hobs* is very dexterous, in Confuting others, by putting a new Sense upon their words, rehearsed by himself; different from what the same Words signifie with other men. And therefore, if You shall have occasion to speak of *Chalk*; He'l tell You that by *Chalk*, he means *Cheese*: and then, if he can prove that what You say of *Chalk*, is not true of *Cheese*; he reckons himself to have gotten a great Victory.[22]

Similarly, G.W. Leibniz (1646–1716) accused Hobbes of changing 'the nature of terms and to speak a language different from that of other men' by maintaining 'that "just" is whatever pleases the most powerful'.[23] Though exaggerating, the critics have a point. Conceptual innovations are indeed a cornerstone of Hobbes's philosophy.[24] His self-declared scientific approach to morals and politics started

---

[21] DCv 11.5; DCv 15.1; L 20.16; L 31.1. Susanne Sreedhar argues that 'the most obedience people *can* give' and '*have* to give are the same; they are coextensive' in 'The Right of Nature and Political Obedience' in Robin Douglass and Johan Olsthoorn (eds), *Hobbes's On the Citizen* (Cambridge, 2020) 85, also 79.

[22] John Wallis, *Hobbius Heauton-timorumenos, or a Consideration of Mr Hobbes His Dialogues* (Oxford, 1662) 154.

[23] G.W. Leibniz, *Political Writings*, ed. Patrick Riley (Cambridge, 1988) 47.

[24] In modern parlance, Hobbes engaged in conceptual engineering. On the nature and felicity conditions of conceptual engineering, see Herman Cappelen, 'Conceptual Engineering: The Master

8   VINDICATING THE 'MORTALL GOD'

from the 'right Definition of Names', essential for gaining general knowledge (L 4.13). Clearing up linguistic sources of error sometimes prompted slight, sometimes sweeping restatements—leaving few major moral and political terms untouched. All true. Yet Hobbes produced his definitional novelties, I submit, not by simple stipulation but by intricate reasoning from widely endorsed starting positions. Hobbes's views on justice are indeed extraordinary. But they cannot be dismissed as chalk victories.

1.2 A CIVIL THEODICY

Hobbes defended an extreme form of political absolutism.[25] Sovereign power, he maintained, is of necessity absolute and arbitrary (L R&C.8). Power is absolute if it is legally unlimited, making the sovereign accountable to no one (but God). 'Power Unlimited, is absolute Soveraignty' (L 22.5). Absolute power, thus understood, implies legal impunity: 'to sovereign power (whatsoever it doth) there belongeth impunity' (EL 20.12).[26] It also implies what Hobbes calls 'Arbitrary government'— rule unrestrained by civil law (L 46.35). Since laws cannot enforce themselves, making the sovereign subject to civil law is to set 'a Judge above him, and a Power to Punish him; which is to make a new Soveraign' (L 29.9). The ambitions of his theory of justice go well beyond establishing political absolutism. Rather than stripping sovereign power from any legal limitation, it seeks to enclothe it with a mantle of justice.[27]

That theoretical objective differs from what we may call 'moral exceptionalism about government'. The last thesis, advocated by early modern reason-of-state theorists and decried by Hugo Grotius (1583–1645), denies that rules of justice are unwaveringly binding for sovereigns. Either because ordinary norms of justice do not apply to civil government at all ('To a King or Sovereign City, nothing is unjust that is profitable'). Or because these norms may and sometimes should be set aside ('no State can be governed without injustice').[28] Rulers cannot keep their hands clean: considerations of power or national security sometimes make it imperative to commit injustices. The last line of reasoning seeks to excuse sovereign injustices

---

Argument' in Alexis Burgess, Herman Cappelen, and David Plunkett (eds), *Conceptual Engineering and Conceptual Ethics* (Oxford, 2020) 132–151.

[25] For a succinct account of Hobbes's defence of political absolutism, see Deborah Baumgold, *Contract Theory in Historical Context: Essays on Grotius, Hobbes, and Locke* (Leiden, 2010) 89–95. On ideas of political absolutism in early modern England more generally, see J.P. Sommerville, *Royalists and Patriots: Politics and Ideology in England, 1603–1640* (Routledge, 2014) 226–250.

[26] Also EL 27.10; DCv 6.12; L 18.7; L 20.3.

[27] Cf. Sommerville, 'Hobbes and Absolutism', 389–391.

[28] Grotius, *War and Peace*, prol. 3.

by appeal to values other than justice; the former holds that for sovereigns realizing those external values *is* justice.

Hobbes, by contrast, argued audaciously for the very impossibility of sovereign injustice. Moreover, his arguments are *not* premised upon separate standards of justice—one for rulers, one for subjects. For Hobbes, the formal meaning of each principle of justice is the same regardless of to whom it applies. This is so even if what norms of justice in practice permit, require, and prohibit is contingent on the empirical conditions agents are in. After all, what an agent must do as a matter of justice depends on what (if anything) she had previously covenanted to do. Equity, it is true, is a virtue of arbitrators alone, calling for impartial and even-handed adjudication of civil disputes. *Leviathan* subsumes distributive justice under equity, thus rendering the principle in this guise inapplicable to citizens (§4.2). Citizens nevertheless remain obligated to do as distributive justice formally instructs—namely, to give each their own. Distributive justice in practice places different demands on rulers than on subjects because the former legally determine what belongs to each. Sovereigns fulfil distributive justice by issuing distributive laws distinguishing *mine* from *thine*. Citizens keep the same principle by obeying those laws. Positional differences thus explain why some passages seem to ascribe different moral standards to sovereigns than to citizens (B 165). Justice formally being the same for all, Hobbes's theory of justice simultaneously aims to morally empower the sovereign and to chain subjects to simple obedience. How did he pull this off?

The main objectives of Hobbes's theory of justice are consequently two. First, establishing that the civil law is the sole authoritative standard of right conduct for citizens: 'there are no authentic doctrines of just and unjust, good and evil, except the laws established in each commonwealth' (DCv P.8).[29] Second, proving that citizens cannot possibly have standing to accuse the sovereign of injustice. 'He cannot be Accused by any of his Subjects, of Injury' (L 20.3). Whether his commands 'be it sin, or not sin, there is no power in *England* that may resist him, or speak evil of him lawfully' (DPS 181). The first objective seeks to ensure that citizens are never morally obligated to disobey civil law. What justice requires of citizens and what is binding law to them cannot possibly be in conflict. On the contrary, justice calls for general legal compliance (commands which citizens had never promised to obey to begin with are no law to them) (§6.2). The second objective aims to eliminate the possibility of justified grievances against the sovereign, to forestall any pretext for sedition.[30]

---

[29] Also EL 29.8; DCv 6.9; DCv 12.2; DCv 17.10, 14; L 18.10; L 26.3–4; L 29.6; L 42.96; L 46.11; DH 13.9; DPS 30; EW 4: 370.

[30] Commentators have duly highlighted Hobbes's practical solution to the potentially destabilizing role of ideologies: political education. Citizens should be taught their duties and doctrines inimical to peace should be stamped out. Less attention has been paid to his moral vindication of the sovereign—part of what has to be taught. S.A. Lloyd, 'Coercion, Ideology, and Education in Hobbes's *Leviathan*' in Andrews Reath et al. (eds), *Reclaiming the History of Ethics: Essays for John Rawls* (Cambridge,

10 VINDICATING THE 'MORTALL GOD'

Leibniz coined the term 'theodicy' (meaning: vindication of God) in his eponymous treatise of 1710. There, Leibniz upheld the moral perfection, wisdom, and power of God in the face of rampant evil.[31] Half a century earlier, Hobbes developed what we may dub a 'civil theodicy'. Hobbes sought to morally vindicate both the deity *and* the civil sovereign, or '*Mortall God*' (L 17.13). At times, he was tempted to buttress his civil theodicy by morally likening the sovereign's authority to God's. The Latin *Leviathan* declares, blasphemously, that 'to speak evill of the Soveraign ruler . . . is a transgression of the third commandment' (LL 30.9) ('thou shalt not take the name of the Lord thy God in vain'—Exod. 20:7). Such parallels notwithstanding, Hobbes's twin vindications of the mortal and eternal God are in fact entirely different. The deity's right to rule derives from irresistible power: 'the Kingdome over men, and the Right of afflicting men at his pleasure, belongeth Naturally to God Almighty; not as Creator, and Gracious; but as Omnipotent' (L 31.5; also DCv 15.5–6). Whatever God does is justified by his power alone. 'Power irresistible justifieth all actions . . . Less power does not' (EW 5: 116; also DCv 1.14; EW 5: 212).[32] This justification is unavailable to humans. Not in principle— 'if there had been any man of Power Irresistible' then he could 'by that Power have ruled . . . according to his own discretion' (L 31.5; also DCv 15.5). But in practice— roughly equal in power, humans cannot impose their will upon others by sheer force alone: 'absolutely irresistible . . . power can be no other than the power divine' (EW 5: 146). Human sovereignty depends on prior consent of the governed (§2.5). Sovereign immunity against accusations of injustice therefore cannot be derived from overwhelming power either. While power is key to Hobbes's divine theodicy, his *civil* theodicy requires a different normative foundation.

Unlike Leibniz's theodicy, Hobbes's vindication of the civil sovereign was negative (the sovereign cannot properly be accused of injustice) rather than positive (he is a paragon of justice). Far from insisting on their moral perfection, Hobbes concedes throughout his works that sovereigns are known to 'seize, rob, and kill' citizens. Albeit patent transgressions of natural law, the sovereign may 'do so rightly [jure], i.e. without inflicting a wrong [injuria] on himself' (DCv 6.13n). Hobbes frankly admits that human rulers can and do flout moral duties by sinning against natural and divine law. 'I have not denied that the sovereign can act inequitably' states the Latin *Leviathan* (LL 18.6). Nearly thirty years earlier, *Elements* read:

1997) 39–46; Geoffrey M. Vaughan, *Behemoth Teaches Leviathan: Thomas Hobbes on Political Education* (Lanham, 2002) 57–58.

[31] G.W. Leibniz, *Theodicy*, ed. Austin Farrer, trans. E.M. Huggard (La Salle, IL, 1985).

[32] Hobbes effectively reduced God's justice to his power, argues Luc Foisneau, 'Omnipotence, Necessity, and Sovereignty' in Patricia Springborg (ed), *The Cambridge Companion to Hobbes's Leviathan* (Cambridge, 2007) 276, 281. On Hobbes's vindication of God's justice, see George Wright, 'Authority and Theodicy in Hobbes's *Leviathan*', *Rivista di Storia della Filosofia* 59 (2004) no. 1: 175–204.

the acts of sovereign power ... when they tend to the hurt of the people in general, they be breaches of the law of nature, and of the divine law; and consequently, the contrary acts are the duties of sovereigns, and required at their hands to the utmost of their endeavour, by God Almighty, under the pain of eternal death. (EL 28.1)[33]

This concession greatly complicated his vindicatory project. Why isn't a sovereign acting 'to the hurt of the people' injuring his citizens? What makes it the case that citizens have no standing to publicly condemn their sovereign for crossing natural law? And why should citizens take civil laws that objectively violate natural law as the final word on what conduct of theirs is just and what unjust?

Hobbes's answers to these questions, this book reveals, are complex and multi-layered. Underpinning his apologetic, I argue, is a sharp demarcation of two spheres of ethical discourse: natural law vs. justice. The laws of nature are general dictates of reason forbidding humans to act in (socially) self-destructive ways. Justice is one of the twenty-odd laws of nature, ordering persons to fulfil their covenants and to give each their due. Both deontic principles are built upon the same normative foundation: enlightened self-interest. 'For every man is assumed to be naturally after his own good; he seeks *Justice* only incidentally, for the sake of *peace*' (DCv 3.21).[34] Justice and natural law nonetheless regulate what are effectively different types of moral obligations, with diverging deontic features. In a nutshell: justice regulates self-assumed obligations, created by voluntarily laying down right to some other party. Obligations of justice are always 'directed'—owed to other contractors. Moreover, flouting these obligations always wrongs the person(s) whose liberty it unjustly hinders. Natural law duties, by contrast, are not typically owed to other persons. Contravening natural law duties is always immoral but not always unjust: sinful conduct often wrongs no one but God. My contention is that Hobbes had to work hard to establish a near-categorical distinction between natural law duties and obligations of justice. Chapter 3 provides an in-depth reconstruction of his two main arguments for separating the two, countering Abizadeh's rival reading.[35] Both arguments hinge upon his idiosyncratic conception of injury as action without right, itself dissected in Chapter 2.

The disentanglement of natural law duties from obligations of justice underpins Hobbes's civil theodicy. It enabled him to hold that even sovereigns sinning against natural law cannot wrong their citizens. Upon this conceptual foundation, Hobbes erected a two-layered defence of sovereign moral unaccountability. The

---

[33] Other passages evincing the possibility of sovereign immoral conduct are EL 21.3; DCv 7.14; L 18.6; L 21.7; L 22.15; L 24.7; EW 4: 371; EW 5: 178; DPS 31.

[34] This passage squares badly with Harvey's thesis that some Hobbesian agents value justice intrinsically, for non-instrumental reasons. Martin Harvey, 'Hobbes and the Value of Justice', *Southern Journal of Philosophy* 42 (2004) no. 4: 443–450.

[35] Arash Abizadeh, *Hobbes and the Two Faces of Ethics* (Cambridge, 2018).

12   VINDICATING THE 'MORTALL GOD'

first layer aims to establish that sovereigns cannot possibly commit injustices or injuries *strictu sensu*. The second layer gainsays citizens the standing to accuse the sovereign of moral wrongdoing in general. Consider the following passage:

> It is true that a Soveraign ... may ordain the doing of many things in pursuit of their Passions, contrary to their own consciences, which is a breach of trust, and of the Law of Nature; but this is not enough to authorise any subject, [1] either to make warre upon, or [2] so much as to accuse of Injustice, or [3] any way to speak evill of their Soveraign. (L 24.7)

Citizens lack the standing to condemn sovereign immorality, Hobbes contends, because they have authorized his every word and action: 'nothing the Soveraign Representative can doe to a Subject, on what pretence soever, can properly be called Injustice, or Injury; because every Subject is Author of every act the Soveraign doth; so that [the sovereign] never wanteth Right to any thing' (L 21.7). Whatever supreme rulers do is done by will and right of each and every citizen. As wronging yourself is impossible, so the person whose every action you have authorized cannot wrong you. The Authorization Argument vindicates the sovereign only from the standpoint of citizens: their authorization ensures that the sovereign cannot injure *them* (L 18.6; L 30.20; EW 5: 177–178). The thesis does not establish that the sovereign cannot commit wrongs or injustices as such (§6.6). Hobbes's doctrine that citizens have no standing whatsoever to voice grievances against their rulers radicalized the position of earlier political absolutists. Consider King James VI and I (1566–1625). Claiming to reign by divine right, the King deplored subjects who 'judge and speake rashly of their Prince'. In response, he proposed to rule so justly and well that citizens 'have no ground to grudge it'.[36] By contrast, Hobbes bluntly declared that citizens cannot permissibly gripe about their government regardless of how their sovereign governs. Political rulers are 'not to be accused of injustice by those that owe subjection to them' (EW 5: 182). Even the most ruthless dictator may not be spoken poorly of.

Equally radical was Hobbes's maxim that subjects cannot possibly be wronged by the sovereign. Other political absolutists had denied citizens the right to resist sovereign wrongdoing, ordering them to patiently suffer such evils. Yet they uniformly accepted that citizens can be wronged by unjust rulers. Even the most despotic power—that of slaveholders over enslaved humans—does not forestall injury: 'a Slave may undoubtedly be injured by his Master'.[37] Early modern political absolutists commonly gainsaid citizens only *enforceable* rights against the sovereign. To unpack this claim, we must turn to the age-old tripartite classification

---

[36] King James VI and I, *Political Writings*, ed. J.P. Sommerville (Cambridge, 1995) 30–31.
[37] Grotius, *War and Peace*, 2.5.28. Also e.g. Pufendorf, *Nature and Nations*, 6.3.8; Christian Thomasius, *Institutes of Divine Jurisprudence*, ed. Thomas Ahnert (Indianapolis, 2011) 3.5.22.

of justice. Early modern jurists had transformed this typology—going back to Aristotle—through their integration of ideas of individual rights (§4.1).[38] *Commutative* justice requires agents to take heed of what belongs to others, forbidding violation of enforceable rights of others. So-called perfect rights can be enforced in court and on the battlefield.[39] *Distributive* justice, by contrast, regulates non-enforceable, imperfect rights. Failure to give another what she has an imperfect right to is morally wrong. Yet it neither grants the victim standing to sue nor to resist. *Universal* justice, finally, captures the remainder of other-regarding morality. Early modern political absolutists generally maintained that sovereigns have no obligations of *commutative* justice to their citizens, corresponding in enforceable rights against government. Yet other norms of justice do govern their interactions with the people. Witness Kant's objection to Hobbes:

> According to [Hobbes], a head of state has no obligation to the people by the contract and cannot do a citizen any wrong (he may make what arrangements he wants about him). This proposition would be quite correct if a wrong were taken to mean an injury that gives the injured party a *coercive right* against the one who wronged him; but stated so generally, the proposition is appalling.[40]

While agreeing that citizens cannot have enforceable rights against the state, Kant deemed it obvious that government policies can be unjust in other ways.[41]

Hobbes stood out by vindicating the sovereign from *all* forms of injustice and injury. This required precluding sovereign violations of commutative, distributive, and universal justice alike. The textbook account of why sovereigns cannot commit injustices is hence incomplete. The sovereign, it goes, on his part made no covenant with his citizens. Injustice being defined as breach of covenant, it follows that nothing the sovereign does can be unjust to citizens. This so-called No Pact Argument safeguards the sovereign from only one form of injustice (i.e. commutative). It is silent on the possibility of sovereign violations of distributive and universal justice. For Hobbes, it is true, only commutative justice merits the name of justice properly speaking. Universal justice goes unmentioned, and what 'men mean by distributive justice . . . is properly termed EQUITY' (EL 17.2). However, a mere change of labels does not suffice to show that citizens are not wronged by

---

[38] Johan Olsthoorn, 'Francisco Suárez and Hugo Grotius on Distributive Justice and Imperfect Rights', *History of Political Thought* 41 (2020) no. 1: 96–119. While wedded to the same moral framework, early modern natural jurisprudents explained the meaning of and differences between these three forms of justice in competing ways.

[39] The Grotian notion that perfect rights can in principle be enforced by war helps explain why Hobbes sees constitutional limits on government power as potentially licensing violent resistance against the sovereign. See Baumgold, *Contract Theory in Historical Context*, 27–49.

[40] Kant, *Practical Philosophy*, 302. Kant's objection is analysed in Gabriella Slomp, 'Kant against Hobbes: Reasoning and Rhetoric', *Journal of Moral Philosophy* 4 (2007) no. 2: 210–218.

[41] E.g. Kant, *Practical Philosophy*, 462.

14 VINDICATING THE 'MORTALL GOD'

sovereigns contravening the renamed principles. Chapter 4 argues that Hobbes in addition had to reconceptualize the idea of merit in order to show that sovereign maldistributions (which he admits occur) cannot possibly fail to give citizens what they deserve by right. Besides, why is a kleptocratic government expropriating 'a good citizen of all his possessions' not thereby acting unjustly towards that subject (LL 19.8)? To defang that concern, Hobbes developed over time a complex theory of property, reconstructed in Chapter 5.

Sovereign *moral* unaccountability, the previous discussion shows, is a more expansive doctrine than sovereign *legal* unaccountability (i.e. political absolutism). Establishing the former does enhance sovereign authority. Indeed, Hobbes's rejection of the popular doctrine of passive obedience should be understood in connection with his stunning vindication of the sovereign. Luther and other political absolutists had urged subjects to neither resist nor carry out unjust commands by superiors. *Behemoth* rejects their doctrine of passive obedience as incoherent: 'Every Law is a command *to do*, or *to forbeare*, neither of these is fulfilled by suffering' (B 173; also DCv 14.23; EW 4: 381). Over time, Hobbes developed a theory of limited individual rights of resistance against the government. *Leviathan* accords citizens inalienable rights to actively resist self-incrimination, imprisonment, and corporal punishments; moreover, it allows citizens to rightfully disobey dangerous and dishonourable commands (including military conscription).[42] Distinctively, Hobbesian rights of resistance are not triggered by injustice. They are remnants of natural rights of self-defence, not given up in the original covenant. Even justly condemned criminals retain the right to resist state punishment (L 21.17). As Green observes, 'injustice cannot justify resistance even though self-defense might'.[43] By conceptually disconnecting rights of resistance from injustice, Hobbes ensures that these rights do not undermine sovereign immunity to moral accusation. This helps explain why citizens generally have no moral reason to join anyone rightfully resisting government orders. For while their fellow subject resists with right, so their sovereign commands by right. Significantly, Hobbes's theory of justice thus rules out multiplier effects of rights of resistance, ensuring that these rights remain at all times individual.

---

[42] On the nature and grounds of individual rights of resistance, see Susanne Sreedhar, *Hobbes on Resistance: Defying the Leviathan* (Cambridge, 2010) 53–88; Patricia Sheridan, 'Resisting the Scaffold: Self-Preservation and Limits of Obligation in Hobbes's *Leviathan*', *Hobbes Studies* 24 (2011) no. 2: 146–157.

[43] Michael Green, 'Authorization and Political Authority in Hobbes', *Journal of the History of Philosophy* 53 (2015) no. 1: 39.

1.3 THE PLACE OF JUSTICE IN HOBBES'S PHILOSOPHY

This monograph provides a historically informed philosophical analysis of Hobbes's idiosyncratic conceptualizations of justice and cognate notions (including right, obligation, merit, property, natural law, civil law, charity, self-defence, just war, and treason). That analysis allows me to reassess the structure and development of his moral theory and to revisit and resolve some long-standing interpretive questions (including around the status of natural law, the grounds and scope of the right to everything, his relation to legal positivism, and reply to the fool). Justice ties together Hobbes's main moral, legal, political, and international doctrines. *Hobbes on Justice* exploits this prism to offer an original and integrated reading of variant strands of his thought and their logical interrelations. Along the way, the book contributes to the history of ideas of justice: an area that has received relatively little attention (contrast the countless studies of past ideas of liberty, democracy, and representation).[44]

The importance of justice for Hobbes's ethics and politics is sometimes down-played: 'arguments from justice... lack the centrality claimed for them by Hobbes'.[45] Despite her attention to Hobbes's anxiety over ideological threats to political stability, Lloyd regards 'justice... of secondary importance to Hobbes'.[46] I do not wish to argue for the relative significance of justice vis-à-vis other political concepts in Hobbes; indeed, I am not sure what such an argument should look like. Suffice it to say in reply that justice often looms large even when the term goes unmentioned. Lloyd decries Hobbes's 'attenuated treatment of justice' as 'perfunctory', 'impoverished, formalistic', and (to modern readers) 'insufficient'.[47] That verdict reflects the common tendency to take Hobbes at his word: justice requires keeping faith, and nothing else. That extremely narrow definition, this book shows, is itself the outcome of a complex argument, developed in part by expunging norms of justice from key domains of social and political life. For instance, Chapter 9 argues that Hobbes develops an extremely undemanding just war theory in part to forestall civic pleas for conscientious disobedience. Similarly, arguments about justice

---

[44] Birds-eye overviews of historical conceptions of justice include Samuel Fleischacker, *A Short History of Distributive Justice* (Cambridge, MA, 2004); David Johnston, *A Brief History of Justice* (Malden, MA, 2011); Mathias Risse, *On Justice: Philosophy, History, Foundations* (Cambridge, 2020) 149–220. On the value of studying how moral concepts have changed over time, see Edward Skidelsky, 'What Moral Philosophers Can Learn from the History of Moral Concepts', *History of European Ideas* 45 (2019) no. 3: 311–321.

[45] Tom Sorell, 'Hobbes and the Morality beyond Justice', *Pacific Philosophical Quarterly* 82 (2001) no. 3/4: 237, also 235–238.

[46] Lloyd, *Ideals as Interests*, 278.

[47] Lloyd, *Ideals as Interests*, 286–287. Foisneau defends the enduring value of Hobbes's narrow conception of justice for philosophical theorizing on justice today, amidst deep societal disagreement over the meaning of the good. Luc Foisneau, 'Hobbes et les Limites de la Justice' in Jauffrey Berthier and Jean Terrel (eds), *Lumières 10: Hobbes: Nouvelles Lectures* (Bordeaux, 2007) 187–202.

16   VINDICATING THE 'MORTALL GOD'

underpin Hobbes's international theory precisely because he wanted justice and injustice to have no place in extra-statist interactions (Chapter 7).

My comprehensive reconstruction of Hobbes's theory of justice is split into five parts, including this introduction (Part I). Part II analyses the basic conceptual elements of this theory—'right', 'wrong', 'injustice', 'injury', 'obligation', 'law', etc.—and unravels the intricate relations between justice and natural law. Part III deals with justice within the state, focusing on Hobbes's accounts of distributive justice, property, and civil law. Part IV turns to the extra-statist domain, taking up questions of war, international morality, enmity, and rebellion. Part V concludes. *Hobbes on Justice* is a long and dense book. Not every reader, I imagine, will be equally riveted by every topic and debate covered (no judgement). In their service, I have done my best to make each chapter self-standing—intelligible on its own and framed around an independently interesting research question.

Various chapters explore Hobbes's subversive gloss on the seminal Roman law definition of justice (*suum cuique tribuere*: 'give each their due'). From *Leviathan* onwards, he equates this definition with distributive justice (relabelled: equity) (L 15.15; L 24.5). According to Hobbes, the sovereign literally gives each citizen their own, by means of distributive civil laws that first create exclusive property rights. Property rights of subjects never exclude the sovereign himself, who retains *dominium* over all they have. The sovereign hence cannot possibly steal from citizens (through taxation or confiscation): what belongs to them is also always his (Chapter 5). *Leviathan's* reinterpretation of the Roman law definition underpins various other doctrines, including that all distributive laws are, in a sense, just to citizens (Chapter 6); and that justice and injustice are non-existent outside the state (Chapter 7). Chapter 6 argues that Hobbes was no legal positivist. Against extant non-positivist readings, I argue that a civil law's (non-)conformity with natural law does not affect its legal validity. Against positivist readings, I contend that Hobbes rejected both the Sources Thesis and the Separability Thesis. An ineliminable conceptual connection obtains between civil law and justice: no civil law can possibly be unjust or injurious to citizens. Immoral laws and decrees are legally valid precisely because and insofar as they have been authorized by citizens. The last chapter sheds new light on Hobbes's much-discussed reply to the fool, by analysing the place of treason in his social contract theory (Chapter 10).

Since Hobbes's views on the rights of war and moral norms beyond the state are by and large ramifications of his domestic concerns—and foremost of his political absolutism and vindicatory project—my integrated reading will help elucidate the relations between justice, natural law, and the laws of nations. Hobbes has become a hallmark figure in international relations theory in part because for him morality and justice have a very limited place outside the state. While conditionally binding contractual agreements are possible between states, thus allowing for the formation of international leagues and alliances,[48] Hobbes denied that such agreements

---

[48] E.g. DCv 2.18; L 14.27; L 20.4; L 21.24; L 22.29; LL 28.23; B 301.

amount to international law. Moreover, international actors may without injustice jettison these agreements the moment they spot a new reasonable cause for fear—whether in other contractors or in third parties (DCv 13.7; L 14.27). Drawing on my conceptual analyses of justice and cognate notions, I offer new insights into the meaning and theoretical significance of *jus gentium*, rights of war, and other norms with extra-statist application. One of my contentions is that Hobbes developed a just war theory of sorts—albeit an unusually lenient one. Machiavelli had maintained that political rulers should sometimes disregard justice for reasons of state. Hobbes, by contrast, moralized reason-of-state positions, thus ensuring that safeguarding national security never requires injustice. Justice and *jus belli* are thus made amenable for a realist position on international relations (Chapters 8 and 9).

The overall picture of Hobbes that emerges from this monograph differs considerably from the liberalized one prevalent in today's literature.[49] *Hobbes on Justice* does not present us with a more just Hobbes. Extant analyses of justice and morality in Hobbes tend to focus on the ways in which these norms *delimit* sovereign right and power. My angle is the opposite. I explore how Hobbes developed a theory of justice to establish sovereign moral unaccountability. His vindicatory project morally *empowered* the sovereign. In order to establish sovereign immunity to accusations of injustice, Hobbes watered down any moral, legal, and constitutional constraints on government power, leaving the sovereign legally unchecked and morally accountable to God alone. This makes his theory of justice most congenial to despotism. That Hobbes defends a despotic conception of sovereignty is another thesis, which this book provides evidence for but lacks space to defend comprehensively. The early works quite explicitly model sovereignty on despotic power, casting citizens in the role of slaves (§5.3). Yet by the time of *Leviathan*, Hobbes had found ways to defend the same unaccountable, arbitrary, and unlimited form of sovereignty through the incorporation (and hence political neutralization) of proto-liberal principles like the rule of law, equity, distributive justice, representation, and even individual rights of resistance. His endorsement and use of such notions should not blind us to the continuing centrality of unbridled political power within his theory. Despotism cloaked in justice is despotism all the same.

1.4 A WORD ON METHOD

This monograph endeavours interpretive truth, as farre as I have hope of obtaining it. Along the way, I seek and use all helps and advantages that modern scholarship

---

[49] On the liberalizing reception of *Leviathan*, see Charles D. Tarlton, 'The Despotical Doctrine of Hobbes, Part 1: The Liberalization of *Leviathan*', *History of Political Thought* 22 (2001) no. 4: 587–618. On the liberal potential of Hobbes's illiberalism, see Noel Malcolm, 'Thomas Hobbes: Liberal Illiberal', *Journal of the British Academy* 4 (2016) 113–136.

affords. The vitality and richness of the field of Hobbes studies is in no small measure due to the fact that academics studying his thought hail from various disciplines. Legal and political theorists, philosophers, intellectual historians, theologians, international relations theorists, literary scholars—all bring their own research agenda and research methods to the texts, developing a plurality of perspectives based on diverse sources and considerations. My own research has been much enriched by engagement with cross-disciplinary scholarship. To reap the fruits of methodological pluralism, some understanding and appreciation of research approaches practised in adjacent fields are required. This section positions my own bespoke approach within existing methodological debates in order to facilitate cross-disciplinary harvests.

Many attempts have been made to characterize diverging methodological approaches to the history of philosophy. As the meanings of some popular categorizations differ across disciplinary lines, these characterizations can themselves be parochial and obscuring. Consider contextualism. Historians of philosophy, Mercer has argued, have silently replaced rational reconstructionism with contextualism. Nowadays, few are mining the classics for insights to solve current philosophical quandaries—criticizing and revising past arguments whenever they fail to give compelling answers to today's pressing questions. Most historians of philosophers nowadays adopt a contextualist approach, which in Mercer's view is driven by the interpretive principle of 'getting it right'. We no longer 'attribute claims or ideas to historical figures without concern for whether or not they are ones the figures would recognize as their own'.[50]

Mercer's *thin* contextualism differs considerably from the *thick* version originally theorized by intellectual historians. Thin contextualism seeks to understand past philosophical works for their own sake and 'on their own terms'—to recover their 'authentic' meaning.[51] It places texts within relevant historical contexts in order to avoid anachronistic interpretations. Thick contextualism, over and above this, seeks to recover what the author intended to do by writing what they did (in the jargon: to recover a work's intended illocutionary force).[52] 'If we want a history of philosophy written in a genuinely historical spirit', Skinner avers, 'we need to make it one of our principal tasks to situate the texts we study within such

---

[50] Christia Mercer, 'The Contextualist Revolution in Early Modern Philosophy', *Journal of the History of Philosophy* 57 (2019) no. 3: 530. The contextualist turn in the history of philosophy had previously been defended by Sarah Hutton, 'Intellectual History and the History of Philosophy', *History of European Ideas* 40 (2014) no. 7: 925–937.

[51] Mercer, 'The Contextualist Revolution', 538, 545. In its strongest form, recovering the 'authentic' meaning of a work requires us 'to think as they thought and to see things in their way'. Quentin Skinner, 'A Reply to My Critics' in James Tully (ed), *Meaning and Context: Quentin Skinner and His Critics* (Cambridge, 1988) 252.

[52] On the distinction between textual and intended meaning, see Skinner, 'A Reply to My Critics', 269–272; Quentin Skinner, *Visions of Politics, Vol. 1: Regarding Method* (Cambridge, 2002) 82. For further discussion, see Adrian Blau, 'Meanings and Understandings in the History of Ideas', *Journal of the Philosophy of History* 14 (2020) no. 2: 232–256.

intellectual contexts as enable us to make sense of what their authors were doing in writing them.[53] The underlying assumption is that 'texts are acts'.[54] Texts are written for a purpose—as interventions in specific local debates. Any interpretation of what Hobbes meant to do by writing *Leviathan* (i.e. what he aimed to achieve thereby) requires thick contextualization. Its intended illocutionary effect cannot be reconstrued without understanding then-prevailing debates and political conditions; intellectual allegiances and expected audiences; what criticisms the work meant to parry; etc. Thin and thick contextualism thus invoke historical contexts for somewhat different purposes—each best served, I contend, by distinct ways of contextualization.

My approach is contextualist in Mercer's thin sense; not in Skinner's thick sense. My aims are primarily exegetical: understanding the structure and foundations of Hobbes's developing theory of justice. My analysis targets Hobbes's *arguments* (rather than his intentions in writing what he did). How did he justify his many extravagant claims about justice? What were the conceptual and doctrinal presuppositions of his arguments? And how did his theory of justice shape and constrain other parts of his thinking? Textual analysis alone is usually not enough to fully grasp the nature and presuppositions of Hobbes's arguments. Hobbes often silently dispensed with potential objections or rival positions—for example when flatly proclaiming that sovereign power has the same extent regardless of how it was acquired (through institution or force of arms) (DCv 9.10; L 20.4). Moreover, many of his basic definitions departed in crucial yet unacknowledged ways from tradition—think of 'injury' (§2.1); 'consent' (§2.5); 'right reason' (§3.4); 'merit' (§4.5); and 'self-defence' (§8.2). Thin contextualization is a key heuristic for unearthing tacit premises, revisions, and elisions. *Hobbes on Justice* frequently cites relevant predecessors (from Aristotle and Aquinas, to Suárez and Grotius) as well as later critics (from Bramhall and Cumberland, to Pufendorf and Leibniz) to bring out idiosyncrasies in Hobbes's thought. Hobbes endeavoured to integrate into his theory many commonplace tropes (such as the Golden Rule). Contrasts with rival theorists can help cut through surface-level similarities, revealing how profoundly he altered the meaning and theoretical significance of such bromides.[55] The same comparisons can help indicate what argumentative steps and conceptual revisions were needed to achieve his theoretical aims (such as denying the existence of natural obligations of justice). Lastly, thin contextualism enables us to position Hobbes in wider traditions of thought (including the history of just war theory and constitutional law).

---

[53] Skinner, *Visions of Politics*, vol. 1, 3.
[54] Skinner, 'A Reply to My Critics', 279; Skinner, *Visions of Politics*, vol. 1, 120.
[55] One reason why Hobbes may have been so hesitant to cite other authors, I venture, is to conceal how brazenly he misconstrued their ideas.

20 VINDICATING THE 'MORTALL GOD'

My thin manner of contextualization may seem haphazard to intellectual historians. I cite rival thinkers from sundry periods and traditions, whenever their definitions, arguments, or positions in my view make for an insightful contrast. Comparisons with rival theorists can be insightful for argumentative reconstruction—uncovering suppressed premises, conceptual idiosyncrasies, loose distinctions, etc.—even if Hobbes never intended to respond to their works; indeed, never read them.[56] This book generally brackets questions about whom Hobbes 'was responding to' or 'drawing on'. Establishing claims of historical influence requires extensive textual and contextual evidence (not collected here).[57] To any intellectual historian reading this book: please keep in mind that I aim to reconstruct the arguments found in Hobbes's works, not to examine what he was doing by writing his treatises.[58] Given my research objectives, it is not imperative for me to situate Hobbes's writings within the particular historical debates in which he meant to intervene; that is, to adopt that form of contextualization designed to recover authorial illocutionary intentions. To be sure, I have greatly benefited from engagement with thick contextualist studies of Hobbes. Awareness of what was at stake in the specific debates in which Hobbes meddled can help us grasp the point of an argument. Yet knowing his polemical intentions in developing an argument is not the same as understanding the logic of the argument itself. And it is the latter that I care about. Whether the comparisons I make really are illuminating, the reader must decide. My point here is that the adopted *manner* of contextualization is well tailored to my specific research objectives. Clearly, my way of contextualizing Hobbes's works can be the right one given my research goals, even if my use of it is bungled.

What do I mean by argumentative reconstruction? Two forms of reconstructionism can be distinguished. Both involve logical analysis and evaluation of past philosophical arguments—but to different degrees and for different goals. Mercer contrasts thin contextualism with *thick* reconstructionism: critically evaluating and reworking past arguments until they seem compelling to us, as partial solutions to philosophical problems troubling us today. Thick reconstructionists are unapologetically revisionist: altering and improving Hobbes's arguments and positions until the resulting overall theory ('inspired by Hobbes') is defensible in its own right.[59] Thick reconstructionists often extrapolate: applying recognizably

---

[56] For an eloquent defence of argumentative reconstruction and its value for (thick) contextualist histories of ideas, see Knud Haakonssen, *Natural Law and Moral Philosophy* (Cambridge, 1996) 11–12.

[57] Establishing influence requires more than spotting doctrinal commonalities, as these may derive from a common source or be arrived at independently. Skinner, *Visions of Politics*, vol. 1, 75–76.

[58] Whether Hobbes believed in the truth of everything he wrote is another issue I remain neutral on. His deep commitment to peace may have prompted him to advance irenic claims he himself deemed false: philosophy for him aims at promoting peace, rather than at truth. Moreover, his own 'doctrine of doctrines' may have constrained his writing: 'subjects cannot rightfully publish doctrines contrary to those laid down by the sovereign as necessary for their peace and defence'. Kinch Hoekstra, 'The End of Philosophy (The Case of Hobbes)', *Proceedings of the Aristotelian Society* 106 (2006) no. 1: 45.

[59] G.S. Kavka, *Hobbesian Moral and Political Theory* (Princeton, 1986) 3. Revisionism comes in degrees. So-called de re interpretations (Brandom's term) do not revise or reject textual claims that we

Hobbesian principles or perspectives to philosophical problems Hobbes himself did not engage with (e.g. medical ethics, terrorism).[60] *Thin* reconstructionism— practised in this book—lacks an 'appropriationist', present-oriented goal.[61] Thin reconstructionism aims to reconstruct the arguments found in past philosophical works on their own terms and for their own sake. Thin reconstructionists do not defend the merits or enduring appeal of past philosophical arguments. Nor are they after their improvement or further development. Even so, parsing past philosophical arguments inevitably requires a degree of logical reconstruction—more so the deeper we dig. Suppressed premises need to be made explicit; underlying conceptualizations spelled out; theoretical interlinkages exposed; ambiguities dispelled; conclusions drawn. Evaluating the logical validity or cogency of the arguments we attribute to Hobbes is often needed to refine our interpretations and to decide between rival readings. Some of the arguments and doctrines I attribute to Hobbes have firm textual support, others are more speculative.[62] All are arrived at through philosophical analysis and put forth as stabs at the most compelling interpretation of what Hobbes said about justice and how he tried to justify that.

The arguments and doctrines I attribute to Hobbes are interpretive proposals— attempts to make sense of the reasoning and conclusions found in his works. My rational reconstructions offer justifications for the substantive claims I take Hobbes to be making, supported by textual evidence and in line with his general theoretical commitments. Not all of my reconstructions will match Hobbes's authorial intentions, for two reasons. First, mapping the structure of an argument requires laying bare its conceptual presuppositions and main theoretical implications. Hobbes may not have been fully cognizant of either.[63] Second, I do not shy away from characterizing his views in modern philosophical terms wherever I believe this enhances scholarly understanding. It is meaningful to inquire, for instance, whether Hobbes 'was' a legal positivist. Legal positivism is a twentieth-century moniker. But as Hobbes had all the conceptual resources needed to affirm or deny whether the moral quality of some civil law matters for its legal validity, we can meaningfully ask to what extent his position is a legal positivist one—thereby

---

now deem mistaken. Yet to determine what exactly follows from them, de re interpretations select auxiliary premises that we now hold true, rather than ones the author would have endorsed (as per 'de dicto interpretations'). Brandom sees both methods of interpretation as equally valid. De re interpretations are best regarded as a third, intermediate form of rational reconstructionism. Robert Brandom, *Tales of the Mighty Dead: Historical Essays in the Metaphysics of Intentionality* (Cambridge, MA, 2002) 94–107.

[60] For examples of such extrapolations, see S.A. Lloyd (ed), *Hobbes Today: Insights for the 21st Century* (Cambridge, 2013); Shane D. Courtland (ed), *Hobbesian Applied Ethics and Public Policy* (Routledge, 2018).

[61] Mogens Lærke, J.E.H. Smith, and Eric Schliesser, 'Introduction' in idem (eds), *Philosophy and Its History: Aims and Methods in the Study of Early Modern Philosophy* (Oxford, 2013) 1.

[62] On the need to report degrees of uncertainty in textual interpretations, see Adrian Blau, 'Uncertainty and the History of Ideas', *History and Theory* 50 (2011) no. 3: 358–372.

[63] On this point, see Michael Rosen, 'The History of Ideas as Philosophy and History', *History of Political Thought* 32 (2011) no. 4: 707–709.

obtaining greater insight into the character of his legal theory and the history of law.[64] Modern-day terminology is sometimes (not always) distorting. For instance, adopting the familiar language of claim-rights, I submit, makes it hard to grasp Hobbes's mature account of injury and directed obligation. The idea of claim-rights renders unintelligible a crucial distinction he makes: the persons wronged by flouting obligations of justice are not necessarily identical to the persons to whom these obligations are owed (§2.4).[65] Whether introducing modern terminology mangles or clarifies Hobbes's ideas is always itself an interpretive question.

A recurring methodological question in this book is whether Hobbes was by his own lights *entitled* to say what he does. One is entitled to hold a thesis if the arguments one advances in support logically establish the thesis. One is not so entitled if the thesis lacks due argumentative support (i.e. argumentative justification). Criteria for entitlement here are logical validity and cogency (rather than soundness: the premises of the argument need not be true). In addition, Hobbes is *required* to hold a particular position if his arguments logically commit him to it.[66] Far from assuming that all Hobbes's views are internally coherent, I explore to what extent they are so.[67] Thin reconstructionism can reveal gaps and other argumentative infelicities—unsupported conclusions, idiosyncratic conceptualizations, invalid inferences, loose distinctions, mutually inconsistent claims, etc.—which 'disentitle' Hobbes from making certain claims or require him to hold others. I do not hesitate to ascribe shaky arguments or unappealing doctrines to Hobbes when the preponderance of textual evidence supports that ascription.

Unlike its thick counterpart, thin reconstructionism rejects the principle of interpretive charity. That principle provides guidance for deciding between competing readings that each have textual support. It admonishes us 'to present each writer's thought in what [we take] to be its strongest form'. Rather than interpreting past arguments and doctrines in the way that is most convincing to us—'the most reasonable interpretation' the text can bear—I am after the textually best-supported reading.[68] Thick reconstructionism is a generally sympathetic interpretive project: mining past philosophical material for gems that, duly cut and

---

[64] Mark Murphy, 'Hobbes (and Austin, and Aquinas) on Law as Command of the Sovereign' in A.P. Martinich and Kinch Hoekstra (eds), *The Oxford Handbook of Hobbes* (Oxford, 2016) 340n.

[65] Curran rightly warns that modern legal terminology risks distorting Hobbes's views on rights—before ironically herself falling victim to its lure. Obsessed with liberty-rights, commentators have failed to recognize 'the claim-rights that Hobbes describes'. Eleanor Curran, 'Lost in Translation. Some Problems with a Hohfeldian Analysis of Hobbesian Rights', *Hobbes Studies* 19 (2006) no. 1: 71.

[66] For further discussion, see the introduction to Susanne Sreedhar, *Hobbes on Sex* (Oxford, forthcoming).

[67] Thus steering clear from Skinner's critique of the 'mythology of coherence' in *Visions of Politics*, vol. 1, 67–72.

[68] John Rawls, *Lectures on the History of Political Philosophy*, ed. Samuel Freeman (Cambridge, MA, 2007) xiii, also 52. For discussion, see Michael Frazer, 'The Modest Professor: Interpretive Charity and Interpretive Humility in John Rawls's *Lectures on the History of Political Philosophy*', *European Journal of Political Theory* 9 (2010) no. 2: 218–226.

polished, help resolve current theoretical quandaries. Thin reconstructionism, by contrast, is non-aligned. I have no skin in the game. I offer you Hobbes's theory of justice as it was, unvarnished, rather than dressed up for maximum present-day appeal.

Besides thin contextualization, this monograph peruses a second heuristic for reconstructive purposes: intertextual comparison. I devote much attention to changes and developments across Hobbes's oeuvre (from the 1640 *Elements* to the posthumously published *Behemoth*). Less to map his intellectual development than as cues for reconstructing his arguments. While few of Hobbes's basic political and philosophical commitments altered significantly over time, supporting arguments were continually added, amended, and sometimes discarded. Tracing how the content or textual location of an argument changes between, say, *Elements* and *Leviathan* can help unearth suppressed premises and hidden theoretical linkages. Intertextual comparison helps determine which claims are theoretically foundational and which secondary. It may also reveal argumentative inertia. Hobbes wrote later works by expanding or condensing earlier material, keeping in place the same general framework—a method dubbed 'serial composition'.[69] Some initial claims or argumentative moves may over time have proved infelicitous by Hobbes's own lights. Some of them may by then have become so foundational (theoretically or expository) that it became preferable to let them stand rather than start anew from scratch. Recognition of intertextual change is complicated by the seminal status of *Leviathan*. We are accustomed to reading Hobbes's other works through the lens of his *magnum opus*, unwittingly filling in the blanks with lines of reasoning found in the 1651 text. I have tried to resist this tendency.

Due to Hobbes's method of serial composition, remnants of older lines of reasoning are frequently found in later texts. Broader theoretical revisions can alter the meaning and implications of such relics, even of ones lifted verbatim from earlier works. Unless stated otherwise, the arguments and positions I attribute to Hobbes should not be taken to be 'present in' some texts but not 'in' others—even if I develop them, in part, to make sense of apparent cross-textual theoretical shifts. My reconstructions go beyond simple interpretive claims ('here he says this, there that'). Consider them rather as general attempts to spell out in full the arguments and doctrines Hobbes develops over time. For ease of reference, I have given catchy labels to the main arguments and doctrines I ascribe to Hobbes; the abbreviations section lists them all.

My exploration of intertextual change has affinities with what Schneewind calls 'internal explanations for philosophical change'.[70] External explanations are

---

[69] Deborah Baumgold, 'The Difficulties of Hobbes Interpretation', *Political Theory* 36 (2008) no. 6: 832–838.

[70] Jerome Schneewind, *Essays on the History of Moral Philosophy* (Oxford, 2010) 150–151. For critical discussion, see James Harris, 'The Pastness of Past Moral Philosophy', *British Journal for the History of Philosophy* 19 (2011) no. 2: 327–338.

24 VINDICATING THE 'MORTALL GOD'

extra-philosophical. Think of changed audiences; altered political or religious contexts; perceived needs to respond to new ideas; growing threats of persecution; etc. The *de facto* turn in *Leviathan* is a salient example of doctrinal change prompted by political events—even if Hobbes's underlying philosophical commitments logically mandated this change.[71] 'An internal explanation', by contrast, 'involves argument and the working out of the full logical implications of a principle or a position'.[72] One powerful explanation for why a philosopher ended up revising their argument is that by their own lights doing so improves their theory: eliminating contradictions; strengthening conclusions; incorporating new insights; removing ambiguities; shedding controversial or redundant premises; achieving theoretical parsimony; better answering real or potential objections; etc.

Hobbes on Justice highlights many such cross-textual improvements. For instance, *Leviathan*'s Authorization Argument shows much more powerfully the impossibility of sovereigns injuring citizens than the Consent Argument it replaces. Even sovereign commands which citizens never consented to obey (such as punitive orders) can be issued in their name and by their authority (rendering them non-injurious). Had he stuck to the earlier Consent Argument, then Hobbes would not have been entitled to call 'non-injurious' those sovereign decrees which individuals may resist without injustice (§6.6). *Leviathan* also introduces stronger and more parsimonious arguments for the state-dependency of property (§5.5) and justice (§7.3). These arguments in turn rest on two other theoretical novelties in *Leviathan*: a novel conception of distributive justice as equity as a positional duty of arbitrators (§4.2) and an accompanying anti-Aristotelian conception of merit in distributive justice (§4.5). Scrutinizing how exactly later arguments amend earlier ones can provide valuable information about the goals these arguments meant to serve and about their perceived strengths and weaknesses. It can also bring to light unexpected theoretical interconnections (e.g. between authorized representation and retained rights of resistance).

Hobbes's tendency to retain older arguments while adding new ones muddles attempts to unravel intertextual development. A characteristic feature of his writings is *argumentative overdetermination*: presenting multiple, sometimes mutually incompatible arguments for the same thesis.[73] Take his signature doctrine that sovereigns cannot be bound by covenant to their citizens. The most concessive of his supporting arguments are based on premises Hobbes did not truly countenance. They have the form: 'you argue that q because p. But even if we grant p (which I have already argued is false), then still q does not follow'. Thus, *if* the sovereign had entered covenants with his citizens (which he has not), then citizens are

---

[71] Kinch Hoekstra, 'The *De Facto* Turn in Hobbes's Political Philosophy' in Tom Sorell and Luc Foisneau (eds), *Leviathan after 350 Years* (Oxford, 2004) 33–73.
[72] Schneewind, *Essays*, 151.
[73] Alison McQueen, 'Hobbes's Strategy of Convergence', *Hobbes Studies* 33 (2020) no. 2: 135–152.

still not allowed to accuse the sovereign of injustice. Otherwise there would be 'no Judge to decide the controversie: it returns therefore to the Sword again . . . contrary to the designe they had in the Institution' (L 18.4) (§6.5). By facially endorsing tenets rejected elsewhere, argumentative overdetermination complicates reconstruction of Hobbes's considered views. I have tried to be attentive throughout to the presence of multiple levels of argumentation, possibly in tension with one another. Throughout, I split and isolate distinct lines of argument Hobbes advances for the same doctrine, evaluating them separately.

Which brings me to another Hobbesian trademark: *definitional convergence*. Definitional convergence occurs when multiple ostensibly distinct definitions are theoretically harmonized by equalizing their extensions. Concepts are extensionally equivalent when their instantiations fully overlap (i.e. when each concept refers to the exact same set of objects). Extensional equivalence differs from identity in meaning. To explain by example: Hobbes equates 'injury' with 'breaking agreements' (EL 16.2; DCv 3.3; L 14.7). Their equivalence is extensional: 'injury' (*sine jure*) means 'action without right', not reneging on agreements. The two notions nevertheless amount to the same thing. Humans, having natural right to everything, can act without right (*sine jure*) only after contractually divesting right to someone else. Every injury is for this reason always also a violation of a promise made (and vice versa) (§2.1). Postulating the *jus omnium in omnia* in addition allowed Hobbes to present converging definitions of 'injury' and 'unjust action'. *Leviathan* defines injustice of actions as '*the not Performance of Covenants*' (L 15.2). Every unjust action is also an injury (and vice versa) because in violating covenants, humans act 'without *jus*, or right; which was transferred or relinquished before' in the agreement (EL 16.2). Unjust action, injury, action without right, and breaking covenant are hence all extensionally equivalent. Which parities hold true by definition and which do so contingently, in virtue of underlying principles, is not always clear. Philosophical analysis must determine what kind of equivalence is involved.

Definitional convergence, the above example indicates, can render terms with distinct meanings mutually interchangeable. Definitional convergence can also pertain to a single notion, defined in clashing ways within a single text. Having formally defined injustice as breach of covenant, *Leviathan* proceeds to call 'Injustice . . . the Inconformity of the Action to the Law' (L 46.31). On that last definition, actions contravening the laws of nature—whose precepts obligate perpetually, without prior contracting—are also unjust. Jarring claims like these have led scholars to attribute to Hobbes two concepts of justice; three notions of obligation; four accounts of equity; and so on. As it happens, *Leviathan*'s two rival definitions of injustice do ultimately converge. A long argument aligns their extensions (more or less). In brief: Hobbes reduces natural and revealed law to civil law, thus making it the case that all unlawful behaviour within the state violates the original pact of simple obedience (§3.5).

Not all clashing definitions are problematic. Some may concern homonyms: distinct concepts that share the same label. The word 'equity', for instance, has two separate meanings in Hobbes. In its narrow sense, equity signifies a specific law of nature commanding arbitrators to adjudicate conflicts even-handedly. More broadly, it denotes the evaluative standard (i.e. natural law as a whole) which judges should use to interpret written law when adjudicating. These two meanings of equity are irreducibly distinct (§4.2). Whether opposing definitions are supposed to align—and whether they do in fact align—are matters of interpretation. It is an open question how internally coherent Hobbes's theory of justice is. For now, the takeaway methodological lesson is to take heed of possible definitional convergences. My reconstruction indicates that Hobbes made systematic use of this tool, brazen conceptual engineer as he was. Definitional convergence enabled him to incorporate rival definitions of contested terms into his theory, thus neutralizing commonplaces and forestalling terminological objections. And it helped him erect an awe-inspiringly complex interlocking system of thought, outlining an encompassing view of human life and politics that is both gripping and outlandish.

PART II
BASIC MORAL CONCEPTS

2

JUSTICE, RIGHTS, AND INJURY

INTRODUCTION

Hobbes went through tremendous lengths to clear the sovereign from all taints of injustice. Over time, he developed multiple capstone arguments to preclude the possibility of sovereign injustice. In addition, he crafted numerous supporting arguments to put in place the conceptual framework buttressing his overarching claims. Additional backing was direly needed: Hobbes constructed his theory of justice out of most unusual conceptual material. This chapter brings out how deeply revisionary were his glosses on terms like justice, rights, injury, wronging, and consent. Conceptual idiosyncrasies, we will see, cement even his simplest argument in defence of sovereign moral unaccountability. The No Pact Argument runs as follows. Since 'those who have obtained *sovereign power* in a commonwealth are not bound by any agreements to anyone, it follows that they can do no *wrong [injuria]* to the citizens. For . . . a *Wrong* is simply the violation of an agreement' (DCv 7.14; also EL 21.3). The same reasoning holds for unjust acts—a term synonymous with injury.

Concerns have been raised over this deceptively simple argument. Are there truly never any covenants between sovereign and citizens? Doubts are triggered by Hobbes's account of how so-called commonwealths *by acquisition* are formed.[1] In commonwealths *by institution*, the sovereign is not a contracting party to the original covenant but a third-party beneficiary. In these commonwealths, sovereign power arises from a mutual covenant between citizens. Fearing each other, citizens agree among themselves to freely grant another person sovereign power by jointly promising to simply obey him (L 17.15). As the sovereign is empowered 'by Covenant onely of one to another, and not of him to any of them; there can happen no breach of Covenant on the part of the Soveraigne' (L 18.4). Things look different in commonwealths by acquisition. Those commonwealths arise when some party seizes sovereign power through armed force (DCv 5.12; L 20.1–2; L 21.11). Sovereigns-by-acquisition *have* contracted with each of their subjects individually—sword in neck. Yet they immediately deliver the thing contracted for

---

[1] E.g. Howard Warrender, *The Political Philosophy of Hobbes* (Oxford, 1957) 133–134, 138; David Gauthier, *The Logic of Leviathan* (Oxford, 1969) 114–115; A.P. Martinich, *Hobbes's Political Philosophy: Interpretation and Interpretations* (Oxford, 2021) 176: '[Hobbes] seems to say that the conquering sovereign becomes a covenanting party in sovereignty by acquisition.' Martinich seeks to explain away his erroneous impression by harmonizing sovereignty-by-acquisition contracts with the third-party beneficiary covenant of sovereignty by institution.

Hobbes on Justice. Johan Olsthoorn, Oxford University Press. © Johan Olsthoorn 2024.
DOI: 10.1093/9780191904585.003.0002

30   JUSTICE, RIGHTS, AND INJURY

('life and liberty') in return for promises of future performance ('simple obedi-ence') (DCv 8.1). Citizens, for their part, have agreed to obey the sovereign indef-initely in either type of commonwealth.

In my view, voiced concerns over sovereignty-by-acquisition are ill-founded, resting on a misunderstanding of Hobbes's concept of covenant. Covenants are contracts involving trust. Contracts are essentially mutual transfers of rights. Rights are always transferred the moment the deal is signed. But oftentimes, the object of the right is not handed over straight away (L 14.10). For example, I may sell you land now for delivery next year. Any contracting party agreeing to future perform-ance has 'on his part' entered a 'PACT, or COVENANT', being trusted in the mean-time (L 14.11; also EL 15.8–9; DCv 2.9–10). Commonwealths by acquisition arise through part-contract, part-covenant agreements. Call such hybrid agreements 'covenants of *single* trust' (§7.1). Sovereigns-by-acquisition do *contract* with each citizen singly, letting them live in return for lifelong obedience. Yet no sovereign on his part ever enters with his subjects a *covenant*: a contract obligating him to future performance ('delivery'). The agreement sovereigns-by-acquisition sign contains no clause forbidding them to retake lives and liberties of released subjects later on (otherwise their contract would have been a covenant). Importantly, injury and unjust action exclusively consist in the violation of *covenants*. Whence their equa-tion with '*Violation of Faith*', that is, with inexcusably failing to do what one was contractually trusted to do (L 14.11).[2] Covenants are the only contracts that can be broken. Someone who performs their part of the deal in full straight away upon signing the agreement cannot possibly break the contract afterwards. Having im-mediately fulfilled their part, nothing sovereigns-by-acquisition do afterwards can count as a violation of covenant (i.e. as injustice).[3] Sovereign breaches of faith are hence impossible, regardless of how sovereignty was obtained.

Hobbes, I conclude, is entitled to the first premise of the No Pact Argument. The second premise—that injustice and injury consist in breaking valid covenants—is generally left unquestioned. Most commentators accept the premise as defin-itional. But what could justify equating injustice and injury with breaking faith? If pushed, many readers will agree with Pufendorf that these definitions are 'false and unreasonable'. Articulating a common objection, Pufendorf countered that hu-mans can be wronged in ways other than by breaking agreements with them: 'such *Right* as being violated produceth an Injury, is not only acquir'd by Covenant, but was given at first by Nature, without the Intervention of any Human Act'.[4]

---

[2] EL 5.7: 'faith ... signifieth the keeping of a promise'.

[3] As noted by G.S. Kavka, *Hobbesian Moral and Political Theory* (Princeton, 1986) 393; Mark Murphy, 'Deviant Uses of "Obligation" in Hobbes' *Leviathan*', *History of Philosophy Quarterly* 11 (1994) no. 3: 283; Luciano Venezia, *Hobbes on Legal Authority and Political Obligation* (New York, 2015) 99–100.

[4] Pufendorf, *Nature and Nations*, 1.7.13. The same objection is raised by Daniel Eggers, 'Injury, Injustice, Iniquity: The Evolution of Hobbes's Theory of Justice', *Intellectual History Review* 24 (2014) no. 2: 169.

INTRODUCTION 31

Consequently, 'a State, or the Sovereign Ruler of it, may do an *Injury* to a private Subject' even absent a mutual contract.[5] In denying this, Hobbes tacitly rejected the existence of natural obligations of justice.

A moment of reflection reveals how extraordinary Hobbes's definitions of injury and unjust action are. For a start, they imply that either humans owe no obligations of justice to their children, parents, and God; or that those obligations first arise through covenants. The same holds true, startlingly, for moral duties. 'The *laws of nature*', Hobbes insists, 'are *immutable and eternal*: what they forbid can never be lawful; what they command never unlawful' (DCv 3.29; also L 15.38). Yet absent some agreement to the contrary, he implies, contravening natural law duties is neither unjust nor injurious to humans harmed by it. Audacious as the second 'definitional' premise is, much theoretical work was required to establish it.

This chapter examines the theoretical grounds and implications of Hobbes's definitions of injury and injustice. By reconstructing the logic behind his deontic vocabulary, I aim to elucidate the nature of obligations of justice. Hobbes's theory of justice, I argue, pivots on a remarkable fourfold equation: (i) 'unjust action'; (ii) 'injury'/'wrong'; (iii) 'action without right'; and (iv) 'breach of covenant'.

> The breaking of an *Agreement* . . . is called a WRONG [INJURIA]. Such an action or failure to act is said to be *unjust* [*injusta*]; so that *wrong* and *unjust* action or failure to act have the same meaning, and both are the same as breaking an agreement or *breaking faith*. It seems that the name *wrong* [*injuria*] is applied to an action or a failure to act, because it is *without right* [*sine jure*], inasmuch as the party which acted or failed to act had already transferred the right to someone else. (DCv 3.3; also EL 16.2; L 14.7)

In what follows, I reconstruct the argumentative moves underpinning this chain of conceptual equivalences, highlighting some subtle yet theoretically significant changes over time. This chapter focuses exclusively on what Hobbes calls 'Commutative Justice . . . the Justice of a Contractor' (L 15.14). The other traditional type of particular justice—'Distributive Justice, the Justice of an Arbitrator' (L 15.15)—comes with a different deontic logic and status. Analysis of how Hobbes reworks distributive justice ('equity') for vindicatory purposes follows in Chapter 4.

As my reconstruction is at times technical, a chapter outline may prepare for what follows. §2.1 analyses Hobbes's definition of 'injury' (*injuria*, wrong) as action without right (*sine jure*). That definition underpins the equation of breaches of covenant with injuries. Contractual alienation of right creates obligations to do what one agreed to—and obligations preclude freedom (or right) to act

---

[5] Pufendorf, *Nature and Nations*, 7.8.4.

32 JUSTICE, RIGHTS, AND INJURY

contrariwise. Hobbes unwaveringly maintained that breaking covenants is both injurious and unjust. Yet the rationale for this equivalence shifts as *Leviathan* redefines the meaning of justice. Significantly, Hobbes never claimed that unjust actions are wrong because they violate another's rights. The implicated rights are always those of the wrongdoer—never the victim's (§2.2). Covenants always involve the alienation of right to some other person, who is wronged if the covenant is broken (§2.3). Yet the person thus injured need not be the covenantee(s) to whom one is bound by justice—it could also be a third-party beneficiary (the sovereign). Hobbes's struggle to account for the potentially diverging directionalities of injury and injustice helps explain why *Leviathan* redefines justice (§2.4). The equation of injury with breach of covenant presupposes that humans cannot lack right absent valid agreements; and that *all* obligations owed to humans are contractually created. To rule out the existence of natural obligations governed by justice, Hobbes had to introduce an extremely thin conception of attributed consent. Babies and enslaved persons alike 'consent' to simply obey their parents/enslavers in exchange for having been kept alive—just as citizens have done in commonwealths by acquisition (§2.5).

2.1 INJURY AS AN ACTION WITHOUT RIGHT

'Injury' (*injuria*) is a technical term for Hobbes. It denotes any action or omission without right.[6] (Though the following analysis applies equally to 'inaction without right'/'unjust inaction', I will for ease speak of 'action without right'/'unjust action'.) Hobbes offers an etymological justification for this definition.

> It seems that the name *wrong* [*injuria*] is applied to an action or failure to act, because it is *without right* [*sine jure*], inasmuch as the party which acted or failed to act had already transferred the right to someone else. (DCv 3.3; also L 14.7)

Equating injury with unjust action was historically commonplace. Suárez, citing the authority of Augustine, held that '*injuria* is nothing more nor less than an unjust act'.[7] Hobbes's conception of injury was nonetheless highly idiosyncratic, both in meaning and in extension. Take glosses on 'injuria' in Roman law. The *Digest* reads: 'Wrong is so called from that which happens not rightly [*non jure fiat*]; for everything which does not come about rightly is said to occur wrongfully.'[8] The

---

[6] Hobbes occasionally talks of (perceived) injury in a looser, non-technical sense, as slights of honour—never positively ('little injuries'). E.g. EL 24.2; EL 28.9; L 6.21; L 27.20.

[7] Suárez, *De Legibus*, 1.2.4: 'nam injuria nihil aliud est quam actus injustus'. Also Isidore of Seville, *The Etymologies*, ed. Stephen Barney et al. (Cambridge, 2006) 5.26.10: '*injuria* is injustice'.

[8] *Digest* 47.10.1: 'Injuria ex eo dicta est, quod non jure fiat: omne enim, quod non jure fit, injuria fieri dicitur.'

Institutes: 'Injuria in its general sense denotes all wrong conduct' [*non jure fit*].[9] These passages explicate injury in terms of general wrongdoing (i.e. conduct contrary to right). Grotius concurred: 'We have seen what constitutes a "right" [*jus*]; and from this concept we derive also the definition of a "wrong" or "injury" [*injuria*], guided by the basic belief that this term refers to whatever is done in opposition to right [*non jure fiat*].'[10]

Hobbes, by contrast, connected injury not to *non jure* (acting <u>contrary to</u> right) but to *sine jure* (acting <u>without</u> right): 'INJURY, as being *Sine Jure*' (L 14.7).[11] The significance of this move lies in the novel explanation it permits of when and why actions are injurious. Due to the natural right to everything—which allows each person 'to have and to do all things' (DCv 1.10)—injuries presuppose the contractual alienation of right. Hence the description of injury as an 'action or omission, without *jus*, or right; which was transferred or relinquished before' (EL 16.2). The link with *sine jure* informs the equation of injury with breach of covenant and explains why injuries are impossible absent valid agreements. Those two conceptual links would not have held had Hobbes agreed with Grotius that injuries are actions *contrary* to right. For why think that breaches of covenant exhaust wrongdoing? Surely actions contravening other laws of nature—for example cruelty, inequity, arrogance, ingratitude—are contrary to right as well. Explicating injury in terms of *sine jure* rather than *non jure* is thus the first step in Hobbes's argument that violating natural law is of itself neither injurious nor unjust. And that thesis, in turn, is indispensable for vindicating sinning sovereigns.

The resulting conception of injury was historically anomalous. Injury was commonly understood at the time to mean 'unlawful harm'.[12] Spinoza, for example, wrote: 'An injury [*injuria*] occurs when a citizen or subject is forced to suffer a harm from someone else, contrary to the civil law, or to an edict of the supreme power.'[13] For the Dutch thinker, unprovoked infliction of harm is rendered unlawful by *civil* law. Other early modern philosophers insisted that humans have natural rights whose violation is injurious. Berating Hobbes, Pufendorf held that in all unprovoked harm 'an Injury is always done, whether a Covenant hath interven'd or not'.[14] Likewise, Cumberland protested that 'every Opposition to, or

---

[9] *Institutes* 4.4.pr: 'Generaliter injuria dicitur omne quod non jure fit.' 'Injuria' was also used in more specific senses, including as signifying a distinct wrong involving disrespect ('contumelia'). David Ibbetson, '*Iniuria*, Roman and English' in Eric Descheemaeker and Helen Scott (eds), *Iniuria and the Common Law* (Oxford, 2013) 39–43.

[10] Hugo Grotius, *Commentary on the Law of Prize and Booty*, ed. M.J. van Ittersum (Indianapolis, 2006) 50: 'quid jus sit vidimus: unde injuria etiam noscitur, generali scilicet notione, ut id significet quidquid non jure fiat.'

[11] Also DCv 3.3: 'Videturque *injuriæ* nomen, inde actioni vel omissioni tribui, quia *sine jure* est.'

[12] Feinberg observes that the meaning of 'harming' and 'injuring' has since reversed. Today 'harm' is normative, 'injury' is not. Joel Feinberg, *Harm to Others* (Oxford, 1984) 106–107.

[13] Baruch Spinoza, 'Theological-Political Treatise' in *The Collected Works of Spinoza*, vol. 2, ed. Edwin Curley (Princeton, 2016) 16.41.

[14] Pufendorf, *Nature and Nations*, 1.7.15.

34 JUSTICE, RIGHTS, AND INJURY

Violation of, another's Right, is an *Injury* by what Law soever that Right accrued to the other'—be it by natural or civil law.[15] In his *Confutations of Mr Hobbes's Principles*, James Tyrrell (1642–1718) inveighed similarly: 'whatever a man enjoys by the right of Nature, it must needs be Injury and injustice to take it away; for every invasion or violation of another's Right or Property, is injury, by whatever Law he enjoys it.'[16] All three critics assumed that injuries consist in violations of another's rights. Endowed with natural rights, people can be wronged in ways other than by breaking covenants with them. Hobbes disagreed, reasoning that injury conceptually implicates the (missing) rights of the wrongdoer rather than any invaded rights of the victim. For this reason, no action, however harmful, can be injurious ('without right') as long as each person retains their natural right to all things. Modern commentators have overlooked this surprising conceptual feature of Hobbesian injury. Eggers, for instance, assumes that 'injury' refers to 'a violation of the rights of a particular individual.'[17] Yet Hobbes is quite clear that what makes injury *sine jure* is that the wrongdoer had previously alienated the right to perform that action.

Once we apprehend Hobbes's wondrous conception of injury as action without right, two otherwise puzzling doctrines start to make sense. The first likens injury to absurdity; the second holds that people are not wronged by infringements of their natural rights.

> *Injury*, or *Injustice*, in the controversies of the world, is somewhat like to that, which in the disputations of Scholers is called *Absurdity*. For as it is there called an Absurdity, to contradict what one maintained in the Beginning: so in the world, it is called Injustice, and Injury, voluntarily to undo that, which from the beginning he had voluntarily done. (L 14.7)

More succinctly: 'And so injury is an absurdity of conversation, as absurdity is a kind of injustice in disputation' (EL 16.2; also DCv 3.3). Commentators have struggled to explain how the analogy with self-contradiction is supposed to be normatively illuminating.[18] What is morally wrong about self-contradiction? And why

---

[15] Cumberland, *Treatise*, 348.

[16] [James Tyrrell], *A Brief Disquisition of the Law of Nature* (London, 1692) 299. His confutations of Hobbes conclude this tract.

[17] Eggers, 'Injury, Injustice, Iniquity', 171, also 176. Tuck's contention that Hobbes's natural law theory is grounded in a ban on 'wanton injury of another' becomes untenable once we appreciate the idiosyncratic nature of Hobbesian injury. Richard Tuck, *Philosophy and Government, 1572–1651* (Cambridge, 1993) 306.

[18] 'Hobbes's analogy between injury and absurdity is, itself, extremely absurd' writes Daniel Eggers, 'Liberty and Contractual Obligation in Hobbes', *Hobbes Studies* 22 (2009) no. 1: 78. Others have suggested, more constructively if exegetically less plausibly, that Hobbesian agents are motivated by fear of (being accused of) self-contradiction. Philip Pettit, *Made with Words: Hobbes on Language, Mind, and Politics* (Princeton, 2008) 61–63; Larry May, *Limiting Leviathan: Hobbes on Law and International Affairs* (Oxford, 2013) 15.

would it be distinctively unjust? The point of the analogy can be grasped by reflecting on what it does *not* say. Omitted is the truism that injury forbids invading the rights of others. The analogy with absurdity instead highlights that the wrong-making feature of injury consists in acting *without right* (as that right had been contracted away before).

Hobbes had good reason to avoid claiming that wrongdoers violate rights of others. After all, that claim would greatly complicate his signature doctrine of a natural right to all things, 'whereby one man invadeth with right, and another with right resisteth' (EL 14.11; also DCv 1.12). Natural rights of self-preservation allow each person to do whatever they deem necessary for survival—including seizing what others have equal right to. Hobbesian natural rights are non-exclusive: 'one could say of anything, *this is mine*, still he could not enjoy it because of his neighbour, who claimed the same thing to be his by equal *right* and with equal force' (DCv 1.11; also EL 14.10). Hobbes's view is not that the wrong done in violating another's rights is justified by the greater moral good of securing personal necessity. It is not because self-defence trumps the rights of others not to be subdued or killed that in 'the war of all against all, any one may legitimately subdue or even kill Men, whenever that seems to be to his advantage' (DCv 8.10). Rather, Hobbes holds that invading another's rights is not *by itself* wrong. On what grounds?

In reply, commentators commonly mention that Hobbesian natural rights are mere liberties, akin to Hohfeldian privileges.[19] Natural rights merely express what is morally permissible for the right-holder to do. They place no moral restraints on others. Invoking a distinction originally coined by Jeremy Bentham (1748–1832), Hobbesian liberty-rights are 'naked' (unprotected by any obligation of others) rather than 'vested' (correlating in obligations of non-interference in others).[20] I fully subscribe to these last interpretative claims. Yet the violability of natural rights, I submit, is not an inbuilt feature of them. Rather, Hobbes's conception of injury as 'action without right' explains why invading the natural rights of others is not by itself wrong. Indeed, violating another's *civil* rights is not of itself wrong or injurious either. Rather, actions (including those infringing rights/liberties of others) are injurious because and only insofar as the wrongdoer had previously forgone the right to perform that action.[21] That curious conceptual claim allowed Hobbes

---

[19] Even Curran, who has argued at length that Hobbes has a philosophically appealing theory of claim-rights, holds that natural rights are violable since they are mere liberties. Eleanor Curran, *Reclaiming the Rights of Hobbesian Subjects* (New York, 2007) 69–71.

[20] Cited in H.L.A. Hart, *Essays on Bentham: Studies in Jurisprudence and Political Theory* (Oxford, 1982) 172. This interpretation goes back at least to Pufendorf, notwithstanding his reservations about calling such naked liberties 'rights'. 'For 'tis ridiculous Trifling to call that Power a *Right*, which should we attempt to exercise, all other Men have an *equal Right* to obstruct or prevent us ... not every natural Licence, or Power of doing a Thing, is properly a *Right*; but such only as includes some moral Effect, with regard to others.' Pufendorf, *Nature and Nations*, 3.5.3; also 1.1.19.

[21] This casts doubt on Mautner's explanation for why injury is impossible outside the state: 'Since there is no natural suum, there is no such thing as injury or injustice in the state of nature.' The non-existence of exclusive natural rights is derivative and not explanatory of the absence of injury in the state of nature. The primary explanation is that no action can be without right ('injurious') as long as each

36 JUSTICE, RIGHTS, AND INJURY

to reduce injury to breaking faith. Significantly, he thus accounted for the nominal wrongfulness of injury without postulating a moral right not to be injured.[22] The cornerstone of his theory of justice, Hobbes's account of injury is strangely counter-intuitive. No wonder it has, until now, been misunderstood by contemporary and modern critics alike.

2.2 JUSTICE, INJUSTICE, AND INJURY

Hobbes's theory of justice is based on a series of conceptual equivalences. It is not always clear which of these definitions are basic and which derivative, holding true in virtue of a combination of other definitions. (Hobbes apparently used the phrase 'by the definition of' for both.) Take 'unjust action'. Each of his political works identifies this notion with both 'injury' and 'breach of covenant'. Which of the two captures the basic meaning of 'unjust action'? The answer, I contend, varies per book.

Both *Elements* and *De Cive* define 'justice of actions' in terms of injury: 'justice and injustice, when they be attributed to actions, signify the same thing with no injury, and injury' (EL 16.4). '[W]hen applied to actions, *Just* means the same as done with right [jure factum], and *Unjust*, done without right [*Injuria*]' (DCv 3.5). Moreover, both works define 'injury' as breach of covenant: 'injury consisteth in violation of covenant, by the definition thereof' (EL 16.3; also EL 21.3). '[A] *Wrong* is simply the violation of an agreement' (DCv 7.14; also DCv 3.3). Breaking covenants is unjust *because* it is injurious. 'The breach or violation of covenant, is that which men call INJURY, consisting in some action or omission, which is therefore called UNJUST' (EL 16.2; also DCv 3.3). Hobbes's reasoning in the early works seems to be that justice prohibits injury, and therefore, by consequence, breaking faith.

Leviathan retains the identification of 'unjust action' with 'injury': 'the injustice of an action, that is to say injury' (L 15.12; also L 14.7; L 15.11). Yet justice is now defined directly in terms of covenant-keeping: 'the nature of Justice, consisteth in keeping of valid Covenants' (L 15.3). 'INJUSTICE, is no other than *the not Performance of Covenants*' (L 15.2).[23] Instead of a maxim forbidding injury/

---

person retains their natural right to everything. Thomas Mautner, 'Natural Law and Natural Rights' in P.R. Anstey (ed), *The Oxford Handbook of British Philosophy in the Seventeenth Century* (Oxford, 2013) 492.

[22] Another historically unusual position. *Neminem laedere* ('harm no one') is one of three basic moral principles in Roman law. Leibniz equated it with 'the precept of mere or strict right...no one is to be injured'. G.W. Leibniz, *Political Writings*, ed. Patrick Riley (Cambridge, 1988) 172. For similar statements, see Cicero, *On Duties*, 1.20; Grotius, *Law of Prize and Booty*, 27.

[23] A change highlighted and variously explained by Luc Foisneau, '*Leviathan*'s Theory of Justice' in Tom Sorell and Luc Foisneau (eds), *Leviathan after 350 Years* (Oxford, 2004) 106–108; Eggers, 'Injury, Injustice, Iniquity', 175. Laird overlooks these cross-textual changes when arguing that Hobbes

wrongdoing, justice has become the natural law duty to keep faith. Injury, in turn, is now defined as injustice of action, rather than as breaking covenant (L 15.11–12). This subtle shift has far-reaching theoretical consequences, explored in depth later on. Discarding the earlier conceptual equivalence, actions with right are no longer *ipso facto* 'just' on the new definition. For not all actions with right are instances of covenant-keeping. Think of things done by natural right outside the state, or of sovereign conduct within it. Thus, combatants who violently resist attacks on their life are acting justly (for: with right) on the earlier definition—even if they are not keeping any pact thereby. Not so on *Leviathan*'s definition of justice. While any just action (i.e. performance of covenant) is done with right, the reverse no longer holds. It remains true in *Leviathan* that any injury is also an unjust action (and vice versa).

Intriguingly, the fourfold conceptual equivalence between (i) 'unjust action'; (ii) 'injury'; (iii) 'action without right'; and (iv) 'breach of covenant' persists despite this rearrangement. While these four terms remain mutually interchangeable, *Leviathan* does alter the logical connections between them. Any unjust action is of necessity without right since injustice consists in performing an action the right to which one has contracted away (i.e. in doing what one has obligated oneself not to do). Breaching faith 'is INJUSTICE, and INJURY, as being *Sine Jure*; the Right being before renounced, or transferred' (L 14.7). Conversely, any action that is injurious/without right is also unjust/a breach of covenant. Yet that claim now holds true not axiomatically but contingently, in virtue of the natural right to all things. Absent any binding agreement to the contrary, we will see, natural right literally allows each person to do anything to anyone (§3.2). Outside the state, 'no action can be Unjust' because by nature 'every man has right to every thing' (L 15.2; also LL 27.3). *Leviathan*'s new definition of justice thus purposefully creates an asymmetry. While any action without right is unjust, it is not the case that any action with right is just.

What is the rationale behind *Leviathan*'s new definition of justice? And what is its theoretical significance? Later on, I will expound three distinct advantages of the redefinition. To anticipate, first, it permits injury and injustice to have diverging directionalities: the same action can be unjust to some and injurious to others. Hobbes needed that conceptual disentanglement to account for the possibility of private wrongs within the commonwealth (§2.4). Second, the redefinition sidesteps an inconvenient implication of *Leviathan*'s novel doctrine of the

---

employed justice in both a narrow and a broad sense, and that he confused the two. For Laird, justice in its narrow sense consists in performance of covenants, in its broad sense in 'whatever was done "with right"' (citing DCv 3.5). Adopting his parlance, *Leviathan* substitutes justice in the narrow sense for that in the broad. John Laird, *Hobbes* (London, 1934) 183. Like Laird, Green attributes a narrower and a broader conception of justice to Hobbes, with the narrower one requiring keeping covenants and the broader one demanding observance of *all* the laws of nature. Michael J. Green, 'Justice and Law in Hobbes', *Oxford Studies in Early Modern Philosophy* 1 (2003) 133–134.

38   JUSTICE, RIGHTS, AND INJURY

true liberties of subjects. By retained natural right, citizens may resist sovereign orders that imperil their lives 'without Injustice' (L 21.10). On the early conception of justice ('action done with right'), any citizen exercising those inalienable rights of resistance would be acting *justly*. By redefining just actions as performances of covenants, Hobbes avoided that riotous implication. Third, the redefinition allows him to affirm that justice and injustice have no place outside the commonwealth. On the early conception of justice, just actions had been omnipresent beyond the state, due to each person's natural right to everything (§7.2).

Leviathan's change in definition notwithstanding, justice and injustice retain their most unusual character. Injustice keeps its close conceptual link with Hobbes's counter-intuitive conception of injury as action without right. Like injury, injustice makes no reference to rights of others. It contrasts sharply, in this respect, with prevailing conceptions of injustice within seventeenth-century natural jurisprudence. From Grotius onwards, it was commonly held that 'the very Nature of Injustice consists in nothing else, but in the Violation of another's Rights'.[24] Locke, for instance, writes: 'the *Idea* to which the Name *Injustice* is given, being the Invasion or Violation of that right'.[25] For Hobbes, justice does command persons not to hinder others in exercising their rights—but only if and because they have contractually obligated themselves to do so. Consequently, trampling on rights of others is by itself neither injurious nor unjust.

To fully appreciate this remarkable point, consider that covenants can create exclusive rights. The original covenant endows each person with exclusive liberty-rights in their own life, body, and person (though crucially not excluding the sovereign) (§5.6). For in that covenant, all citizens jointly lay down their natural rights to invade others to heighten personal security: 'when we make societies or commonwealths, we lay down our right to kill' (EW 5: 153).[26] Physically harming fellow citizens without provocation henceforth becomes unjust. Yet harming others is not wrong or unjust *because* they violate their exclusive rights to bodily integrity. Rather, they are so because they void self-incurred obligations not to hinder others in the enjoyment of their bodies. Put differently, justice prohibits persons from acting without right; it does not demand respect for the rights of others.

This brings us to a last peculiarity of Hobbes's conception of justice. Remarkably, it presupposes only so-called liberty-rights. Actions are just if the agent has the liberty-right so to act; unjust when they lack that liberty-right. Claim-rights do not figure in these definitions. By contrast, the rights conceptually implicated in, for instance, Grotius's conception of justice are more akin to claim-rights. 'Justice

---

[24] Grotius, *War and Peace*, Prol.45: 'cum tamen injustitia non aliam naturam habeat quam alieni usurpationem'. Also Grotius, *War and Peace*, Prol.10, 2.12.9.2.

[25] John Locke, *An Essay Concerning Human Understanding*, ed. P.H. Nidditch (Oxford, 1975) 4.3.18. Also Cumberland, *Treatise*, 328; Samuel Pufendorf, *The Whole Duty of Man, According to the Law of Nature*, ed. Ian Hunter and David Saunders (Indianapolis, 2003) 1.2.15.

[26] Curran, *Reclaiming the Rights*, 72–76, 100, 110–111, 165–168.

properly and strictly taken' regulates so-called perfects rights.[27] Perfect rights are enforceable—actionable in courts and on battlefields. For Grotius, justice forbids taking from or denying others what they have an enforceable claim to.

Looking back, we may with reason object that Hobbes's theoretical achievements so far are merely verbal. As injury/wrong is defined as action without right, so injustice is wrong in virtue of being an action without right. Yet what is *morally* wrong about acting without right/breaking covenants? Hobbes's argument that injury and injustice by definition consist in acts without right provides neither moral nor prudential reason to abstain from injustice.[28] As it happens, Hobbes does provide a normative explanation of the wrongness of injustice later on. Forbidden by natural law, injustice is a moral vice since it always tends to bring war and violent death closer. The 'Goodnesse' of justice, in turn, consists in it being a 'meanes of peaceable, sociable, and comfortable living' (L 15.40).

2.3 TURNING INJURY AND INJUSTICE INTO DIRECTED CONCEPTS

I have been arguing that Hobbes conceptualized 'injury'/'injustice' idiosyncratically as actions without right (rather than as rights-violations). This unprecedented account normatively foregrounds the wrongdoer rather than their victim. It also precludes a common way of semantically differentiating 'injustice' from 'injury'. Namely, by calling a wrongful action 'unjust' when judging the wrongdoer and 'injurious' when eyeing the victim. As Hobbes's critic Roger Coke (1628–1704) put it:

> Injustice differs from Injury, only in agencie and patiencie, in him who does, and in him who suffers. It is injustice for any man, unjustly to make use of any law of God or man, or Temporal power . . . to the hurt or prejudice of another; and such hurt or prejudice, is injury to whom it is done.[29]

For Hobbes, both injustice and injury reside in what Coke calls 'agencie'. The rights conceptually implicated in unjust acts are those of the wrongdoer alone. Hobbes

---

[27] Grotius, *War and Peace*, 1.1.8.1.

[28] As noted by Stephen Darwall, *British Moralists and the Internal 'Ought', 1640–1740* (Cambridge, 1995) 55–57. Hobbes's use of deontic language therefore gives us no insight into the character of his moral theory. Deontological readings have generally failed to appreciate this point. Indeed, their conflation of a conceptual with a normative argument goes some way to explain the inadequacy of such interpretations. E.g. Martin Harvey, 'Teasing a Limited Deontological Theory of Morals out of Hobbes', *The Philosophical Forum* 35 (2004) no. 1: 36–40.

[29] Roger Coke, *Elements of Power & Subjection* (London, 1660) 4.1.24. Also Pufendorf, *Nature and Nations*, 1.7.14–15. On Coke as a critic of Hobbes, see John Parkin, *Taming the Leviathan* (Cambridge, 2007) 229–232.

40 JUSTICE, RIGHTS, AND INJURY

therefore needed a further argument to explain who (if anyone) is injured by actions without right.

Hobbes was adamant that 'the Injustice of an Action, (that is to say Injury,) supposeth an individuall person Injured; namely him, to whom the Covenant was made' (L 15.12). What makes it the case that any and every injustice injures another person? What prevents the possibility of 'free-floating injuries'—actions that are wrong (noun) without wronging (verb) anyone in particular? Persons are not morally free to contravene natural law duties. Immoral actions thus seem to be injuries—actions without right—even if they involve no breach of covenant and wrong no one. Hobbes made free-floating injuries impossible in part by postulating a universal right to all things, grounded in human natural equality. Outside the state, I will argue, each person equally has blanket permissions vis-à-vis other humans to 'do whatever he pleases, or whatever seems right to him' (DCv 11.4). Even objectively wrong actions crossing natural law are performed with right if done in good faith—and which actions are done sincerely only God knows. Besides, equals can legitimately accuse each other of wrongdoing only by appeal to a common standard of law. And no such standard exists outside the state. Chapter 3 dissects Hobbes's twin arguments for this controversial doctrine (§3.3–§3.4).

This section analyses another supporting premise: rights are always alienated *to* some other party (who is wronged by any subsequent violation of obligation).[30] Obligations, for Hobbes, essentially consist in the absence of right. 'Right' is conceived as a kind of liberty; 'obligation', he associates with law. 'LAW, determineth, and bindeth to one of them: so that Law, and Right, differ as much, as Obligation, and Liberty; which in one and the same matter are inconsistent' (L 14.3).[31] In Hohfeldian terms, obligation is for Hobbes the opposite of right—not its correlative.[32] Since obligations (to φ) consist in lack of right (not to φ), they can be created *de novo* by laying down right:

> Right is layd aside, either by simply Renouncing it; or by Transferring it to another. By *Simply* RENOUNCING; when he cares not to whom the benefit thereof redoundeth. By TRANSFERRING; when he intendeth the benefit thereof to some certain person, or persons. And when a man hath in either manner abandoned, or granted away his Right; then is he said to be OBLIGED, or BOUND, not to hinder those, to whom such Right is granted, or abandoned, from the benefit of it: and that he *Ought*, and it is his DUTY, not to make voyd that voluntary act of his

---

[30] Arash Abizadeh, *Hobbes and the Two Faces of Ethics* (Cambridge, 2018) 191–195.

[31] On the opposition between right and obligation, see also EL 29.5; DCv 2.10; DCv 14.1, 3; L 26.43; DPS 37.

[32] W.N. Hohfeld, *Fundamental Legal Conceptions*, ed. W.W. Cook (New Haven, 1923) 36. For a defence of the interpretive value of this framework, see Arthur Yates, 'A Hohfeldian Analysis of Hobbesian Rights', *Law and Philosophy* 32 (2013) no. 4: 405–434.

own: and that such hindrance is INIUSTICE, and INIURY, as being *Sine Jure*; the Right being before renounced, or transferred. (L 14.7)

Elements and *De Cive* likewise distinguish between divesting right through transfer and through renunciation. (I shall use 'alienating right' as a general term for laying down right in either manner.) Yet these early works suggest that only *transference* of right involves some other party.[33] Only rights-transfers require acceptance by the intended recipient to be felicitous (EL 15.4; DCv 2.5). Renouncing a right consists in simply declaring that one 'no longer wants it to be licit for him to do some specific thing which previously he might *rightly do*' (DCv 2.4; also EL 15.3). This claim is enigmatic. To whom is one accountable for any subsequent illicit conduct? And why should acting contrary to a unilaterally renounced right be called 'unjust'? Is anyone wronged or any agreement broken thereby?[34] The inclusion in *Elements/De Cive* of unilateral renunciation of right hints at the possibility of free-floating injuries: actions without right that wrong no one.

Leviathan eliminates this puzzling possibility. Both renunciation and transference of right are now said to involve another party: 'when a man hath <u>in either manner</u> abandoned, or granted away his Right; then is he said to be OBLIGED, or BOUND, not to hinder those, to whom such Right is granted, or abandoned, from the benefit of it' (L 14.7). Both ways of alienating right create obligations not to hinder the beneficiary of the rights-divestment. The difference between the two ways of divesting right is that in renunciation, the right is not granted to a specific party but is left up for grabs, as 'he cares not to whom the benefit thereof redoundeth'. *Leviathan* does not specify to whom one becomes obligated upon renouncing right. The Latin *Leviathan* clarifies that the right is then cast away 'to the people generally, not giving it to any individual' (LL 14.7).

Hobbes's talk about 'transferring rights' is liable to misunderstanding. It brings to mind a transaction, where one person holding some right passes it on to another person. First the right was mine, then the transaction makes it yours. That is not Hobbes's view: 'he that renounceth, or passeth away his Right, <u>giveth not</u> to any other man a Right which he had not before; because there is nothing to which every man had not Right by Nature' (L 14.6). No new rights are acquired in the original covenant since any 'recipient' 'already had a right to all things *before the transfer of the right*; hence the transferor could not give him a <u>new</u> *right*' (DCv 2.4; also EL 15.3; L 28.2). Recipients are instead said to receive the 'benefit' of the alienated right. 'To *lay downe* a mans *Right* to any thing, is to *devest* himselfe of the *Liberty*, of hindring another of the benefit of his own *Right* to the same'

---

[33] EL 15.3; DCv 2.4. A rights-transfer botched due to non-acceptance of the other party does not result in renunciation of right, 'for the reason why I wished to give it to one particular person lies in him alone and not in others' (DCv 2.5; also EL 15.4).

[34] A.P. Martinich, *The Two Gods of Leviathan: Thomas Hobbes on Religion and Politics* (Cambridge, 1992) 77–78.

42   JUSTICE, RIGHTS, AND INJURY

(L 14.6). Non-exclusive and unprotected, natural rights are useless when held in common (EL 14.10; DCv 1.11; LL 31.4). The collective alienation of right in the original covenant first makes possessing natural rights beneficial. Covenanters obligate themselves not to hinder the beneficiary of the rights-transfer, by promising to 'standeth out of his way, that he may freely enjoy the right which he previously possessed' (LL 14.6).

Citizens and the sovereign alike are beneficiaries of this collective rights-alienation. Crucially, Hobbes's social contract is composed of two covenants. Each is necessary for forming a commonwealth—and each involves the alienation of different rights. In the so-called 'Covenant of Peace', individuals mutually lay down their invasive rights, as dictated by the second law of nature (L 14.31). It commands each to '*lay down this right to all things; and be contented with so much liberty against other men, as he would allow other men against himselfe*' (L 14.5; also EL 15.2; DCv 2.3). The first collective rights-divestment takes the form of a mutual promise not to hinder any fellow citizens in the enjoyment of their retained liberties. This promise renders exclusive certain pre-existing natural liberties all have, including rights to their own body, life, and person. By renouncing their invasive rights of nature, citizens mutually grant fellow citizens a sphere of personal freedom, theirs alone to enjoy (§3.6; §5.6). Mutual fear and self-serving partiality would swiftly doom any covenant of peace unless a common power is instituted to keep potential pact breakers in line. That common power is the government, set up in the second covenant ('the covenant of Subjection'—L 21.24). While no covenant of peace can last without an accompanying covenant of subjection, the two covenants remain analytically distinct: different rights are alienated to different parties in each.

The sovereign is the sole beneficiary of the collective rights-alienation in the covenant of subjection. In commonwealths by acquisition and institution alike, all subjects have empowered and authorized him through renunciation of their rights of self-government *to* him (L 17.13). People subject themselves to the rule of another by promising simple obedience—that is, by agreeing not to resist their ruler's future orders, whatever their content (EL 19.10; DCv 5.11; DCv 8.1). The obligations citizens jointly contract into remove as many impediments to the exercise of the sovereign's natural right. As Hobbes explains when discussing the grounds of the 'right of Punishing': 'Subjects did not give the Soveraign that right; but onely in laying down theirs, strengthned him to use his own, as he should think fit . . . so that it was not given, but left to him, and to him onely' (L 28.2). The same mechanism applies to the sovereign's right to govern generally. This *jus regnandi* derives from natural rights of self-defence—which permits individuals to 'subdue' and 'master' all others (EL 22.9; L 13.4) (§8.2). The right to everything, in other words, includes a natural right 'to reign over all the rest' (L 31.5; also EL 22.2; DCv 15.5). Due to human natural equality of power, this natural right (like all others) is useless unless others climb down. Subjects really only promise not to hinder the sovereign in the exercise of his natural right to rule. Their promises of simple obedience empower the sovereign by removing resistance (i.e. hindrances to his freedom) (EL 19.10; EL 22.2; DCv 5.7). As Gauthier puts it, 'natural right becomes sovereign right, not by its own augmentation, but by the diminution of the rights of others'.[35] Notice that the provided analysis of rights-transfer in the original covenant supports my contention that injustice for Hobbes does not conceptually imply rights-violations.

The above analysis evinces that *all* self-incurred obligations are created by laying down right to some other party—at least in *Leviathan*. Another Hobbesian doctrine supports the same. Obligations owed to yourself are impossible: 'he that is bound to himself only is not bound' (L 26.6). This is so because '[a]ll obligations are determinable at the will of the obliger' (EL 15.12). Obligations are absolved by restitution of right. 'Forgivenesse [is] a re-transferring of that Right, in which the obligation consisted' (L 14.26). Anyone obligated to themselves alone is free to release themselves at will. This means one was never bound. 'For he that can oblige, can also, when he will, release; and he that can release himself when he will, is not obliged' (EW 5: 144).[36] Observe that this argument only applies to obligations that permit release. It does not hold for natural law requirements, which bind in virtue of rational agency and for which one remains perpetually accountable to God.

Combined with the natural right to everything, Hobbes's directional account of rights-alienation explains why free-floating injuries and injustices are impossible. It turns injury into an essentially relational concept: any action without right injures another person. And it ensures that justice of actions essentially governs obligations people have *to* others ('directed' obligations, in modern jargon) (§3.1).[37] Put differently, wrongdoers not only *act wrongly* by breaking covenant, they thereby also always *wrong someone*.[38] On *Leviathan*'s account, unjust actions likewise are always unjust *to* at least one other person. Because injustice and injury conceptually implicate the (missing) rights of the wrongdoer alone, establishing their directionality required considerable further argument. Hobbes would have been spared that task had he adopted the common view that injustice/injury consist in invading another's rights.

It may seem that the person wronged by breaking faith must be the covenantee.[39] That view is defended in *Elements*: 'in all violation of covenant . . . the

---

[35] Gauthier, *The Logic of Leviathan*, 110.

[36] Also DCv 6.14; DCv 7.7; DCv 12.4. This principle can be traced back to Roman law, *Digest* 45.1.108.1: 'No promise can be valid if it lies wholly within the choice of the promisor.'

[37] Simon Căbulea May, 'Directed Duties', *Philosophy Compass* 10 (2015) no. 8: 523: 'Directed duties are duties that an agent owes to some party – a party who would be wronged if the duty were violated.' See also Gopal Sreenivasan, 'Duties and Their Direction', *Ethics* 120 (2010) no. 3: 464–494; Stephen Darwall, *Morality, Authority, and Law: Essays in Second-Personal Ethics I* (Oxford, 2013) 27–42.

[38] Warrender, *The Political Philosophy of Hobbes*, 133, overlooks this point when claiming that Hobbes can safeguard even *covenanting* sovereigns from accusations of injustice: 'it is not necessary that the sovereign be shown to be incapable of breaking covenant provided that the judgement on this matter be left to God.'

[39] As argued by Eggers, 'Injury, Injustice, Inequity', 172.

44   JUSTICE, RIGHTS, AND INJURY

injury is done <u>only</u> to him to whom the covenant was made' (EL 16.3). *De Cive* enlarges who can be wronged: 'a wrong [injuriam] can only be done to someone with whom an *agreement* has been made, or to whom something has been given as a gift, or promised by *agreement*' (DCv 3.4; also DCv 3.6; DCv 7.14). That alteration is required by Hobbes's social contract theory. In commonwealths by institution, the sovereign is not a contracting party to the original covenant but its beneficiary. Citizens mutually agree to freely give up their rights of self-government to him, by promising simple obedience (L 17.13). Such 'GIFT, FREE-GIFT, GRACE', Hobbes insists, involves no 'Contract' between donors and recipient (L 14.12; also EL 15.7; DCv 2.8).[40] Citizens owe it to each other as well to not hinder the thus-empowered third-party beneficiary.

> Thus by the agreements made between individuals which bind them to each other and by the gift of right which they are obliged to the ruler to respect, the power of government is secured by a double obligation [duplici obligatione] on the part of the citizens, an obligation to their fellow citizens and an obligation to their rulers. (DCv 6.20; also DCv 7.14; L 18.3)

Does this double obligation mean that citizens and the sovereign alike are wronged ('injured') by crimes—unjust breaches of the *pactum generale obedientiae*? Must the person to whom one is obligated to perform a covenant and the person wronged upon its violation be the same? Hobbes's recognition of, and struggle with, that additional complexity lies behind a major change in his theory of justice between *De Cive* and *Leviathan*.

2.4 INJURY AND LOSS

Across his works, Hobbes carefully distinguished between injury and harm (loss, damage; Latin: *damnum*). 'Injury' is a normative notion ('action without right'). 'Damnum' is non-moralized, signifying a setback to one's interests (due to events or the actions of others). Persons can be harmed without being injured; the reverse is possible too. '[M]any times the injury is received by one man, when the damage redoundeth to another' (L 15.12; also EL 16.3; DCv 3.4). For example,

> when the Master commandeth his servant to give mony to a stranger; if it be not done, the Injury is done to the Master, whom he [the servant] had before

---

[40] May argues that by mixing the notion of covenant and free-gift transfer, Hobbes 'forms the new notion of third-party beneficiary contract'. Larry May, 'Hobbes's Contract Theory', *Journal of the History of Philosophy* 18 (1980) no. 2: 205, 207. Mutual transfer of right hence 'does not require that any party to the contract transfer his right to any other party to the contract'. Martinich, *Two Gods*, 153.

Covenanted to obey; but the dammage redoundeth to the stranger, to whom he [the servant] had no Obligation; and therefore could not Injure him. (L 15.12; also LL 15.10; DCv 3.4)

Hobbes's non-moralized conception of loss/damnum was unusual. According to Roman law, '[n]o one commits a wrong [*damnum*] against another unless he does something which he has no right to do'.[41] Grotius even took 'damnum' itself to mean rights-deprivation. 'The Word *Damnum*, Damage' signifies that 'a Man has less than his Right'.[42] Pufendorf agreed: 'Damage [*Damnum*] . . . implies all Hurt, Spoil or Diminution of whatsoever is already actually our own'—that is, of whatever we are entitled to by perfect right.[43]

Hobbes's key rationale for revising the meaning of 'damnum' is to deprive citizens of reasons for resentment. Hobbes regarded the uniquely human capacity to distinguish injury from loss a major cause of civil unrest (DCv 5.5; L 17.11; DH 10.3). '[I]njury, how light soever the damage, is always grievous' (EL 24.2). Citizens not only resent injuries done to themselves. They are also indignant about harms others wrongfully suffer. '*Anger* for great hurt done to another, when we conceive the same to be done by Injury, INDIGNATION' (L 6.21; also L 30.23). Sedition looms if citizens experience losses incurred by government regulation as personal affronts. The disaffected will 'believe that their rebellion is just, their discontents grounded upon great injuries' (EL 27.14). Bees, by contrast, live together at ease in part because 'they have no conception of right and wrong, but only of pleasure and pain, and therefore also no CENSURE of one another, nor of their commander' (EL 19.5). In response, Hobbes insisted that a sovereign arbitrarily depriving citizens of their goods, livelihoods, or even lives does them no injury. He only causes them loss.

Hobbes worked hard to conceptually establish that 'no one may think that a *wrong* [injuriam] is anything but a breach of faith or agreements' (DCv 3.6). Reducing 'injury' to 'breach of covenant' and the concomitant sharp distinction between injury and loss greatly supported his vindicatory project. It underpinned his No Pact Argument: having made no covenant with his citizens, the sovereign can do them no wrong. Hobbes unflinchingly endorsed the counter-intuitive implications of this view in *De Cive*:

> So too in a commonwealth, if one harms anyone with whom he has no agreement, he causes *loss* [*damnum*] to the person he maltreats, but does a *wrong* [*injuriam*] only to the holder of authority over the whole commonwealth. For if the victim

---

[41] *Digest* 50.17.151: 'Nemo damnum facit, nisi qui id fecit, quod facere jus non habet.'

[42] Grotius, *War and Peace*, 2.17.2, also 2.17.4: 'to have less than is due, and consequently to suffer Damage [*damnum*]'.

[43] Pufendorf, *Nature and Nations*, 3.1.3.

46   JUSTICE, RIGHTS, AND INJURY

of the harm should claim to have been wronged, the person who did the action would say, *What are you to me? Why should I act at your pleasure rather than my own, since I am not preventing you from acting at your discretion, not mine?* I do not see how one could fault that response, when no agreement had been made. (DCv 3.4)

I take it that this passage will seem outrageous to any reader who is not a banker. Commenting on this passage, Pufendorf exclaimed: 'No sane person should consider that excuse reasonable.'[44] The passage has no parallel in *Leviathan*—even though the contrast between *injuria* and *damnum* is retained.[45] Perhaps the '*what are you to me?*' line is dropped because it does not adequately capture the moral relations the original covenant establishes between sovereign and citizens. Sovereigns-by-institution are obliged by natural law to be grateful to citizens, in virtue of being the beneficiary of their free gift—even if acts of ingratitude are by definition neither unjust nor injurious (EL 16.6–7; DCv 3.8; L 15.16).

Rejecting any fixed conceptual connection between injury and harm/damage, Hobbes equated injury with injustice and breaking faith instead. This triple equation had a curious implication due to a twist in his social contract theory. In the original covenant of subjection, citizens promise simple obedience to the sovereign *and* to each other. They thereby establish 'a double obligation' (DCv 6.20). Crimes—unjustified transgressions of civil law (L 27.2–3)—are unjust qua breaches of this mutual agreement. It follows that 'what is Unjust, is <u>unjust to all</u>'— that is, to the sovereign and to all fellow citizens alike (DCv 3.4n).

Recall that *Elements* and *De Cive* define 'injury' as 'breach of covenant'. On this account, crimes injure every citizen alike, victim or not. Call this implausible doctrine *Collective Victimhood*. The first edition of *De Cive* affirms this doctrine explicitly: 'if a citizen fails to show obedience to the sovereign power, he is a *wrongdoer [injurius] ... both against his fellow citizens* on the ground that each man has agreed with every other man to show obedience, *and against the sovereign*' (DCv 7.14). *Collective Victimhood* has three counter-intuitive implications. First, any crime injures an exceptionally large number of people: all members of the commonwealth. Second, every crime injures all citizens *equally*. Third, the fact that a thief steals *your* goods (and not someone else's) is irrelevant for whether the theft she commits injures *you*.[46] For the wrong done in unlawfully seizing

---

[44] Samuel Pufendorf, *The Pufendorf Lectures*, ed. Bo Lindberg (Stockholm, 2014) 67.

[45] Deborah Baumgold (ed), *Three-Text Edition of Thomas Hobbes's Political Theory* (Cambridge, 2017) 165–166.

[46] This is not because Hobbes is committed to 'moral occasionalism' (in Feinberg's felicitous phrase). On Feinberg's reading, Hobbesian citizens have 'obligations toward one another; but the obligations (here is the twist) will not be owed directly *to* promisees, creditors, parents, and the like, but rather to God alone, or to the members of some elite, or to a single sovereign under God'. On the interpretation advanced here, citizens *do* have directed obligations to each other—albeit overly general ones. Joel Feinberg, 'The Nature and Value of Rights', *Journal of Value Inquiry* 4 (1970) no. 4: 247.

another's goods consists exclusively, on the early account, in reneging on the original promise made to you and to everybody else to obey the civil laws.[47]

Hobbes first dealt with *Collective Victimhood* in a remark added to the second edition of *De Cive*.

> The word Injustice has meaning in relation to law; Wrong [Injuriæ] in relation to law and a specific Person. For what is Unjust, is unjust to all; but there can be a Wrong which is not a wrong against me or against him, but against someone else, and sometimes not against any private person at all, but against the commonwealth only, and even a wrong which is against neither man nor commonwealth, but against God alone. (DCv 3.4n)

Hobbes conceptually disentangled injustice and injury, I submit, to render it possible for crimes, though equally *unjust* to all, to *injure* only specific persons.[48] As breaches of the mutual promise of simple obedience, crimes are unjust to everyone. Yet only the person to whom right is alienated, Hobbes now emphasized, can be wronged. 'There can therefore be no wrong against a particular man [injuria in hunc] except after transfer of a right <u>to him</u>' (DCv 3.4n). From 1647 onwards, Hobbes held that the mere act of covenanting creates obligations owed to other covenantees—even if no right is alienated *to* these covenantees. *Leviathan* corroborates this. Revoking the original 'gift of right' to the sovereign (had this been licit, counterfactually) would require unanimity, 'for any one man dissenting, all the rest should break their Covenant made to that man, which is injustice' (L 18.3). In this case, the specific rights the multitude seeks to revoke ('Soveraignty', or the right to 'beareth their Person') were evidently not alienated to the dissenter but to the sovereign alone. This passage indicates that flouting directed obligations created by covenanting is unjust to all covenanters, even if those obligations (absences of liberty) are created by alienating rights to a third party.[49]

---

[47] The social contract theory advanced in *Elements* and *De Cive* can capture the special moral relation between promisers and promisees (the former owing performance *to* the latter). Its weakness lies rather in its over-generalization of that relation. On the need for philosophical theories of promising to account for the directionality of obligations, see Margaret Gilbert, 'Scanlon on Promissory Obligation: The Problem of Promisees' Rights', *Journal of Philosophy* 101 (2004) no. 2: 83–109; Stephen Darwall, *Honor, History, and Relationship* (Oxford, 2013) 131–154.

[48] Eggers's alternative explanation for this disentanglement must be rejected: 'Hobbes wanted to sever the conceptual link between injury and injustice in order to be able to apply the terms "iniustitia" or "injustice" to forms of morally wrong behaviour that do not imply the violation of valid covenants.' As Chapter 3 shows, Hobbes in fact worked hard to separate the domains of natural law and justice of actions. Overlooking the significance of to whom rights are alienated, Eggers considers but dismisses the possibility that breaking covenant can be unjust to some and injurious to others. Eggers, 'Injury, Injustice, Iniquity', 173.

[49] My reconstruction departs on this point from Abizadeh, *Two Faces of Ethics*, 192. Abizadeh takes directed obligations to be owed only to the person to whom right is alienated. He is led to this view because he assumes erroneously that directed obligations correlate in claim-rights; and because he holds that claim-rights are created by receiving the 'benefit' of an alienated right. My account of the potentially diverging directionalities of directed obligations vs. injuries sticks closer to Hobbes's logic by avoiding distorting mention of claim-rights.

48   JUSTICE, RIGHTS, AND INJURY

Hobbes's struggle to adequately explain the diverging directionalities of injury and injustice continued in *Leviathan*. 'All breaches of the Law, are offences against the Common-wealth: but there be some, that are <u>also</u> against private Persons' (L 30.15). Sovereigns are guilty of 'iniquity' should they pardon crimes committed against citizens without the latter's consent. For the normative standing 'to pardon an injury belongs to him who has suffered it' (LL 30.16; also DPS 42; DPS 179).

> All breaches of the Law ... that concern the Common-wealth onely, may without breach of Equity be pardoned; for every man may pardon what is done against himselfe, according to his own discretion. But an offence [injuria] against a private man, cannot in Equity be pardoned, without the consent of him that is injured; or reasonable satisfaction. (L 30.15; LL 30.16; also L 28.18)

Which crimes exactly are private offences, injuring specific citizens (whilst being unjust to all)? *Leviathan* offers textual support for two mutually inconsistent explanations. The first restricts injuries against private persons to breaches of private contracts: 'private men may remit to one another their debts; but not robberies or other violences, whereby they are endammaged; because the detaining of Debt, <u>is an Injury to themselves</u>; but Robbery and Violence, are Injuries to the Person of the Common-wealth' (L 15.12). While private parties have the authority to enforce or remit contractual obligations between themselves, 'harm inflicted contrary to the commonwealth's laws, e.g. theft, murder, and so on, is not punished at the discretion of the man who suffers loss [damnum]' (DCv 3.4n). These passages deny, curiously, that criminal offences like robbery and murder are injuries to their victims. (Such crimes *are* unjust to them and to everyone else, as violations of the original covenant.) Transgressing civil law, the first explanation states, injures the sovereign alone. Victims suffer mere loss instead.

The first explanation jars with passages elsewhere. We read of 'Murder, Felonies, and other Injuries as are done to any Subject' (DPS 43; also L 27.41, 51; LL 30.16). Moreover, public and private crimes, *Leviathan* adds, are not different kinds of crimes but rival perspectives on the same crime: 'in almost all Crimes there is an Injury done, not onely to some Private men, but also to the Common-wealth; <u>the same Crime</u>, when the accusation is in the name of the Common-wealth, is called a Publique Crime; and when in the name of a Private man, a Private Crime' (L 27.54). These passages suggest that some public crimes *do* leave their victims injured, providing them with standing to legally accuse. What entitles Hobbes to say this?

Recall that subjects have jointly made two distinct covenants, each involving the alienation of a different set of natural rights. Besides alienating their rights of self-government to the sovereign in the pact of subjection, subjects have also mutually renounced their rights of war in the covenant of peace. That last divestment in effect provides all citizens with a set of exclusive liberty-rights vis-à-vis each other. The obligations—lack of right—thus incurred first render it wrongful/injurious for citizens to kill and subjugate one another, even without any civil law prohibiting murder and enslavement (§3.6). On *Leviathan*'s second explanation, I propose, public crimes are without right towards their victims specifically in virtue of this mutual 'Covenant of Peace' (L 14.31). To injure a person on this account means unjustly hindering their enjoyment of retained liberty-rights. In sum, the first explanation portrays the sovereign as the sole beneficiary of the collective rights-alienation grounding duties of political obligation; the second highlights that all citizens receive the benefit from the collective renunciation of the warlike right to everything.

Leviathan's new definition of justice as keeping faith completes the conceptual rearrangement began in DCv 3.4n. Breach of covenant is now primarily defined as 'unjust' rather than as 'injury' (as the early works had it). That revision opens up the conceptual space needed to deny that breaking faith injures all covenantees alike, by pushing 'injury' further down the conceptual line. Conceptually severing injustice and injury allowed Hobbes to acknowledge a distinction of sorts between criminal and private law. *Leviathan*'s covenant-based definition of justice thus helps solve a problem in Hobbes's criminal theory—up to a point. That problem (labelled *Collective Victimhood*) initially arose, I have argued, because of Hobbes's remarkable denial that injury consists in violating another's rights. That denial made it hard for him to explain why injuries ('actions without right') wrong assaulted persons specifically, by dint of being assaulted. He eventually reached a solution: an action without right wrongs only those individuals whose personal liberties the action unjustly hinders.

2.5 ABSOLUTE NATURAL FREEDOM

Hobbes principally advanced conceptual arguments to establish his fourfold equation between (i) 'unjust action'; (ii) 'injury'/'wrong'; (iii) 'action without right'; and (iv) 'breach of covenant'. The equation nonetheless has various theoretical presuppositions—controversial ones, requiring their own supporting arguments. Saliently, breaking faith is co-extensive with the other three notions in virtue of Hobbes's trademark doctrine of a natural right to everything. Any action without right must be breaking an agreement since 'before men bound themselves by any agreements with each other, every man was permitted to do anything to anybody, and to possess, use and enjoy whatever he wanted and could get' (DCv 1.10; also EL 14.10; L 14.4). The fourfold equation holds true only insofar as humans have a natural right to *literally* everything. Many scholars doubt that Hobbes can uphold such a practically unlimited right.[50] I believe that he can. Proof for this must

---

[50] E.g. Warrender, *The Political Philosophy of Hobbes*, 59–61; Kavka, *Hobbesian Moral and Political Theory*, 300–302; Susanne Sreedhar, *Hobbes on Resistance* (Cambridge, 2010) 12–13. Pufendorf had

50   JUSTICE, RIGHTS, AND INJURY

follow later. Hobbes justified the natural right to all things in various ways; some coming with qualifications and limiting conditions, others without. Complex as the grounds of the *jus in omnia* are, a full reconstruction will unfold across various sections (§3.2–§3.4; §5.1; §7.1; §8.1).

The claim that all obligations of justice arise through covenants in addition logically presupposes that there are no natural obligations of justice. That last thesis Hobbes supported through a two-step argument: (1) natural law duties are no obligations of justice (barring covenants to the contrary); (2) all directed obligations are conventional in origin—created through consensual alienation of right to another party. The first step is analysed in Chapter 3; the second I turn to now.

Above, I argued that all obligations of justice are directed ('owed') to another person (§2.3). This section analyses Hobbes's thesis that all directed obligations are voluntarily assumed. *Leviathan* boldly asserts this view: 'there being no Obligation on any man, which ariseth not from some Act of his own; for all men equally, are by Nature Free' (L 21.10). In Abizadeh's words: 'There are no pre-conventional or natural directed obligations.'[51] Obligation and liberty-right being opposites, the absence of natural obligations owed to other humans equals absolute natural freedom. Hobbes's contemporaries scolded him for portraying the human natural condition as one of absolute liberty. Two objections recurred time and time again: Hobbes would have ignored, impiously, the natural obligations children owe their parents and the natural duties rational creatures owe to God.[52] This section validates the first critique. All directed obligations, including filial ones, are contracted into. Hobbes established this thesis, I contend, by means of a 'vanishingly thin' conception of (attributed) consent.[53]

Hobbes's state of nature has two defining characteristics: (i) *equality* of right; and (ii) absolute *freedom* (from political obligations, from directed ones).[54] In the natural condition equality reigns: 'no one is subject to anyone else' (DCv 14.5). Absolute freedom vis-à-vis humans is the corollary of natural equality of right: 'absolute Liberty, such as is theirs, that neither are Soveraigns, nor Subjects' (L 31.1).

---

already argued that Hobbes's natural right of self-preservation cannot possibly extend to 'a Licence of doing *any* thing to *any* Person', since such 'an unbounded and injurious Licence could never by any Man in his Wits, be thought a likely Means for the lasting Preservation of himself'. Pufendorf, *Nature and Nations*, 2.2.3.

[51] Abizadeh, *Two Faces of Ethics*, 192.

[52] For an example of the first criticism, see Robert Filmer, *Patriarcha and Other Writings*, ed. J.P. Sommerville (Cambridge, 1991) 187–188, 191–192. For an example of the second, see Leibniz to Hobbes in *The Correspondence of Thomas Hobbes*, vol. 2, ed. Noel Malcolm (Oxford, 1994) 717.

[53] Kinch Hoekstra, 'The *De Facto* Turn in Hobbes's Political Philosophy' in Tom Sorell and Luc Foisneau (eds), *Leviathan after 350 Years* (Oxford, 2004) 67.

[54] Hobbes characterizes the state of nature in diverging ways. Not all seamlessly align. For a helpful overview, see S.A. Lloyd, 'The State of Nature as a Continuum Concept' in Marcus Adams (ed), *A Companion to Hobbes* (Blackwell-Wiley, 2021) 157–163. For natural equality of right as a defining feature of the state of nature, see DCv 9.2; DCv 12.1. Ditto for absolute freedom, see DCv 6.18; DCv 7.18; DCv 15.1; DH 13.8.

The absence of mutual relations of authority and subjection amounts to natural equal freedom. Both characteristics are premised in turn on the non-existence of natural directed obligations. For Hobbes, I submit, subjection first comes about by taking on directed obligations of obedience.

Are babies really born absolutely free and equal in right? The state of nature depicts 'men as if they had just emerged from the earth like mushrooms and grown up without any obligation to each other [ad alterum obligatione]' (DCv 8.1). The hypothetical phrasing suggests infants are not actually born free, 'without covenants or subjection one to another, as if they were . . . all at once created male and female' (EL 22.2). As Hobbes explains elsewhere, a child 'who as soon as he is born is in the power and under the authority' of their parents is not in a 'pure natural state' (DCv 1.10n). Infants immediately acquire filial obligations. And these obligations, it seems, must be natural ones. After all, lacking reason, 'children . . . had never power to make any covenant, or to understand the consequences therof' (L 26.12). Nor can they authorize another to act on their behalf (L 16.10). These passages notwithstanding, Hobbes valiantly endeavoured to derive filial obligations 'from the Childs Consent' (L 20.4).[55]

To rule out natural directed obligations, I contend, Hobbes argued that parental authority is a type of sovereignty by acquisition, presupposing a covenant of absolute submission. For Hobbes, all human authority ('dominion') is essentially the same in kind—whether parental, despotic, or political.[56] All such authority is called 'sovereign' when supreme. Hence 'originally the Father of every man was also his Soveraign Lord' (L 30.11; also L 22.26). Recall that sovereignty can arise in two ways: by mutual institution or by force ('acquisition'). 'Soveraign Power is acquired by Force' when individuals agree to be ruled by him 'that hath their lives and liberty in his Power' (L 20.1).[57] Sovereigns-by-institution, by contrast, do not have the proverbial sword in the neck of their subjects *before* being enthroned. Two examples of sovereignty-by-acquisition recur across his works: despotic rule over vanquished enemies and parental rule over offspring.[58] 'Soveraign Power' is

---

[55] In doing so, Hobbes broke new ground. His contemporaries generally agreed that children are born subject to the natural government of their parents, owing natural obligations of obedience. They disagreed, however, over the ground, duration, and limits of natural subjection of progeny. For Grotius, human authority can spring from 'generation' as well as from consent and crime. Filmer grounded parental authority in divine right; Locke and Tyrrell in parental duties to preserve and raise their offspring. Barring Filmer, all three thinkers maintained that children become free and equal upon reaching maturity and that parents' powers over their offspring are limited in extent. Grotius, *War and Peace*, 2.5.1; Filmer, *Patriarcha*, 6–7; Locke, *Second Treatise*, 6.55–67; James Tyrrell, *Patriarcha non Monarcha* (London, 1681) 18–19.

[56] E.g. EL 23.10; DCv 9.10; L 20.14; DPS 190–191. The *locus classicus* of the idea that the authority to govern states and families is identical in kind is Plato, 'Statesman' in *Complete Works*, ed. J.M. Cooper (Indianapolis, 1997) 259b. Hobbes's reductionist account of human authority was highlighted long ago by R.W.K. Hinton, 'Husbands, Fathers and Conquerors', *Political Studies* 16 (1968) no. 1: 55–57.

[57] Also EL 22.2; DCv 8.1; DCv 9.10; L 17.15; L 20.14.

[58] To be precise, *Leviathan* introduces the notion of sovereignty-by-acquisition to merge parental and despotic dominion. Both forms of dominion generate what the early works had called a 'natural commonwealth' in opposition to commonwealths by institution (DCv 5.12; also EL 19.11). They

52   JUSTICE, RIGHTS, AND INJURY

seized 'by Naturall force; as when a man maketh his children, to submit themselves, and their children to his government, as being able to destroy them if they refuse' (L 17.15; also L 21.11).

Outside the state, dominion over children originally accrues to their mothers (DCv 9.2; L 20.5). Maternal authority equals sovereignty-by-acquisition because every newborn initially lives at the mercy of their mommy—and she will raise her child only on condition that he 'shall not be her enemy... when he grows up' (DCv 9.3). Every baby is presumed to consent to receiving life and care in exchange for simple obedience, their covenant of subjection forestalling future enmity: 'it is to be <u>presumed</u>, that he which giveth sustenance to another, whereby to strengthen him, hath received a promise of obedience in consideration thereof' (EL 23.3; also EL 14.13; DCv 1.14). Filial obligations originate in a tacit pact of 'most absolute subjection' to one's caregiver—rendering infants liable to be sold, given away 'in adoption or servitude to others', killed for rebellion, and sacrificed for peace (EL 23.8). On no other terms, Hobbes claims implausibly, would anyone be willing to rear their offspring. 'And in this way in the state of nature every woman who gives birth becomes a *mother* and a *lord* [domina]' (DCv 9.3). Filial obligations need not be owed to one's biological parents. The child 'ought to obey him by whom it is preserved', regardless of kinship (L 20.5; also EL 23.8; DCv 1.10n; DCv 9.4). The obligations children owe their caregiver, Hobbes stresses, 'arose from the gift of life'—'not by *generation* but by *looking after* him' (DCv 9.4; also EL 23.3). That gift, I have pointed out, is not exactly free. It is granted in exchange for lifelong obedience. Notice that Hobbes's argument assumes that parents do not owe their children any support absent a pact of filial subjection.

Unable to speak or reason, newborns cannot make covenants. But they can be *presumed* to consent to the socially necessary conditions of their upbringing—and for Hobbes, tacit consent creates real obligations. Promises of simple obedience can be 'either expresse, or tacite'. Anyone who lives 'under their Protection openly ... is understood to submit himself to the Government' (L R&C.7).[59] Similarly, infants are '<u>supposed</u> to promise obedience, to him, in whose power it is to save, or destroy him' (L 20.5; also EW 5: 180). Filial obligations vanish the moment the parent refuses to look after the child; just as duties to obey the civil sovereign become void the moment the commonwealth becomes manifestly unwilling or incapable to provide protection (L 21.21; L 29.23). The tacit pact of submission babies promptly 'sign' with their caregiver allowed Hobbes to claim that the human

---

had differentiated the two kinds of commonwealth by subjects' reason for submission (i.e. whom they feared: their prospective ruler vs. each other). *Leviathan's* merger resulted in an additional differentiating feature: namely, the manner in which sovereign power is obtained (mutual institution vs. natural force).

[59] On tacit consent in Hobbes's contract theory, see Kavka, *Hobbesian Moral and Political Theory*, 391–398; Mark Murphy, 'Hobbes on Tacit Covenants', *Hobbes Studies* 7 (1994) no. 1: 69–94.

condition of birth truly is one of absolute freedom, devoid of any natural obligations owed to others. In this respect, humans and mushrooms alike come into this world 'as if a man were the author of himself and knew no other kin'.[60]

Born free, babies are entirely dependent on the grace of their overpowering mother. Persons defeated in war, Hobbes maintained, are similarly dependent on the mercy of their conquerors. Both infants and the vanquished are entrusted with their lives on the same condition of absolute submission. The claim that sovereignty could be obtained through victory in war was a common one. George Lawson (1598–1678) called 'a victory obtained by a just and necessary war . . . a most common title of most sovereigns in the world'.[61] Such conquests could be validated either by natural law (restricting rights of conquest to just belligerents) or by the customary law of nations (extending them indiscriminately to all). In either way, conquest could justify involuntary subjection—the former insofar as the defeated party had forfeited basic rights by engaging in unjust aggression; the latter as a generally accepted international practice.[62] Hobbes's just war theory, we shall see, has no place for either rights-forfeiture (§8.2) or international customary law (§9.2). Hobbes grounded sovereignty seized through war in consent instead. 'The conqueror makes no law over the conquered by virtue of his power; but by virtue of their assent, that promised obedience for the saving of their lives' (EW 5: 180). 'It is not therefore the Victory, that giveth the right of Dominion over the Vanquished, but his own Covenant' (L 20.11; also DCv 8.1; L R&C.7). In sum, all sovereignty ('dominion'), whether acquired by institution or natural force, presupposes the consent of the governed.[63]

What entitled Hobbes to claim that sovereignty-by-acquisition derives from the consent of the forcibly subjected? What conception of consent lies behind his conventionalization of obligations of obedience of children and the vanquished alike? As is well known, neither coercion nor duress excludes consent for Hobbes (EL 15.13; DCv 2.16; L 14.27). As Pateman perceptively notes, the 'postulated agreement of the infant' is 'one example of Hobbes' identification

---

[60] William Shakespeare, 'The Tragedy of Coriolanus' in *The Norton Shakespeare*, second edition, ed. Stephen Greenblatt (New York, 2008) 5.3.

[61] George Lawson, *Politica Sacra et Civilis*, ed. Conal Condran (Cambridge, 1992) 61. Also, Bodin, *Six Books*, 200–201; Grotius, *War and Peace*, 3.8.1–4; Pufendorf, *Nature and Nations*, 7.6.16.

[62] E.g. Grotius, *War and Peace*, 2.5.32; Locke, *Second Treatise*, 16.178: '*a lawful Conqueror . . .* has an Absolute Power over the Lives of those, who by an Unjust War have forfeited them'.

[63] At least in *Leviathan*. In *Elements/De Cive*, human dominion can exceptionally derive from brute power alone, without consent. Slaveholders have 'supreme dominion' over enchained subjects deprived of all corporeal freedom (DCv 8.5; also EL 22.4). *Leviathan* drops this claim. Baumgold (ed), *Three-Text Edition*, 283. So-called 'bound slaves' have no obligation to their *domini* whatsoever: they may justly resist or kill them. Directed obligations derive from agreements, and agreements presuppose 'a promise from one who is trusted' (DCv 8.3; also EL 22.3, 7; DCv 17.6; L 20.10–12). No bonds of trust exist between enchained people and their captors (L 21.22). Slaveholders' 'supreme dominion' over them must, by elimination, derive from their irresistible power.

54   JUSTICE, RIGHTS, AND INJURY

of enforced submission with voluntary agreement'.[64] My analysis further indicates that consent must mean 'attributed consent'. For only attributed consent—*assuming* a given will—can account for the tacit covenant newborns make with their mothers: agreeing to be nursed and raised in return for future obedience (DCv 9.3; L 20.4).[65] Few today would assent to such a notion of consent. Attributed consent, moreover, results in *real* rights-alienation for Hobbes—babies are obligated to simply obey their parents in virtue of the pact of absolute submission they are presumed to have made. By dint of that same pact, 'a parent is incapable of wronging a *child*' (DCv 9.7). For Hobbes, the state of nature—the war of all against all—was a threateningly real possibility. Even so, his thinly stretched accounts of consent and covenanting make his theory of obligation, if not hypothetical, then wildly specious.

CONCLUSION

Defining injury as action without right (rather than as rights-violations) greatly supported Hobbes's vindicatory project. This unprecedented definition helped establish that subjects cannot possibly be wronged/injured by their rulers. For as long as persons act *with right*, injury is impossible—no matter how grievously rights/liberties of others are hindered along the way. Hobbes offers two reasons why the sovereign never lacks right towards his citizens. First, as the early works stress, the sovereign has not contractually divested any right to them, keeping intact his original right of nature. Sovereigns-by-acquisition, it is true, have contractually granted their subjects life and liberty in return for lifelong obedience. But they made no promise to refrain from killing or confining innocent subjects later on (since peace and social stability may require this). Second, *Leviathan* adds that each individual citizen has authorized their ruler unconditionally, giving him 'the right to doe what he pleased' (L 21.7). Chapter 6 further analyses the meaning of individual authorization and its place within Hobbes's civil theodicy.

This chapter started with a conceptual analysis of Hobbes's deontic vocabulary, laying bare the peculiar accounts of injustice, rights, and injury that scaffold his theory of justice. It ended with a brief analysis of the nature and grounds of parental dominion. Disparate though these topics may seem at first, they turn out to be deeply theoretically intertwined. Hobbes *had* to conventionalize children's obligations of obedience to their parents to be entitled to claim that every 'obligation arises from an agreement' (DCv 8.3). Theoretical pressure, moreover, ran

---

[64] Carole Pateman, *The Sexual Contract* (Cambridge, 1988) 44–45. For critical discussion, see Meghan Robison, 'Mother Lords: Original Maternal Dominion and the Practice of Preservation in Hobbes', *Hypatia* 38 (2023) no. 1: 65–85.

[65] Hoekstra, 'The *De Facto* Turn', 67–69. Hoekstra's article offers an illuminating analysis of the tension between power and consent as grounds of authority in Hobbes.

both ways. By grounding all directed obligations, including filial ones, in consent, Hobbes dramatically weakened the standards of what counts as consent. Establishing that all obligations of justice owed to humans are voluntarily assumed was a huge theoretical undertaking, logically requiring numerous conceptual and doctrinal revisions. We are not even halfway yet. Chapter 3 reconstructs the status of natural law duties, to explain when and why immoral conduct is neither unjust nor injurious to the persons it harms.

3

JUSTICE AND NATURAL LAW

INTRODUCTION

Complicating his ambition to rule out all sovereign injustice, Hobbes frankly concedes across his works that rulers can and sometimes do sin against natural law. 'One cannot deny that a prince sometimes may have a mind to act wickedly' (DCv 6.13n). We read about sovereigns who start wars against foreign countries 'out of ambition, or of vain-glory' (EL 28.9); immorally drain their citizens of resources to enrich their favourites (DCv 6.13n);[1] adjudicate legal cases partially and deny subjects charged with crime a fair trial (L 26.24); 'hang a man for making his apparel otherwise' than legally instructed (EW 4: 371); and send citizens to death in order to sleep with their wives (L 21.7; alluding to 2 Sam. 11:2–12:14).[2] Hobbes had good reason to admit that sovereigns can and do act immorally. His political works double as mirrors for princes, outlining how absolute rulers ought to govern in order to secure enduring peace and social stability.[3] Sovereigns who govern in violation of the laws of nature invite civil unrest, he warned, if not outright rebellion (L 31.40).

Hobbes is adamant that sovereign immorality, however heinous, never amounts to injustice or injury. 'It is true that they that have Soveraigne power, may commit Iniquity; but not Injustice, or Injury in the proper signification' (L 18.6). Which arguments prop up this doctrine? One standard reply is that injustice and injury consist in breaking covenants; since the sovereign did not covenant with anyone, it follows that he can act neither unjustly nor injuriously. This reply begs the question. What warrants the claim that sovereigns can act unjustly only by breaking faith? Why don't immoral actions and commands by the sovereign merit the moniker 'injustice'? Violations of natural law were traditionally regarded as unjust.[4] Hobbes's own abridged translation of Aristotle's *Rhetoric* (1637) attests to this: '*Unjust*, in the opinion of all men, is that which is contrary to the *law of nature*' (EW 6: 445; also EW 6: 447). On what grounds then did he later proclaim sovereign contraventions of natural law to be 'not unjust'? Does it have to do with the

---

[1] On this 'great and inevitable inconvenience' of all civil government, see L 19.8; EL 24.5; DCv 10.6; DPS 12.

[2] On immoral conduct by the sovereign, see also EL 28.1; DCv 6.13; DCv 7.14; DCv 13.4; L 24.7; LL 18.6; EW 5: 178. On immoral laws, see L 22.15; DPS 31.

[3] For discussion, see Gerald M. Mara, 'Hobbes's Counsel to Sovereigns', *The Journal of Politics* 50 (1988) no. 2: 390–411.

[4] E.g. Aquinas, *Summa Theologica*, 1a.2ae.94.6, 1a.2ae.96.4.

Hobbes on Justice. Johan Olsthoorn, Oxford University Press. © Johan Olsthoorn 2024.
DOI: 10.1093/9780191904585.003.0003

special status of the sovereign? Or with the status of natural law duties generally—are violations of natural law as such for some reason never unjust?

Hobbes supported his civil theodicy by systematically reinterpreting the meaning of basic moral terms and rearranging their conceptual interrelations. This chapter provides a comprehensive reconstruction of the theoretical grounds and implications of what we may call his 'separation of natural law from justice'. Hobbes worked hard to conceptually disentangle the domains of natural law and of justice of actions—so that he could coherently maintain that violations of natural law are not by definition unjust. Or, if you will, that people are not required to keep all natural law duties on pain of injustice. Since unjust actions are always also injuries, this disentanglement further required showing that transgressing natural law is not injurious *per se*. Injuries are actions without right. Hobbes hence had to explain how it can be that offences against natural law are not necessarily actions without right. How and in what sense can Hobbesian agents have a right to act immorally? In reconstructing why sinning against natural law need not involve injuries/acts without right, this chapter simultaneously explains in greater detail the theoretical underpinnings of Hobbes's triple identification of injury and unjust action with actions without right (§2.1 and §2.2).

Judging by recent scholarship, Hobbes's separation of natural law from justice was not unsuccessful. Abizadeh has recently argued that justice and natural law regulate distinct *kinds* of moral duties for Hobbes.[5] In a nutshell: obligations of justice are always conventionally assumed, created by laying down right to someone else. And always directed: *owed* to the person to whom right is alienated (such that violation of the obligation wrongs them). Natural law duties, by contrast, are immutable and eternal, obliging in virtue of 'our rational nature' (DCv 3.30). Various passages suggest that natural law duties are non-directed: *not* owed to other humans. When sovereigns or pre-statist individuals violate natural law, Hobbes maintains, then their malfeasance (however harmful) never wrongs other people. Sovereigns can in 'many ways . . . sin against natural law, by *cruelty*, for example . . . or other vices, which do not come under the strict and accurate signification of *wrong* [injuriæ]' (DCv 7.14). With respect to pre-statist individuals we read: 'nothing that one does in a purely natural state is a wrong against anyone, at least against any man. Not that it is impossible in such a state to sin against God or to violate the Natural Laws' (DCv 1.10n).

This chapter shows that the distinction between (directed) obligations of justice and (non-directed) natural law duties was not simply posited by Hobbes. On the contrary, it was the end product of some complicated lines of reasoning. My reconstruction of the underlying argumentation indicates, *contra* Abizadeh, that obligations of justice and natural law duties differ in character only contingently

---

[5] Arash Abizadeh, *Hobbes and the Two Faces of Ethics* (Cambridge, 2018).

(rather than intrinsically) (§3.1). The two differ in kind only insofar as an external principle applies: rights of private judgement, grounded in human natural equality of right. Immoral conduct does not wrong others, I contend, only because and insofar as the sinner enjoys rights of private judgement. For anyone who has forgone that right (i.e. citizens) actions contravening natural law *do* wrong other humans. Sovereign violations of natural law are neither unjust nor injurious in part because he possesses rights of private judgement. Hobbes offers two distinct arguments for why rights of private judgement block due accusation of moral wrongdoing (a doctrine labelled *Sinning with Right*) (§3.2). The first declares it impossible to accuse others of sinning outside the state for epistemic reasons, granting all in effect a natural right to everything vis-à-vis humans (§3.3). The second states more boldly that pre-statist moral accusation is impossible in principle: warranted blame presupposes a common standard of law—and civil legislation first creates that standard (§3.4). The 'question of Injury, depending on the Law of Nature' becomes conceivable only once natural law is incorporated into the legal system (L 26.17) (§3.5 and §3.6). The chapter ends with a discussion of the contrast between justice of manners vs. justice of actions (§3.7).

3.1 ARE NATURAL LAW DUTIES MERELY PRUDENTIAL?

Why is a sovereign violating his natural law duties not thereby acting unjustly towards his citizens? One answer is that transgressions of natural law as such *never* count as injustice or injury—for no one. Abizadeh provides the most sophisticated defence of this reading. He argues that obligations of justice and natural law duties are categorically different. Obligations of justice are directed: *owed* to another party ('the obliger') who is wronged if the obligation is violated (EL 15.12).[6] Natural law duties, by contrast, are non-directed. They merely 'articulate the reasons agents have to preserve themselves' and 'no one is intrinsically accountable to others for complying with such reasons'.[7] Violating natural law is imprudent— but never as such unjust or injurious (except perhaps vis-à-vis God). To be sure, people defy natural law whenever they break obligations of justice without excuse. For justice is itself a precept of natural law, obliging us to keep whatever obligations we have taken upon us (L 15.1). Yet the natural law duty of justice is not itself owed

---

[6] Gopal Sreenivasan, 'Duties and Their Direction', *Ethics* 120 (2010) no. 3: 467; Simon Căbulea May, 'Directed Duties', *Philosophy Compass* 10 (2015) no. 8: 523. What it is that makes a duty a directed duty, and in virtue of what duties are directed to one party rather than to another, are contested questions among philosophers today.

[7] Abizadeh, *Two Faces of Ethics*, 217, also 5, 9. In modern jargon, natural law duties articulate 'reasons of the good'; obligations of justice 'reasons of the right'. Stephen Darwall explores to what extent Hobbes's laws of nature can be interpreted as expressing reasons of the right in *Modern Moral Philosophy: From Grotius to Kant* (Cambridge, 2023) 39–61.

to others. Only the obligations created by covenanting are (which justice orders us to keep).[8]

To further clarify the distinction, consider what it means to owe a duty to some other party. I can imagine having a duty to abstain from punching you, without thinking that I owe it *to you* not to punch you. (I might owe this duty to my therapist, whom I had promised to stop clobbering people.) Your existence gives my duty content and application. Yet you are not the target of our duty; the duty itself is not directed at you. Consequently, you can neither *demand* that I not punch you, as something due *to you*, nor release me from my duty (by consenting to be punched by me). And if punching you does not wrong *you* (however much it may hurt), then it is not up to you to demand redress or forgive me either.[9]

Directed obligations thus provide the obliger with special normative standing against the obligee. Indeed, 'the normative significance of the concept of direction is precisely that it ties duties to individual's moral status'.[10] This distinctive standing is central to Abizadeh's 'bifurcated' reading of Hobbes's ethics. Humans are morally accountable to others, he argues, only for living up to obligations of justice.[11] The obliger, he notes, has unique control over the obligation. Only they can release the obligee from their obligation through forgiveness of what is owed: 'the restitution of liberty; as being a re-transferring of that Right, in which the obligation consisted' (L 14.26; also DCv 2.15). Abizadeh's main point about moral accountability is a more general one: only violations of obligations of justice warrant moral accusation (censure, condemnation). No one can be held morally accountable by others for breaking the laws of nature (imprudent though doing so is).[12]

---

[8] Abizadeh, *Two Faces of Ethics*, 226–227. Directed obligations of justice had previously been distinguished from non-directed natural law duties by G.S. Kavka, *Hobbesian Moral and Political Theory* (Princeton, 1986) 304; Daniel Eggers, 'Liberty and Contractual Obligation in Hobbes', *Hobbes Studies* 22 (2009) no. 1: 86, 98–101. The focus on directionality makes Abizadeh's interpretation stand out in the crowded debate over whether Hobbes's ethics has place for 'genuine' moral obligations. Various scholars had previously distinguished 'prudential' natural law requirements from 'deontological' obligations of justice: e.g. Mark Peacock, 'Obligation and Advantage in Hobbes' *Leviathan*', *Canadian Journal of Philosophy* 40 (2010) no. 3: 433–458. Others regard all Hobbesian duties as merely prudential, obligations of justice included: e.g. Thomas Nagel, 'Hobbes's Concept of Obligation', *The Philosophical Review* 68 (1959) no. 1: 68–83; Jean Hampton, *Hobbes and the Social Contract Tradition* (Cambridge, 1986) 27–57. Lastly, for the view that all duties are deontological, see e.g. A.E. Taylor, 'The Ethical Doctrine of Hobbes', *Philosophy* 13 (1938) no. 52: 406–424; Howard Warrender, 'Obligations and Rights in Hobbes', *Philosophy* 37 (1962) no. 142: 352–355.

[9] Joel Feinberg, 'The Nature and Value of Rights', *The Journal of Value Inquiry* 4 (1970) no. 4: 243–257; Michael Thompson, 'What Is It to Wrong Someone? A Puzzle about Justice' in R. Jay Wallace et al. (eds), *Reason and Value: Themes from the Philosophy of Joseph Raz* (Oxford, 2004) 333–384. Compare Seneca's dictum: 'this word "to owe" is not appropriate except between two people'. Seneca, *On Benefits*, ed. Miriam Griffin and Brad Inwood (Chicago, 2011) 5.8.3.

[10] Simon Căbulea May, 'Moral Status and the Direction of Duties', *Ethics* 123 (2010) no. 1: 121.

[11] Abizadeh, *Two Faces of Ethics*, 191–195, 199–208. On the normative standings implied by directed vs. non-directed duties, respectively, see Stephen Darwall, *Morality, Authority, and Law* (Oxford, 2013) 27–42.

[12] Abizadeh, *Two Faces of Ethics*, 199.

60   JUSTICE AND NATURAL LAW

Formal differences no doubt exist between obligations of justice and natural law duties. Most saliently, the two types of requirements differ with respect to their normative origins, scope, and content. All obligations of justice are voluntarily assumed, created by contractually alienating right to another party; natural obligations of justice being non-existent (§2.5). Only those who made covenants can have obligations of justice. And these obligations bind, not by dint of their content (which may vary per pact), but because promise-keeping in general is conducive to peace.[13] Natural law duties, by contrast, 'obligate by nature', that is, in virtue of human rationality (DCv 16.10; also L 40.1). These duties do not 'arise from the consent of men ... for if they originated in human consent, they could also be abolished by human consent; but they are immutable' (DCv 14.2). Furthermore, the eternal law of nature imposes the same set of moral duties upon all rational agents. Obligations of justice and natural law duties undoubtedly differ in *these* three ways. The contested question is whether the two in addition differ in terms of directionality, such that only obligations of justice are owed to other people?

Indisputably, Hobbes's laws of nature have other-affecting content. They prescribe traditional moral virtues: justice, gratitude, sociability, mercy, modesty, equity, etc. (DCv 3.31; L 15.40). These virtues are called 'moral' 'because they concern men's manners and conversation [interaction] one towards another' (EL 18.1). The *'moral virtues'*, Hobbes writes, 'relate to men's duties [officia] towards each other' (DCv 15.8; also DCv 16.10; L 42.37). Indeed, 'every violation of Natural Laws' results from failure to recognize what 'duties towards other men are necessary to their own preservation' (DCv 2.1n). On Abizadeh's reading, 'the naturall Duties of one man to another' enjoined by the laws of nature are no ordinary duties (L 31.7).[14] They are not owed to other humans; their violation constitutes no injury or injustice; and we lack the normative standing to hold one another intrinsically accountable for living up to them.[15] Absent an agreement to the contrary, humans cannot *demand* of their natural equals that they abstain from inflicting harm upon them. The normative standing to hold people accountable for the moral quality of their actions derives from pacts alone. Consequently, all that we can demand of others is that they forgo injury (by fulfilling obligations of justice owed to us). Moreover, we can demand this only of people with whom we entered covenants. In short: no agreement, no standing to condemn.

This would make Hobbes's natural law theory highly counter-intuitive. Consider: the eternal law of nature prohibits cruelty—'to hurt one another without reason' (EL 16.10; also DCv 3.11; L 15.19). While natural law obliges all to abstain

---

[13] In Cudworth's terms, the duty to perform obligations of justice lies for Hobbes 'not in the materiality of the action promised, but in the formality of keeping faith and performing covenants'. Ralph Cudworth, *A Treatise Concerning Eternal and Immutable Morality*, ed. Sarah Hutton (Cambridge, 1996) 21.

[14] Abizadeh, *Two Faces of Ethics*, 221.

[15] Abizadeh, *Two Faces of Ethics*, 205.

from gratuitous violence, no one owes it *to others* not to cruelly torture them (barring a non-torture pact) (DCv 7.14). Despite its oddity, Abizadeh's interpretation has ample textual support. In the state of nature, '[w]hat is done of necessity, or in pursuit of peace, or for self-preservation is done rightly. Apart from this, all infliction of harm on men is a violation of natural Law and a wrong against God' (DCv 3.27n). *Ex silentio*, no wrong is done to the person harmed. According to an unparalleled passage in *De Cive* (examined in §2.4), the same holds true within the state:

> So too in a commonwealth, if one harms anyone with whom he has no agreement, he causes *loss* [*damnum*] to the person he maltreats, but does a *wrong* [*injuriam*] only to the holder of authority over the whole commonwealth. For if the victim of the harm should claim to have been wronged, the person who did the action would say, *What are you to me? Why should I act at your pleasure rather than my own, since I am not preventing you from acting at your discretion, not mine?* I do not see how one could fault that response, when no agreement had been made. (DCv 3.4)

Less deleteriously, ingratitude 'is not to be called injury' either, 'seeing in this case there passeth no covenant' (EL 16.7; also DCv 3.8; L 15.16). These passages imply that humans, born free and equal, have no obligation to comply with the demands of others absent an agreement to the contrary (not even reasonable demands against maltreatment). That implication has conceptual backing: 'injury consisteth in violation of covenant, by the definition thereof' (EL 16.3). Yet what warrants defining injury/wrong so narrowly?

Why are humans not by nature accountable to each other for fulfilling their natural law duties? And why does immoral conduct not wrong the persons harmed by it? The reason could lie either in the character of natural law duties or in some external principle (such as human natural equality). Abizadeh favours the former explanation. Natural law duties, he contends, are not the kind of normative requirements that can be owed to others. They are merely prudential requirements. Not obligations in the proper sense, for which people are intrinsically accountable to others: 'to violate natural law is not itself to fail to do anything for which one is accountable to anyone'.[16] Transgressing natural law is imprudent. But it does not make one liable to moral censure: condemnation and accusation. Flouting natural law at most makes one liable to be criticized for acting irrationally and foolishly.

In support, Abizadeh cites *De Cive*'s discussion of sin.[17] In its broad sense, sin [peccatum] means 'imprudent action' (i.e. conduct contrary to right reason) (DCv 14.16). This notion of sin applies to all irrational conduct, regardless of whether it contravenes some law. A narrower sense of sin is 'culpable evil' [malum

---

[16] Abizadeh, *Two Faces of Ethics*, 188.
[17] Abizadeh, *Two Faces of Ethics*, 188–189.

culpae]—any action for which one can be 'blamed with reason'. So understood, sin presupposes law. Culpable sins, Hobbes claims, consist exclusively in breaches of civil law (the only shared evaluative standard, the sole one people can agree on) (DCv 14.17). Pre-statist individuals, he implies, can sin against natural law only in the wide sense of imprudence. Such sins, it seems, are not *morally* blameworthy: others cannot appropriately react to them with moral censure or condemnation.[18] Violating the laws of nature—the natural dictates of right reason—is undoubtedly stupid (DCv 2.1n). The contested question is whether humans are by nature morally unaccountable to one another because trespasses against natural law are mere 'sins of imprudence' outside a legal system (DCv 14.19).

Significantly, *Leviathan* ditches the distinction between imprudent vs. blameworthy sins.[19] A new contrast explains in which ways immoral conduct can be wrong: sin vs. crime. Dropping the broader sense of sin (disconnected from law), *Leviathan* now defines 'sin' as any transgression of law, be it of natural or civil law. Crimes are transgressions of law that are humanly observable, in word or deed: 'sin is the transgression of any law whatsoever, whereas crime is only that transgression which can be judged by a human judge, or with which one man can charge another' (LL 27.2; also EW 5: 229, 234; DPS 47). Hence 'every Crime is a sinne; but not every sinne a Crime' (L 27.2). A haughty mental attitude is constitutive of sin. 'A *Sinne*, is ... a Transgression of a Law' mixed with 'Contempt of the Legislator' (L 27.1; also L 29.15). Crooked intentions can be sinful even when they do not break out into action. 'A Sin may be in the thought or secret purpose of a Man' (DPS 46–47). Thus, 'the *Intention*, or purpose to transgresse' civil law is sin but no crime (L 27.1). Since natural law binds in conscience, individuals can break its precepts merely by having foul intentions. Only when ill will reveals itself in action do transgressions of natural law count as crimes. In sum, crossing the laws of nature is always sinful but not always a crime (even if what 'is done against the Natural Law ... is usually called a sin, not a crime') (LLA 2.34).

The sin vs. crime contrast informs a rival explanation for why sins against natural law are beyond reproach outside the state: such sins are undetectable by humans. Immoral conduct is no crime in the state of nature because people are, for reasons outlined later, by nature in no position to charge others with wrongdoing: 'the Civill Law ceasing, Crimes cease: for there being no other Law remaining, but that of Nature, there is no place for Accusation' (L 27.3). Within the state, citizens' actions contravening natural law *are* crimes. 'Ignorance of the Law of

---

[18] According to Hobbes, we blame both persons and inanimate creatures ('fire', 'horses') when they displease us. Yet only towards rational, reason-responsive agents do we feel malice and resentment (EW 5: 52–54).

[19] Deborah Baumgold (ed), *Three-Text Edition of Thomas Hobbes's Political Theory* (Cambridge, 2017) 400–402. Hobbes had introduced the notion of 'sins of imprudence' to show that atheists are only guilty of imprudence, not of injustice (DCv 14.19n). On Hobbes's changing account of sin, see Laurens van Apeldoorn, 'Hobbes on Evil' in Thomas Nys and Stephen de Wijze (eds), *The Routledge Handbook of the Philosophy of Evil* (London, 2019) 72–75.

Nature Excuseth no man … if he <u>do</u> anything contrary to that Law, it is a Crime' (L 27.4). To 'leaveth the Law of Nature … is a certain Offence' (L 27.20). The *Dialogue* discusses the judicial status of plotted evil foiled by accident. 'Malice prepensed', Hobbes writes, is not 'contrary to any Statute'. Crossing 'the Law of Reason it is a sin, and such a sin as a Man may be Accused of, and Convicted, and consequently a Crime' (DPS 122–123; also LLA 2.34).

Leviathan's revision of the meaning of sin spells trouble for Abizadeh. Ditching the concept of 'sins of imprudence', Hobbes now argues that pre-statist individuals are morally unaccountable to one another because their wrongdoing is humanly imperceptible (somehow). Within the state, human judges *can* detect and condemn certain breaches of natural law by citizens—breaches that therefore count as crimes. Moreover, citizens can wrong their fellow subjects through mere violations of natural law. *Leviathan* contrasts 'injury, or crime' hinging 'upon a written Law' from 'a question of Injury, depending on the Law of Nature' (L 26.17–18). Natural law duties, this suggests, *can* be directed in principle. This raises the question of how exactly the normative status of natural law changes within the state— and what this tells us about supposed character differences between natural law duties and obligations of justice. Before turning to these questions, I will provide a novel explanation for why sinning individuals act with right in the state of nature. An explanation that does not rest on natural law duties being 'merely prudential' requirements.[20]

3.2 SINNING WITH RIGHT

Some scholars maintain that natural law is not operative outside the commonwealth. According to Goldsmith, for instance, the state of nature 'describes that area in which morality does not exist'.[21] This is mistaken. The laws of nature are indeed generally silent in the warlike condition of nature (EL 19.2; DCv 5.2; DPS 36). Yet only in the sense that they need not be *practised*. The laws of nature primarily bind in conscience, ceaselessly obliging all individuals to sincerely endeavour to seek peace.[22] Moreover, 'there are some natural laws' that should be observed 'even within war' (DCv 3.27n). Hobbes himself mentions laws forbidding drunkenness and cruelty; the natural law forbidding incitement of hatred arguably qualifies too (L 15.20). Pre-statist individuals, I conclude, *can* sin against natural law—both in will and deed.

---

[20] Abizadeh, *Two Faces of Ethics*, 21–22, 218.
[21] M.M. Goldsmith, *Hobbes's Science of Politics* (New York, 1966) 173. Gauthier claims that 'there are no *moral* distinctions within the state of nature'—but he does so on the assumption that the laws of nature are not 'themselves moral principles'. David Gauthier, 'Thomas Hobbes: Moral Theorist', *The Journal of Philosophy* 76 (1979) no. 10: 550–551.
[22] EL 17.10; DCv 3.27n; DCv 3.30; DCv 4.21; L 15.36–7.

64   JUSTICE AND NATURAL LAW

Moreover, many *do* sin outside the state. Absent threats of legal punishment, 'most men are disinclined to observe' the laws of nature, 'however well they recognize them'. Some may do so rightfully, out of just fear. Others are driven by 'iniquitous [iniquo] desire' to sin (DCv 3.27; also L 17.2). Injustice and injury against humans are nevertheless non-existent in the state of nature—due to each person's natural right to everything: 'when the Soveraign Power ceaseth, Crime also ceaseth: there is no just and unjust, because of the right of all people to all things' (LL 27.3). How to reconcile these claims? Why do sins against natural law not count as injustices in the state of nature? And why do those pre-statist trespasses not wrong the people harmed by them? In sum, what could give humans the right to act immorally towards others?

Chapter 2 uncovered Hobbes's idiosyncratic conception of injury (§2.1). To recapitulate: injuring/wronging another person does not mean violating *their* rights. Rather, injury/wrong consist in acting towards another person *without right*: 'INJURY, consisting in some action or omission . . . without *jus*, or right' (EL 16.2; also DCv 3.3; L 14.7). The universal *jus in omnia* renders injury impossible prior to contractual divestment of right (to someone else). For this reason, every action without right is a breach of covenant. Injury and injustice of action are synonymous for the same reason (EL 16.4; DCv 3.5; L 15.12). To understand why pre-statist violations of natural law do not constitute injustices or injuries towards other humans, we thus have to examine why and in what sense persons 'can violate the laws of nature, even while in possession of the right to all things'.[23] Call this paradoxical thesis *Sinning with Right*. Hobbes is wedded to this thesis by dint of accepting the existence of pre-statist transgressions of natural law whilst defining injury and injustice as breach of covenant.[24] What entitles Hobbes to affirm *Sinning with Right*? What made it coherent for him to uphold this doctrine?

My contention is that Hobbes develops two distinct but interrelated lines of argument for *Sinning with Right*. Both arguments aim to establish that humans cannot with reason be accused of moral wrongdoing outside the state, thus granting all a natural right to everything vis-à-vis others. 'In the condition of Nature, where every man is Judge, there is no place for Accusation' (L 14.30). Moreover, both arguments ultimately ground natural immunity to moral accusation in human natural equality (rather than in the essence of natural law duties). Each argument

---

[23] Abizadeh, *Two Faces of Ethics*, 243. Abizadeh unravels the paradox by reiterating that natural law duties oblige merely prudentially, while the right of nature consists in the absence of directed obligations. On his reading, humans have no obligations owed to others to abstain from 'foolishly' breaking natural law.

[24] Green dismisses a view tantamount to *Sinning with Right* by arguing that violating natural law *is* unjust and injurious as 'a failure to do the right thing'. In his view, sins against natural law are violations of 'general justice'—a wider notion than justice-as-keeping-covenants. Green's proposal is textually untenable, contradicting Hobbes's triple equation of unjust action with injury and breaking covenant (EL 16.2; DCv 3.3; L 14.7). Michael J. Green, 'Justice and Law in Hobbes', *Oxford Studies in Early Modern Philosophy* 1 (2003) 134, also 126–134.

interprets this immunity in diverging ways, however. The first argument declares it epistemically impossible to accuse others of sinning outside the state. It starts from Hobbes's trademark thesis that in hazardous conditions humans may justifiably decide to suspend practice of the laws of nature. Naturally subject to none but God, each person may rightfully judge for themselves whether in present circumstances peaceful or warlike conduct best aids their self-preservation. Others cannot know for sure with which intentions self-judging humans resort to war—reluctantly or aggressively. Call this first argument *Untraceable Intentions*.

The second argument is more ambitious: it altogether denies humans the normative standing to hold their equals morally accountable absent a legal system. Natural law, it points out, curbs individual right only as law. Law is the binding command of a superior to a subject. Although the laws of nature are divine commands, as long as all remain equal no one is obliged to accept another's interpretation of these laws as binding law to them. Natural law first becomes law *between* humans by sovereign legislation. The introduction of an interpersonally binding moral standard first makes it possible to legitimately call out one's equals for contravening natural law. Call this argument *No Accusation without Law*. Both arguments are found across Hobbes's works. Both, moreover, establish that humans can act with right vis-à-vis other humans even if they knowingly sin. Yet only *No Accusation without Law*, I contend, helps underpin his moral vindication of the sovereign.

3.3 UNTRACEABLE INTENTIONS

Untraceable Intentions is the first argument for the doctrine *Sinning with Right*. It begins with the right of nature.

> The RIGHT OF NATURE . . . is the Liberty each man hath, to use his own power, as he will himselfe, for the preservation of his own Nature; that is to say, of his own Life; and consequently, of doing any thing, which in his own Judgement, and Reason, hee shall conceive to be the aptest means thereunto. (L 14.1)

The right of nature is a naked liberty-right. It expresses what is morally permissible for the right-holder to do (rather than what they can rightfully claim against others) without imposing any obligations upon others. The early works nonetheless suggest that the right of nature endows the right-holder with some moral standing towards others—namely, non-blameworthiness (when acting within its confines). What people cannot be blamed for, Hobbes reasons, is what they have right to do: 'that which is not against reason, men call RIGHT, or *jus*, or <u>blameless liberty</u> of using our own natural power and ability. It is therefore a *right of nature*: that every man may preserve his own life and limbs, with all the power he hath' (EL

66 JUSTICE AND NATURAL LAW

14.6).[25] In *Elements/De Cive*, Hobbes justifies the right of nature by arguing that protecting life and limb is neither 'absurd, nor reprehensible, nor contrary to right reason': 'we cannot be blamed for looking out for ourselves' (DCv 1.7). *Leviathan*'s truncated discussion of natural right omits this justification, dropping all reference to 'blameless liberty'. Commentators generally take this as an oversight on Hobbes's part, rather than as signalling a theoretical shift.[26] I disagree. *Leviathan*'s account, I will argue, is actually incompatible with his earlier conceptualization of natural right in terms of blameless liberty (§3.4).

The right of nature morally permits each person to protect their life and limbs in *whatever* way they judge best. It includes 'the right to <u>use any means and to do any action</u> by which he can preserve himself' (DCv 1.8; also EL 14.6–7; L 14.1). In the bellicose condition of nature, people may rightfully seek their self-protection by resorting to violence and deception—the 'two Cardinall vertues' in war (L 13.13; also DCv ED.2). The right of nature thus veritably gives rise to 'a *Right to all things, or a Right of war*' (DCv 5.1). No forms of warfare are morally off-limits: 'the summe of the Right of Nature ... is *By all means we can, to defend our selves*' (L 14.4) (§8.1). Naturally, self-preservation is ultimately best served by bringing about peace. Reason hence obliges people to act peacefully whenever they judge doing so safe.

The laws of nature are 'Articles of Peace': general precepts of reason, dictating the socially necessary means to peace so that agents can survive and thrive amidst others (L 13.14).[27] The 'means of Peace' prescribed by natural law are the moral virtues (L 15.40; also DCv 15.8). Crucially, Hobbes declares it irrational to act on these moral virtues when surrounded by people of hostile intent. Reason itself dictates that we abstain from carrying out the laws of nature in perilous conditions. Otherwise one 'should but make himselfe a prey to others, and procure his own certain ruine, contrary to the ground of all Lawes of Nature, which tend to Natures preservation' (L 15.36; also DCv 3.27; L 14.5). To require humans to act morally outside of an effective legal system would leave 'the good ... without

---

[25] Blamelessness is central to many reconstructions of Hobbes's right of nature. E.g. S.A. Lloyd, *Morality in the Philosophy of Thomas Hobbes* (Cambridge, 2009) 60, 71–72; Susanne Sreedhar, *Hobbes on Resistance* (Cambridge, 2010) 13–14. Some commentators interpret 'blameless liberty' in a non-moralized manner. E.g. Tommy L. Lott, 'Hobbes's Right of Nature', *History of Philosophy Quarterly* 9 (1992) no. 2: 171; Alan Cromartie, 'The *Elements* and Hobbesian Moral Thinking', *History of Political Thought* 32 (2011) no. 1: 37.

[26] E.g. Annabel Brett, *Changes of State: Nature and the Limits of the City in Early Modern Natural Law* (Princeton, 2011) 109–111.

[27] *Leviathan* clarifies the relation between (i) natural law; (ii) natural right; and (iii) general rules of reason. The early works had integrated the right of nature into the fundamental law of nature, by equating the latter with the norm '*to seek peace when it can be had; when it cannot, to look for aid in war*' (DCv 2.2; also EL 15.1). *Leviathan* calls the same disjunctive a 'generall rule of Reason' instead. This relabelling allowed Hobbes to narrow down the fundamental law of nature to the precept '*seek Peace, and follow it*', while still identifying the right of nature with unlimited freedom of self-defence (L 14.4). I follow *Leviathan* throughout in only subsuming the precepts of peace under natural law, thus fully excluding the right of nature from its domain.

defence against the wicked' (EL 17.10). Such a demand is both unreasonable and self-defeating.[28]

The natural right of self-preservation therefore grants humans the freedom to *set aside* morality as a standard of action. In the state of nature, humans may rightfully refrain from practising the precepts of natural law. In Hobbes's terms, natural law does not always bind *in foro externo*.

> a law of nature gives rise to an obligation in *the internal Court [in Foro interno]* or *in conscience* always and everywhere; but in *the external court [in foro externo]* it gives rise to obligation only when it can be kept with safety. (DCv 3.27; also EL 17.10; L 15.36)

The laws of nature are immutably obliging in the sense that they ceaselessly bind in conscience—that is, 'to a desire they should take place' (L 15.36). Our will should always be geared towards peace. Yet if keeping these precepts in practice is deemed dangerous, then we may rightfully take up arms instead (DCv 5.1; L 17.2).

Some scholars maintain that natural law delimits the rightful exercise of the right of nature: 'this right is not a blank check, and it *never* permits us to harm others in the ways the Laws of Nature forbid'.[29] This is false. The right of nature, I have argued, allows humans to *set aside* the laws of nature (dictating the means of peace) as a standard of action in hostile conditions. Its precepts do not obligate in practice (*in foro externo*) whenever they are bracketed as too unsafe to act on. Clearly, when natural law is thus-sidelined, it cannot delimit what persons may rightfully do. Everything is permitted if peace is deemed out of reach: 'each person has the right to defend himself by all ways and means' (LL 14.4). Moreover, people sideline moral precepts by authority of the right of nature. By natural right, all decide for themselves whether conditions are such that practising natural law is rational and safe, and hence morally obligatory.

Outside the state, the right of nature entitles each person to adopt whatever means *they judge* best promotes their preservation at that particular moment— be they weapons of war or instruments of peace. 'By natural right [jure naturali] *one is oneself the judge* whether the means he is to use and the action he intends to take are necessary to the preservation of his life and limbs or not' (DCv 1.9). Letting someone else judge your fate, we might think, could be dangerous: others may prove ignorant or malicious. Hobbes provides a different reason for why each

---

[28] Some deny that the point of the dispensation clause is to make space for rights of self-defence. Green, for instance, argues that practising natural law when few do so is not rationally required because it is futile—widespread moral compliance is needed to produce the social good that natural law aims at (i.e. peace). Michael J. Green, 'Hobbes's Minimalist Moral Theory' in Marcus Adams (ed), *A Companion to Hobbes* (Malden, MA, 2021) 171–183.

[29] Lloyd, *Morality*, 117.

68 JUSTICE AND NATURAL LAW

person must be entitled to judge for themselves the danger they are in. That reason lies in human natural equality.

> For if it were contrary to right reason, that I should be my own judge of my danger, someone else would judge it; since someone else is judging a matter that concerns me, then <u>because we are equal by nature</u> [quia æquales natura sumus], I will be judge of what concerns him. (DCv 1.9; also EL 14.8; EL 19.1)

Hobbes is not claiming here that all by natural right may judge for themselves what the natural law precepts *are*. Rather, each is to judge for themselves whether *empirical conditions* are such that acting morally is expected to most effectively promote self-preservation—or such that unleashing war does.

Natural human equality makes the right of nature a subjective right. Hobbes provides two distinct accounts of how the right of nature is based in rights of personal judgement. The first morally restricts what people may do by natural right, the second does not. Various passages place a right intention condition on the due exercise of the right of nature. Only 'what is done of necessity, or in pursuit of peace, or for self-preservation is done rightly' (DCv 3.27n). As a subjective right, it allows us to do what is objectively detrimental to self-preservation—provided that we act in good faith: 'in the judgement of the person actually doing it, what is done is rightly done, even if it is a wrong, and so is rightly done' (DCv 1.10n; also DPS 192). Other passages state bluntly that each is by nature allowed 'to do whatsoever he listeth to whom he listeth', without qualification (EL 14.10).[30] This apparent inconsistency has long troubled commentators.[31] Attention to the relational dimension of law and right helps dissolve the tension. In the state of nature, all are entirely free to do as they wish vis-à-vis other humans, while in relation to God all are ceaselessly obliged to sincerely pursue peace as a means to self-preservation. *Untraceable Intentions* attributes to all an 'originall right to do what he please' vis-à-vis their fellows on the ground that the right intention condition is uncheckable by humans (L 15.13). The human inability to read each other's minds, I contend, transforms a morally qualified natural right into a blanket right to sin.

Outside the state, mistaken judgements about potential threats will be rife. Fearful and distrustful, people are liable to mistake an open hand for a clenched fist. Many more will worry about others misjudging *their* motives, providing

---

[30] Also e.g. EL 20.5; EL 20.18; DCv 11.4; L 14.5; L 15.22.

[31] E.g. Howard Warrender, *The Political Philosophy of Hobbes* (Oxford, 1957) 59–61; Kavka, *Hobbesian Moral and Political Theory*, 300–302; Sreedhar, *Hobbes on Resistance*, 12–13; Abizadeh, *Two Faces of Ethics*, 242–244. Some might wish to resolve the quandary by declaring humans psychologically incapable of violating the right intention condition: we are hard-wired to pursue self-preservation and to act on what our conscience (i.e. judgement) tells us is best in this regard. This solution is textually untenable, being gainsaid by Hobbes's frequent admissions that humans can and do sin against natural law (both outside the commonwealth and within it).

yet more reason to be safe than sorry.[32] Inaccurate assessments of danger do not render a person's resort to violence morally wrongful. For all that is required to observe natural law is the will to observe them, based on 'a *bona fide* estimation' of the situation.[33] God 'taketh the will for the deed, both in good and evil actions' (EL 18.10; also EL 25.10; DCv 4.21; L 43.20). In short, pre-statist individuals sin by acting against their better judgement, swayed by passion. 'For a mans Conscience, and his Judgement is the same thing' (L 29.7; also EL 25.12).[34]

'*The laws of nature* are a matter of *conscience*' (DCv 4.21). They are so, we now see, in two separate ways.[35] First, in conditions of war, natural law duties can be fully discharged through a good conscience alone. Outside the state, people do not actually need to act justly, modestly, or sociably to meet the requirements of natural law. An 'unfeigned and constant' willingness to observe these precepts suffices (L 15.39). Second, the divine enforcer of these laws checks for compliance by inspecting our conscience. 'God that seeth the thoughts of man, can lay it to his charge' (L 27.2). Indeed, actions congruent to natural law are nonetheless wrongful in the eyes of God 'if the agent believes it to be contrary' (DCv 3.28; also EL 17.13; L 15.37). Persons, this shows, can contravene natural law in two distinct ways. *Sins* against natural law require a wrongful intention. Not all actions contrary to natural law (the dictates of right reason) are sins, however. Some are honest mistakes—well-intended yet imprudent acts that foreseeably bring war and death closer. God does not mind the latter. In sum, the 'Court of Naturall Justice' is 'in the Conscience onely; where not Man, but God raigneth' (L 30.30).[36]

'In the state of nature', Hobbes declares, 'there is in all men a will to do harm, but not for the same reason or with equal culpability' (DCv 1.4; also DCv ED.2). Some resort to violence out of just fear. Others out of sheer wickedness. Only the latter sin against natural law—failing to observe morality against their better judgement. Why does wanton and vain-glorious violence not wrong those harmed by it? *Untraceable Intentions* replies that it is epistemically impossible for others to determine whether pre-statist individuals are wilfully breaking natural law. We cannot know on what grounds people choose to resort to violence—out of fear or depravity. Mindreading is beyond us. 'For seeing no man (but God alone) knoweth the heart

---

[32] This is so because 'we cannot tell the good and the bad apart' (DCv P.12). The opacity of intentions greatly reinforces extra-statist conflict, as Marshall Missner already pointed out in 'Skepticism and Hobbes's Political Philosophy', *Journal of the History of Ideas* 44 (1983) no. 3: 414–416, 426.

[33] Warrender, *The Political Philosophy of Hobbes*, 59.

[34] On Hobbes's conception of conscience, see Mark Hanin, 'Thomas Hobbes's Theory of Conscience', *History of Political Thought* 33 (2012) no. 1: 55–85; Richard Sorabji, *Moral Conscience through the Ages* (Oxford, 2014) 139–142.

[35] Warrender, *The Political Philosophy of Hobbes*, 70–73.

[36] Hobbes's insistence that 'there ought to be no Power over the Consciences of men, but the Word it selfe' was an anti-Catholic one (L 47.20). The court of conscience was historically regarded as one where priests judge. Witness Francisco de Vitoria, *Political Writings*, ed. Anthony Pagden and Jeremy Lawrance (Cambridge, 1991) 238: 'Yet since this is a case of conscience, it is the business of the priests, that is to say of the Church, to pass sentence upon it.'

70   JUSTICE AND NATURAL LAW

or conscience of a man, unless it break out into action' (EL 25.3). To be sure, moral dispositions that reveal themselves in word or action *can* be judged: 'actions, and words, for those onely are known, and may be accused; and of that which cannot be accused, there is no Judg at all, but God, that knoweth the heart' (L 42.80; also L 8.10; L 42.19, 29).[37] Yet in conditions of hostility, the same action could have been prompted by morally opposite intentions. I might have defrauded you out of greed or in dread of your malice—others cannot tell.[38] Moreover, humans by nature disagree passionately over what natural law requires (DH 13.9). Even blatant wrongdoers may declare that they are sincerely following *their* own interpretation of natural law—and who could prove them wrong? Opaque as our intentions are, humans cannot accuse one another of acting without right (i.e. committing wrongs/injuries) outside the state: 'of Intentions, which never appear by any outward act, there is no place for humane accusation' (L 27.2).

Observe that *Untraceable Intentions* establishes that pre-statist individuals can sin with right only in the sense of impunity. The argument does not deny that pre-statist violations of natural law are wrongful. It states that for epistemic reasons humans cannot reasonably accuse others of breaking its precepts in the perilous state of nature. All therefore have *in effect* a 'libertie to do all they list' vis-à-vis fellow humans (L 15.22). Not *in principle*—the right of nature does not licence immorality on this argument.[39] 'In a state of nature', Hobbes writes, 'Just and Unjust [Justum & Injustum] should be judged not from actions but from the intention and conscience of the agents' (DCv 3.27n). Intentions being untraceable in war, it follows that there is no place for moral accusation outside the state.

With one exception. Pre-statist malefactors who publicly announce their sins *can* be accused of moral wrongdoing. Think of the fool who 'declares he thinks it reason to deceive those that help him' (L 15.5). The fool trumpets that he acts viciously for reasons of short-term advantage, considering himself unbound by general precepts of reason and reciprocity. All can ascertain his foolish intentions by attending to his words.[40] *Untraceable Intentions* provides no reason why loudly announced wrongdoing should not count as unjust and injurious. After all, breaches of natural law are with right vis-à-vis other humans on this argument only in virtue

---

[37] Similarly, 'inner faith' is not subject to civil jurisdiction because humans cannot detect it in each other (L 40.2; L 42.43).

[38] This crucial point is overlooked by David Boonin-Vail, *Thomas Hobbes and the Science of Moral Virtue* (Cambridge, 1994) 145–160.

[39] As rightly pointed out by S.A. Lloyd, 'Hobbes's Self-Effacing Natural Law Theory', *Pacific Philosophical Quarterly* 82 (2001) no. 3–4: 296–298. Confusing right reason with the laws of nature (i.e. the *general* rules of reason), Lloyd proceeds to conclude erroneously that 'the right of nature is thus a *product* of the law of nature'. In truth, the right of nature is the natural liberty *reason* declares all humans must have. It entitles all to judge for themselves whether the laws of nature can rightfully be suspended.

[40] The fool's noisy denunciation of justice—'with his tongue' (L 15.4)—has been highlighted before, albeit to different effect, by Kinch Hoekstra, 'Nothing to Declare? Hobbes and the Advocate of Injustice', *Political Theory* 27 (1999) no. 2: 230–235. Hoekstra argues that fools can also publicly declare their unjust intentions by engaging in 'conspicuous action'. This I deny is possible outside the state.

of their general undetectability. *Untraceable Intentions*, I conclude, cannot establish *Sinning with Right* in full.

Untraceable Intentions has another important limit. It only applies in war. The existence of security, established by empowering a sovereign punisher, removes the pretext that practising morality is unsafe. Where all act morally, so should you. For this reason, *Untraceable Intentions* is of little help in vindicating the sovereign. Barring conflicts with foreign enemies, the sovereign cannot avail himself of the excuse that practising natural law is too risky for him. The general right to set aside morality as a standard of action in dangerous circumstances cannot render sovereign failures to adhere by natural law *de facto* rightful vis-à-vis humans. For the same reason, *Untraceable Intentions* cannot by itself justify Hobbes's conceptualizations of justice and injury. It cannot explain why sinful failure to practice natural law in conditions of safety wrongs God alone—and hence why among humans '*wrong* [injuriam] is simply the violation of an agreement' (DCv 7.14).

3.4 NO ACCUSATION WITHOUT LAW

Myriad passages evince that sovereigns and pre-statist individuals alike can sin against natural law, and thereby wrong God.[41] What does it mean to injure the deity? Injuries are defined as actions without right. Right (i.e. freedom) can be removed in two ways: (i) through voluntary alienation of right; (ii) through imposition of law by a superior—since 'right is that liberty which law leaveth us' (EL 29.5). Naturally equal in right and power, people can be subject to a human superior only after entering a covenant of submission (involving voluntary alienation of right). God, by contrast, has the right to legislate without agreement of the subjected, by dint of his irresistible power (DCv 15.4–5; L 31.5) (§1.2). Persons lack right vis-à-vis God insofar as the deity binds them to observe divine laws (including the laws of nature). Consequently, persons wrong God by wilfully breaking his laws. To restate the puzzle posed by *Sinning with Right*: how can people bound by natural law lack right vis-à-vis God—and yet have right vis-à-vis other humans?

No Accusation without Law provides a second argument for *Sinning with Right* (thus-stated). It establishes general natural immunity to moral accusation in the following manner. Moral accusation presupposes the existence of a common standard of law. To condemn another's action as morally wrong is to declare that it deviated without excuse from what natural law requires. Outside the state, each individual's own reason is the yardstick of natural law for them personally (DCv 2.1n; DCv 12.1; L 29.7). In accusing others of wrongdoing, pre-statist individuals inevitably impose upon others their own interpretation of natural law

---

[41] On sovereign misconduct wronging God, see EL 21.3; DCv 6.13; L 21.7; L 22.15; EW 5: 178. On pre-statist conduct wronging God, see DCv 1.10n; DCv 3.4n; DCv 3.27n.

72 JUSTICE AND NATURAL LAW

(i.e. their own standard of reason). Humans being naturally equal, no one is obligated to accept as authoritative another's opinion of what natural law means and requires: 'those who are outside the state are not obliged to follow another's opinion' in anything (DH 13.8). Rightful accusations of moral wrongdoing are for this reason impossible absent a legal system. Had pre-statist individuals been epistemically capable of accusing others of transgressing natural law, they would still lack the right to do so.

The laws of nature, some might counter, surely form a common moral standard in the state of nature? The dictates of right reason are divine commands after all, unwaveringly obliging all rational agents. Besides, all are capable of finding out what natural law requires by rational reflection. The answer is vintage Hobbes. Amidst war and disagreement, who decides what right reason calls for? No common standard of right reason can be found in nature itself (L 5.3; L 6.7). Right reason is always the reason of someone: 'seeing right reason is not existent [*in rerum naturâ*], the reason of some man, or men, must supply the place thereof' (EL 29.8).[42] Within the state, the sovereign's will is by general consent turned into the standard of right reason (DPS 158). All have to rely on their private reason 'outside of a Commonwealth, where no one can distinguish right reason from false except by making comparison with his own' (DCv 2.1n). Even if some pre-statist individuals manage to discover the full moral law through correct ratiocination, their true conclusions are not therefore law to others nor likely to find widespread acceptance. People's moral judgements generally reflect their own passions and interests after all, producing fierce disagreement over right and wrong (§6.3). In the state of nature, there are hence as many interpretations of natural law as there are individuals (DH 13.8). Hobbes concludes: 'in the condition of men that have no other Law but their own Appetites, there can be no generall Rule of Good, and Evil Actions' (L 46.32). 'Therefore a common standard for virtues and vices doth not appear except in civil life; this standard cannot . . . be other than the laws of each and every state' (DH 13.9; also DCv 12.1; L 29.6). Bramhall is appalled: 'by right reason he understands the arbitrary edicts of an elective Governoour'.[43]

Outside a legal system, I have argued, individuals cannot make judgements about right and wrong except by reference to their own reason. As such, their verdicts carry no normative weight vis-à-vis their equals. By nature free and equal, humans have the right to ignore the moral criticism of others:

> amid such diversity of opinion, what is rationally to be blamed is not to be measured by one man's reason more than by another's, because of the equality of

---

[42] Thus breaking with tradition—cf. e.g. Cicero, *The Republic*, 3.33. On Hobbes's creative reworking of this age-old notion, see Robert A. Greene, 'Thomas Hobbes and the Term "Right Reason": Participation to Calculation', *History of European Ideas* 41 (2015) no. 8: 997–1028; Johan Olsthoorn, 'On the Absence of Moral Goodness in Hobbes's Ethics', *The Journal of Ethics* 24 (2020) no. 2: 254–259.

[43] John Bramhall, *Castigations of Mr. Hobbes* (London, 1657) 199.

human nature; and since there exists no reason other than the reasons of *individuals* and the reason of *the commonwealth*, it follows that the commonwealth must determine what is *to be blamed with reason*; so that a *fault*, i.e. a SIN, is what anyone does, fails to do, says or wills contrary to *the reason of the commonwealth*, i.e. against the laws. (DCv 14.17)

Equals can be legitimately accused of wrongdoing only by appeal to a common authoritative standard. Civil law is the only such standard. In its absence, Hobbes concludes, people cannot be appropriately blamed by others for anything. That is why 'culpable sins' presuppose the state (§3.1).

No Accusation without Law entails that all are by nature beyond human reproach. Not because their actions are morally spotless—far from it. But rather because outside the commonwealth people lack the standing to morally censure their equals: any such condemnation inadmissibly imposes *their* personal interpretation of right and wrong upon others. Absent common rules to which accusers can appeal, moral condemnations are mere expressions of their private opinion, which others may rightfully ignore. *No Accusation without Law* thus derives natural rights of private judgement from the non-existence of shared law. It differs, in this respect, from *Untraceable Intentions*. That argument had grounded natural rights of private judgement in the epistemic impossibility of warranted accusation in war. The two arguments thus provide different explanations for how the right of nature, as a subjective right, extends to an unlimited right vis-à-vis fellow humans to do as one pleases.

No Accusation without Law is in tension, I believe, with Hobbes's initial conceptualization of natural right as 'blameless liberty' (EL 14.6). Recall that in *Elements/De Cive*, natural right permits all to do whatever is not 'reprehensible, nor contrary to right reason' (DCv 1.7). The concept of 'blameless liberty' conceptually presupposes shared norms. The rule Hobbes invokes to determine which actions are blameless is right reason. Yet who determines what right reason means and requires? Outside the state, people can make moral judgements only by appeal to their own interpretation of right reason. Humans being naturally equal, their verdicts obligate no one—and likely clash with others' assessments. This makes Hobbes's early conception of natural right practically useless. What one may do blamelessly is not something people will agree upon in the state of nature. Worse, even had such agreement been possible, equals could not with reason invoke it to authoritatively tell others right from wrong. Verdicts of blame and blamelessness, *No Accusation without Law* states, presuppose the existence of civil law. Without it, humans have vis-à-vis others literally right to do 'any thing he liketh' (L 14.5). This insight, I conjecture, explains why *Leviathan* makes no mention of blameless liberty. The same explains why Hobbes drops the derivation of the right of nature, found in earlier works. After all, that derivation was based on showing that unlimited rights of self-defence are not contrary to right reason/natural law (EL 14.6–10;

74   JUSTICE AND NATURAL LAW

DCv 1.7–10).[44] To be sure, *Leviathan* continues to deduce the right to everything from rights of self-defence (L 14.4). After all, in the eyes of God, pre-statist individuals have right only to what they sincerely judge aids their self-defence. Yet vis-à-vis fellow humans, all are entitled to do as they please. That postulate Hobbes now derives directly from human natural equality.

Untraceable Intentions had not questioned the existence of common standards of right reason. Instead it points out that, amidst hostility, the right of nature permits all to judge for themselves whether these common precepts bind in practice. It thereby made individual immunity to moral accusation dependent on the existence of war. *No Accusation without Law* removes this major practical limitation on the scope of natural right. It declares people altogether unaccountable to others for the moral quality of their conduct—on grounds of natural equality: 'the Civill Law ceasing, Crimes cease: for there being no other Law remaining, but that of Nature, there is no place for Accusation; every man being his own Judge, and accused onely by his own Conscience, and cleared by the Uprightnesse of his own Intention' (L 27.3). *Untraceable Intentions* posits a natural right to judge for oneself when natural law must be practised. *No Accusation without Law* is bolder, entitling pre-statist individuals to follow their own judgement, whatever it is. From natural freedom and equality Locke derived a general ban on wanton harm: 'being all equal and independent, no one ought to harm another in his Life, Health, Liberty or Possessions'.[45] Hobbes drew the opposite conclusion. By nature free and equal, humans are under no directed obligation, owed to others, to act in accordance with another's will—not even their reasonable desire not to be maltreated.

3.5 NATURAL LAW, DIVINE LAW, AND CIVIL LAW

The laws of nature have a dual status in Hobbes. They can be regarded as mere dictates of reason or as true laws.

> These dictates of Reason, men use to call by the name of Lawes, but improperly: for they are but Conclusions, or Theoremes concerning what conduceth to the conservation and defence of themselves; whereas Law, properly is the word of him, that by right hath command over others. But yet if we consider the same Theoremes, as delivered in the word of God, that by right commandeth all things; then are they properly called Lawes. (L 15.41; also EL 17.12; EL 18.1; EW 4: 284–285)[46]

---

[44] Baumgold (ed), *Three-Text Edition*, 135–137.

[45] Locke, *Second Treatise*, 2.6.

[46] *De Cive* adds that the word of God is Holy Scripture (DCv 3.33). Parallel passages omit this clause, which jars with Hobbes's view that God issues commands through revelation *and* through natural reason. Other considerations, discussed in this section, further discredit Undersrud's suggestion that

NATURAL LAW, DIVINE LAW, AND CIVIL LAW   75

Laws are commands issued by a superior to a subject previously obligated to obey their orders (L 26.2) (§6.2). Natural law, Hobbes emphasizes, is law qua divine command. 'There is no doubt but they were made Laws by God himselfe' (L 42.37). These 'Lawes, (such of them as oblige all Mankind,) in respect of God, as he is the Author of Nature, are *Naturall*; and in respect of the same God, as he is King of Kings, are *Lawes*' (L 30.30). The laws of nature are binding law to all those who acknowledge God's authority and providence; only to atheists are these rules mere dictates of reason (L 31.4).[47]

Like many of his contemporaries, Hobbes recognized two categories of divine law. '*Divine law* is twofold: *natural* (or *moral*) and *positive*' (DCv 14.4; also L R&C.17).[48] Divine natural law is eternal, immutable, and universally binding.[49] It consists of: (1) the laws of nature, enjoining the necessary means to self-preservation; and (2) general rules found out by right reason regarding the due honour and worship of God (DCv 15.8; DCv 15.15–16; L 31.7). The first category has two subtypes: (1a) moral laws, prescribing moral virtues as means to peace; (1b) rules prescribing non-moral personal virtues such as temperance, prudence, and courage. While not being means to peace, possession of those last virtues does reliably promote the agent's self-preservation, and are as such dictated by natural law (DCv 3.32; L 15.34; DH 13.9). While many passages seemingly equate the two, the moral law is really only a subset of natural law.[50] All natural laws are divine laws (EL 29.7; L 26.39). God promulgates the divine natural laws through natural reason, whence they are called 'dictates of right reason' (DCv 15.3; L 31.3). Divine positive law, by contrast, is neither eternal nor universally binding. It consists of 'posited' law—that is, God's commandments to specific people at specific times (L 26.39). The deity issues positive laws by means of revelation and prophecy (L 31.4).

the laws of nature are divine law only qua biblical commands. David Undersrud, 'On Natural Law and Civil Law in the Political Philosophy of Hobbes', *History of Political Thought* 35 (2014) no. 4: 690, 712.

[47] Whether Hobbes was sincere in equating natural law with divine commands—that is, whether he personally believed in a law-giving deity—is a question I side-step. This book aims to reconstruct arguments about justice and morality found in Hobbes's works, not to speculate about his inner thoughts and beliefs. For rival takes on Hobbes's personal investment in divine law ethics, see Edwin Curley, '"I Durst Not Write so Boldly": Or How to Read Hobbes's Theological-Political Treatise' in Emilia Giancotti (eds), *Hobbes e Spinoza* (Naples, 1992) 497–593; A.P. Martinich, *The Two Gods of Leviathan* (Cambridge, 1992) 100–127; Greg Forster, 'Divine Law and Human Law in Hobbes's *Leviathan*', *History of Political Thought* 24 (2003) no. 2: 189–217.

[48] E.g. Suárez, *De Legibus*, 1.3.9, 14; Grotius, *War and Peace*, 1.1.15.

[49] On the laws of nature being divine, see e.g. EL 17.12; EL 18.1; EL 29.7; DCv 3.33; L 15.41; L 29.9; LLA 2.34. On their being eternal and unalterable, see e.g. EL 18.4; DCv 3.29; DCv 4.20; DCv 14.2, 4; DCv 16.10; L 15.38; L 26.24; L 33.22; DPS 157; B 264. On their being universally binding, see e.g. L 26.9, 13; L 30.30; L 42.37. The natural dictates of right reason bind all rational persons—not all humans. Natural law does not govern people incapable of reasoning: 'over naturall fooles, children, or mad-men there is no Law... nor are they capable of the title of just, or unjust' (L 26.12; also L 27.23; DPS 34).

[50] Bernard Gert, *Hobbes: Prince of Peace* (Malden, MA, 2010) 75, 79. See e.g. EL 18.1; EL 25.11; EL 29.7; DCv 3.31; DCv 4.1; L 26.36, 40. The equation is a canon law doctrine, found on the first page of Gratian's *Decretum* (c.1150).

76   JUSTICE AND NATURAL LAW

Divine positive laws are binding only to those who have covenanted with God (i.e. Jews, Christians) (DCv 16.10). The divine positive laws found in Scripture reissue the entire natural moral law, without amendment or addition (EL 29.7; DCv 4.1; L 43.5). Lastly, all human law is positive law.

Leviathan reiterates the claim that natural law is law qua divine command (L 15.41). Yet it adds the sweeping thesis that natural law is truly law only within the commonwealth.

> For the Lawes of Nature . . . in the condition of meer Nature . . . are not properly Lawes, but qualities that dispose men to peace, and to obedience. When a Common-wealth is once settled, then they are actually Lawes, and not before; as being then the commands of the Common-wealth; and therefore also Civill Lawes. (L 26.8; also DH 13.9)

Only qua civil law is natural law truly law. 'For though it be naturally reasonable; yet it is by the Soveraigne Power that it is Law' (L 26.22). How to reconcile this novel doctrine with passages calling natural law the product of divine legislation?

Some commentators attempt to harmonize these facially conflicting claims by positing *two* states of natures. In the primary one, the laws of nature are moral virtues disposing men to peace; in the secondary one, where God reigns, they are laws proper.[51] That interpretive proposal cannot explain the puzzle at hand, to wit that natural law is not actually law beyond the commonwealth. The proposal is nevertheless illustrative of how scholars generally approach the conundrum. They take Hobbes to be asking: when do the laws of nature have the status of law *to individuals* governed by these norms? Thus construed, the answer hinges on what grounds God's right to rule and what ensures epistemic access to his legislative will.[52] In my view, Hobbes is asking an entirely different question: when does natural/divine law have the status of law *among humans*? When can humans invoke natural law as a norm obliging others?

The early works had assumed that God's natural and positive laws are truly law outside the state. The sovereign is tasked to authoritatively settle any interpretive dispute over their meaning and content. 'The *interpretation* of *natural laws*', we read, 'depends on the authority of the commonwealth, i.e. of the man or council which has been granted sovereign power . . . whatever God commands, he commands through its voice' (DCv 15.17). Whether a particular action is sinful—that is, a wilful breach of natural law—likewise always requires human interpretation (DCv 17.25). God himself willed the sovereign 'to be the *interpreter of right reason*,

---

[51] Michael Byron, *Submission and Subjection in Leviathan* (New York, 2015) 67–69; also Martinich, *Two Gods*, 76–87.

[52] E.g. David Gauthier, 'Hobbes: The Laws of Nature', *Pacific Philosophical Quarterly* 82 (2001) no. 3/4: 258–284; Kinch Hoekstra, 'Hobbes on Law, Nature and Reason', *Journal of the History of Philosophy* 41 (2003) no. 1: 111–120.

i.e. of his [natural] laws' (DCv 15.17). The sovereign is the ultimate arbiter of the meaning of revealed law as well: 'the *interpretation* of holy scripture, i.e. the *right to settle* all *disputes*, should depend on and be derived from the Authority of the man or group of men in whose hands lies the sovereignty in the commonwealth' (DCv 17.27; also EL 26.11).

Elements/De Cive nowhere suggest that the divine laws (natural and positive) are first made law among humans through civil legislation. That bold claim is new to *Leviathan*.[53] Consider its statements about the legal status of the Bible: 'are not the Scriptures, in all places where they are Law, made Law by the Authority of the Common-wealth, and consequently, a part of the Civill Law?' (L 46.38). 'The Scriptures themselves were made law to us here, by the authority of the common-wealth, and are therefore part of the civil law' (EW 4: 369).[54] Civil legislation is needed to make the Bible binding law for two reasons. First, how else could we know which books contain God's revealed word? The deity has directly revealed his positive laws to only a select few. Non-prophets, to whom God has not spoken supernaturally, are not obliged to 'take for Gods Law' whatever their equals claim the deity has told them (L 33.24). 'For though God be the Sovereign of all the world, we are not bound to take for his Law, whatsoever is propounded by every man in his name' (L 42.46; also L 40.6). Religious conflict would be endless had we been obliged to take for God's commandments all 'dreams, and fancies' of the super-stitious (L 26.40; also EW 5: 290). Only the 'Soveraign Prophet'—that is, the civil ruler—can authoritatively settle 'in the name of God' what God's revealed word is (L 36.20; also L 40.2). For this reason, 'those Books only are Canonicall, that is, Law, in every nation, which are established for such by the Soveraign Authority' (L 33.1).[55] Second, large chunks of the Bible take the form of counsel, not law. Jesus Christ was no lawgiver (L 43.5). The Gospel consequently contains no 'Laws, but onely good, and safe advice' on how to attain salvation, which all 'may without injustice refuse to observe' (L 42.43). For this reason, too, 'the New Testament is there only Law, where the lawfull Civill Power hath made it so' (L 42.44).

Other parts of the Bible *are* law prior to civil legislation—namely all 'Morall Doctrine consonant to Reason; the Dictates whereof are Laws, not *made*, but *Eternall*' (L 33.22). Again, that natural law is divine law does not suffice to make its precepts law between humans. For a start, outside of a Christian commonwealth, many lack firm knowledge that the dictates of right reason are in fact divine com-mandments.[56] More importantly, people are mutually obligated to take as binding

---

[53] This major shift has been overlooked in the debate over whether Hobbes's religious and ecclesias-tical views change over time. Compare e.g. Lodi Nauta, 'Hobbes on Religion and the Church between *The Elements of Law* and *Leviathan*: A Dramatic Change of Direction?', *Journal of the History of Ideas* 63 (2002) no. 4: 577–598.

[54] Also EW 4: 339; EW 4: 363–364; EW 5: 179; L 42.80; L 43.5; DH 14.4. Johann Sommerville, *Thomas Hobbes: Political Ideas in Historical Context* (London, 1992) 97: 'divine positive law therefore collapses into human law'.

[55] Martinich, *Two Gods*, 316–320.

[56] Undersrud, 'Natural Law and Civil Law', 688–689.

78 JUSTICE AND NATURAL LAW

law over them only what the sovereign declares so: 'law obliges not, nor is Law to any, but to them that acknowledge it to be the act of the Soveraign' (L 42.37). As commands issued by an irresistible lawgiver, natural and revealed law are binding law to God's subjects. Yet these laws do not interpret themselves. And even sound interpretations of divine commands are not law to those free to disobey the interpreter. As Hobbes asks rhetorically, 'would you have every Man to every other Man alledge for Law his own particular Reason?' (DPS 26). Outside the state, the benchmark of natural law is for each their private reason: 'he that is subject to no Civill Law . . . has no other rule to follow but his own reason' (L 29.7). In such conditions, all are 'at liberty, and have no law but from themselves' (EL 20.6). Sovereign legislation is needed to make natural law *interpersonally* binding: 'the laws of nature . . . being not known by men for any thing but their own natural reason, they were but theorems, tending to peace, and those uncertain, as being but conclusions of particular men, <u>and therefore not properly laws</u>' (EW 4: 284–285). In this way, Hobbes reduces all law to civil law: 'all Lawes, written, and unwritten, have their Authority, and force, from the Will of the Common-wealth' (L 26.10).

The reason natural law is not properly law outside the commonwealth, I conclude, has nothing to do with the rampant insecurity there. Civil law certainly provides the safety needed to render natural law obligatory *in foro externo*, thereby making it morally obligatory for all to practice natural law. Yet legal protection does not suffice to turn these precepts into interpersonal law.[57] That requires in addition authoritative specification, interpretation, and penal enforcement by a common legal superior (L 26.8). In every commonwealth, all moral precepts become part of the legal code: 'for natural law, when the state is constituted, become part of the civil law' (DH 13.9) (§6.5). Only when natural law is thus turned into interpersonal law, *No Accusation without Law* states, can humans lack the right vis-à-vis others to sin. Only then can their immoral conduct be unjust and injurious to others—such that compliance with natural law is no longer a matter between the agent and God alone.

3.6 NATURAL LAW DUTIES OF CITIZENS

Abizadeh correctly observes that 'natural laws are not properly laws for which anyone is accountable until incorporated into civil law'.[58] He does not explain why and how natural law duties become directed upon inclusion within the legal system. This section provides an interpretation of the deontic status of citizens' natural law duties that aligns with my novel account of why these duties are non-directed outside the commonwealth.

---

[57] *Contra* Warrender, *The Political Philosophy of Hobbes*, 80.
[58] Abizadeh, *Two Faces of Ethics*, 236.

Contra Abizadeh, I have argued that the non-directed character of natural law duties is best understood as a contingent rather than an inbuilt feature. Their initial non-directedness is not a consequence of *how* natural law duties bind (i.e. what kind of obligation they impose: their supposed merely prudential character). It follows rather from Hobbes's relational conception of injury/wrong as any action towards another person vis-à-vis whom the wrongdoer lacked the right so to act (§2.3). Being acts without right, no injustice or injury can be committed against humans as long as all enjoy a veritable right to everything. Consequently, the correct interpretive questions to ask are: when and why do trespasses against natural law not wrong/injure the persons harmed by them? Under which conditions do humans have the right vis-à-vis their fellows to sin? My answer is: as long as persons are entitled to follow their own judgements about what (if anything) morality demands in practice. Unrestricted rights of private judgement, grounded in human natural equality, ensure that pre-statist individuals cannot be accused by others of injury (i.e. of acting without right). Private judgement turns the right of nature into an unlimited right vis-à-vis others to do as one wishes, precluding all interpersonal injustice and injury (i.e. acts *sine jure*). In the state of nature, I have argued, humans sin with right because the fog of war renders immoral conduct undetectable in practice; and because prevailing natural equality of right bars all moral condemnation in principle. The introduction of a legal system enables moral censure in two ways. Each is necessary for humans to be able to hold each other morally accountable. First, legal protection makes it mandatory to keep natural law in practice—rendering moral wrongdoing humanly detectable (as per *Untraceable Intentions*). Second, it provides a common standard of law to which equals can appeal so they can admissibly censure and sue wrongdoers (in line with *No Accusation without Law*).

Citizens whose conduct inexcusably violates natural law duties, I have argued, *are* guilty of injustice and injury towards their co-nationals. But in what ways exactly? How can we reconcile the directed nature of natural law duties of citizens with Hobbes's quadruple equation of (i) 'unjust action'; (ii) 'injury'/'wrong'; (iii) 'action without right'; and (iv) breach of covenant? If immoral conduct is not essentially but contingently non-injurious, in virtue of pre-statist rights of private judgement, what then ensures that all injuries/acts without right are also injustices/violations of covenant? The answer, in short, is that covenants are needed for the laws of nature to become law proper. Civil laws are obligatory to citizens in virtue of their original promise of general obedience. The sovereign lawgiver converts natural law into civil law. By interpreting, specifying, and enforcing its precepts, he makes it crystal clear to his citizens that he wishes them to follow these moral rules (to assume otherwise 'were a great contumely'—L 26.26). Crimes against natural law as incorporated into the legal system ('unwritten civil law') are hence always unjust qua breaches of faith. Citizens owe it to the sovereign and to each other to obey natural law qua civil law. This takes the sting out of DCv

80   JUSTICE AND NATURAL LAW

3.4: 'in a commonwealth, if one harms anyone with whom he has no agreement, he [merely] causes *loss* to the person he maltreats'. Wantonly harming fellow citizens is always an unjust violation of agreement because the natural laws forbidding it have lawlike status within the state, courtesy of sovereign legislation. While the original covenant is a precondition for the laws of nature becoming actual laws, the authority of civil law itself rests on the third law of nature: 'natural law commands that all civil laws be observed in virtue of the natural law which forbids the violation of agreements' (DCv 14.10).[59] This does not make Hobbes's argument circular. For natural law can steadfastly obligate individuals *without* having the status of law.

In short, citizens are under a self-assumed obligation of justice, owed to *all* members of the commonwealth, to abide by all precepts of natural law (as incorporated within the legal system). In addition, I maintain, their violations of natural law duties can wrong *specific* co-citizens. Recall Hobbes's belated conceptual disentanglement of injury from injustice of action (§2.4). From the 1647 edition of *De Cive* onwards, wrongs/injuries no longer by definition *consist in* breaking agreements (even if they must *involve* the same). Every felony, Hobbes now maintains, is unjust towards all citizens by dint of breaking their mutual pact of obedience. Yet crimes may wrong/injure only the victim, whose personal liberties the lawbreaker unjustly hinders. This disentanglement, I have indicated, solves a problem in Hobbes's criminal theory. It also opens up theoretical space for the thought that citizens' immoral conduct is injurious/without right vis-à-vis fellow subjects merely as a transgression of natural law. Let me explain.

Recall that citizens have not only alienated their right of self-government to the sovereign (by promising non-resistance in all things not contrary to divine law).[60] As instructed by the second law of nature, upon entering the commonwealth individuals have also jointly laid down their invasive rights of nature, retaining only '*so much liberty against other men, as he would allow other men against himself*' (L 14.5; also EL 15.2; DCv 2.3). In the so-called covenant of peace, citizens obligate themselves not to violently intrude on the retained equal liberties of others (§2.3; §5.6). Only threats of state punishment can make this armistice last (L 14.31; L 17.4). After all, without an accompanying covenant of subjection, all would retain their natural right of self-government, allowing them to shelve the initial covenant of peace whenever *they* judge that self-preservation is best served by renewing the war (§7.1). Exiting the state of war requires forming a commonwealth. For without an additional covenant of subjection, any covenant of peace swiftly becomes null. With it, though, the truce can endure. Overlooking this point, commentators

---

[59]   Also DCv 14.21, 23; L 26.8; L 30.4; L 43.5; B 195.
[60]   E.g. EL 25.1; DCv 8.1; DCv 15.1; DCv 18.13; L 26.40; L 30.1.

rarely consider the normative effects the covenant of peace has within the commonwealth: how it informs the mutual rights and duties of citizens.[61]

By mutually renouncing their natural right to everything, individuals simultaneously bind themselves to comply with the precepts of natural law—for two reasons. First, the law of nature determines how much natural liberty each equally shall retain. The Golden Rule—the sum of natural law—captures it: '*Do not that to another, which thou wouldest not have done to thy selfe*' (L 15.35; also L 14.5).[62] Second, humans truly had right to everything only because and insofar as they were permitted to forgo practising morality in hostile conditions. By forswearing their invasive rights, citizens simultaneously obligate themselves to abide by natural law in practice (*in foro externo*). In effect, upon joining the commonwealth subjects mutually promise each other to henceforth behave morally by renouncing resort to a rival standard of action: war.[63] Consequently, any citizen who acts unsociably towards a co-national thereby *injures* that person because she had freely renounced the right to act unsociably upon entering the state. Moreover, her unsociable conduct wrongs *that person* specifically whose enjoyment of retained liberty-rights she so unjustly hinders (§2.4). Hobbes's conceptual disentanglement of injury from injustice of action thus allows him to hold that citizens' immoral conduct is without right and a wrong/injury *to* others merely qua violation of natural law (forbidding all uncivil behaviour).

Natural law duties of citizens, I have argued, are directed: their violation is unjust to all and injurious to anyone whose retained liberty-rights it tramples upon. Their injustice consists in a violation of the original covenant of obedience. For civil legislation first makes the precepts of right reason interpersonally law and obligatory in practice. Not civil legislation but the original covenant of peace removes the right to act immorally vis-à-vis humans. Citizens lack the right/freedom to act cruelly, hatefully, unsociably, etc. towards co-nationals by dint of the collective rights-renunciation enjoined by the second law of nature. Subsequent sins against natural law can qualify as injuries towards fellow citizens not just indirectly, as breaches of unwritten civil law. But also directly, because subjects have mutually renounced their rights of war upon joining the commonwealth. This is so even though what legally constitutes an injury is determined by the sovereign. He authoritatively specifies what counts as cruelty, hatred, unsociability, etc. through legislation and adjudication—thus first creating a shared standard of morality (§6.3).

---

[61] But see Eleanor Curran, *Reclaiming the Rights of Hobbesian Subjects* (Basingstoke, 2007) 72–76, 100, 110–111, 165–168.

[62] Allusions to the Golden Rule recur in EL 18.6; EL 29.7; DCv 4.12; L 26.13; L 42.11.

[63] This makes natural right normatively prior to natural law duties—yet only insofar as the latter are seen as binding in practice. I firmly reject Strauss's misguided view that Hobbes 'asserted the primacy of natural rights' over natural law in general, on the grounds that 'all duties are derivative from the fundamental and inalienable right of self-preservation'. Leo Strauss, *Natural Right and History* (Chicago, 1953) 181–183; also Leo Strauss, *The Political Philosophy of Hobbes: Its Basis and Its Genesis* (Chicago, 1952) viii–ix.

82 JUSTICE AND NATURAL LAW

Leviathan's innovative reduction of natural and revealed law to civil law enabled Hobbes to tighten the link between justice and law. Regardless of what kind of law is transgressed (written or unwritten), all crimes—that is, all humanly detectable breaches of law—are now unjust violations of agreement. Justice essentially consists in keeping faith. And yet this duty indirectly requires keeping *every* law— eternal ones included—because all interpersonally binding law is ultimately civil law. Consequently, the 'virtue of a subject is comprehended wholly in obedience to the laws of the commonwealth' (B 165). Moreover, the same ensures that every action of citizens that crosses natural law is an unjust offence against the sovereign's orders. *Leviathan's* reductionism about law enables Hobbes to broaden the extension of 'unjust action' to include the violation of *any* law whatsoever—while clinging to his narrow definition of justice as keeping valid agreements. Thus, we read that: 'Injustice . . . is the Inconformity of the Action to the Law' (L 46.31). 'Lawes are the Rules of Just, and Unjust; nothing being reputed Unjust, that is not contrary to <u>some</u> Law' (L 26.4). 'What is unjust, but the transgression of a law? *Law* therefore was before unjust' (EW 4: 370).[64] This definitional convergence makes *Leviathan's* theory of justice more parsimonious and unified than commonly believed.[65]

Though everywhere incorporated into civil law, natural law retains some unique deontic features. Most importantly, it remains possible for citizens and the sovereign alike to flout natural law without breaking civil law. Evidently so for supreme rulers: not subject to civil law, all sovereign moral wrongdoing—in will and deed— injures God alone. For citizens, all actions prohibited by natural law are now in addition legally banned by civil law. Yet citizens can still sin against natural law alone—by having wrongful intentions (DCv 14.14; L 27.2). Being humanly undetectable, such 'sins of the mind' are neither crimes nor transgressions of civil law (which governs words and actions only). Despite its legal incorporation, natural law continues to be a moral standard separate to civil law: governing not actions but what Hobbes calls *manners*.

---

[64] Also e.g. EW 1: 74; EW 5: 152; DH 10.5; DPS 31; DPS 36; B 44.

[65] According to Kavka, 'Hobbes offers two accounts of unjust actions . . . The narrower account of injustice defines it as failing to perform one's part of a covenant. The wider account defines injustice as any breach of obligation.' *Leviathan* harmonizes both accounts by establishing that every action transgressing law is simultaneously a failure to perform the original covenant. Kavka, *Hobbesian Moral and Political Theory*, 304, also 305–306, 344, 377. The same harmonizing move allows Hobbes to declare 'unjust' any action by citizens contravening natural law, while holding fast to his equation of injustice with injury. *Contra* Daniel Eggers, 'Injury, Injustice, Iniquity: The Evolution of Hobbes's Theory of Justice', *Intellectual History Review* 24 (2014) no. 2: 173–174.

3.7 THE VIRTUE OF JUSTICE

To complete my reconstruction of the relation between justice and natural law, I turn to Hobbes's distinction between the justice of actions vs. that of manners, found across his works. According to Hobbes, the meaning and criteria for 'just' and 'unjust' differ depending on whether the terms apply to actions or persons. Consider *Elements*:

> For justice and injustice, when they be attributed to actions, signify the same thing with no injury, and injury; and denominate the action just, or unjust, but not the man so; for they denominate him guilty, or not guilty. But when justice and injustice are attributed to men, they signify proneness and affection, and inclination of nature, that is to say, passions of the mind apt to produce just and unjust actions. (EL 16.4; also DCv 3.5; DCv 14.18)

The contrast recurs in *Leviathan*, with this difference that 'just action' now means 'keeping covenants' rather than 'no injury' (L 15.10) (§2.2). The meaning of justice of *persons* stays the same over time. Persons are just if they are reliably disposed to act justly—however the latter is understood: '[W]hen a man is said to be just, or unjust, not the action, but the passion, and aptitude to do such actions is considered' (EL 16.4). Insofar as someone is acting justly, they are called 'not Just, but *Guiltlesse*' (L 15.11; also EL 25.10; DCv 3.5). Clearly, not all people free from guilt are just persons. People refrain from committing injustices for manifold reasons. Not all these reasons reflect a mind steadily inclined to justice. *Being* just requires abstaining from law-breaking, not in fear of punishment but 'because the law so instructs' (DCv 3.5). Someone who keeps on weighing the pros and cons of abstaining vs. engaging in crime, measuring his actions 'by the apparent benefit of what he is to do', cannot be called just. 'A Just man ... taketh all the care he can, that his Actions may be all Just'—without constant calculation of short-term advantage (L 15.10). Indeed, the just man scorns law-breaking so much that he 'condemns what he has done unjustly, even though the action is unknown to others' (LL 15.9). Just people, Hobbes intimates, are few and far between. Most mortals need threats of punishment to 'frame and make their will to justice' (EW 5: 152).[66]

---

[66] Existing literature on the subject is largely framed around the dispute over psychological egoism: is it psychologically possible for Hobbesian agents to act out of a sense of justice? E.g. Taylor, 'The Ethical Doctrine of Hobbes', 408–409; Martin Harvey, 'A Defense of Hobbes's "Just Man"', *Hobbes Studies* 15 (2002) no. 1: 68–86; Boonin-Vail, *Science of Moral Virtue*, 112–113, 149–150, 164–165, 182–186. Though I cannot defend this claim here, I see no tension between Hobbes's psychological egoism and passages about just persons—the latter may well be motivated by considerations of enlightened (rather than apparent) self-interest. Corsa argues that magnanimity ('greatness of soul') motivates people to be just. A.J. Corsa, 'Thomas Hobbes: Magnanimity, Felicity and Justice', *Hobbes Studies* 26 (2013) no. 2: 147–150.

84　JUSTICE AND NATURAL LAW

Just persons have good manners. 'This Justice of the Manners', Hobbes writes, 'is that which is meant, where Justice is called a Vertue; and Injustice a Vice' (L 15.10; also EL 16.4). '[M]anners, if they be good, are called *virtues*, if evil, *vices*' (DH 13.8). *Moral* virtues, in turn, are 'those qualities of man-kind, that concern their living together in Peace, and Unity' (L 11.1).[67] They are 'habits of the mind that conduce to Peace, and Charity' (L 26.36). Manners are dispositions 'so strengthened by habit, that they beget their actions with ease and with reason unresisting' (DH 13.8). For the just, promise-keeping comes naturally, with the gentle ease of habit. Just persons may once in a while commit injustices—all flesh is weak and mistakes happen. Occasional mishaps need not mean that their law-abiding habits and convictions are lost:

a Righteous man, does not lose that Title, by one, or a few unjust Actions, that proceed from sudden Passion, or mistake of Things, or Persons: nor does an Unrighteous man, lose his character, for such Actions, as he does, or forbeares to do, for feare: because his Will is not framed by the Justice, but by the apparent benefit of what he is to do. (L 15.10)[68]

The laws of nature principally prescribe good manners (i.e. moral virtues) (DCv 3.31). Hobbes calls the 'Doctrine of the Lawes of Nature' 'the science of Vertue and Vice' (L 15.40). He even boasts to have pioneered this science (EW 7: 471).[69] His breakthrough insight was that the goodness of the laws of nature lies in their being necessary means of peace. Virtue does not lie 'in a certain mean between two extremes' as Aristotle had falsely believed (DCv 3.32; also L 15.40; EW 5: 267; B 165).[70] The science of moral virtue spells out those moral dispositions that render humans suitable for living together in peace—'the *moral virtues*, the bringers of peace' (DCv 15.8). Hobbes claims to have uncovered general causal connections between moral actions and dispositions on the one hand, and peace on the other. The laws of nature are eternal and immutable in part because these general causal tendencies hold true universally. 'Injustice, Ingratitude, Arrogance, Pride, Iniquity, Acception of persons, and the rest, can never be made lawfull. For it can never be that Warre shall preserve life, and Peace destroy it' (L 15.38).

---

[67] Also DCv 15.8; DH 13.8–9; DH 15.4.

[68] Also EL 16.4; EL 25.10; DCv 3.5; DCv 18.12; LL 15.9–10; L 43.20.

[69] A demonstrative moral science is possible since we make and hence can know its principles or causes (DH 10.5). For discussion, see Marcus Adams, 'Hobbes's Laws of Nature in *Leviathan* as a Synthetic Demonstration', *Philosophers' Imprint* 19 (2019) no. 5: 1–23. I presume that 'the Science of Naturall Justice' is the science of natural law (L 31.41). For a rival gloss on natural justice, see Matthew Hoye, 'Natural Justice, Law, and Virtue in Hobbes's *Leviathan*', *Hobbes Studies* 32 (2019) no. 2: 179–208.

[70] Quentin Skinner, *Reason and Rhetoric in the Philosophy of Hobbes* (Cambridge, 1996) 323–326. On Aristotle's doctrine of the mean, see Ioannis Evrigenis, 'The Doctrine of the Mean in Aristotle's Ethical and Political Theory', *History of Political Thought* 20 (1999) no. 3: 393–416.

Which virtues does a person need to possess to qualify as just? Hobbes provides two distinct answers.[71] In a narrow sense, people are just when they possess the virtue of justice. The virtue of justice consists in 'that habit by which we stand to covenants' (EL 17.14).[72] Or as Hobbes sometimes puts it, in 'the will to give every one his owne' (L 43.4). 'Thus a person who has a constant will of giving to every man his own, even if his actions may sometimes have been unjust, is nevertheless himself just' (LL 15.9). Justice so-understood is only one of the moral virtues enjoined by natural law. In a broader, more demanding sense, people are just when they possess all the moral virtues. That is, when they have a constant disposition to observe *all* the laws of nature. As *Elements* states: 'the observation of the law of nature ... is that for which a man is called just or righteous (in that sense in which justice is taken not for the absence of all guilt, but for the endeavour, and constant will to do that which is just)' (EL 25.10). *De Cive* likewise reserves the title 'JUST' for 'anyone who makes every effort to conform all his actions to the *precepts of nature*' (DCv 3.30). It adds that '*the laws of nature* are a matter of *conscience*, i.e. *the just man* is the man who makes every effort to fulfil them' (DCv 4.21; also L 15.39). The divine inspector of our conscience requires obedience to all his laws, demanding 'the will to live rightly' (DCv 18.6n; also DCv 18.12; L 43.19–20). This broader sense of justice of persons, as consisting in a willingness to observe all laws of nature, helps explain why Hobbes sometimes calls violations of *any* law of nature 'unjust before God' (EL 21.3; also L 42.43; EW 5: 178).

The will of unjust people is geared towards their short-term benefit. They have no scruples about engaging in crime when they think it will profit them. Such an attitude to the law reflects unjust manners: 'the Injustice of Manners, is the disposition, or aptitude to do Injurie; and is Injustice before it proceed to Act; and without supposing any individuall person injured' (L 15.12).[73] Threats of state punishment may keep unjust people in check by momentarily convincing them that crime does not pay. Even if their actions abide by law, their will continues to express contempt for the legislator. Disdaining sovereign authority, only risk of punishment renders them obedient. Hobbes argues that unjust manners result from poor reasoning. Correctly thinking through the long-term consequences of actions reveals that a contented life requires peace, and peace requires observing the laws of nature. The willingness to transgress civil law results from flawed reasoning about what conduces to self-preservation and is as such a sin against natural law, even before crime is done.

---

[71] Boonin-Vail, *Science of Moral Virtue*, 109–111.

[72] Also DCv 3.5; L 4.8; L 15.10; L 26.12; EW 5: 115.

[73] Also L 30.13: 'not onely the unjust facts [actions], but the designes and intentions to do them, (though by accident hindred,) are Injustice; which consisteth in the pravity of the will, as well as the irregularity of the act'. DCv 14.18 confusingly makes the same point using Greek terms: 'lawlessness of actions is adíkēma, *unjust action*; lawlessness of disposition is adikía and kakía, *injustice and evil*'. The Greek terms are cited in Justinian's *Institutes* 4.4, albeit to different effect: 'fault [culpa], which the Greeks call adíkēma ... inequity and injustice [iniquitas et injustitia], which the Greeks call adikía'.

CONCLUSION

Hobbes did not vindicate sinning sovereigns by pronouncing their misdeeds mere foolishness, unapt for moral censure. Rather, violating natural law duties is neither unjust nor injurious vis-à-vis others because and insofar as rights of private judgement shield sinners from all warranted moral accusation. The same 'originall right to do what he please' renders sovereign trespasses against natural law 'not unjust' (for: with right) vis-à-vis humans (L 15.13). Like pre-statist individuals, the sovereign is free from all directed obligations owed to others, being 'Subject to none but God' (DPS 41). By natural right entitled to determine for himself what the law of nature means and requires, he is beholden 'to God, the author of that law, and to none but him' (L 30.1).[74] Even if he knowingly does wrong—his reason warped by passion—that is something between him and the deity alone.

Sovereigns have absolute rights of private judgement for somewhat different reasons than pre-statist individuals do. Unlike pre-statist individuals, rulers do not occupy a state of war vis-à-vis their citizens. This renders *Untraceable Intentions* inapplicable: the reason subjects cannot possibly accuse their lord of wrongdoing is not because the fog of war renders his intentions indiscernible to them. Another dissimilarity is that sovereigns have been given the right to sin by their subjects. Citizens have authorized their ruler unreservedly, granting him 'the right to doe what he pleased' for their common security. Consequently, the sovereign 'never wanted Right to any thing otherwise, than as he himself is the Subject of God, and bound thereby to observe the laws of Nature' (L 21.7; also DCv 6.13) (§6.6). General moral unaccountability underwrites sovereign impunity. Should they sin against natural law, their 'malice is left to God alone to punish' (LLA 2.34). What to call sins against natural law that neither breach pledged faith nor civil law? From *Leviathan* onwards, Hobbes's preferred term for non-criminal breaches of natural law, I submit, is inequity. 'But in what cases the Commands of Soveraigns are contrary to Equity, and the Law of Nature, is to be considered hereafter', in the next chapter (L 24.7).

---

[74] Also DCv 13.2; L 29.9; LL 21.10; DPS 15, 26, 32.

PART III
JUSTICE WITHIN THE STATE

4

DISTRIBUTIVE JUSTICE AND EQUITY

INTRODUCTION[*]

'[T]he nature of Justice', *Leviathan* states, 'consisteth in keeping of valid Covenants' (L 15.3). This definition of justice has struck commentators as seeming 'not only excessively narrow but positively untrue'.[1] It excludes both criminal and distributive justice and makes no reference to either equality, desert, or fairness. Some of these aspects of justice, we shall see, are accounted for by Hobbes—under the heading of equity: '[what] men mean by distributive justice . . . is properly termed EQUITY' (EL 17.2). Equity is a moral and legal notion traditionally associated with fairness and even-handedness, invoked to correct unreasonable adjudications arising from the application of general laws to particular cases.[2] Why did Hobbes subsume distributive justice under this category? And what conceptual revisions were required to justify this reclassification?

This chapter examines the rationale for and grounds and implications of Hobbes's redefinition of distributive justice as equity.[3] I argue that this unprecedented reformulation served to forestall the possibility of unjust distributive laws, thus safeguarding the sovereign from taints of distributive injustice. Governments, Hobbes admits, can allocate rights and goods iniquitously, by failing to treat citizens as equals. Yet such maldistributions are not unjust/injurious, properly speaking—they do not wrong citizens. They are merely iniquitous. To be entitled to this position, Hobbes had to do more than simply substitute one word ('inequity') for another ('injustice'). Various conceptual linkages had to be reconceived. Tracing his attempts at theoretical validation, this chapter documents

---

[*] The main argument of this chapter first appeared in Johan Olsthoorn, 'Hobbes's Account of Distributive Justice as Equity', *British Journal for the History of Philosophy* 21 (2013) no. 1: 13–33. §4.1 and §4.5 rework material from Johan Olsthoorn, 'Francisco Suárez and Hugo Grotius on Distributive Justice and Imperfect Rights', *History of Political Thought* 41 (2020) no. 1: 96–119.

[1] D.D. Raphael, *Concepts of Justice* (Oxford, 2001) 66. Also D.D. Raphael, 'Hobbes on Justice' in G.A.J. Rogers and Alan Ryan (eds), *Perspectives on Thomas Hobbes* (Oxford, 1988) 153; Daniel Eggers, 'Injury, Injustice, Iniquity: The Evolution of Hobbes's Theory of Justice', *Intellectual History Review* 24 (2014) no. 2: 169.

[2] On the history and meaning of equity in the British context, see Stuart E. Prall, 'The Development of Equity in Tudor England', *American Journal of Legal History* 8 (1964) no. 1: 1–19; Michael Lobban, *A History of the Philosophy of Law in the Common Law World, 1600–1900* (Dordrecht, 2007) 20–90.

[3] This redefinition is mentioned by G.S. Kavka, *Hobbesian Moral and Political Theory* (Princeton, 1986) 376; William Mathie, 'Justice and Equity' in Craig Walton and Paul Johnston (eds), *Hobbes's Science of Natural Justice* (Dordrecht, 1987) 259; Raphael, *Concepts*, 76; Perez Zagorin, *Hobbes and the Law of Nature* (Princeton, 2010) 93. What made this relabelling conceptually possible for Hobbes has been left unexplored.

Hobbes on Justice. Johan Olsthoorn, Oxford University Press. © Johan Olsthoorn 2024.
DOI: 10.1093/9780191904585.003.0004

90 DISTRIBUTIVE JUSTICE AND EQUITY

significant and hitherto overlooked changes in his accounts of distributive justice, highlighting several key departures from tradition (§4.2 and §4.3).

Leviathan completes Hobbes's whitewashing of sovereign maldistributions by introducing a novel conception of merit in distributive justice as due by grace alone. Merit is no longer a criterion independent of and prior to a distribution, stipulating how goods and rights should be allocated ('more to the more worthy, less to the less worthy'—DCv 3.6). In *Leviathan*, distributions do not track but create merit: you deserve what the sovereign gives you. Distributive laws therefore cannot fail to give what is due (which, Hobbes concedes, would be unjust). The same doctrine allowed him to claim that the institution of property rights *is* justice—in demarcating *mine* and *thine* the sovereign truly gives each their own (§4.5). *Leviathan*'s Merit-Grace Argument, I contend, is more successful in protecting the sovereign from allegations of maldistribution than the earlier Liberality Argument. For it applies also to distributions of goods that are not one's own. The final section examines the moral limits equity sets to the legal apportionment of rights and goods. These limits, I argue, are procedural and do not curb Hobbes's political absolutism: citizens cannot invoke equity to claim a fair share of distributed goods (§4.6).

4.1 COMMUTATIVE AND DISTRIBUTIVE JUSTICE

Hobbes introduces the notions of justice and equity when criticizing the received distinction between commutative and distributive justice ('the sense wherein it useth to be expounded, is not right'—L 15.14; also EL 16.5; DCv 3.6). This distinction can be traced back to *Nicomachean Ethics*.[4] There, Aristotle distinguished universal from particular justice and then subdivided the latter further. Universal justice (A) is equivalent to the whole of morality, 'not without qualification, but in relation to another person'.[5] Universal justice consists of all social virtues, including for instance beneficence and gratitude (hence the saying 'in justice is every virtue comprehended'). Particular justice (B) is a specific virtue aiming at fair equality. It comes in two main types.[6] Commutative justice (B1)—sometimes translated as corrective justice—regulates interactions, both voluntary (like selling, hiring, and lending at interest) and involuntary ones (like theft, murder, and 'enticing away slaves').[7] It demands that people get what they deserve in these 'commutations'

---

[4] Izhak Englard, *Corrective and Distributive Justice from Aristotle to Modern Times* (Oxford, 2009).

[5] Aristotle, *Nicomachean Ethics*, 5.1 (1129a20).

[6] Whether reciprocal justice, which demands that goods exchanged are of equal value and is mentioned by Aristotle later on, should be regarded as a third type of particular justice is contested. For an argument in favour, see Theodore Scaltsas, 'Reciprocal Justice in Aristotle's *Nicomachean Ethics*', *Archiv für Geschichte der Philosophie* 77 (1995) no. 3: 259–260.

[7] Aristotle, *Nicomachean Ethics*, 5.2 (1131a).

and requires rectification if they do not. Aristotle contended that commutative justice targets numerical equality: each individual involved in the exchange counts equally, regardless of their personal worth or merit. This makes commutative justice non-comparative.[8] By contrast, distributive justice (B2) is comparative. It calls for allocating common goods (including honours, the spoils of war, and political offices) in proportion to prospective recipients' merit.[9] How much a person ought to receive of a scarce resource divided amongst a group depends on their worth relative to others'. As Aristotle put it, 'all men agree that what is just in distribution must be according to merit [ἀξία]'.[10] Distributive justice requires so-called geometric equality: 'that whole is to whole as each part is to each part'.[11]

Thomas Aquinas (1225–1274) further developed Aristotle's typology. He proposed another difference between the two kinds of particular justice: each aims to establish and preserve different orderings. Commutative justice deals with mutual interactions between private citizens. Distributive justice, on the other hand, regulates the order of the community to the individual.[12] Another significant aspect of Aquinas's account was his identification of particular justice with the Roman law definition of justice: 'to render to each their own' (*suum cuique tribuere*).[13] Each person's own 'is what is due to him according to equality of proportion'—be it numerical (commutative justice) or geometric equality (distributive justice).[14] For Aquinas, commutative and distributive justice are different measures to determine what is due to a person. They do not respond to distinct kinds of 'due' (rights).

Francisco Suárez (1548–1617) and Hugo Grotius (1583–1645) both rejected the two standard Thomist ways of differentiating commutative from distributive justice: by the kinds of equality they implicate (numerical vs. geometric) and the social relations they regulate (private vs. communal).[15] As Suárez argued in the lecture series *De justitia et jure* (1584), commutative justice does sometimes require repayment according to geometric equality—such as when an indebted person lacks the means to repay all her creditors. Nor does commutative justice exclusively govern private interactions and distributive justice public–private affairs. States should keep their contractual obligations and pay hired soldiers as a matter of commutative justice. And while commutative justice usually deals with

---

[8] On this concept, see Joel Feinberg, 'Noncomparative Justice', *The Philosophical Review* 83 (1974) no. 3: 297–338.

[9] Aristotle, *Nicomachean Ethics*, 5.2–5; Aristotle, *Politics*, 5.1 (1301b30–1302a8). According to Keyt, distributive justice is concerned primarily with the distribution of political authority for Aristotle, and only secondarily with material goods. David Keyt, 'Aristotle's Theory of Distributive Justice' in David Keyt and F.D. Miller (eds), *A Companion to Aristotle's Politics* (Oxford, 1991) 238–278.

[10] Aristotle, *Nicomachean Ethics*, 5.3 (1131a25).

[11] Aristotle, *Nicomachean Ethics*, 5.3 (1131b).

[12] Aquinas, *Summa Theologica*, 2a.2ae.61.1.

[13] Aquinas, *Summa Theologica*, 2a.2ae.58.11. The Roman law definition of justice is found at *Institutes* 1.1; *Digest* 1.1.10.

[14] Aquinas, *Summa Theologica*, 2a.2ae.58.11.

[15] Grotius, *War and Peace*, 1.1.8, 2.20.2.

92 DISTRIBUTIVE JUSTICE AND EQUITY

interactions and distributive justice with distributions, this functional difference is not universal: a just sentence falls under commutative justice although it distributes punishments.[16] The essential difference between commutative and distributive justice, Suárez and Grotius held, lies instead in the kinds of rights they regulate. While commutative justice demands respect for the perfect rights belonging to each, distributive justice has regard for imperfect rights. Both thinkers thus incorporated the modern idea of subjective rights as moral powers into the received Aristotelian typology of justice.[17]

What Hobbes calls 'justice' is a modification of the received notion of commutative justice, while 'distributive justice' is relabelled equity. Rather than rehashing standard objections against the Thomist understanding of the distinction, Hobbes fundamentally revised the meaning of both notions. By subsuming distributive justice under equity, he turned commutative justice into the whole of justice. As Pufendorf observed: 'Hobbes . . . seems to reduce justice to but one kind, namely keeping faith and fulfilling one's agreements'.[18]

Hobbes ostensibly followed tradition in maintaining that commutative justice calls for honouring the duty to fulfil agreements made: 'To speak properly, Commutative Justice, is the Justice of a Contractor; that is, a Performance of Covenant' (L 15.14). '[B]arter, sale, purchase, borrowing, payment of loan, letting, hiring, and all other actions of mutually contracting parties' all fall under commutative justice (DCv 3.6; also EL 16.5; L 15.14).[19] At first sight a continuation of earlier conceptions, Hobbes in fact significantly narrowed the domain of commutative justice.[20] Commutative justice traditionally required that equality is observed in both voluntary interactions (contracts, etc.) and involuntary ones (theft, assault, etc.). According to Aristotle, assaults upend equality: 'when one party is struck, and the other strikes, or one kills, and the other is killed, the suffering and the action are divided unequally'. By penalizing the wrongdoer, 'the judges restores equality' by equalizing suffering across the parties.[21] Aquinas likewise held

[16] Joachim Giers, *Die Gerechtigkeitslehre des jungen Suárez* (Freiburg im Breisgau, 1958) 102–105 (cf. 176–180 for discussion). Suárez' denial that distributive justice essentially deals with proportionate equality is highlighted by Daniel Schwartz, 'Suárez on Distributive Justice' in idem (ed), *Interpreting Suárez: Critical Essays* (Cambridge, 2012) 166–168, 175.

[17] The two thinkers conceptualized perfect and imperfect rights differently, however. For Suárez, commutative justice regulates rights in things (*jus in rem*) and distributive justice rights to receive things (*jus ad rem*). For Grotius, both *jus in rem* and *jus ad rem* are perfect rights governed by commutative justice. Distributive justice for him regulates non-enforceable 'aptitudes' (a new concept of rights, to which he applies the old name of 'imperfect right'). Olsthoorn, 'Francisco Suárez and Hugo Grotius'.

[18] Pufendorf, *Nature and Nations*, 1.7.13; also G.W. Leibniz, *Political Writings*, ed. Patrick Riley (Cambridge, 1988) 60. Pufendorf proceeded to complain that Hobbes collapsed two Ciceronian precepts of justice ('do not harm others' and 'keep your promises') into one. Hobbes did so by making the possibility of injury conditional on the exchange of promises. Cicero, *On Duties*, 1.20–23.

[19] Aquinas, *Summa Theologica*, 2a.2ae.61.3, subsumes the same set of actions under commutative justice.

[20] *Contra* J.P. Sommerville, *Thomas Hobbes: Political Ideas in Historical Context* (London, 1992) 48: 'Hobbes' key innovation in the analysis of justice was to insist that it is always concerned with contracts' yet 'the extent and significance of this innovation should not be exaggerated'.

[21] Aristotle, *Nicomachean Ethics*, 5.4 (1132a).

that crimes against another's person and property should be redressed as a matter of commutative justice.[22] And Grotius wrote in an early work that commutative justice 'is concerned not only with the preservation of equality among individuals, but also . . . with the punishment of persons who are injuring the community'.[23] Hobbes's gloss on commutative justice makes no reference to *involuntary* interactions. It merely requires performance of valid covenants, not restoring equality by punishing criminals.

To be sure, commutative justice does indirectly forbid citizens to commit burglary, assault, and other 'involuntary interactions'. Commutative justice requires nothing else than keeping faith (L 15.1–2). Yet since all citizens are presumed to have promised simple obedience to a common lawgiver, keeping faith for them requires obeying the civil laws: 'we should not violate our Faith, that is, a commandement to obey our Civill Soveraigns, which wee constituted over us, by mutuall pact one with another' (L 43.5).[24] While different states criminalize different conduct, justice everywhere requires citizens 'not to violate the laws' (DH 13.9).[25] While thus agreeing that commutative justice orders citizens to abstain from crime, Hobbes denies that the principle demands rectifying inequalities *resulting* from crime. After all, the sovereign did not contractually obligate himself to either prosecute criminals or to restore to victims what was stolen from them.[26] Rulers hence cannot fall foul of commutative justice by failing to punish felony. Indeed, as we shall see, punitive justice for Hobbes falls under distributive justice or equity instead.

Besides reducing commutative justice to the natural law duty to perform covenants, Hobbes stripped the principle of its capacity to assess the moral quality of laws and agreements. He ridiculed the idea that commutative justice demands that things exchanged are of equal value: 'As if it were Injustice to sell dearer than we buy' (L 15.14). Justice forbids injuring others. Why think high prices wrong willing customers? (DCv 3.6). The fair value is merely the price buyers are willing to pay. 'The value of all things contracted for, is measured by the Appetite of the Contractors; and therefore the just value, is that which they be contended to give' (L 15.14).[27] Mutual consent, rather than equality or fairness, is the standard by which commutative justice determines whether each party in an exchange gets

---

[22] Aquinas, *Summa Theologica*, 2a.2ae.61.3.

[23] Hugo Grotius, *Commentary on the Law of Prize and Booty*, ed. M.J. van Ittersum (Indianapolis, 2006) 37, also 28–29.

[24] Also DCv 14.10, 21, 23; L 26.8; L 30.4; B 195.

[25] Also DCv 18.12; L 42.96; L 43.4–5; L 46.31; DPS 36; B 44; B 165.

[26] *Contra* Arthur Yates, 'A Hohfeldian Analysis of Hobbesian Rights', *Law and Philosophy* 32 (2013) no. 4: 430–431.

[27] On Hobbes's 'demand theory of value', see EL 16.5; DCv 3.6; L 10.16; L 38.25; L 41.2. Compare C.B. Macpherson, *The Political Theory of Possessive Individualism* (Oxford, 1962) 63: 'Since there is no measure of value except market price, every exchange of values between freely contracting persons is by definition an exchange of equal values'. Also Luc Foisneau, '*Leviathan*'s Theory of Justice' in Tom Sorell and Luc Foisneau (eds), *Leviathan after 350 Years* (Oxford, 2004) 111–112.

94   DISTRIBUTIVE JUSTICE AND EQUITY

what they deserve. The conditions of a lawful contract are dictated by demand, not by justice. Any (social) contract entered is just, by virtue of having been entered.[28]

Pufendorf articulated the obvious objection:

> Indeed so far is it from being rational to resolve all Justice into Performance of Covenants, that on the contrary, before we can know whether any Covenant is to be perform'd, we ought to be certain that it was entred upon, either by the Command, or with the Permission of the Laws of Nature; that is, that it was *justly* made.[29]

One might reply, in Hobbes's defence, that the laws of nature dictate entering the original covenant upon equal terms. True enough. Yet equal terms are not required because the agreement would otherwise be *unfair*. But rather because Hobbes thinks there is no *demand* for any other terms: 'men that think themselves equall, will not enter into Conditions of Peace, but upon Equall termes' (L 15.21; also EL 17.1–2; DCv 3.13–14). Needing no measure of fair exchange other than mutual consent, Hobbes turned commutative justice into the virtue to keep agreements made. This redefinition greatly supported his vindicatory project: as the sovereign on his part has entered no pact with his subjects, the laws he issues cannot possibly cross commutative justice. In what follows, I argue that Hobbes required a substantive additional argument to be entitled to declare 'unjust distributive laws' likewise impossible.

4.2 EQUITY

Hobbes, like Suárez and Grotius before him, uses the term 'equity' (Greek: *epieikeia*; Latin: *aequitas*) in at least two distinct senses.[30] Equity in the broad sense (also called 'common equity'—L 26.17) signifies the 'unwritten' principles of fairness according to which judges should adjudicate conflicts and interpret statute law. The principles of equity are the same as the common laws of England and the laws of

---

[28] Covenants can nonetheless misfire. Persons may lack the right they mean to transfer (e.g. because they had already transferred the same right to someone else before—DCv 2.17). And even if they possess the right in question, it may be inalienable (think of rights not to resist capital punishment). Such covenants are not unjust—they simply cannot be validly made.

[29] Pufendorf, *Nature and Nations*, 1.7.13.

[30] Grotius, *War and Peace*, 3.20.47; Suárez, *De Legibus*, 1.2.9–10: '*aequitas* is customarily interpreted as having a twofold sense. In one sense, it stands for natural equity, which is identical with natural justice... in another sense, however, [equity is] a prudent moderation of the written law, transcending the exact literal interpretation of the latter'. The former maps onto Hobbes's equity in the broad sense, the second onto equity in the narrow sense. Dennis Klimchuk, 'Hobbes on Equity' in David Dyzenhaus and Thomas Poole (eds), *Hobbes and the Law* (Cambridge, 2012) 165–185, argues that Hobbes uses 'equity' in no less than four senses.

nature, dictated by God through reason.[31] Where the law is silent or needs further interpretation (and every law requires interpretation—L 26.21), judges should follow the spirit (the legislator's intention) over the letter of the law. 'For it is not the words of the law but the meaning of the legislator which is the rule of actions' (DCv 17.25; also L 26.11; L 26.20; DPS 81–82). Importantly, 'the Intention of the Legislator is alwayes supposed to be Equity' (to suggest otherwise 'were a great contumely') (L 26.26).[32] Subordinate judges are thus duty-bound to interpret civil law equitably in their rulings, on pain of misconstruing the sovereign's will. In this way, equity effectively comes to govern the administration of legal justice.[33] Hobbes followed received legal theory in maintaining that equity regulates the application of general laws to particular cases. Yet he departed from the commonplace view, going back to Aristotle, that the equitable is a rectification of the legally just.[34] Equity amends not 'the Law, but the Judgments only when they are Erroneous' (DPS 86–87).[35] In the later works, 'iniquity' is used to signify any non-criminal breach of natural law: 'For what is done contrary to the law of nature is called inequitable [iniquum]; what is done contrary to the civil law, unjust [injustum]' (LL 18.6; also DPS 31).[36] Presumably, Hobbes had in mind here equity in the broad sense.

Hobbes also employed 'equity' in a narrow sense. *Leviathan's* eleventh law of nature prescribes equity as a specific moral duty of arbitrators. Here, equity commands an even-handed adjudication of controversies, prohibiting corruption and partiality in judgement on the grounds that this deters 'men from the use of Judges and Arbitrators', thus inviting conflict (L 15.23). Confusingly, equity thus signifies both the evaluative standard according to which judges should interpret written law *and* the specific moral duty of arbitrators to judge impartially.[37] Arbitrators

---

[31] This point is made most emphatically in the *Dialogue*: DPS 26, 31–32, 74–76, 81; also L 36.6; B 156; B 264. For discussion, see Alan Cromartie, 'General Introduction' in Alan Cromartie and Quentin Skinner (eds), *Thomas Hobbes: A Dialogue between a Philosopher and a Student* (Oxford, 2005) xxvi–xlv.

[32] Also DCv 14.14; L 26.7, 14–15, 23; DPS 73, 81–84.

[33] David Dyzenhaus has examined in detail the role of subordinate judges in Hobbes's legal theory, most recently in *The Long Arc of Legality: Hobbes, Kelsen, Hart* (Cambridge, 2022) 111–115, 136–143.

[34] Aristotle, *Nicomachean Ethics*, 5.10. On Aristotle on equity, see Jacques Brunschwig, 'The Aristotelian Theory of Equity' in Michael Frede and Gisela Striker (eds), *Rationality in Greek Thought* (Oxford, 1996) 115–156; Allan Beever, 'Aristotle on Equity, Law, and Justice', *Legal Theory* 10 (2004) no. 1: 33–50; Annie Hewitt, 'Universal Justice and *Epieikeia* in Aristotle', *Polis* 25 (2008) no. 1: 115–130.

[35] Equity cannot correct law itself, Hobbes reasons speciously, since the law of reason cannot clash with civil law: 'It cannot be that a Written Law should be against Reason: For nothing is more reasonable than that every Man should obey the Law, which he hath himself assented to' (DPS 81).

[36] Eggers, 'Injury, Injustice, Iniquity', 177–180.

[37] The same dual use of equity is present in Grotius. Johan Olsthoorn, 'Two Ways of Theorizing Collective Ownership of the Earth' in James Penner and Michael Otsuka (eds), *Property Theory: Legal and Political Perspectives* (Cambridge, 2018) 203. Corbin overlooks the connection between equity as even-handedness vs. equity as the substantive moral norms guiding adjudication by legal arbitrators. This may explain why he claims, wrongly, that equity in the last sense is unique to the *Dialogue*. Thomas A. Corbin, 'On Equity and Inequity in Thomas Hobbes's *Dialogue*', *Southern Journal of Philosophy* 60 (2022) no. 4: 518–539.

96 DISTRIBUTIVE JUSTICE AND EQUITY

observe the natural law duty of equity when they sincerely endeavour to administer justice even-handedly (EL 17.7). That is, when they sincerely attempt to adjudicate in line with equity in the broad sense (i.e. with natural law/common law/reason). Judges may erroneously issue rulings that contradict natural law, thereby contravening equity in the broad sense—without violating equity in its narrow sense (the specific natural law precept commanding impartial adjudication). Think of an unbiased judge who through flawed reasoning misinterprets what sociability requires, producing an unreasonably harsh verdict. Across his works, Hobbes subsumed distributive justice under equity in the narrow sense.

It has not been sufficiently appreciated hitherto how radically Hobbes's accounts of equity (in the narrow sense) and distributive justice change from *Elements* to *Leviathan*. Their (i) address; (ii) meaning; (iii) opposing vice; and (iv) distributive currency are all restructured; as is (v) the kind of equality implicated by equity.[38] The early works portray equity primarily as a duty of citizens, whereas *Leviathan* depicts it as a duty of public officials (including the sovereign). In *Elements* and *De Cive*, equity commands citizens to acknowledge natural equality by not claiming more for oneself than one allows to others (on pain of *pleonexia*). In *Leviathan*, by contrast, equity orders judges to adjudicate impartially (on pain of *prosopolepsia*). And by 1651, distributive justice has come to regulate the division of common goods rather than one's own. These changes are theoretically interlinked. The rationale behind these shifts becomes apparent by studying the limits of Hobbes's earlier accounts.

Distributive justice pops us at two distinct points in *Elements* and *De Cive*. It first appears in a critique of the received view that distributive justice requires geometric equality:

> distributive justice, which consisteth in the distribution of our own benefits; seeing a thing is therefore said to be our own, because we may dispose of it at our own pleasure: it can be no injury to any man, though our liberality be further extended towards another, than towards him; unless we be thereto obliged by covenant: and then the injustice consisteth in the violation of that covenant, and not in the inequality of distribution. (EL 16.5; also DCv 3.6; DCv 3.32)

We are free to dispose of our own goods as we want (EL 22.5; DCv 2.16). Justice does not require us to give away what is ours in line with equality or recipients' merit. Less deserving persons can be preferred without injustice. 'Christ himself, witnesses to this in the Gospel' (DCv 3.6). By modelling distributive justice on liberality (a 'supply theory of distributive justice'), Hobbes turned it into

---

[38] Some of these changes are mapped in Klimchuk, 'Hobbes on Equity', 166–169, and Lee Ward, 'Equity and Political Economy in Thomas Hobbes', *American Journal of Political Science* 64 (2020) no. 4: 826–829 (emphasizing the increasingly public nature of distributive justice).

a non-comparative principle.[39] Yet this Liberality Argument, advanced in the early works, has clear limitations. It applies only to resources owned by the distributor.[40] This assumption jars with legal adjudication: surely sentences handed out by a judge are not hers to freely distribute at will.[41] Moreover, giving *less* to someone than they deserve remains unjust—leaving open the possibility of sovereign injustice. *Elements* states so explicitly: 'To give a man more than his due, is no injustice, <u>though it be to give him less</u>' (EL 17.14). Similarly, *De Cive* prohibits unequal apportionments of rights on the ground that this insults those who are not favoured (DCv 3.15; also EL 16.12).

Building on the Liberality Argument, *Elements* contends that distributive justice is not a distributive norm but a virtue of human equality. The distinction between commutative and distributive justice, Hobbes complained, 'is not well made, inasmuch as injury, which is the injustice of action, consisteth not in the inequality of the things changed, or distributed, but in the inequality that men (contrary to nature and reason) assume unto themselves above their fellows' (EL 16.5). Distributive justice (better: equity) rather prohibits 'covetousness' or 'pleonexia': taking or demanding more than one's fair share (EL 17.2; EL 18.6). This is a novel move. Pleonexia was Aristotle's term for the vice opposing particular justice of *either* kind (i.e. commutative and distributive). The unjust person is characterized by a 'greedy' and 'grasping' trait, covetous of more than their due share of public honours or material goods.[42] *Elements* depicts such encroaching as the distinctive vice opposing 'distributive justice . . . properly termed EQUITY': the pleonectic person fails to 'alloweth to every man alike' (EL 17.2). *Elements* thus effectively turns distributive justice from a norm regulating the fair allocation of resources into a norm requiring people to be content with equal shares (EL 18.6).

De Cive again links distributive justice (but not equity) to the vice of pleonexia: 'To allow *equal* rights to *equals* is the same as the principle of proportionality. Observance of this law is called *Modesty*, its violation *pleonexia*' (DCv

---

[39] By contrast, King James VI and I had maintained that 'trew Liberalitie' must align with 'that proportionall discretion, that every man may be served according to his measure, wherein respect must be had to his ranke, deserts, and necessitie'. King James VI and I, *Political Writings*, ed. J.P. Sommerville (Cambridge, 1995) 48.

[40] Aquinas, *Summa Theologica*, 2a.2ae.63.1, stressed that distributive justice exclusively governs the allocation of common goods, while liberality concerns the division of private goods. Nicole Reinhardt, *Voices of Conscience: Royal Confessors and Political Counsel in Seventeenth-Century Spain and France* (Oxford, 2016) 140, 144–146.

[41] If 'the judge is merely a distributor of property over which he personally has no right', Suárez maintained, then he has no right to 'award the property by his own decision to either one of the parties to the litigation, as he might choose'. Francisco Suárez, 'On Charity' in *Suárez: Selections from Three Works*, ed. Thomas Pink (Indianapolis, 2015) 13.6.4. Also Samuel Rachel, *Dissertations on the Law of Nature and of Nations*, ed. Ludwig von Bar (Washington, 1916) 118.

[42] Aristotle, *Nicomachean Ethics*, 5.1 (1129b). On the nature of pleonexia, see David Keyt, 'Injustice and Pleonexia in Aristotle', *Southern Journal of Philosophy* 27 (1988) suppl. 251–257; David Sachs, 'Notes on Unfairly Gaining More: Pleonexia' in Rosalind Hursthouse, Gavin Lawrence, and Warren Quinn (eds), *Virtues and Reasons* (Oxford, 1995) 176–183.

98   DISTRIBUTIVE JUSTICE AND EQUITY

3.14; also DCv 3.6; DCv 4.12). The text proceeds to introduce a new law of nature prescribing equity or fairness 'in awarding rights to others' (DCv 3.15; also DCv 4.13; DCv 14.14; cf. EL 17.7; EL 18.7). The vice opposing equity, so understood, is discrimination (*prosopolepsia*). *De Cive* thus omits the earlier equation of distributive justice with equity. It does so because it associates equity with impartial adjudication and allocation instead: 'if we ever have to distribute *Right* to others, this law forbids us from giving more or less to one person than to another as a favour' (DCv 3.15). *De Cive* continues to portray distributive justice as a virtue of citizens rather than of adjudicators alone—perhaps to prevent the question of distributive unfairness in civil legislation from arising.

Leviathan finally severs the link between distributive justice and the vice of pleonexia. The natural duty of citizens to allow equal rights to all others—to have no 'desire of more than their share'—it calls 'modesty'; its opposing vice 'pleonexia' (L 15.22). This revision allowed Hobbes to reinstate *Elements'* equation of distributive justice with equity. He did so by turning distributive justice as equity into a natural law duty of arbitrators, prohibiting corruption and partiality. One of those laws of nature that 'obliges not all, but only some condition of men' (LL 26.13), equity becomes in essence the justice of judges and legislators:

> Distributive Justice, the Justice of an Arbitrator; that is to say, the act of defining what is Just. Wherein, (being trusted by them that make him Arbitrator,) if he performe his Trust, he is said to distribute to every man his own: and this is indeed Just Distribution, and may be called (though improperly) Distributive Justice; but more properly, Equity; which also is a Law of Nature. (L 15.15)[43]

Equity demands that arbitrators (those who are 'trusted to judge between man and man') 'deale Equally' between various contenders in distributions of any sort— rights, goods, honour, even punishment (L 15.23; also L 15.31). The vices opposing this duty are now corruption and partiality ('acception of persons') (L 15.24). 'Acception of persons' had been the distinct sin opposing distributive justice at least since Aquinas.[44] *Leviathan* reverts, in this respect, to tradition. Equity regulates the handing out of sentences and the distribution of rights and goods alike. 'The observance of this law, from the equall distribution to each man, of that which in reason belongeth to him, is called EQUITY, and (as I have sayd before) distributive Justice' (L 15.24). Equity prohibits the punishing of innocents as contrary to

---

[43] By turning equity into a 'sovereign virtue', Hobbes comes closer to the Thomist view that commutative justice concerns the mutual dealings of citizens amongst each other, while distributive justice governs 'the order of the whole towards the part' (i.e. of the community to each individual). Aquinas, *Summa Theologica*, 2a.2ae.61.1. It also chimes better with *Leviathan*'s account of why private property is a product of civil legislation (§4.5; §5.5; §7.3).

[44] Aquinas, *Summa Theologica*, 2a.2ae.63.1. On scholastic discussions of 'acception of persons', see Reinhardt, *Voices of Conscience*, 136–146. On corruption more generally, see Adrian Blau, 'Hobbes on Corruption', *History of Political Thought* 30 (2009) no. 4: 596–616.

'an equall distribution of justice' (L 28.22; also L 26.24). Criminal justice thus falls under distributive justice—or better: under equity.

4.3 EQUALITY

What does distributive justice have to do with fair and impartial jurisprudence, we may wonder?[45] The answer is that both require acknowledgement of human equality. Distributive justice is linked to equality across Hobbes's works. Yet the kind of equality it calls for changes as distributive justice is transformed from a virtue of private individuals into a virtue of public officials. *Elements/De Cive* had linked distributive justice with human natural equality *of worth*. The natural law duty to acknowledge each person's 'equality of worth' requires 'attribution of the equality of benefit and respect' (EL 17.2; also EL 18.6). While neither numerical nor geometrical equality is relevant to justice, *De Cive* suggested that 'perhaps . . . justice is some kind of equality' after all. '[S]ince we are all equal by nature, one may not take for himself more *right* than he allows to another, unless he got this *right* by agreement' (DCv 3.6; also DCv 3.14; DCv 4.12). As a duty of individuals, distributive justice demands acknowledgement of each person's equal worth by not retaining or seizing more rights than one allows to others.

Across his works, Hobbes dismisses Aristotle's doctrine of natural aristocracy as contrary to reason and experience: 'there are very few so foolish, that had not rather governe themselves, than be governed by others' (L 15.21). Humans 'naturally love Liberty, and Dominion over others' (L 17.1; also L 36.19). Therefore, they won't renounce their right to all things and submit to a sovereign save upon equal terms. The moral imperative to acknowledge others as our natural equals for the sake of peace holds regardless of whether humans are in fact naturally equal in worth:

> If nature therefore have made men equall; that equalitie is to be acknowledged: or if Nature have made men unequall; yet because men that think themselves equall, will not enter into conditions of Peace but upon Equall termes, such equalitie must be admitted. (L 15.21; also EL 17.1; DCv 3.13)[46]

While *Elements* and *De Cive* link the natural law duty to enter the commonwealth upon equal terms to distributive justice ('the principle of proportionality'), *Leviathan* deems it a matter of modesty alone, thus severing the earlier link

---

[45] With Raphael, *Concepts*, 77–78.

[46] Kari Saastamoinen, 'Hobbes and Pufendorf on Natural Equality and Civil Sovereignty' in Ian Hunter and David Saunders (eds), *Natural Law and Civil Sovereignty* (New York, 2002) 193–195, 200; Kinch Hoekstra, 'Hobbesian Equality' in S.A. Lloyd (ed), *Hobbes Today* (Cambridge, 2013) 76–112.

100   DISTRIBUTIVE JUSTICE AND EQUITY

between distributive justice and the natural duty to acknowledge human equality of worth.

What kind of equality then informs *Leviathan*'s new conception of distributive justice as the justice of arbitrators? In what manner should arbitrators acknowledge human equality? In *Elements* and *De Cive*, distributive justice forbids self-favouring (on pain of pleonexia): one must regard oneself as equal in worth to all others when dividing benefits amongst oneself and others. In *Leviathan*, distributive justice instead requires arbitrators to regard as equals those between whom they adjudicate: it forbids favouring either party (on pain of prosopolepsia). Equity demands that judges 'deale Equally' between contenders (L 15.23). It calls for equality before the law. Like offences should be punished equally, irrespective of the offender's social status:

> the rich, and mighty ... may have no greater hope of impunity, when they doe violence, dishonour, or any Injury to the meaner sort, than when one of these, does the like to one of them: For in this consisteth Equity. (L 30.15; also L 27.13–15)

Equity prohibits corruption. Indeed, the Latin *Leviathan* translates 'corruption and partiality' as 'iniquitate' (LL 26.23; cf. L 26.24). 'The enriching of a favourite or flatterer' is a 'great and inevitable inconvenience' of all regime types (L 19.8).[47] Judges violate equity not only by misusing their public office for private gain but also by being partial (usually 'towards the great') (L 30.16). Equitable and impartial adjudication requires a judge to be patient, insensitive to bribes, and *'able in judgment to devest himselfe of all feare, anger, hatred, love,* and *compassion'* (L 26.28).

Furthermore, equity regulates the fair division of burdens for providing public goods, including foremost internal and external peace. 'To Equall Justice, appertaineth also the Equall imposition of Taxes' (L 30.17). The relevant equality is determined by the principle of proportionality, associated with distributive justice. Taxes, Hobbes contends, should be imposed relative to the benefits each person derives from government rather than relative to their ability to pay. 'For the burdens of the commonwealth being the price that we pay for the benefit thereof, they ought to be measured thereby' (EL 28.5). That benefit is for each alike: 'the enjoyment of life, which is equally dear to poor, and rich' (L 30.17). On these grounds, Hobbes argues that the fairest tax regime is a regressive one: equity calls for taxing consumption rather than wealth (the two main forms of taxation at the time).[48]

---

[47] Also EL 24.5; DCv 10.6. The *Dialogue* downplays the disruptive effects of a corrupt monarch—money spent on favourites 'falls down again upon the Common People' (DPS 25).

[48] EL 28.5; DCv 13.10–11; L 30.17. For discussion, see Mathie, 'Justice and Equity', 260–261. Neil McArthur argues, based on a misreading of DCv 13.11, that Hobbes 'favors some principle of progressive taxation' in '"Thrown amongst Many": Hobbes on Taxation and Fiscal Policy' in S.A. Lloyd (ed), *Hobbes Today* (Cambridge, 2013) 188.

Suárez, by contrast, had held that tax burdens must be commensurate with citizens' abilities to pay: 'the imposition of equal burdens upon all persons, without regard to the strength or capacity of each, is also contrary to reason and to justice'.[49]

Subsequent laws of nature spell out implications of equity for fair arbitration—including in division of resources. What cannot be divided must be enjoyed in common. If this is impossible, then equity requires that lot determines who is to possess the thing (first). 'For equall distribution, is of the Law of Nature; and other means of equall distribution cannot be imagined' (L 15.26).[50] Such egalitarian-sounding phrases should not be mistaken for a commitment to material equality. For Hobbes, equity counteracts favouritism and partiality rather than social inequalities. It calls for procedural, not outcome equality (§4.6). Addressing social needs is a matter of charity (L 30.18). Moreover, distributive justice governs the distribution of common goods, not the redistribution of private ones. Summing up, equity enjoins fair distributions and impartial jurisprudence; and impartiality and fairness require treating humans as equals.

The relation between judicial impartiality (equity) and a fair allocation of common goods (distributive justice) in *Leviathan* should now be clear. On Hobbes's mature view, distributive justice is a subclass of equity in the narrow sense. The natural law precept of equity demands that arbitrators deal equally between contenders, impartially and without regard of either person or rank. Distributive justice, then, commands treating humans as equals when distributing rights, benefits, respect, etc. The connection between 'equity' and 'equality' provides distributive justice with its content. For Hobbes, distributive justice is a non-comparative principle: arbitrators are not required to compare the worthiness of prospective recipients and allot goods accordingly. Rather, judges must treat all subjects as equal before the law (regardless of whether they are truly naturally equal in worth) since prickly subjects are wont to stir sedition otherwise.[51] Distributive justice as equity thus requires impartial divisions rather than divisions proportionate to merit. What's more, *Leviathan* reinterprets merit such that it can no longer function as the regulating principle of distributive justice.

4.4 VINDICATING SOVEREIGN MALDISTRIBUTIONS

To establish that rulers cannot act unjustly, Hobbes advanced the so-called No Pact Argument. The sovereign cannot violate commutative justice by failing to

---

[49] Suárez, *De Legibus*, 1.9.16, also 5.16.1. For an overview of ideas on taxation in Suárez and his contemporaries, see Harro Höpfl, *Jesuit Political Thought: The Society of Jesus and the State, c.1540–1640* (Cambridge, 2004) 306–313.

[50] EL 17.3–5; EL 18.7; DCv 3.16–18; DCv 4.14–15; L 15.25–28.

[51] Judges need not regard *themselves* as naturally equal in worth to those subject to their decision—as distributive justice had required of private individuals in *Elements/De Cive*.

102 DISTRIBUTIVE JUSTICE AND EQUITY

keep faith since he on his part did not enter any covenants. Previous chapters reconstructed the conceptual presuppositions of this argument. Here I scrutinize its limits. The No Pact Argument cannot by itself fully vindicate supreme rulers if only because it does not obviate their violations of *distributive* justice (e.g. by accepting bribes in legal adjudication or by routinely granting government contracts to family members). Hobbes did not render sovereign maldistributions, like sovereign breaches of faith, impossible. While non-covenanting rulers cannot renege on pledged faith, they can and do distribute rights and goods iniquitously. Hobbes's vindicatory project would therefore have faltered had he conceded that sovereigns commit injustice in failing to allocate to citizens what is their due.

To tackle this challenge, Hobbes argued that violations of distributive justice are mere sins against natural law. This allowed him to draw on a remarkable feature of his moral theory: those not subject to civil law do not wrong other humans by violating natural law duties (§3.4). The sovereign's iniquitous conduct is morally wrong yet it injures no one but God (L 21.7; LL 21.10). A sovereign, despoiling subjects to favour friends, 'may do so rightly, i.e. without inflicting a wrong on himself', though not 'without violating natural laws and wronging God' (DCv 6.13n; also DCv 7.14). Why don't iniquitous distributions constitute injustices or injuries proper? What justifies Hobbes's equation of distributive justice with equity?

Unjust distributive laws are impossible only when the sovereign's distribution of rights and goods cannot possibly wrong his citizens. An unfair division of goods constitutes no breach of contract: the citizens authorized the sovereign 'to distribute to every man his own' without stipulating the terms of this division. Indeed, Hobbes is emphatic that people do not 'covenant so much, as that his sentence shall be just; for that were to make the parties judges of the sentence'—reigniting the potential for violent disagreement (EL 17.7). More is needed, however, to establish that distributive laws cannot injure/wrong subjects. In the early works, Hobbes established the justness of distributions by defending an argument analogous to the 'demand account of commutative justice'—that is, by denying the existence of any standard of fairness regulating the allocation of goods. This 'supply theory of distributive justice' likens distributive justice to liberality. It assumes that distributive justice 'consists in the distribution of our own benefits' (EL 16.5). Since we may dispose of what is ours in whatever way pleases us, distributive justice does not in fact regulate how we ought to allocate goods (EL 16.5; EL 22.5; DCv 3.6).

The Liberality Argument cannot plausibly be extended to justify all sovereign conduct (in accordance with *Leviathan*'s reconceptualization of distributive justice as the justice of arbitrators). For not all rights and goods doled out by the sovereign can sensibly be considered his own. To be sure, Hobbes had the theoretical resources to attribute ultimate ownership of all material resources within the commonwealth to the sovereign (§5.3). Still, it would be a stretch to hold that distributive justice poses no restrictions on the just imposition of tax burdens or on legal sentencing on the grounds that the sovereign is free to hand out his own property. In *De Cive*, Hobbes admits that complaints about unfair taxation laws are sometimes 'justified, namely when the burdens of the commonwealth are imposed on the citizens unequally' (DCv 13.10). 'It is in the interest of the public peace to remove a justified complaint [justam querimoniam], and consequently it is a duty of sovereigns to ensure that public burdens are equally borne' (DCv 13.10). *Elements* likewise avers that grievances over taxation are 'not real; <u>unless</u> more be exacted than is necessary' (EL 24.2).

In *Leviathan*, Hobbes developed a different argument to forestall rightful complaints of maldistribution—one that also applies to the distribution of things that are not one's own. That argument grants that a principle of fairness regulates the division of goods but denies that that standard is responsive to pre-existing rights or merit. *Leviathan* thereby establishes, better than earlier texts, that distributive justice is a principle of equity rather than of justice. The new argument supplements Hobbes's authorization doctrine. The sovereign cannot act without right vis-à-vis his citizens since each citizen has individually authorized 'all the Soveraign doth'; and 'he that doth any thing by authority from another, doth therein no injury to him by whose authority he acteth' (L 18.6). The Authorization Argument does not however suffice to establish that distributive justice is not a standard of justice. At most, it shows that such violations are towards citizens not unjust/injurious (in the sense of 'without right').

Leviathan's new argument was premised on a reinterpretation of the traditional Roman law definition of justice associated with Ulpian (c.170–223): 'justice is the constant and perpetual will to give everyone his due/own' [*suum cuique tribuere*].[52] Scholastics took this formula to signify both commutative and distributive justice.[53] Hobbes identified the formula exclusively with distributive justice. This equation creates a tension. The *suum cuique* formula conceptually implicates rights, merit, and desert: failing to give another their due wrongs the right-holder. (As we will see, Hobbes did not follow Grotius in defending a less robust kind of 'due' specific to distributive justice.) Equity has no such conceptual implications. How then can both capture distributive justice? To align Ulpian's definition with his own conception of distributive justice as equity, Hobbes had to develop a novel account of the ground of merit in distributive justice, to which I turn now.

---

[52] *Institutes*, 1.1; *Digest*, 1.1.10. Earlier versions of the formula are found in Plato, *The Republic*, 331e; Cicero, *The Republic*, 3.18–19. The *Institutes* are discussed in L 26.29–36. On Hobbes's relation to the Roman law tradition, see Daniel Lee, 'Hobbes and the Civil Law' in David Dyzenhaus and Thomas Poole (eds), *Hobbes and the Law* (Cambridge, 2012) 210–235.

[53] E.g. Aquinas, *Summa Theologica*, 2a.2ae.58.1; Suárez, *De Legibus*, 1.2.4.

4.5 MERIT

Recall that on the Aristotelian theory, distributive justice calls for allocating common goods according to merit. Agamemnon regarded it unjust to be assigned a share of war loot smaller than Achilles's—considering himself his equal in worth. For Aristotle, one's merit depends on one's excellence, wealth, and status (e.g. freedom vs. enslavement). Oligarchies and aristocracies organize political offices based on different criteria of merit (wealth vs. excellence, respectively). Across his works, Hobbes flatly denies that distributive justice requires doling out goods in proportion to recipients' worth. The early works establish this contention by likening distributive justice to liberality: we are free to dispose of our own goods as we like. Drawing on a scholastic theological distinction, *Leviathan* established the same by reconceptualizing merit in distributive justice itself. Distributions of any kind are unencumbered by principles of proportionality as the merit pertaining to distributive justice is due by grace alone.

Chapter 10 of *Leviathan* contains Hobbes's only in-depth analysis of 'merit'.[54] There, he distinguished between worth, worthiness, and merit:

> WORTHINESSE, is a thing different from the worth, or value of a man; and also from his merit, or desert; and consisteth in a particular power, or ability for that, whereof he is said to be worthy: which particular ability, is usually named FITNESSE, or *Aptitude*. (L 10.53)

The concept of 'aptitude' as meaning 'worthiness' came from Grotius. The Dutch jurist juxtaposed two kinds of rights. Perfect rights are those rights whose infringement provides the right-holder with the legal standing to sue within the state and with a just cause for war outside it.[55] Grotius recognized three types of perfect rights: powers over ourselves and over others [*potestas*]; property rights in external resources [*dominium*]; and the right to demand what is due [*creditum*].[56] Imperfect right, by contrast, denotes 'Aptitude or Merit, which doth not contain in it a Right strictly so called, but gives Occasion to it'.[57] Imperfect rights express one's *worthiness* to receive a perfect right; they denote that it is fitting or proper for the right-holder to be accorded something. For Hugo to have an imperfect right

---

[54] Hobbes's analyses of merit have received little sustained attention. Foisneau, 'Leviathan's Theory', 110–113, draws attention to *Leviathan*'s redefinitions of merit, interpreting them as attempts to develop a theory of justice suitable to commercial society and free markets. Foisneau overlooks how congenial these redefinitions are to Hobbes's political projects.

[55] Grotius, *War and Peace*, 2.1.2.1: 'as many *Sources* as there are of *judicial* Actions, so many *Causes* may there be of *War*'. On the place of perfect and imperfect rights in Grotius's just war theory, see Johan Olsthoorn, 'Grotius and the Early Modern Tradition' in Larry May (ed), *The Cambridge Handbook of the Just War* (Cambridge, 2018) 47–50.

[56] Grotius, *War and Peace*, 1.1.5.

[57] Grotius, *War and Peace*, 2.20.2.2.

to amnesty, for instance, means that the world would be morally better for him to receive reprieve—even though Hugo cannot *claim* amnesty as his due. Imperfect rights do not entail the distinct moral authority to demand whatever one is worthy to receive. More generally, infringements of aptitudes do not warrant punishment;[58] are unenforceable in court or on the battlefield;[59] and resulting damage or loss need not be compensated.[60]

Significantly, Grotius linked imperfect rights ('aptitudes') to distributive justice, and perfect rights to commutative justice.

> Justice properly and strictly taken, which respects . . . *perfect Right*, and is called by Aristotle . . . *Justice of Contracts* . . . *Attributive Justice*, stiled by Aristotle *Distributive*, respects Aptitude or *imperfect Right*, the attendant of those Virtues that are beneficial to others, as Liberality, Mercy, and Prudent Administration of Government.[61]

Grotius accepted the Aristotelian view that distributive justice calls for dividing resources according to merit/worthiness (relabelled: 'imperfect right'). But he insisted that those who, unjustly, fail to receive their due by worthiness lack the standing to sue or initiate war in response. For this reason, rulers cannot be held legally accountable for maldistributions, though they may be liable to moral criticism (§1.2).[62]

Notwithstanding the congeniality of Grotius's account with political absolutism, Hobbes sidelined it in pursuit of a greater prize: fully absolving sovereigns from all possible injustices—including unjust infringements of citizens' unenforceable rights. To this end, he rejected Grotius's claim that distributive justice requires allocating rights or goods in line with aptitudes/worthiness. Grotius, he insinuated, had confused merit with worth and worthiness.

> a man may be Worthy of Riches, Office, and Employment, that neverthelesse, can plead no right to have it before another; and therefore cannot be said to merit or deserve it. For Merit, praesupposeth a right, and that the thing deserved is <u>due by promise</u>. (L 10.54)

To merit *x* is to have an exclusive right to receive *x*—'to have it as DUE'. Merit neither is, nor results from, 'a particular ability . . . named FITNESSE, or *Aptitude*' (L 10.53).

---

[58] Grotius, *War and Peace*, 2.20.20.1.
[59] Grotius, *War and Peace*, 2.22.16, 2.25.3.4.
[60] Grotius, *War and Peace*, 2.17.3.1, 2.17.9, 2.17.13.
[61] Grotius, *War and Peace*, 1.1.8.1; also 2.17.3.1.
[62] Grotius acknowledged that rulers can have contractual duties, due by commutative justice, to appoint only persons worthy of office: 'For he, to whom the Power of making Magistrates is committed, is bound to the Commonwealth to make choice of such a Person as is fit for the Office; and the Commonwealth has properly a Right to require this of him'. Grotius, *War and Peace*, 2.17.3.2.

As the Latin *Leviathan* puts it: 'merit is never called "worthiness" [*Dignitas*]; for they differ insofar as <u>merit presupposes a right resulting from a promise</u>, whereas worthiness does not presuppose a right' (LL 10.53). Nor is 'the *Value*, or WORTH of a man' identical to, or a ground of, merit (L 10.16).

In Hobbes's view, merit can derive only from contract or free gift (L 14.17). Consequently, no one merits special treatment on grounds of personal abilities, wealth, or excellence. All social distinctions of honour and rank are of civil origin and established by the sovereign's grace. 'The Inequality of Subjects, proceedeth from the Acts of Soveraign Power' (L 30.16; also L 18.15; L 27.13). By disentangling merit from worth and worthiness, Hobbes rendered mute the claims of ambitious (pleonectic) men who consider themselves worthy of offices and public esteem (EL 27.3). Reminding the nobility that their high rank 'has arisen not from some real excellence in them, but from the will of the sovereign ruler' should also stop them from treating their fellow subjects with 'uncivil disdain' (LL 30.16). The dismissal of the civic relevance of natural inequalities of worth (should they exist) ensured, lastly, that all subjects are 'equall, and without any honour at all ... in the presence of the Soveraign' (L 18.19).[63]

Hobbes distinguished two types of merit. One relates to commutative, the other to distributive justice:

> Merit (besides that which is by Covenant, where the performance on one part, meriteth the performance of the other part, and falls under Justice Commutative, not Distributive,) is not due by Justice; but is rewarded of Grace onely. (L 15.14)

For Grotius, perfect and imperfect rights capture two distinct ways in which things can be due as a matter of justice: whether by perfect right or '*By way of Decency and Fitness*'.[64] For Hobbes, merit in distributive justice is not due in some less rigorous way than merit by contract. All merit or due presupposes the same kind of right. The two kinds of merit differ rather in their grounds for legitimate claims: 'In Contract, I merit by virtue of my own power, and the Contractors need; but in this case of Free gift, I am enabled to Merit onely by the benignity of the Giver' (L 14.17; also L 28.24).

Hobbes linked the two concepts of merit to the scholastic distinction between *meritum condigni* and *meritum congrui* (L 14.17; EW 4: 380–381). Aquinas had glossed that distinction as follows. To merit *ex condigni* is to deserve a reward proportionate to the good we do as such. We merit *ex congrui* for our works insofar as they contribute ('are congruent') to God's purpose and glory.[65] The distinction

---

[63] Teresa Bejan, 'Hobbes and Hats', *American Political Science Review* 117 (2023) no. 4: 1195–1196, 1198.

[64] Grotius, *War and Peace*, 2.7.10.1.

[65] Aquinas, *Summa Theologica*, 1a.2ae.114.

later figured in Reformation debates about whether and in what sense performing good works makes humans deserving of salvation. Lutherans argued that depraved humanity cannot do anything to deserve salvation by their own accord (*ex condigni*). Redemption is freely given by God to undeserving sinners to whom he owed nothing in advance. The elected hence merit eternal life *ex congrui*.[66] Although Hobbes's endorsement of the Lutheran (non-Pelagian) view on redemption has independent textual support (L 26.41; L 41.2–3), his explanation of *meritum congrui* and *meritum condigni* in the context of covenants no doubt serves political purposes.[67] By making merit in distributive justice the result of grace or free gift alone, Hobbes ensured that distributions cannot fail to render each their due.

Consider his gloss on the two forms of merit:

> Merit *ex condigno*, is when a thing is deserved by pact; as when I say the labourer is worthy of his hire, I mean *meritum ex condigno*. But when a man of his own grace throweth money among the people, with an intention that what part soever of it any of them could catch he should have, he that catcheth merits it, not by pact, <u>nor by precedent merit</u>, as a labourer, but because it was congruent to the purpose of him that cast it amongst them. (EW 4: 381)

For earlier theorists, distributive justice regulates any division of resources, even those enacted by a person 'of his own grace'. The duties imposed by distributive justice are conditional. *If* one decides to hand out, say, academic offices, *then* one must do so in accordance with the merit of contenders. According to Suárez, distributive justice requires allotting pledged public prizes to the best candidate. When adjudicating a contested case, judges are likewise bound by distributive justice to compare the merits of the contenders' claims and to decide accordingly. 'For that is an act of distributive justice, in which the more worthy party is to receive the preference; and he is the more worthy party who enjoys the more probable right'.[68] The claim that the person most suitable for the job deserves to get it, Hobbes countered, conflates worthiness with merit.

What Hobbes calls a just distribution is not the allocation of goods proportionate to recipients' worthiness, but the creation of merit by freely granting

---

[66] A.P. Martinich, *The Two Gods of Leviathan* (Cambridge, 1992) 138–142; Schwartz, 'Suárez on Distributive Justice', 171–173.

[67] Here I disagree with Martinich who sees 'no explanation for [Hobbes's] attempt to understand these terms [*meritum congrui* versus *meritum condigni*] other than a deep intellectual commitment to theology. I would be willing to rest my entire thesis about Hobbes's religious thought on the fact that he weaves these theological concepts into his initial discussion of a covenant, if there were not so much other evidence for his commitment to the Christian religion'. Martinich, *Two Gods*, 142.

[68] Suárez, 'On Charity', 13.6.2. For Suárez, in all such cases, the worthiest contender has an enforceable claim to the contested good as a matter of distributive justice: 'this is not a matter of proportion but of *right*; the right that the worthiest candidate has to the thing, in comparison to the less worthy' (quoted in Schwartz, 'Suárez on Distributive Justice', 167).

108 DISTRIBUTIVE JUSTICE AND EQUITY

away rights. Merit is not prior to the distribution of rights, but the result of this distribution. Thus revised, merit can no longer function as the regulating principle of distributive justice. Rewards cannot be responsive to merit, since merit comes about by being rewarded exclusive rights.[69] Interestingly, Hobbes arrived at this conclusion without denying that distributive justice demands that each is given what they merit (in a sense). It is hence not the natural duty to acknowledge equal human worth that subverts the Aristotelian theory of justice. Had Hobbes simply transplanted a meritocratic for an egalitarian distributive scheme, then humans, deemed naturally equal in worth, could all have claimed to deserve an equal share of the goods distributed. Instead, by making merit the result of grace alone, *Leviathan* eliminates all grounds for entitlement-claims to distributive shares.[70]

Leviathan's Merit-Grace Argument is an improvement upon the earlier Liberality Argument (from Hobbes's perspective). It focuses, not on the rights of the giver, but on those of recipients. Rather than asserting that distributors cannot wrong recipients since each is free to give away what is theirs as they see fit, it argues that people do not have rights of any kind *to receive* distributed goods. They cannot have any: all such rights are the result of distributions. Unlike the Liberality Argument, *Leviathan's* Merit-Grace Argument leaves open the possibility that distributions are morally flawed in some other way than by failing to give people their due. Namely by involving procedural shortcomings, such as undue partiality.

The Merit-Grace Argument underlies a crucial if somewhat neglected aspect of Hobbes's political theory: the institution of private property. Immediately after defining injustice as the non-performance of covenants in *Leviathan*, Hobbes cites the Roman law definition of justice: *'Justice is the constant Will of giving to every man his own'* (L 15.3).[71] He interprets 'the ordinary definition of Justice in the Schooles' in a startling way: 'own' means 'private property'.[72] The sovereign gives each citizen their own by issuing distributive civil laws spelling out what exclusively belongs to whom:

> the Introduction of *Propriety* ... consisteth in the Lawes, which none can make that have not the Soveraign Power. And this they well knew of old, who called that *Nomos*, (that is to say, *Distribution*,) which we call Law; and defined Justice, by *distributing* to every man *his own*. (L 24.5; also DPS 35)

---

[69] In the 1643 *Anti-White*, Hobbes had still proclaimed merit to be distinct from and prior to the reward: 'In whatever is worthy of anything the possession of merit must be prior to the object deserved' (AW 37.2). Cf. Aquinas, *Summa Theologica*, 1a.2ae.114.1: 'Merit and reward refer to the same, for a reward means something given anyone in return for work or toil'.

[70] In claiming that Hobbes 'follows the egalitarian conception of human entitlement and rejects the meritarian', Raphael, *Concepts*, 79, misses this point.

[71] Ulpian's definition is also mentioned or hinted at in DCv ED.9; DCv 17.10; DCv 18.3; L 15.22; L 18.3; L 24.5; L 26.8; L 30.12; L 43.4; DPS 8–10, 35. *Elements* pays lip service to the formula twice, both times half-heartedly (EL 17.14; EL 22.5).

[72] Foisneau, *'Leviathan's* Theory', 110.

As the philosopher in the *Dialogue* asks: 'What mean you by his own? How can that be given me which is my own already? Or, if it be not my own, how can Justice make it mine?' His discussion partner, a lawyer, answers that natural law dictates that 'Lands and Goods' must be distributed, so 'that each Man may know what is proper to him, so as none other might pretend a right thereunto, or disturb him in the use of the same'. Hobbes then adds, in an outright abuse of Ulpian's dictum, '[t]his distribution is Justice, and this properly is the same which we say is ones own' (DPS 10). This subversive gloss on justice, we shall see, underpins two mature doctrines of Hobbes. To wit, that the sovereign creates private property rights *ex nihilo* through distributive civil laws (§5.5); and that unjust actions are impossible prior to the legal establishment of property rights. 'Where there is no *Own*, that is, no Propriety, there is no Injustice' (L 15.3) (§7.3).

Leviathan associates the Roman law definition of justice with equity. The sovereign 'distribute[s] to every man his own: and this is indeed Just Distribution, and may be called (though improperly) Distributive Justice; but more properly, Equity' (L 15.15). In distributing goods, the sovereign is simply 'performing his Trust' (L 15.15). A convenient implication is that any iniquitous institution of property rights is but 'a breach of trust, and of the Law of Nature; but this is not enough to authorise any subject, either to make warre upon, or so much as to accuse of Injustice, or any way to speak evill of their Soveraign' (L 24.7). Citizens cannot meaningfully appeal to principles of distributive justice to morally criticize legal property regulations. Subjects have neither enforceable nor non-enforceable rights to receive distributive shares. 'Subjects . . . have no title at all to demand any part of the Land, or any thing else but security' (DPS 193). Moreover, they lack the standing to morally criticize iniquitous distributive laws, in part due to their unconditional authorization of the sovereign.

For Hobbes, distributive justice thus refers both to a virtue of arbitrators (equity) and to the legal arrangements of rights and goods produced through government arbitration. *Leviathan* calls distributive justice 'the act of defining what is Just' (L 15.15). By instituting property rights, the sovereign indirectly determines what is just and unjust for citizens—that is, what goods they must let others enjoy as theirs alone (L 18.10; L 26.38). Remarkably, in the very same move the sovereign renders each their due. Even inequitable distributions of property do so. Clearly, the manner in which exclusive property rights are instituted cannot be unjust when justice *is* this distribution. Distributive justice can hence no longer serve as a standard to assess the substantive rightness of the resulting distribution. Hobbes's subversive reading proves Ulpian's definition to be an empty formula. The question of *what* is each own cannot be decided by the maxim but is presupposed.[73]

---

[73] Patricia Springborg, '*Behemoth* and Hobbes's Science of Just and Unjust' in Tomaž Mastnak (ed), *Hobbes's Behemoth: Religion and Democracy* (Exeter, 2009) 164, 168. The same point is made more generally by Hans Kelsen, 'What Is Justice?' in idem, *What Is Justice?* (Los Angeles, 1971) 1–24.

110 DISTRIBUTIVE JUSTICE AND EQUITY

Hobbes cleverly exploited the dictum's silence about what constitutes each own, interpreting 'jus' in line with his conventionalist theory of property. Due to this positive twist, Ulpian's definition loses its critical potential. Following a similar line of argument, Hüning concludes that distributive justice for Hobbes orders only that 'there should be distribution'—it says nothing about the form the distribution should take.[74] That conclusion is misleading. It ignores the moral constraints distributive justice as a virtue of arbitrators places on *the process* of distributing property rights. Although justice has no say in it, the institution of civil rights is not morally arbitrary.

4.6 EQUITY AS PROCEDURAL JUSTICE

Scholarly discussions of equity often aim to 'soften' Hobbes's political absolutism, stressing the limits natural law sets to the sovereign's conduct or legislative powers.[75] What kind of standard equity poses is disputed, crucial though it is for understanding why distributive justice is subsumed under equity. My contention is that equity places only procedural constraints on distributions: such allocations must be made in an impartial and even-handed manner. Equity is silent on what makes for a just distributive *outcome*—on the particular arrangements of rights distributions must produce. For Hobbes, iniquity can only be of a formal or procedural kind since there is no independent criterion specifying what counts as a just division of rights and goods, independent of and prior to distribution. Hobbes eliminated such procedure-independent standards by reconceptualizing merit in distributive justice. This made his theory of distributive justice historically anomalous. For Aristotle, justice requires that goods are distributed in proportion to recipients' merit. According to Suárez, the worthiest candidate has an enforceable claim to receive their due share as a matter of distributive justice. Grotius denied that distributive justice concerns enforceable rights ('perfect rights'). Yet he accepted that distributions must align with imperfect rights ('worthiness'). Hobbes, by contrast, has no such 'patterned' theory of distributive justice.[76] There is no pattern of entitlements which distributive justice as equity *can* respect. For what is due (rights, merit) is first determined by distributive justice in the sovereign act of defining 'just' and 'unjust'.

---

[74] Dieter Hüning, 'From the Virtue of Justice to the Concept of Legal Order: The Significance of the *suum cuique tribuere* in Hobbes's Political Philosophy' in Ian Hunter and David Saunders (eds), *Natural Law and Civil Sovereignty* (New York, 2002) 146.

[75] Mathie, 'Justice and Equity'; Larry May, *Limiting Leviathan: Hobbes on Law and International Affairs* (Oxford, 2013) 82–84. Zagorin, *Hobbes*, 84, even speaks of Hobbes's 'very moral sovereign' in this regard. For a critique, see Tom Sorell, 'Law and Equity in Hobbes', *Critical Review of International Social and Political Philosophy* 19 (2016) no. 1: 29–46.

[76] In terminology adapted from Robert Nozick, *Anarchy, State and Utopia* (Oxford, 1974) 156–157.

As a form of procedural justice, equity regulates *how* rights and goods should be distributed. In its narrow sense, equity requires that the division procedures are fair and properly followed. It orders the sovereign to treat citizens impartially, as equals, when apportioning goods. Accepting bribes and punishing rich offenders more mildly than poor ones violates equity. Not because burdens and benefits thereby end up in the wrong hands (there is no criterion to determine whether the outcome is fair or not). But because the process of division is unfair: some are treated as 'more equal' than others (prosopolepsia). Elsewhere we read that the sovereign is required by natural law to distribute benefits according to 'Equity, and the Common Good', that is, 'to the common Peace and Security' (L 24.6–7). Hobbes presumably had in mind here equity in the broad sense (identical to the entire law of nature) since crossing any law of nature hampers peace.

Some commentators contend, to the contrary, that Hobbes *does* advance a substantive interpretation of the principle of equity. 'Hobbes's claim that common property should be distributed in terms of equity signifies a moral claim intelligible in terms of retained rights individuals have to a share of common property in civil society.'[77] In support, they cite the various natural laws spelling out what makes for an equal distribution of resources. 'For equall distribution, is of the Law of Nature; and other means of equall distribution cannot be imagined' (L 15.26).[78] In reply: 'equall distribution' must here refer to the process, rather than the outcome. The following consideration proves this. Goods that can neither be divided nor enjoyed in common, Hobbes insists, should be distributed by lot—whether natural (primogeniture) or arbitrary (first seizure). Distribution by lot unavoidably results in unequal shares. Indeed, primogeniture was denounced by some of Hobbes's contemporaries for the stark inequalities in wealth it produced.[79] Hobbes nonetheless regarded division by lot as equal: 'in this case lottery is the only form equality can take' (DCv 3.17). His reasoning presupposes that equity is a form of procedural justice: contenders must be treated impartially, as equals, to forestall grounds for complaint.[80]

A better objection is the following. While holding true for divisions of goods and property, regarding equity as a form of procedural justice seems untenable

---

[77] Ward, 'Equity and Political Economy', 829; also Klimchuk, 'Hobbes on Equity', 170.

[78] Also EL 17.3–5; EL 18.7; DCv 3.16–18; DCv 4.15; L 15.26–28.

[79] E.g. James Harrington, *The Commonwealth of Oceana and A System of Politics*, ed. J.G.A. Pocock (Cambridge, 1992) 105–109. For a general overview, see Michael Austin, 'The Genesis Narrative and the Primogeniture Debate in Seventeenth-Century England', *The Journal of English and Germanic Philology* 98 (1999) no. 1: 17–39.

[80] James likewise argues that for Hobbes 'equity is not equality of distribution by its very nature' as it has 'no essential reference to an outcome of equal distribution per se'. Rather, 'a requirement of equal distribution' arises because 'the parties are moral equals . . . such that any difference in how they are treated . . . must have relevant, sufficient grounds'. Aaron James, *Fairness in Practice: A Social Contract for a Global Economy* (Oxford, 2012) 136. While correctly observing that equity calls for treating persons as equals, rather than for equality of outcomes, James's interpretation of the normative foundation of Hobbesian equity seems otherwise overly moralized.

112 DISTRIBUTIVE JUSTICE AND EQUITY

for criminal justice—subsumed by Hobbes under equity (in the narrow sense). A procedure-independent standard for correctness clearly exists for criminal justice: to wit, whether the accused actually committed the crime they are charged with. Whenever an innocent person is convicted after a fair trial or a guilty one acquitted, neither gets what they deserve, and justice is not served. As innocents deserve not to be punished, inequitable punishment can be substantially, and not only procedurally, unjust. According to Hobbes, punishing innocents violates at least three laws of nature: the ones forbidding revenge, ingratitude, and iniquity. Equity commands 'an equall distribution of Justice; which is Punishing the Innocent is not observed' (L 28.22; also L 26.24). Just punishment *must* track guilt and innocence, the objection goes, on pain of rendering these moral norms practically meaningless.

The objection has merit: criminal justice in Hobbes cannot plausibly be reduced to procedural justice alone. Several passages imply that the justice of legal verdicts depends on whether they match criminal desert. 'For all Judges, Soveraign and subordinate, if they refuse to heare Proofe, refuse to do Justice: <u>for though the Sentence be Just</u>, yet the Judges that condemn without hearing the Proofes offered, are Unjust Judges' (L 26.24). To condemn a person without a fair trial is iniquitous—a violation of the natural law commanding impartial, even-handed adjudication. Inequitable adjudication by unjust judges, Hobbes claims here, can nonetheless result in just sentences. The underlined clause is best read as imparting that legal sentences can additionally be unjust in failing to give defendants what they deserve—sanction or absolution. Hobbes discusses several legal excuses that make punishment inappropriate. Subjects 'cannot justly be condemned by the Soveraign' for doing as instructed, for instance (L 27.27). Nor can they be 'rightly punished' for breaking 'a law [that] has not been declared and promulgated' (LLA 2.32). Justice in punishment, this suggests, requires that those innocent of wrongdoing go free.[81] Moreover, equity forbids punishing malefactors more harshly for their crime than is customary (LL 27.8).

Complicating matters, the sovereign's will is the sole authoritative standard of just and unjust within the state (§6.3). Subjects have obligated themselves to take his laws and sentences as the unquestionable public verdict on right and wrong. 'No Man may presume to dispute of what he does, much less to resist him' (DPS 41). Even inequitable legal decisions are 'Law to the party pleading' (L 26.24). Presumably, subjects are not to contest definite legal verdicts of guilt and innocence either—not even when justice miscarriages. This higher-order consideration may explain why some passages portray innocence as posterior to and established

---

[81] Compare Hobbes's apologetic that only people who deserve mistreatment suffer under tyranny: 'when a *Nero* or a *Caligula* is in power, no one can suffer undeservedly . . . for those who are troublesome or insolent towards him deserve their punishment . . . Only the ambitious suffer, the rest are protected from being wronged [by the sovereign] by the powerful' (DCv 10.7).

EQUITY AS PROCEDURAL JUSTICE 113

by criminal proceedings. 'Innocent is he that acquitteth himselfe Judicially, and is acknowledged for Innocent by the Judge' (L 26.24). Punishing innocents, on this account, means sanctioning someone legally declared non-guilty for the very crime they are exonerated from. 'Here you see, *An Innocent man, Judicially acquitted, notwithstanding his Innocency* ... after his acquittal, *upon a Presumption in Law*, condemned to lose all the goods he hath' (L 26.24; also DPS 177–178). Jesus Christ was innocent in this sense when Pilate gave him up for crucifixion 'unjustly, without finding fault in him [sine causa]' (L 42.131). Even someone so outrageously maltreated has no standing to accuse the sovereign of injustice because of their prior authorization:

> For though the action be against the law of Nature, as being contrary to Equitie, (as was the killing of [the innocent] *Uriah*, by [king] *David*;) yet it was not an Injurie to *Uriah*; but to *God*. Not to *Uriah*, because the right to doe what he pleased, was given him by *Uriah* himself; And yet to *God*, because *David* was *Gods* subject; and prohibited all Iniquitie by the law of Nature. (L 21.7, citing Ps. 51:4)[82]

The sovereign can behead someone whose legal innocence he acknowledges without committing an injustice to that person. '[T]he holder of sovereign power may not only set any penalty he pleases for any offence he wishes, but may also, from anger and greed, put innocent citizens to death who have done nothing against the laws' (DCv 10.7). Such malign treatment is, however, iniquitous and contrary to natural law.

Does this mean that the sovereign owes us something after all, namely fair trials and non-discrimination in allocations of civil rights and goods? Not quite. Citizens have no right of any kind to be treated as equals. As with any dictate of right reason, equitable conduct is both morally right and prudential for the sovereign: partiality and corruption lead to war (DCv 13.17; L 15.23). Yet natural law is only enforceable when incorporated into the civil law—and the sovereign is above that law (§3.4 and §3.5).[83] Some commentators have pointed out that equity nonetheless constitutes 'a standard for appeal to citizens' against the sovereign.[84] Citizens, it is true, may take legal action against the sovereign 'as a matter of natural equity'. However, in line with Hobbes's political absolutism, such appeals do not aim to settle 'what the holder of *sovereign power* may rightly do, but what he *willed*'—as is

---

[82] Dyzenhaus, *The Long Arc*, 123–127, concludes his long discussion of this passage by pronouncing King David's order 'ultra vires or outside the limits of sovereign authority'. David would have 'stepped out of his artificial role as sovereign and into a state-of-nature relationship of hostility with Uriah'. That conclusion must be rejected as incompatible with Uriah's enduring authorization of David's deeply iniquitous command to have him killed (§10.3). For a rival non-absolutist gloss on the verse, see John Milton, *Political Writings*, ed. Martin Dzelzainis (Cambridge, 1991) 96.

[83] EL 27.6; DCv 12.4; L 26.8; L 29.9; L 30.1; LL 21.10; DPS 26.

[84] Mathie, 'Justice and Equity', 258; Zagorin, *Hobbes*, 93.

114　DISTRIBUTIVE JUSTICE AND EQUITY

manifested in existing civil laws (DCv 6.15; also L 21.19). Lawsuits, in other words, seek to clarify what is law to citizens (not what the sovereign should have decided). This also holds true for criminal procedures. These aim to determine 'not whether the commonwealth can take away [the accused's] life by its own absolute right'—it certainly can—'but whether it <u>intended</u> that his life should be taken away <u>under that law</u>' (DCv 12.4).

Hobbes is adamant that equity can never oppose or overrule civil laws: judges invoke natural law to interpret, not to correct, civil law (DPS 81–82, 86–87). What counts as equitable is, moreover, ultimately determined by the sovereign's will 'and not according to anyone else's reason' (DCv 6.15).[85] If 'a wrong Sentence' is 'given by authority of the Soveraign, if he know and allow it', then his tacit consent suffices to repeal the old for 'a new Law' (L 26.24; also L 27.27). Finally, citizens have no standing to sue in response to sovereign commands issued (not by precedent law but) 'in Virtue of his Power' (L 21.19).[86] As such extra-legal commands are not formulated as written general rules, they are not the kind of orders which judges can interpret equitably. For all these reasons, citizens' standing to sue their ruler based on natural equity delimits neither the sovereign's legislative nor his extra-judicial powers.[87]

My interpretation of equity as a form of procedural justice chimes well with the 'politics' of the state of nature. According to Hobbes, humans are prone to disagree and fight over questions of *mine* and *thine*—biased as we are towards our own interests. While we cannot agree on any substantial division of goods, on who owes what to whom, we can agree to institute an arbitrator to decide on such distributions in (we hope) a fair, equal, and impartial manner. Indeed, given our natural love for 'Liberty, and Dominion over others', Hobbes believes that these are the only conditions on which we can agree. For the sake of peace, reason commands us to not contest legal distributions of common goods, however corrupt they may seem. For the same reason, natural law instructs the sovereign to divide benefits and burdens equally and impartially, in order to avoid giving cause for unrest and sedition amongst citizens who, in their pride, are prone to be affronted by unequal treatment (EL 28.5). Though united in their irenic purpose, these moral precepts enjoin facially opposing directives: citizens are obligated to suffer the unequal, biased, and corrupt treatment that sovereigns are duty-bound to forgo. How can the same laws of nature place such disparate demands on differently positioned

---

[85] Also L 26.11, 26; DPS 16–17, 26–27, 81.

[86] On the sovereign prerogative to govern extra-legally in Hobbes, see Thomas Poole, *Reason of State: Law, Prerogative and Empire* (Cambridge, 2015) 51–56.

[87] Laurens van Apeldoorn, 'Hobbes on Property: Between Legal Certainty and Sovereign Discretion', *Hobbes Studies* 34 (2021) no. 1: 65–67, 73–75. Sovereigns are nonetheless well advised to 'lend an ear to the complaints of citizens, and, whenever necessary, appoint a special court of inquiry into [corrupt] judges' (DCv 13.17; also DPS 28).

agents? Because these laws bid persons to refrain from doing what (given human nature) foreseeably triggers unrest—even if any ensuing agitation is itself unjust.

CONCLUSION

This chapter has shown how Hobbes redefined distributive justice as equity to render unjust distributive laws an oxymoron, thus removing a salient ground for citizens to accuse the sovereign of injustice. Doing so required more than simply replacing one word ('distributive justice') by another ('equity'). He also needed to make sure that government distributions cannot fail to give what is due (which he acknowledged would be unjust). Hobbes did so by reinterpreting the meaning of 'own' in the Roman law formula in a positivist manner, as civil rights created by distributive laws. The sovereign renders each their due by instituting exclusive property rights. To theoretically support this revision, Hobbes reconceived the grounds for merit in distributive justice, making it the result of free gifts alone (first achieved in *Leviathan*). As a result, distributive justice no longer calls for honouring the 'worth' of those involved in the distribution; rather, it commands a procedurally fair and impartial distribution, unaffected by favouritism and corruption. Without a criterion stipulating what a substantively just distribution looks like, Hobbes leaves it to the sovereign to determine what is due to whom. Chapter 5 argues that *Leviathan*'s novel account of distributive justice as a virtue of arbitrators allowed Hobbes to radicalize his conventionalist theory of private property.

5

JUSTICE AND PROPERTY

INTRODUCTION*

Throughout his works, Hobbes holds that the sovereign 'may take away from us, not only our Lands, Goods, and Liberties, but our Lives also if he will' (DPS 42). Such unbridled power need not worry subjects, he added soothingly. Subjection to the sovereign's vast uncontrolled power is preferable to living in fear of all and sundry: 'Outside the commonwealth anyone may be killed and robbed by anyone; within a commonwealth by only one person' (DCv 10.1). What's more, keeping citizens safe and prosperous is in the long-term interest of rulers. Profit and duty, properly understood, coincide for sovereigns: both demand promoting the common good of the people (EL 28.1; DCv 13.2). To be sure, rulers do not always reign rationally and morally. Conceding this, Hobbes stresses that sovereigns governing contrary to natural law sin against God alone (L 30.1). Depriving a subject 'of all he possesseth' for personal gain or to please favourites is morally wrong (L 19.8). But it does no injustice or injury to the fleeced subject. That position, safe to say, was highly controversial at the time even among defenders of absolute sovereignty. Bodin, for instance, gainsaid even the most absolute ruler the legal power to raise taxes without explicit consent of the governed: 'it is not in the power of any prince in the world, at his pleasure to raise taxes upon the people, no more than to take another mans goods from him'.[1] Subject to natural law, absolute sovereigns are forbidden 'to rob and spoil other men from their goods'.[2] Unlawful seizure of property is paradigmatically unjust. What argument did Hobbes advance to prove that all-powerful sovereigns commit no injustice by usurping citizens' property?

Some passages grant that rulers can 'rob' [spoliabit] subjects from their belongings, while stressing that such robbery, though immoral, constitutes no injustice or injury (DCv 6.13n; DCv 10.1). That reply begs the present question: what makes it the case that the sovereign does not wrong subjects by dispossessing them for no good reason? Hobbes's considered view, this chapter argues, is that sovereigns *cannot* possibly rob, defraud, or steal from their citizens. His supporting reasons

---

* This chapter reworks material from Johan Olsthoorn, 'Hobbes on Justice, Property Rights, and Self-Ownership', *History of Political Thought* 36 (2015) no. 3: 471–498. That article is framed as a critique of the 'possessive individualist' reading of Hobbes advanced by C.B. Macpherson in *The Political Theory of Possessive Individualism: Hobbes to Locke* (Oxford, 1962) and several smaller writings.

[1] Bodin, *Six Books*, 97. For discussion, see Quentin Skinner, *The Foundations of Modern Political Thought*, vol. 2 (Cambridge, 1978) 295–297.

[2] Bodin, *Six Books*, 109. Natural and divine law legally limit the power of absolute rulers in Bodin, according to Daniel Lee, *The Right of Sovereignty* (Oxford, 2021) 24–27.

Hobbes on Justice. Johan Olsthoorn, Oxford University Press. © Johan Olsthoorn 2024.
DOI: 10.1093/9780191904585.003.0005

INTRODUCTION   117

are two. First, private property rights are purely legal artefacts, forged by distributive civil laws. The sovereign is empowered to alter these laws at will—including by legally redirecting resources to himself or others (annulling individual property rights along the way). Second, the sovereign *ex officio* owns everything within the commonwealth—and one cannot steal from oneself. Either way, private property rights do not legally constrain the sovereign.

This chapter offers an in-depth study of the changing conceptual relations between justice, law, and property rights in Hobbes. Hobbes's views on property are seldom discussed in detail.[3] One explanation for this general neglect is that his position is difficult to miss: time and time again, we read that private property rights are introduced by the civil laws and remain fully dependent on the will of the sovereign.[4] As we *know* what his views on property are, why study them further? My reconstruction shows that Hobbes's theory of property is actually quite complex and multilayered, changing considerably over time. Its two capstone doctrines remain fixed across his works: (1) private property rights existentially presuppose a legal system and (2) do not exclude the sovereign. Yet over time, Hobbes introduces new arguments for both doctrines, revising the legal status of private property along the way.

Elements and *De Cive* contain two distinct arguments for the first doctrine (dubbed *Statism about Property*). The Security and the Precision Argument, both premised on commutative justice, presuppose pre-legal claims to property rendered secure and determinate by civil law (§5.2). Neither argument explains why private property rights leave the sovereign unencumbered. For that doctrine, the early works rely on a separate argument. The Allotment Argument models sovereignty on the power of a slaveholder over their slaves and conceptualizes citizens' property rights as borrowed from the stock of their master (who owns everything) (§5.3).

Leviathan, Chapter 4 has shown, turns distributive justice as equity into the specific natural law duty of arbitrators 'to distribute to every man his own' (L 15.15). This revised account of distributive justice underpinned a new and bolder argument for his two doctrines about property. The Creation Argument explains at once why property presupposes civil law *and* why it does not exclude the sovereign. It holds that the sovereign creates property rights *ex nihilo* by issuing distributive laws and decrees which literally allot to each their own. Legally unbound, he can make and unmake property rights at will through civil legislation (§5.5).

---

[3] Important exceptions are B.B. Lopata, 'Property Theory in Hobbes', *Political Theory* 1 (1973) no. 2: 203–218; Y.C. Zarka, 'La Propriété chez Hobbes', *Archives de Philosophie* 55 (1992) no. 4: 587–605; Laurens van Apeldoorn, 'Property and Despotic Sovereignty' in Robin Douglass and Johan Olsthoorn (eds), *Hobbes's On the Citizen* (Cambridge, 2020) 108–125; Laurens van Apeldoorn, 'Hobbes on Property: Between Legal Certainty and Sovereign Discretion', *Hobbes Studies* 34 (2021) no. 1: 58–79.

[4] E.g. EL 24.2; EL 27.8; DCv ED.9; DCv 6.15; DCv 12.7; DCv 14.9; DCv 17.10; L 15.3; L 18.10; L 24.5; DPS 9–10; DPS 36–37; DPS 199–200.

118   JUSTICE AND PROPERTY

The Creation Argument no longer conceives of property rights as natural liberties to enjoy things rendered exclusive 'by means of the laws and the power of the whole commonwealth' (DCv 6.15). Rather, property rights are now purely legal rights to exclude other citizens from enjoying resources (§5.4). *Leviathan* retains the Allotment Argument for good reason. Its reconceptualization of distributive justice nonetheless helps explain the diminishing argumentative centrality of despotic sovereignty in Hobbes's mature thought. The final section argues that Hobbes's radically conventionalist theory of property only applies to rights in external resources. Exclusive rights in one's body and person derive not from the civil laws that protect them but from the mutual pact of peace (§5.6).

5.1 WHY *MINE* AND *THINE* PRESUPPOSE THE STATE

The question of why private property is non-existent in Hobbes's state of nature differs from that of how civil law makes possible the existence of private property within the state—even if civil law partly serves to remedy internecine extra-statist conflict over *mine* and *thine*. This section tackles the first question. Outside the state, people can and do rightfully possess resources—possibly even many. Yet exclusionary rights to things are non-existent. For the right of nature permits all to seize any good they themselves judge conducive for their preservation. 'Every man by nature hath right to all things, that is to say, to do whatsoever he listeth to whom he listeth, to possess, use, and enjoy all things he will and can' (EL 14.10). As possessing more goods heightens personal security in a war of all against all, so each can by right lay claim to everything. Hence 'in the state of nature where all things are common to all men, the same thing is both yours and another's' (DCv 14.7).[5] Liable to rightful invasion by everyone else, natural rights to external goods are utterly useless outside the state (EL 14.10; EL 20.2; DCv 1.11).

In support of these contentions, Hobbes cited a commonplace: 'Nature hath given all things to all men' (EL 14.10; DCv ED.9; DCv 1.10). Early modern theorists generally maintained that natural resources and spaces initially belonged to humanity in common (in some sense). Hobbes subverted the platitude's received meaning in at least three ways. First, for him, the natural right to use the earth and its resources in common is not an exclusive right. Natural rights are unprotected ('naked'): others are under no obligation to respect them (§2.1). Second, Hobbes was a *legal* institutionalist about property, not a *social* one: the convention instituting private property does not predate the state.[6] Third, nothing is

---

[5] Also EL 24.2; EL 27.8; DCv ED.9; DCv 4.4; DCv 6.15; DCv 12.7; DCv 14.9; DPS 9. Compare L 24.5: 'every thing is his that getteth it, and keepeth it by force; which is neither *Propriety*, nor *Community*; but *Uncertainty*'.

[6] In terminology adopted from Anna Stilz, *Territorial Sovereignty: A Philosophical Exploration* (Oxford, 2019) 36–37.

WHY *MINE* AND *THINE* PRESUPPOSE THE STATE   119

exclusively ours as long as others retain their right to all things. The communality of goods extends 'even to one anothers body' (L 14.4), 'to one another's persons' (EL 15.2), and to 'their lives' (L 21.6). This section handles each point in turn.

Grotius, Locke, and Pufendorf all maintained that we have by nature the right to use natural resources in common with the rest of humanity. For Grotius, this right is an exclusionary right, restricting the moral freedom of others. Others wrong us in preventing us from making use of the earth in common, for example by dispossessing us from what we have taken from the common stock for private use.

> *All Things . . . were at first common* . . . From hence it was, that every Man converted what he could to his own Use, and consumed whatever was to be consumed; and such a Use of the Right common to all Men did at that Time supply the Place of Property, for no Man could justly take from another, what he had thus first taken to himself.[7]

Grotius would thus have rejected Hobbes's contention that 'where all things are *common*, nothing can be *proper* to any one man' (DCv 6.15). Following Hobbes, Pufendorf dismissed Grotius's contention that natural rights to use the earth in common are violable. By nature 'others might lawfully take from us, what we had before actually mark'd out for our own Use'. Absent mutual agreement to the contrary, humans are 'under no obligation to forbear invading and plundering'.[8] Private property rights, including exclusive rights of use, are conventional in origin: 'that one Man's seizing on a thing should be understood to exclude the Right of all others to the same thing, could not proceed but from mutual Agreement'.[9]

Like Pufendorf, Grotius advanced a social contract theory of property:

> the Original of Property . . . resulted from a certain Compact and Agreement, either expressly, as by a Division; or else tacitly, as by Seizure. For as soon as living in common was no longer approved of, all Men were supposed, and ought to be supposed to have consented, that each should appropriate to himself, by Right of first Possession, what could not have been divided.[10]

This position was conceptually open to Grotius since for him naturally violable rights of common use do not amount to full-fledged property rights. Property inseparably involves the right to recover—a legal incident missing in rights of

---

[7] Grotius, *War and Peace*, 2.2.2.1, also 1.2.1.5.

[8] Pufendorf, *Nature and Nations*, 4.4.5.

[9] Pufendorf, *Nature and Nations*, 4.4.4.

[10] Grotius, *War and Peace*, 2.2.2.5. On the compact instituting property, see also Grotius, *War and Peace*, 2.10.1.2–4, 3.2.1.1. First seizure results in property rights in virtue of this (tacit) agreement. The principle of first seizure should be distinguished from mere occupation, which creates rights of exclusive use and has place under conditions of communality of goods as well.

common use.[11] Exercising the original right to use the earth in common does not establish rights beyond exclusive use and possession. It hence neither requires nor entails the acquisition of private property. Grotius could therefore coherently hold that even *after* the introduction of private property, some rights of common use persist. Humans may 'have a Right to enjoy in common those Things that are already become the Properties of other Persons'.[12] Rights of necessity and innocent use conditionally entitle persons to use resources and spaces privately owned by others. Exercising these use-rights does not alter ownership status. 'This then is a Sort of Right to take, without a Right of acquiring.'[13]

Locke begged to differ. For him, any right to a thing counts as property: 'the *Idea* of *Property*, being a right to any thing'.[14] Rights of exclusive use therefore require private appropriation from the commons: 'being given for the use of Men, there must <u>of necessity</u> be a means *to appropriate* them some way or other before they can be of any use'.[15] Locke invoked the property each person has in their own labour to show 'how Men might come to have a *property* in several parts of that which God gave Mankind in common, and that without any express Compact of all the Commoners'.[16] We can unilaterally acquire full private property rights in originally common external things by labouring upon them (subject to the sufficiency and spoilage provisos). Locke's non-conventionalist account of the origin of private property set him apart from Grotius, Hobbes, and Pufendorf.

Next, for Grotius and Pufendorf, the social contract instituting private property is (supposed to have been) formed and binding in the state of nature.[17] Not so for Hobbes. His conflict-ridden natural condition has no place for stable conventions. People, subject to passions and partial to their own interests, cannot even agree on what natural law requires in practice (DH 13.8–9). The only thing humans agree on is that the natural condition must be left by instituting a final arbitrator to authoritatively decide on all things that might fall into controversy, including *mine* and *thine* (EL 29.8; DCv 6.9). Even if (counterfactually) a set of property rules had been instituted by general consent outside the state, anyone deeming it too risky to abide by those instituted rules might by natural right disregard them. For the right of nature allows everyone to use their own judgement and power to preserve themselves in whatever way they consider best—suspending practising morality in perilous conditions (§3.3; §7.1). Outside the Hobbesian state, there can therefore 'be

---

[11] Hugo Grotius, *Introduction to the Jurisprudence of Holland*, ed. R.W. Lee (Oxford, 1926) 2.3.4: 'ownership [*eigendom*] consists in the right to recover lost possession'.

[12] Grotius, *War and Peace*, 2.2.6.1.

[13] Grotius, *War and Peace*, 3.13.1.1.

[14] John Locke, *An Essay Concerning Human Understanding*, ed. P.H. Nidditch (Oxford, 1975) 4.3.18.

[15] Locke, *Second Treatise*, 5.26.

[16] Locke, *Second Treatise*, 5.25. For further discussion, see Johan Olsthoorn, 'Between Starvation and Spoilage: Conceptual Foundations of Locke's Theory of Original Appropriation', *Archiv für Geschichte der Philosophie* 106 (2024) no. 2: 236–266.

[17] Pufendorf, *Nature and Nations*, 8.5.2.

WHY *MINE* AND *THINE* PRESUPPOSE THE STATE   121

no Propriety, no Dominion, no *Mine* and *Thine* distinct; but onely that to be every mans, that he can get; and for so long, as he can keep it' (L 13.13). Private property presupposes the state: '*property* and commonwealth came into being together' (DCv 6.15). Indeed, 'your *property* [is] as extensive as the commonwealth wishes and lasts for just as long' (DCv 12.7).[18]

Lastly, original collective ownership of the earth did not, for the likes of Grotius, Pufendorf, and Locke, mean that *nothing* is exclusively our own by nature. By nature, humans have exclusive rights to their lives, body, actions, and freedom. 'A Man's Life is his own by Nature', Grotius writes, 'and so is his Body, his Limbs, his Reputation, his Honour, and his Actions'.[19] These natural property rights in ourselves cannot be violated without injustice: 'For our Lives, Limbs, and Liberties, had still been properly our own, and could not have been, (without manifest Injustice) invaded'.[20] Pufendorf likewise claimed that agents by nature have a right to their own 'life, body, chastity and liberty'.[21] And Locke famously maintained that 'every Man has a *Property* in his own *Person*. This no Body has any Right to but himself'.[22] Invading another's natural property rights is unjust and a wrong (*injuria*) to the right-holder. Hobbes, by contrast, recognized no morally inviolable natural *suum*. 'Without law every thing is in such sorts every Mans, as he may take, possess and enjoy without wrong to any Man, every thing, Lands, Beasts, Fruits, and even the bodies of other Men' (DPS 9). *Nothing* is exclusively ours by nature— not even our lives, limbs, liberty, or labour.[23] This makes Hobbes's rejection of pre-political property rights enormously consequential.

Goldsmith has pointed out that 'Hobbes did not achieve his radical position in regard to property rights easily'.[24] *Elements*, it is true, already states that private property rights are 'derived from the sovereign power' (EL 24.2).[25] Yet Goldsmith

---

[18] Also EL 24.2; EL 27.8; DCv ED: 9; DCv 14.9; DCv 17.10; L 15.3; L 18.10; L 24.5; DPS 9–10; DPS 36–37.

[19] Grotius, *War and Peace*, 2.17.2.1.

[20] Grotius, *War and Peace*, 1.2.1.5.

[21] Samuel Pufendorf, *The Whole Duty of Man*, ed. Ian Hunter and David Saunders (Indianapolis, 2003) 1.6.3; also Pufendorf, *Nature and Nations*, 3.1.1.

[22] Locke, *Second Treatise*, 5.27.

[23] Thomas Mautner, 'Natural Law and Natural Rights' in Peter R. Anstey (ed), *The Oxford Handbook of British Philosophy in the Seventeenth Century* (Oxford, 2013) 492–494, argues that Hobbes's rejection of a natural *suum* underpins the most salient differences between his theory of justice and those of other early modern natural lawyers. His dismissal of a natural *suum* has also been highlighted by Martin Harvey in 'Grotius and Hobbes', *British Journal for the History of Philosophy* 14 (2006) no. 1: 41–44, and 'Hobbes's Voluntarist Theory of Morals', *Hobbes Studies* 22 (2009) no. 1: 51–55. On the natural *suum* in seventeenth-century natural law theory, see also Karl Olivecrona, 'The Two Levels in Natural Law Thinking', ed. Thomas Mautner, *Jurisprudence* 1 (2010) no. 2: 197–224; James Tully, *A Discourse on Property: John Locke and His Adversaries* (Cambridge, 1980) 80–90, 112–114; Stephen Buckle, *Natural Law and the Theory of Property* (Oxford, 1991) 29–37, 77–80, 91–92, 169–174.

[24] M.M. Goldsmith, *Hobbes's Science of Politics* (New York, 1966) 199. Also M.M. Goldsmith, 'Introduction' in *Hobbes: The Elements of Law*, ed. Ferdinand Tönnies (London, 1969) xi–xiii.

[25] Also EL 20.2; EL 27.8. Goldsmith therefore exaggerates when stating: 'In the *Elements of Law* men are expected to acquire property in the state of nature'. Goldsmith, 'Introduction', xiii. Compare Johann Sommerville, 'Lofty Science and Local Politics' in Tom Sorell (ed), *The Cambridge Companion to Hobbes* (Cambridge, 1996) 256–258. Richard Tuck, *Hobbes* (Oxford, 1989) 70, has argued on different

122   JUSTICE AND PROPERTY

shows, citing a crossed-out paragraph in Hobbes's hand in a manuscript of *Elements*, that Hobbes initially accepted pre-political property rights acquired through mutual agreement. In its oldest version, the paragraph stated: 'Of the law of nature also it is: that entering into peace every man be allowed those rights which he had acquired by the covenants of others. That is to say, right against him that have covenanted'. In its newer form: 'men entering in peace, retain what they have acquired'.[26] I believe that Hobbes's early struggle with pre-political property rights explains two interpretive problems. The first concerns an anomalous remnant of natural self-ownership (§5.6). The second concerns the question of in what sense private property presupposes the existence of a legal system.

5.2 ENFORCING THE JUSTICE OF CONTRACTORS

How does civil law make possible the existence of private property rights? Two stylized explanations are found in Hobbes's early works: the Security and Precision Arguments.[27] The Security Argument declares private property rights non-existent outside the state on the grounds that in war all may by right seize whatever they judge assists their survival. A legal system helps bring about internal peace by promising to punish pact breakers and perpetrators. The provision of domestic security through law enforcement has several implications pertinent to property. Once law and order reign, morality no longer allows agents to take what belongs to others (to heighten personal security). Reneging on agreements in fear of danger likewise becomes morally impermissible. Finally, it means that individuals no longer have to protect much-needed external goods by their own judgement and strength alone.[28]

---

grounds that there is 'a minimal level of private property, at least of a kind, in the state of nature'. The fundamental right of nature would imply that 'everyone is entitled to the material objects necessary for their survival: food, water, housing, and so on'. This is mistaken: since pre-political rights to material resources are non-exclusive and unprotected, they do not qualify as private property.

[26] Hobbes, *The Elements of Law*, ed. Ferdinand Tönnies (London, 1969) 89n. The preceding paragraph (EL 17.2) states: 'Seeing then many rights are retained, when we enter into peace one with another, reason and the law of nature dictateth, *Whatsoever right any man requireth to retain, he allow to every other man to retain the same*'. In later works, the equal terms of covenanting dictated by natural law require all to retain the same basic liberties (rather than any pre-political possessions) (DCv 3.14; L 15.22). Deborah Baumgold (ed), *Three-Text Edition of Thomas Hobbes's Political Theory* (Cambridge, 2017) 177–178.

[27] The names are borrowed from Jeremy Waldron. He attributes similar considerations to Locke in *The Right to Private Property* (Oxford, 1988) 162–167.

[28] The chaos and violence in Hobbes's state of nature is that of a lawless and fearful multitude, as in Thucydides, *The Peloponnesian War*, 1.2 (EW 8: 2 in Hobbes's translation). Not that of an irrational and immature people, waiting for a lawgiver, as in Cicero, *De Inventione*, ed. H.M. Hubbell (Cambridge, MA, 1949) 1.2; Cicero, *Speech on Behalf of Publius Sestius*, ed. Robert A. Kaster (Oxford, 2006) §91: 'in the state of nature, before the time when either natural or civil law had been codified, human beings once wandered at random, dispersed over the earth, and possessed only the goods that murder and

The Security Argument chimes with Hobbes's insistence on the general invalidity of covenants outside the commonwealth, making it a popular explanation for why private property presupposes civil law.[29] Absent some coercive power to compel men to keep their agreements, just fear voids any contract by which agents bind themselves to abstain from taking what another possesses (§7.1).[30] 'Covenants, without the Sword, are but Words, and of no strength to secure a man at all' (L 17.2). On the Security Argument, the state does not create property rights but merely provide the safety necessary for private contracts establishing exclusive rights to things to be valid. As the Latin *Leviathan* explains: 'before the names of Just, and Unjust can have place, there must be some civil power which can avenge the violation of covenants, and assure to each person that property of his which he has acquired by covenants' (LL 15.3).

The Security Argument has clear textual support: 'each man has his own *right* and *property* by particular contracts, so that one man may say of *one thing* and another of *another thing* that it is his own' (DCv 6.1). The argument seems to imply, impractically, that exclusive rights require myriad bilateral contracts secured by civil law. *Elements* suggests that a person can acquire property outside the commonwealth if another agrees to give away by covenant 'his right of common' (EL 17.3). As an older variant points out, this right holds only 'against him that have covenanted' (their lord, presumably).[31] Incalculable bilateral agreements would thus be needed for private property to arise.[32] Given each person's natural right to everything, the first such property-establishing contracts would have involved no transfers of rights to particular resources. Rather, individuals would have promised one another to refrain from interfering with goods enjoyed by others. 'Whoever therefore acquires a *right* in men's natural state, does so simply in order to enjoy his *original right* in security and without justified interference' (DCv 2.4).

The worry about impracticality can be alleviated by construing the Security Argument in a more encompassing manner. Besides enforcing private contracts of property, a legal system provides general protection. Outside the state, '*dominion* and *property* have no place ... because there is as yet none of that security which we showed above [DCv 5.3] was a prerequisite of the practice of the *natural laws*'

---

bloodshed enabled them to seize or retain through physical force'. A relapse to the state of nature is hence less fanciful for Hobbes and Thucydides than for Cicero.

[29] E.g. A.P. Martinich, *A Hobbes Dictionary* (Cambridge, MA, 1995) 236; Luc Foisneau, '*Leviathan*'s Theory of Justice' in Tom Sorell and Luc Foisneau (eds), *Leviathan after 350 Years* (Oxford, 2004) 109; Christopher Pierson, *Just Property*, vol. I (Oxford, 2013) 172–173. Sommerville attributes a version of the Security Argument to Hobbes: people cannot institute a scheme of property rights in the natural condition, because the agreement it presupposes cannot be rendered binding due to the prevailing insecurity. J.P. Sommerville, *Thomas Hobbes: Political Ideas in Historical Context* (London, 1992) 54–56, 165; Sommerville, 'Lofty Science', 257.

[30] EL 15.10; DCv 2.11; L 14.18–19; L 15.3.

[31] Hobbes, *The Elements of Law*, ed. Tönnies, 89n.

[32] Goldsmith, 'Introduction', xii.

124   JUSTICE AND PROPERTY

(DCv 6.1). Once peace obtains, individuals can no longer with reason judge it necessary to seize goods possessed by another to heighten personal security. The sovereign's provision of domestic peace would thus by itself suffice for people to acquire exclusive rights to their possessions—not because such rights are positively granted to them, but because peace invalidates the invasive rights of all others to their possessions. Private property rights are thus conceived as natural rights to resources rendered exclusive through the indirect delimitation of everyone else's natural rights. The argument thus construed, in effect, restates in reverse Hobbes's reasons for why in hostile conditions each person is by natural right authorized to seize each and any resource for the sake of self-defence.

Strengthening this more encompassing reading, upon entering conditions of peace citizens mutually agree to give up their natural right to everything—as dictated by the second law of nature (EL 15.2; DCv 2.3; L 14.5) (§2.3; §3.6). Some natural rights are retained: 'as right to governe their owne bodies; enjoy aire, water, motion, waies to go from place to place; and all things else, without which a man cannot live, or not live well' (L 15.22; also EL 17.2; DCv 3.14).[33] Natural law requires individuals to accept equal terms, each keeping the same amount of natural liberties. The universal renunciation of invasive rights allows everyone to safely seek to procure 'such things as are necessary to commodious living . . . by their Industry' (L 13.14). People hence no longer have to make private contracts with everyone else in order to acquire exclusive rights to a resource: 'men entering into *peace* retain many common [communia] *rights* and acquire many private [propria] rights'—including the means to acquire private property through lawful industry (DCv 3.14). The sovereign is duty-bound to render resulting property rights secure, thus allowing citizens to safely enjoy the fruits of their labour (DCv 13.6; L 30.1).[34] He does so by penalizing wrongdoing and prosecuting thieves (DCv 6.4). The Security Argument chimes well with *De Cive*'s definition of property: 'a person's property is what he can keep for himself by means of the laws and the power of the commonwealth' (DCv 6.15; also DCv 14.7).

The Security Argument (which, construed broadly, applies to the maxims of natural law generally) was from the start accompanied by the Precision Argument. The Precision Argument states that for property to be practically efficacious some measure of precision is required, which humans, in perennial and passionate disagreement, cannot agree upon.[35] Sovereign arbitrage is needed to authoritatively

---

[33] Some natural rights are retained because divesting them is either unnecessary for or contrary to the social contract's purposes (self-preservation amidst multitudes). Other rights are inalienable (humans cannot reasonably be expected to agree to patiently suffer death). DCv 2.18; L 14.8; L 20.10–17; Susanne Sreedhar, *Hobbes on Resistance* (Cambridge, 2010) 40–52.

[34] Sreedhar, *Hobbes on Resistance*, 65–66.

[35] Versions of the Precision Argument are ascribed to Hobbes by Jean Hampton, *Hobbes and the Social Contract Tradition* (Cambridge, 1986) 99–100; Philip Pettit, *Made with Words* (Princeton, 2008) 130–131.

specify what each person is due.[36] The civil law, Hobbes stresses, is the only agreed-upon measure of *mine* and *thine*:

> [A]ll disputes arise from the fact that men's opinions differ about *mine* and *yours*, *just* and *unjust* . . . and everyone decides them by his own judgement. Consequently, it is the responsibility of the same *Sovereign Power* to come up with rules or measures that will be common to all, and to publish them openly, so that each man may know by them what he should call *his own* and what *another's*. (DCv 6.9)

Consider an example adapted from Waldron.[37] Suppose that everyone agrees that Ahmed has a right to the field by the old oak tree. Yet absent agreement about where this field begins and ends (or which is the oak tree in question), Ahmed's property right will be nigh worthless. On the Precision Argument, law is needed to provide an authoritative public set of rules determining what belongs to whom. Hence the publicity requirement: the sovereign should 'make known the common measure' of *mine* and *thine* (EL 20.10).

The Security and Precision Arguments, I contend, are best understood as supplementary accounts for *Statism about Property*. For neither argument adequately explains how people come to acquire rights to tradeable resources (other than to their labour) to begin with. Both arguments assume the existence of provisional claims to property which the state merely needs to enforce and specify. But where could these provisional titles come from? Unlike other early modern jurisprudents, Hobbes spelled out no set of pre-legal rules determining how citizens can acquire exclusive rights by legitimately appropriating things from the commons—suggesting an additional role for civil law.[38] In the original covenant, we have seen, people acquire some exclusive rights, as everyone else obligates themselves to abstain from interfering. While including rights to one's body and person, these retained rights do not divvy up external resources previously held in common. The Security Argument hence cannot by itself explain how citizens can 'make good that Propriety, which by mutuall Contract men acquire, in recompense of the universal Right they abandon' (L 15.3). Indeed, subsequent laws of nature assign a moral duty to the sovereign to distribute what cannot be enjoyed in common without hampering peace.[39] The sovereign must

---

[36] EL 20.10; EL 29.8; DCv 6.9; DCv 17.10, 12; EW 4: 378. Cf. L 6.7; L 46.11; DH 13.8–9.

[37] Waldron, *The Right to Private Property*, 163.

[38] 'Hobbes said very little about how property was acquired and transferred – the very questions which made up the bulk of the work of early modern common lawyers.' Michael Lobban, 'Thomas Hobbes and the Common Law' in David Dyzenhaus and Thomas Poole (eds), *Hobbes and the Law* (Cambridge, 2012) 40, also 61–62.

[39] L 15.24–26; cf. EL 17.3–5; DCv 3.16–18.

126 JUSTICE AND PROPERTY

set out to every subject his propriety, and distinct lands and goods, upon which he may exercise and have the benefit of his own industry, and without which men would fall out amongst themselves . . . every man encroaching and usurping as much of the common benefit as he can, which tendeth to quarrel and sedition. (EL 28.5)

Such divisions, governed by distributive justice, come to inform a different explanation for why private property presupposes civil law (§5.5).

Both the Security and the Precision Argument assume the existence of provisional pre-legal claims to property (i.e. *de facto* possessions). By enforcing and authoritatively specifying private contracts, the state elevates such pre-legal claims into legally effective property rights. As Zarka writes, 'political power does not give property its content, but its legal efficacy'.[40] On this line of reasoning, civil law is instrumental for (rather than constitutive of) private property. The two arguments make sense in relation to commutative justice: 'the Justice of a Contractor' (L 15.14). Let citizens privately buy, sell, barter, borrow, and lend. The state, 'as guarantor of private contracts, and particularly of private property', will make sure that these contracts are kept, keeping in line potential pact-breakers and peacefully resolving conflicts between contracting parties.[41] 'Since justice is embodied in keeping covenants', Foisneau writes, 'and the state guarantees that these covenants will be honoured, Hobbes is right to say that the state gives meaning to the terms "just" and "unjust".[42] In Macpherson's words, the task of the state is to 'enforce the rules necessary for the operation of a [market society]'.[43] Premised upon commutative justice (requiring the performance of valid covenants), the Security and Precision Arguments assign to the state the limited task of setting up the legal conditions required for private contractors to be able to mutually engage in commercial transactions. Liberal as this theory of property sounds, it was accompanied from the start by an argument from slavery.

5.3 PRIVATE PROPERTY AS *PECULIUM*

Throughout his works, Hobbes insists that citizens may uphold property rights only against fellow subjects—not against the sovereign. 'Propriety therefore being derived from the sovereign power, is not to be pretended against the same' (EL 24.2).[44] Citizens are, for this reason, wrong to deem taxation injurious or to feel

---

[40] Zarka, 'La Propriété', 589: 'le pouvoir politique ne donne pas à la propriété sa matière, mais son effectivité juridique'.

[41] Foisneau, '*Leviathan*'s Theory', 109, 114.

[42] Foisneau, '*Leviathan*'s Theory', 109.

[43] Macpherson, *Possessive Individualism*, 98, also 19, 29. Also Neil McArthur, '"Thrown amongst Many": Hobbes on Taxation and Fiscal Policy' in S.A. Lloyd (ed), *Hobbes Today* (Cambridge, 2013) 181.

[44] Also EL 27.8; DCv 6.15; DCv 8.5; DCv 12.7; L 20.16; L 24.7; L 29.10–11, 18; L 30.14; DPS 200.

PRIVATE PROPERTY AS *PECULIUM*   127

entitled 'to contribute nothing to the public, but what they please' (EL 27.8). Neither the Security nor the Precision Argument explains why private property rights diminish the liberties of fellow citizens only. Why would enforcing private contracts and peacefully arbitrating disputes between contracting parties entitle the sovereign to set aside citizens' property rights? The two discovered arguments for *Statism about Property* do not justify by themselves why private property rights do not restrict sovereign power.

Elements and *De Cive* advance a separate argument for that last claim. The sovereign has *dominium* over whatever citizens have—just as a slaveholder owns all that belongs to her slaves (EL 22.4; DCv 8.5). Private property rights, so the Allotment Argument states, are what the sovereign permits citizens to keep for themselves, out of his estate. Hobbes did not merely claim that citizens are legally liable to be taxed and subject to eminent domain: the state power to take private property for public use.[45] His contention is a bolder one. The commonwealth and its sovereign representative necessarily have *dominium* over all the citizens have from the start. Hobbes denied that subjects' 'Propriety in their riches is such, as to exclude <u>the Dominion, which the Common-wealth hath over the same</u>' (L 30.14). Citizens do have property rights in external resources of some kind. But those rights do not amount to full ownership. At most, citizens have revocable rights to use and enjoy what they possess. What is treated as theirs really belongs to the sovereign.

The Allotment Argument models the rights Hobbesian citizens have in their property on the peculium held by enslaved people in Roman times. Justinian's *Digest* defines 'peculium' as follows: 'the property which the slave, with his master's permission, keeps in a separate account of his own, less anything owed to the master'.[46] Enslaved people had no legal standing in court.[47] Yet they could be allotted property by their master, allowing them to engage in all sorts of business transactions with third parties. Through thrift and wise investments, some enslaved people amassed enough money to buy themselves free. The institution of peculium thus incentivized enslaved persons to be docile and financially prudent. Another advantage this legal institution gave to slaveholders is that they immediately came to own whatever their enslaved subjects acquired by engaging in business transactions (a separate administrative act was needed to add new acquisitions

---

[45] The doctrine of eminent domain is already found in Grotius, *War and Peace*, 3.20.7.1. For a historical overview, see Arthur Lenhoff, 'Development of the Concept of Eminent Domain', *Columbia Law Review* 42 (1942) no. 4: 596–638.

[46] *Digest* 15.1.5. The legal status of the peculium is expounded in *Digest* 15.1 and *Digest* 33.8. Compare the definition in Florentinus, *Institutes*, 11: 'A peculium is made up of anything a slave has been able to save by his own economies or has been given by a third party in return for meritorious services or has been allowed by his master to keep as his own.' Quoted in Richard Gamauf, 'Slaves Doing Business: The Role of Roman Law in the Economy of a Roman Household', *European Review of History* 16 (2009) no. 3: 342. For further discussion, see W.W. Buckland, *The Roman Law of Slavery* (Cambridge, 1970) 187–238.

[47] *Digest* 50.17.32: 'As far as concerns the civil law slaves are regarded as not existing' [*pro nullis habentur*].

128   JUSTICE AND PROPERTY

to the peculium). Moreover, the slaveholder's legal liability was restricted to the value of the peculium, shielding her from losses.[48] Peculia could be quite substantial and contain property of any kind, including land and 'underslaves and their peculium'.[49] Enslaved people belonging to the peculium of other slaves were held 'vicariously'.[50] Hobbes's works display awareness of Roman slavery law and practice, contrasting 'servants subordinate', held vicariously, with 'servants immediate' (EL 22.7–8).

Hobbes stated expressly that non-enchained enslaved humans can hold property.[51] They do so, moreover, in the same way as citizens do:

> There is therefore nothing that the *slave* can keep as *his own* against his *Master*. By allotment from his *Master* however, he does have *property* and *Dominion* over things that are *his own* in the sense that he can keep and protect them against a *fellow slave*; in the same way in which it was shown that a citizen has nothing which is properly *his own*, against the will of the *commonwealth*, or of the holder of sovereign power; but each citizen does have *things that are his own* against his fellow citizens. (DCv 8.5; also EL 22.4)

The Allotment Argument generalizes Hobbes's claim that servants can hold property distinct from one another 'by the dispensation, and for the benefit of their master' by extending it to all citizens (EL 22.4). The argument assumes that the sovereign owns everything belonging to his citizens, just as slaveholders own everything held by their enslaved subjects. This supposition has textual support: 'the riches and treasure of the sovereign, is the dominion he hath over the riches of his subjects' (EL 24.1).

Further support is found in Hobbes's highly provocative doctrine that the sovereign holds the exact same rights and powers over citizens as slaveholders hold over enslaved people. 'The subjection of them who institute a commonwealth amongst themselves, is no less absolute, than the subjection of servants' (EL 23.9; also EL 20.16). The distinction between 'a *free citizen* and a *slave*' comes down to this: 'the FREE MAN is one who serves only the commonwealth, while the SLAVE serves also his fellow citizens' (DCv 8.9). As Lee observes, for Hobbes 'the despotic *dominium* over a state is not simply one kind or style of rulership' but rather 'the only kind

---

[48] In line with *Digest* 50.17.133: 'Our condition can be improved but not worsened by our slaves'.
[49] *Digest* 15.1.7.4.
[50] Gamauf, 'Slaves Doing Business', 337.
[51] Across his works, Hobbes distinguished between enslaved people 'held in prison, workhouses, or bonds' and those entrusted with their physical liberty (EL 22.3; DCv 8.4; L 20.10, 12; cf. L 45.13). No bond of trust and hence no obligations exist between enslaved people held in corporeal bondage and their *domini*. Inhabiting a state of war, bonded slaves may flee and kill their slaveholder without injustice. On Hobbes's conception of slavery, see Deborah Baumgold, 'Slavery Discourse before the Restoration: The Barbary Coast, Justinian's *Digest*, and Hobbes's Political Theory', *History of European Ideas* 36 (2010) no. 4: 412–418; Daniel Luban, 'Hobbesian Slavery', *Political Theory* 46 (2018) no. 5: 726–748.

PRIVATE PROPERTY AS *PECULIUM*   129

of rulership'.[52] Hobbes's early works conceptualize 'right . . . over the person of another' in terms of 'property or dominion' (rather than authority: *potestas*) (EL 22.1). Indeed, *De Cive* explicitly equates sovereign authority, sovereign power, and dominion: 'SUMMAM POTESTATEM, sive SUMMUM IMPERIUM sive DOMINIUM' (DCv 5.11). This chain of equivalence allowed Hobbes to claim that the sovereign *ex officio* owns everything their citizens possess: 'he who has *Dominion* over a *person* has *Dominion* over everything that is hers'—offspring included (DCv 9.5; also EL 22.4–5; L 20.8). Hence 'whatever the servant acquires is acquired by the master' (LL 20.13).[53]

Early modern political theorists were wont to distinguish between sovereignty obtained by institution and sovereignty seized through conquest in war. The distinction was deemed to bear on the extent of the rights sovereigns have over their subjects. Witness Pufendorf:

> There is a great difference between [1] a *Prince* that has rais'd his own Kingdom, collected, as it were, his own Subjects, and who was at first the Universal, Absolute *Proprietor* of every thing in the Common-wealth, and [2] Another freely call'd to Government and invested with *Sovereign Power*, by Persons already in Possession of their distinct *Proprieties*.[54]

By the law of nations, conquerors acquire rights of ownership in everything their subdued enemies possessed—even in their persons. 'The law of all peoples also instantly makes us owner of things captured from an enemy. This even makes slaves of free captives'.[55] Those subjected to sovereigns-by-acquisition, therefore, 'can have no better Right to What they possess, than the *Roman Slaves* had to what they got by their own labour, that is, a *Precarious* Possession revocable at Pleasure, whenever the *Prince* thinks fit'.[56] Pufendorf proceeded to berate Hobbes for confounding the rights of sovereignty by acquisition from those by institution. With reason: after equating sovereignty by conquest with despotic rule, Hobbes professed that 'the Rights and Consequences of . . . *Despoticall* Dominion, are the very

---

[52] Daniel Lee, 'Sovereignty and Dominium: The Foundations of Hobbesian Statehood' in Robin Douglass and Johan Olsthoorn (eds), *Hobbes's On the Citizen* (Cambridge, 2020) 136–137.

[53] The provided analysis accords with and supplements that of Van Apeldoorn, 'Property and Despotic Sovereignty', 109: 'sovereigns, by virtue of their sovereignty, *necessarily* and *fully* own their subjects and all they possess' in *De Cive*. Van Apeldoorn examines the conceptual relations between sovereignty and property. This chapter focuses on the kind of property titles citizens hold.

[54] Pufendorf, *Nature and Nations*, 8.5.1.

[55] *Institutes* 2.1.17. This Roman law principle was central to sixteenth-century justifications of the Spanish colonial conquests. See e.g. Francisco de Vitoria, *Political Writings*, ed. Anthony Pagden and Jeremy Lawrance (Cambridge, 1991) 283; Suárez, *De Legibus*, 2.18.8. Hobbes endorsed the same 'Law of War' in DPS 191–193. Locke tried to safeguard individual property rights against state government by denying that just conquerors come to own the goods of the vanquished. His position, he admitted, 'will seem a strange Doctrine' to many. Locke, *Second Treatise*, 16.180.

[56] Pufendorf, *Nature and Nations*, 8.5.1.

130   JUSTICE AND PROPERTY

same with those of a Sovereign by Institution' (L 20.14). The two differ only 'in origin and manner of formation', not in essence (DCv 9.10; also EL 23.10; L 20.3). By modelling sovereignty on the despotic rule of masters over slaves, Hobbes justified a key premise of the Allotment Argument: sovereigns are lord over everything their citizens possess.[57]

The Allotment Argument implies that citizens do not have complete ownership over their goods: 'those who have a *Lord* [*Dominus*] do not have *Dominion*' (DCv 12.7).[58] Theirs is merely a right to enjoy goods owned by someone else—the sovereign. Various passages suggest that citizens are indeed merely accorded rights of exclusive possession, use, and usufruct—rather than full ownership: 'a thing is yours in the sense that all are prohibited from obstructing your ability *to use and enjoy* it at all times in security and at your discretion. What is required for a man to have property in goods is not that he may be able *to use them*, but that he alone be able *to use them*' (DCv 14.7).[59]

The Allotment Argument allows us to make sense of an otherwise obscure passage in *De Cive*. It states that private property originated in each person's renunciation of their *jus in omnia* to the commonwealth: 'Tell me, then, where this *property* came to you from, if not from the commonwealth? And from where did it come to the commonwealth, except that each man transferred his right to the commonwealth?' (DCv 12.7). The passage suggests, puzzlingly, that the sovereign redistributes on behalf of the commonwealth rights received in the original covenant.[60] This claim is intelligible on a despotic conception of sovereignty. If Hobbesian sovereignty is identical to despotic rule, then the original covenant mirrors a self-enslavement contract. Sovereigns come to own everything their subjects possess in virtue of being granted sovereignty (i.e. *dominium*). Citizens are allowed to exclusively enjoy and use some of the sovereign's resources—privileges revocable at any time. Taxation and expropriation, accordingly, are not inroads on private property but alterations of the terms of enjoyment.

Elements and *De Cive*, I have argued, model the property relations between citizens and sovereigns on that between Roman slaves and slaveholders. To be sure, the normative conditions of Hobbesian slave-citizens and people enslaved in Roman times differ in manifold ways—if only because Hobbes's sovereign is the only enslaver around. The commonwealth being one dominion held by a single

---

[57] The despotic conception of sovereignty, modelling the ruler on a slaveholder, was theorized—and condemned—by Bodin. In 'despotic' or 'seigneurial' government, the sovereign has 'become lord [*dominus*] of the goods and persons of his subjects, by law of arms and lawful war, governing them as the master [*paterfamilias*] of a family doth his slaves'. Bodin, *Six Books*, 200. For discussion, see Daniel Lee, '"Office Is a Thing Borrowed": Jean Bodin on Offices and Seigneurial Government', *Political Theory* 41 (2013) no. 3: 412–416.

[58] *Leviathan* appears to offer a revised definition of the dominion—one to which citizens can lay claim: 'the Right of possession, is called Dominion' (L 16.4).

[59] Translation altered: '... non ut quit iis possit uti, sed possit solus'. Also EL 24.2; DCv 14.6; L 24.7; DPS 10; DPS 199–200.

[60] Sommerville, *Thomas Hobbes*, 95.

sovereign lord, enslaved people cannot use their peculium to buy themselves out of their master's dominion. Without glossing over such salient differences, the Allotment Argument highlights one common feature: citizens' property rights do not exclude the sovereign because such rights are held 'as a concession' from their master/owner (DCv 6.15n).

Lee, cited earlier for his documentation of *De Cive*'s equation of sovereignty with the *dominium* of masters over slaves, observes that Hobbes 'seems to change his tune' in *Leviathan*.[61] Dominion and slavery cease to be linked to commonwealths by institution. 'Dominion is acquired two wayes; By Generation, and by Conquest'—no longer by institution (L 20.4). The Latin *Leviathan* goes further still, making generation the sole ground of dominion (LL 20.5). The shift, Lee contends, reflects not any theoretical change but rather a change in readership. To placate an English audience, Hobbes proved 'exceptionally skilled in concealing the centrality of dominion in *Leviathan*'.[62] Against this reading, §5.5 argues that *Leviathan*'s introduction of the Creation Argument partially obviates Hobbes's argumentative need for despotic sovereignty. The Creation Argument can explain (up to a point) why private property does not exclude the sovereign without attributing ultimate ownership to him. This, I conjecture, induced Hobbes to loosen the strict equation of sovereignty with *dominium* and property—while holding fast to unbridled sovereign power. The Creation Argument crowns Hobbes's developing account of the nature of distributive laws, to which I turn first.

5.4 FROM DISTRIBUTIVE LAWS TO DISTRIBUTIVE JUSTICE

Each of Hobbes's political works contradistinguishes two kinds of civil laws through their respective addressees (EL 29.6; DCv 14.6–7; L 26.38). Penal laws speak to public officers, proclaiming the penalties that should be inflicted for specific crimes. *Elements* opposes penal laws to laws plain and simple: 'thou shalt not steal, is simply a law; but this: he that stealeth an ox, shall restore four-fold, is a penal [law]' (EL 29.6). By the time of *De Cive*, Hobbes had realized that the command 'thou shall not steal' is meaningless absent prior legal determination of what counts as property: 'I was alerted by the very name of justice (by which is meant a constant will to give every man *his right*) to ask first how it is that anyone ever spoke of something as *his own* rather than *another's*' (DCv ED.9). This insight induced him to introduce a novel counterpart to penal laws.[63] Distributive laws speak to

---

[61] Lee, 'Sovereignty and Dominium', 137.

[62] Lee, 'Sovereignty and Dominium', 138. Arash Abizadeh, 'Sovereign Jurisdiction, Territorial Rights, and Membership in Hobbes' in A.P. Martinich and Kinch Hoekstra (eds), *The Oxford Handbook of Hobbes* (Oxford, 2016) 404, likewise highlights *Leviathan*'s shift away from the earlier despotic conception of sovereignty, which appeared 'to conflate jurisdictional authority with ownership'.

[63] This insight was not original to Hobbes. See Suárez, *De Legibus*, 2.17.9: 'the prohibition against stealing has no application unless there has been a division of property and property rights'. Other basic

132 JUSTICE AND PROPERTY

citizens, authoritatively determining what belongs to each: 'the law by which his own right is distributed to each man, that is, the law which lays out the rules for all things, by which we may know what belongs to us and what to others' (DCv 14.6).

Distributive civil laws are necessary since by nature nothing counts as theft or murder:

> *Theft, Murder, Adultery* and all *wrongs* are forbidden by the laws of nature, but what is to count as a *theft* on the part of a citizen or as *murder* or *adultery* or a *wrongful act* is to be determined by the *civil*, not the *natural, law* ... what counts as *ours*, what as *another's* is a question for the civil law. (DCv 6.16; also DCv 14.9; DCv 17.10)[64]

Since the natural right to everything renders all things common to all outside the state, 'it was consequently not possible to encroach on what was another's' (DCv 14.9). Exclusionary rights originate within the state and presuppose distributive civil laws. While theft is morally wrong by nature, what counts as theft is conventional through-and-through—because property rights are so. 'For if, notwithstanding the law of nature's prohibition of theft, adultery, etc., the civil law commands such an infringement, the act does not count as theft, adultery, etc.' (DCv 14.10). In support, Hobbes cites the Spartan practice to encourage male adolescents to pilfer goods possessed by others. To permit this 'was simply to make a law that anything so acquired *belonged to them* not to *the other*' (DCv 6.16). This new doctrine radicalizes the view expounded in *Elements*. There, civil law settles private conflicts over the meaning of *mine* and *thine*, rather than first give content to such terms (EL 29.8).

On *De Cive's* account, the distinction between distributive and penal law is not real but conceptual: they are two '*parts* of the same law' (DCv 14.7). To have property is to have a right to a thing secured by the sovereign's law and power (DCv 6.15). Secure possession requires 'prohibiting others from obstruction' through fear of punishment. Without appended sanctions a distributive law 'achieves nothing' (DCv 14.7; also DCv 13.17).[65] The reason is confounding:

> in the state of nature where all things are common to all men, the same thing is both yours and another's so that what the law defines as yours was also yours

---

moral norms have no application either, the Jesuit maintained, unless certain empirical conditions are met. For instance, 'the precept requiring justice in contracts' has no import 'unless one assumes the existence of commercial intercourse among men'.

[64] These three passages have no parallel in either *Elements* or *Leviathan*. Baumgold (ed), *Three-Text Edition*, 229–230, 384, 472–473.

[65] For this reason, every civil law must be understood to come with penalties (DCv 14.8).

before the law, and does not cease to be yours after the law, even though it is in the possession of another. (DCv 14.7)

If others can with impunity (albeit wrongfully) take my goods, then my property rights remain of as 'little use and benefit' as they were outside the state, 'when another as strong, or stronger than himself, hath right to the same' (EL 14.10; also DCv 1.11). Still, as citizens lay down their right to all things upon joining the commonwealth, it is hard to understand why 'what the law defines as yours was also yours before the law'.

In what follows, I argue that *De Cive*'s account of distributive laws is theoretically muddled—and subsequently ameliorated in *Leviathan*. The initial confusion springs from Hobbes's contrasting conceptualizations of laws as obligations, and of rights as liberties.[66] The two jointly inspired an unusual conception of property rights. Property rights, for Hobbes, consist not in claim-rights but in protected and exclusive liberties to use and enjoy some resource.[67] Property, thus understood, presupposes civil law since humans, roughly equal in power, cannot exercise exclusive control over a resource except by force of law.[68] Laws are essentially fetters, removing freedom; while 'a *right* is a *natural liberty* not created by laws but left by them' (DCv 14.3).[69] *De Cive* accordingly conceives of the distribution of private property rights, not as enabling citizen's conduct, but as curtailing it by diminishing the amount of lawful actions open to fellow citizens. Civil laws give each their due by removing the freedom to hinder fellow citizens in enjoying what they possess, through the imposition of legal penalties upon infringement. The distributive part of law 'forbids wrongs to be done', that is, 'to violate what is another's [*aliena invadere*]', whereas the penal part punishes such wrongs (DCv 14.7, 9). Hobbes concluded that distributive civil laws cannot *give* citizens new rights to anything (i.e. freedoms of use and enjoyment). Rather they render things exclusively yours by imposing obligations upon everyone else to back off. Hence the claim that 'what the law defines as yours was also yours before the law' (DCv 14.7). In line with the Security and Precision Arguments, *De Cive* thus assumes 'an instrumental, not a constitutive, relation between the exclusive rights introduced by distributive laws, and the existence of property'.[70]

---

[66] EL 29.5; DCv 14.3; L 14.3; L 26.43; DPS 37.

[67] Liberty is foundational to Hobbes's concepts of legal and political rights, argues Eleanor Curran, 'Blinded by the Light of Hohfeld: Hobbes's Notion of Liberty', *Jurisprudence* 1 (2010) no. 1: 100–104.

[68] Van Apeldoorn, 'Property and Despotic Sovereignty', 110, argues that in *De Cive* property 'is not secured by exclusivity of *right* but by exclusivity of *power*'. If true, this makes private property in principle possible outside the state. Had there been anyone with irresistible power, then they could have effectively laid exclusive claim to a resource. According to Van Apeldoorn, the sovereign has *dominium* over his subjects, including over enchained slaves owing him no obedience, by virtue of his eminent power.

[69] DCv 14.3: 'Est autem *jus, libertas naturalis*, a legibus non constituta, sed relicta'.

[70] Van Apeldoorn, 'Property and Despotic Sovereignty', 113.

134   JUSTICE AND PROPERTY

A moment of reflection reveals the theoretical infelicity of *De Cive*'s conception of property rights as natural liberties to enjoy things rendered exclusive by law. The equation of rights with liberties left by the law neither entails nor requires that property rights derive from natural rights to things. Distributive civil laws determine how citizens obtain exclusive titles to things, which they are henceforth free to use and enjoy. Those liberties exist in virtue of the law—that is, due to its authoritative stipulation and enforcement of rules of property. But they need not be conceived as *natural* liberties. Rather, civil law can be productive of freedom by spelling out on what terms people can acquire and hold property rights. Indeed, it has to do so, because subjects have *alienated* their right to all things—that is, their moral freedom to seize and hold any resource whatsoever.

De Cive conceived of private property as built upon natural liberties: property in *x* consists in a natural freedom to enjoy *x* rendered exclusive by distributive law and protected by penal law. *Leviathan*, I contend, no longer grounds property rights in remnant natural liberties. Such rights are now fully constituted by distributive civil law: 'the Propriety which a subject hath in his lands, <u>consisteth in</u> a right to exclude all other subjects from the use of them' (L 24.7).[71] The altered nature and status of property is reflected in *Leviathan*'s revised account of distributive law. Gone are the suggestions that distributive laws achieve nothing without appended sanctions. Distributive and penal laws are now portrayed as different kinds of laws (rather than as distinct parts of the same law).[72] Their content otherwise remains the same. Penal laws spell out penalties for wrongdoing while '*Distributive* are those that determine the Rights of the Subjects, declaring to every man what it is, by which he acquireth and holdeth a propriety in lands, or goods, and a right or liberty of action' (L 26.38). The shift I have highlighted is a subtle one: whether property includes, as a constitutive element, natural liberty. It does so in *De Cive*, not in *Leviathan*. Yet in both texts, distributive laws determine what is due to each citizen. And in both, penal laws are required to provide the protection needed to render private property secure (L 29.10).

Distributive laws are general rules about how and on what terms citizens can rightfully hold, acquire, and transfer goods (rules of contracts, of inheritance, etc.). '[W]hat Goods [a person] may enjoy, and what Actions he may doe, without being molested by any of his fellow Subjects: And this is it men call *Propriety*' (L 18.10). All such rules are conventional and instituted by the sovereign legislator.[73] Some distributive civil laws are general in reach (if sometimes quite specific in

---

[71] As also argued by Van Apeldoorn, 'Hobbes on Property', 67–70.

[72] As noted by M.M. Goldsmith, 'Hobbes on Law' in Tom Sorell (ed), *The Cambridge Companion to Hobbes* (Cambridge, 1996) 276. Further reasons for this shift are given in §6.2.

[73] L 24.10; L 26.38; DCv 17.10: 'Our Saviour . . . gave no rules by which a citizen could know how to distinguish what is *his own* from what is *another's*, nor what were the appropriate formulae, words or circumstances for *giving, passing, entering upon*, and *possessing* a thing, so that it would be regarded as rightly belonging to the *recipient, entrant* or *possessor*. The only inference possible is that individual citizens should get those rules from the commonwealth'.

content): '*let that be yours which you have caught with your own net in the sea*' (DCv 14.7). Others are concrete hand-outs (e.g. of spoils of war) to particular persons. Hobbes mentions divisions of land by the victorious Israelites to the twelve tribes by lot (Josh. 13–22) and by William the Conqueror to '*English-men* and others'.[74] 'In this Distribution, the First Law, is for Division of the Land it selfe' (L 24.6).[75] Distributive laws establish both what and in what way citizens can trade, thus creating the legal framework enabling commercial transactions. Liberties permitted to citizens by (the silence of) the law include the right 'to buy, and sell, and otherwise contract with one another' (L 21.6).

5.5 THE CREATIVE JUSTICE OF ARBITRATORS

Rather than merely providing the legal conditions that enable individuals to obtain effective property rights, the sovereign creates property rights *ex nihilo* on the Creation Argument. The sovereign introduces private property by literally giving each their own through distributive civil laws. In an allusion to Cicero's *De legibus*, Hobbes wrote:

> the Introduction of *Propriety* ... is the act onely of the Soveraign; and consisteth in the Lawes, which none can make that have not the Soveraign Power. And this they well knew of old, who called that *Nomos*, (that is to say, *Distribution*,) which we call Law; and defined Justice, by *distributing* to every man *his own*. (L 24.5)[76]

Natural law commands that 'Lands and Goods' must be distributed so 'that each Man may know what is proper to him, so as none other might pretend a right thereunto, or disturb him in the use of the same'. 'This distribution', Hobbes claims, 'is Justice, and this properly is the same which we say is ones own' (DPS 10). This radically conventionalist theory of property is defended at length in *Leviathan* and the *Dialogue*.[77] It is not yet clearly worked out in the earlier works since its complete

---

[74] L 24.6; L 42.61; DPS 193–201; B 266.

[75] Hobbes's law 'for Division of the Land' has no affinities with ancient agrarian laws, revitalized by the Leveller movement. Agrarian laws, as advocated by Plato and Harrington, limited the amount of land persons could legally hold for reasons of political stability. By contrast, Hobbes places no upper limits on permissible holdings; does not need the legally instituted division to be preserved; and is silent on any potentially destabilizing consequences of concentration of wealth in land. On intellectual debates over agrarian laws in early modern England, see Eric Nelson, *The Greek Tradition in Republican Thought* (Cambridge, 2004) 89–100, 112–125; Pierson, *Just Property*, 193–207.

[76] Cicero, 'The Laws' in *The Republic* and *The Laws*, ed. Niall Rudd (Oxford, 1998) 1.19: 'they think that law, whose function is to enjoin right action and to forbid wrong-doing, is wisdom. And they believe it received its Greek name [*nomos*] from giving each his own ... If this assertion is correct, as on the whole I think it is, the origin of justice must be derived from law'. Also Suárez, *De Legibus*, 1.1.9.

[77] L 15.15; L 24.5–10; DPS 9–10, 36, 192–195.

136   JUSTICE AND PROPERTY

statement includes a purely legal conception of property as well as a conception of distributive justice as a virtue of arbitrators (both first introduced in *Leviathan*).[78]

The Creation Argument is premised upon distributive justice, understood as the will 'to distribute to every man his own' (L 15.15). The maxim 'give each their due' (*suum cuique tribuere*) is often understood metaphorically as 'respect each other's rights'.[79] Hobbes glosses the dictum in a similar figurative manner when applying it to citizens. 'Justice is but the will to give every one his owne, that is to say, the will to obey the Laws' demarcating *mine* from *thine* (LL 43.4; also L 26.8; LL 15.9). Citizens fulfil 'Justice' by 'taking from no man what is his' (L 30.12). What distributive justice requires of citizens can be fully accounted for by commutative justice: they must abstain from intruding upon what civil law declares is another's by dint of their promise to simply obey the sovereign lawgiver (a pledge commutative justice orders them to keep).[80] The same is not true for the non-covenanting sovereign. When applied to arbitrators, Hobbes interprets 'tribuere' non-metaphorically. Recall that distributive justice *as equity* is 'the Justice of an Arbitrator' (L 15.15). Arbitrators fulfil distributive justice by literally giving each their own, that is, by instituting 'propriety'. Witness the *Dialogue*: 'Justice is the constant will of giving to every Man his own; that is to say, of giving to every Man that which is his Right, in such a manner as to Exclude the Right of all Men else to the same thing' (DPS 35; also DPS 9–10). It is hard to see how citizens can respect another person's right (to *x*) in such a way as to exclude the right of all others (to *x*).

Like any sovereign act, the institution of property is arbitrary in the sense that it depends entirely on the sovereign's will and discretion (L 24.6).[81] This does not mean that the distribution of property is morally arbitrary or of necessity extra-legal. It is not. The natural law of equity (in the narrow sense) regulates distributive acts (§4.6). Distributive laws and decrees must divide rights and goods impartially and even-handedly (i.e. without respect of persons) on pain of iniquity:

> if *a man be trusted to judge between man and man*, it is a precept of the Law of Nature, *that he deale Equally between them* ... The observance of this law, from the equall distribution to each man, of that which in reason belongeth to him, is called EQUITY, and ... distributive Justice. (L 15.23–24)

Subsequent laws of nature spell out which procedures are equitable for different kinds of goods.[82] For example, things which can neither be divided nor peacefully

---

[78] *De Cive* alludes to the *suum cuique* formula several times (DCv ED.9; DCv 17.10; DCv 18.3) but hints only once at its future use as 'sovereign virtue' (DCv 14.6, on distributive laws). *De Cive* still depicts distributive justice as a virtue of citizens (DCv 3.6, 15, 32). Furthermore, not the sovereign, but 'humans have distributed what nature had placed in common' (DCv ED.9).

[79] E.g. Aquinas, *Summa Theologica*, 2a.2ae.58.1.

[80] Michael J. Green, 'Justice and Law in Hobbes', *Oxford Studies in Early Modern Philosophy* 1 (2003) 114.

[81] For Hobbes's use of 'arbitrary', see L 24.8; L 28.10; L 31.10–11; L 46.35; L R&C.8.

[82] EL 17.3–5; EL 18.7; DCv 3.16–18; DCv 4.14–15; L 15.25–28.

enjoyed in common 'ought to be adjudged to the First Possessor; and in some cases to the First-Borne, as acquired by Lot' (L 15.28). It does not follow that primogeniture and first seizure generate provisional claims to property which are afterwards validated by civil law. The laws of nature provide moral guidelines to arbitrators on how to impartially distribute rights and goods. They do not themselves allocate rights. To merit something—'to have it as DUE'—is to have a right to it by either contract or free gift; not by natural law (L 14.17; also L 10.54; LL 10.53) (§4.5). Inequitable laws are legally valid and binding to citizens, creating property rights just the same. Sovereigns are accountable for abiding by the natural law of equity to God alone (L 24.7). To his subjects, who have authorized his every action, his word is law: 'whatsoever is commanded by the Soveraign power, is as to the Subject (though not so always in the sight of God) justified by the Command; for of such command every Subject is the Author' (L 22.15).[83] The possibility of legally valid inequitable laws shows that distributive laws create property rights *ex nihilo*, even though the sovereign is morally and rationally obliged to distribute goods equitably.[84]

The Creation Argument, as reconstructed here, allowed Hobbes to defend in a theoretically more parsimonious and politically less outrageous manner his two main doctrines regarding private property: (1) such rights presuppose the existence of a legal system and (2) leave the sovereign unencumbered. Above, I argued that the Security and Precision Arguments, prevalent in the early works, provide no satisfactory explanation as to why private property rights diminish the liberties of fellow citizens only. To that end, *Elements* and *De Cive* advanced the Allotment Argument: citizens hold property rights by dispensation of their sovereign overlord, who can revoke their rights to enjoy what he owns at will. In modelling sovereignty on despotic rule and citizenship on slavery, the Allotment Argument will have shocked Hobbes's audience. Even Bodin decried rulers who treat 'the goods' and 'bodies of his subjects' as their own, calling it a mark of tyranny.[85]

The Creation Argument, I contend, allowed Hobbes to render private property legally revocable without assuming sovereign *dominium* over all the citizens possess. The argument conceives of property rights as purely legal constructs: legal freedoms of citizens to hold and enjoy goods, rendered exclusive through the selective imposition of duties on all other subjects to refrain from interfering with the same. This allows at once for a straightforward explanation, built upon

---

[83] Also EL 21.3; EL 28.1; DCv 6.13n; DCv 7.14; L 18.6; L 21.7; L 24.7; L 26.23; EW 5: 177–178; DPS 31.

[84] The same analysis applies to the sovereign's duty to provide necessities of life to those unable to work (L 30.18; LL 30.18). This duty, too, is owed only to God. Interpreting the laws of nature as guidelines for how property rights must be allocated, rather than as themselves allocating these rights, dissolves the tension Pierson perceives between the sovereign's absolutism and the 'rather extraordinary account of the proper basis of the initial allocation of property' expressed by natural law. Pierson, *Just Property*, 176–177, 187.

[85] Bodin, *Six Books*, 212.

138   JUSTICE AND PROPERTY

well-established Hobbesian grounds, of why private property rights do not curb sovereign authority. The sovereign is not subject to civil law.[86] As the sole legislator, he can at will alter and repeal distributive laws—and hence the property rights they institute.[87] To be sure, subjects can sue the sovereign to determine their rights in disputes with the state over debt, taxes, compulsory service, punishment, and 'right of possession of lands or goods' (L 21.19).[88] Such lawsuits, I argued in §4.6, serve to clarify what the sovereign's will is as expressed in existing civil law (DCv 6.15; DCv 12.4). Should the sovereign dislike the way subordinate judges settle such lawsuits, then he is free to issue new distributive laws and decrees, amending the legal rights and properties of citizens accordingly. The government is thus empowered to legally cancel financial debts owed to citizens at will.

That justification for legal expropriation is not implied by the Security and Precision Arguments. These two arguments portray civil law as an enabling rather than a constitutive condition of private property: civil laws render secure and determinate pre-legal claims to property. Unbound by such laws and generally entitled to make and unmake laws at will, the sovereign can lawfully jettison such civil laws. Yet *that* legal power does not give the sovereign ownership over what citizens have: it merely results in rendering their possessions insecure and indeterminate. The early works did argue that the sovereign can expropriate at will—albeit on the distinct ground that there is 'nothing that the *slave* can keep as *his own* against his *Master*' (DCv 8.5; also EL 22.4).

That so-called Allotment Argument, I submit, remains needed in *Leviathan*. For the Creation Argument cannot explain why extra-legal and contra-legal confiscations are no forms of theft. Taxation and expropriation, Hobbes claims, do not have to take place by law. The sovereign may 'demand, or take any thing by pretence of his Power' (foreclosing civic lawsuits). His seizure of civic possessions by sheer force is lawful since 'all that is done by him in Vertue of his Power, is done by the Authority of every Subject' (L 21.19). This gave Hobbes reason to continue to affirm complete sovereign *dominium* over whatever the citizens have in later texts: 'he that hath Dominion over the person of a man, hath Dominion over all that is his' (L 20.8; also L 20.13; DPS 199–200). That doctrine, however, is no longer entailed by his conception of property. As Van Apeldoorn has argued, the early works had conceptualized property as natural rights to things rendered effective by pre-eminent power: 'what one *de facto* controls or possesses ... *by means* of positive law and the *potentia* of the commonwealth'.[89] Property in essence being effective control over persons or things, the sovereign owns everything within

---

[86] E.g. EL 27.6; DCv 6.14; DCv 13.2; L 26.6; L 29.9.

[87] Abizadeh, 'Sovereign Jurisdiction', 405–406. Bodin had first made the power to repeal and abrogate law essential to sovereignty, argues Daniel Lee, 'Unmaking Law: Jean Bodin on Law, Equity and Legal Change', *History of Political Thought* 39 (2018) no. 2: 269–296.

[88] On the sovereign's right to request unpaid services from citizens for the public good, see L 28.24.

[89] Van Apeldoorn, 'Property and Despotic Sovereignty', 110–111.

the state's territory in virtue of his supreme power.[90] The same is not implied by *Leviathan's* purely legal conception of property rights.

Leviathan's change in argument did not make for a change in doctrine. Sovereign power remains despotic in reach, wholly unrestricted by individual property rights. By 1651, Hobbes had worked out a way to support the same absolutist conclusions through the more benign idea of distributive civil laws—rather than by deducing them from the despotic claim that sovereigns by definition own everything that citizens have. Hobbes could thus portray rights to external resources as created by distributive laws, rather than as allotted to citizens from the sovereign's estate. *Leviathan*, I conclude, shed rather than concealed the despotic assumptions underpinning its theory of property.[91] Thanks to the Creation Argument, *Leviathan* no longer needs to invoke a despotic conception of sovereignty to explain why private property does not delimit the sovereign legislator. Distributive laws, with their veneer of legality, served Hobbes's legally untrammelled sovereign almost as well.

5.6 THE STATUS AND LIMITS OF PROPERTY IN ONESELF

So far I have focused on rights in external things. Yet in line with seventeenth-century usage, Hobbes understands 'property' and 'propriety' (*proprietas*) in a broad sense, as including anything persons can lawfully claim as their own 'in such manner as to Exclude the Right of all Men else to the same thing' (DPS 35).[92] Property—synonymous with *mine* and *thine* (L 24.5)—can cover both material and immaterial things:

> concerning Mens Titles . . . some Goods are Corporeal, as Lands, Money, Cattel, Corn, and the like, which may be handled, or seen; and some Incorporeal, as Priviledges, Liberties, Dignities, Offices, and many other good things, meer Creatures of the Law, and cannot be handled or seen: And both of these kinds are concerning *Meum*, and *Tuum*. (DPS 45)[93]

Property also includes rights in our body: 'Of things held in propriety, those that are dearest to a man are his own life, & limbs; and in the next degree, (in most men,)

---

[90] Van Apeldoorn, 'Property and Despotic Sovereignty', 117–125.

[91] *Pace* Lee, 'Sovereignty and Dominium', 138.

[92] A similarly broad sense of 'property' is found in Locke, *Second Treatise*, 15.173. *Leviathan* consistently employs the term 'propriety' to signify exclusive rights; it uses 'property' only in its technical sense of 'accident' (L 24.10; L 31.37; L 38.4; L 42.50; L 44.23). Other works use 'property' and 'propriety' interchangeably (e.g. EL 22.5, 8; EL 27.8; DPS 36).

[93] The distinction between corporeal and incorporeal things was central to Roman property law. Incorporeal things are 'things that cannot be touched', such as legal rights and obligations (*Institutes* 2.2.1–2; *Digest* 1.8.1.1).

140 JUSTICE AND PROPERTY

those that concern conjugall affection; and after them riches and means of living'
(L 30.12). In its most general sense, 'propriety' means anything that is 'proper' to
a person, including a 'right or liberty of action' (L 26.38; also DCv 17.10). '[W]hat
Goods [a man] may enjoy, and what Actions he may doe, without being molested
by any of his fellow Subjects: And this is it men call *Propriety*' (L 18.10). This broad
understanding of property might make one think that distributive civil laws bring
into existence *all* exclusive rights citizens have—including personal rights in their
lives, limbs, and labour. That would be a mistake: the Creation Argument only applies to rights in external things.

Two arguments against extending Hobbes's radically conventionalist argument
to all civil rights are found in the literature. Exclusive pre-legal rights in one's own
body and person can be based either in natural self-ownership or in the original
covenant of peace citizens mutually enter. The textual evidence for attributing
natural self-ownership to Hobbes is slim. According to Macpherson, Hobbes's
political theory assumes the idea of a possessive market society in which '[t]he individual is essentially the proprietor of his own person and capacities, for which
he owes nothing to society'.[94] In support, he cites Hobbes's endorsement of labour
markets: 'a mans Labour also, is a commodity exchangeable for benefit, as well as
any other thing' (L 24.4). That passage is indecisive: the right to commercially sell
one's labour need not be a natural right. It might well have been instituted by civil
law. Moreover, Hobbes elsewhere repudiates as specious such reasoning about
justice: 'that whatsoever a man can get by his own Industry, and hazard, is his own'
(L 27.10).

Zarka likewise attributes natural property rights in oneself to Hobbes: 'this dependency [of property on the state] cannot be justified except by reference to a
more fundamental absolute: the property each has in his own body and limbs'.[95]
In support, he cites Hobbes's only explicit endorsement of natural self-ownership.
EL 23.1 states, in the context of parental rights over offspring: 'every man by the
law of nature, hath right or propriety to his own body'. Significantly, Hobbes justified the claim by reference to EL 17.2—the passage Goldsmith discovered was
amended. So Hobbes's only explicit endorsement of natural self-ownership pur-
ports to be validated by a passage that was deleted from later manuscript versions
of *Elements*. In all likelihood, he ditched the idea of natural self-ownership while
revising *Elements*, forgetting to remove the reference to it in *Element*'s chapter on
patrimonial kingdoms. Parallel passages to EL 17.2 and EL 23.1 in *De Cive* and
Leviathan confirm this hypothesis: nil references to natural self-ownership.[96]

---

[94] Macpherson, *Possessive Individualism*, 263, also 53–68, 105–106, 263–265; C.B. Macpherson,
'Introduction' in idem (ed), *Hobbes: Leviathan* (Baltimore, 1968) 48–51.

[95] Zarka, 'La Propriété', 595: 'Mais cette relativité ne peut se justifier que par référence à un absolu
plus fondamental, la propriété que chacun a sur son corps et sur ses members'.

[96] Compare EL 17.2 with DCv 3.14; L 15.22; L 21.11–12. Compare EL 23.1 with DCv 9.1–2; L 20.4–
5. Baumgold (ed), *Three-Text Edition*, 177–178, 286.

Moreover, natural self-ownership jars with each person's natural right to everything, extending 'even to one anothers body' (L 14.4). In the bellicose state of nature, exclusive rights in one's life, body, and person are non-existent since natural rights of self-preservation allow each individual to seize and conquer everything and everyone: 'any one may legitimately subdue or even kill Men, whenever that seems to be to his advantage' (DCv 8.10). The rationale behind these claims is not that self-defence trumps the rights of other agents not to be harmed. Hobbes's view is rather that natural rights, being naked liberties, impose no obligations upon others. '[F]or where there is no law, there no killing, nor any thing else can be unjust' (EW 4: 253/EW 5: 152).[97] The definition of injustice as '*the not Performance of Covenant*' further presupposes a rejection of violable natural rights (L 15.2). All injuries and injustices are breaches of promises because nothing is due to us by nature. Had Hobbes allowed for a natural *suum* whose infringement is unjust, then he could not coherently have claimed that a '*wrong* and *unjust* action or failure to act have the same meaning, and both are the same as breaking an agreement or *breaking faith*' (DCv 3.3).[98]

A more promising pre-legal ground for exclusive property in one's 'own life, & limbs' is the original covenant of peace. The second law of nature specifies the conditions of that covenant. It commands each person to 'be willing, when others are so too, as farre-forth, as for Peace, and defence of himselfe he shall think it necessary, to lay down his right to all things; and be contented with so much liberty against other men, as he would allow other men against himselfe' (L 14.5; also EL 15.2; DCv 2.3). Rights to invade another's body and person are clearly incompatible with peace. As Curran has argued, citizens should hence be understood to have renounced such 'invasive rights under the second law of nature'.[99] The collective renunciation of natural rights to kill and subjugate others for personal security suffices to render exclusive everyone's liberty-rights in their own life and person. This attests that these rights are not created by distributive laws.

In being based on pre-legal claims, originating in the pact of peace, citizens' exclusive rights to their body and person rely on civil law in ways spelled out by the Security and Precision Arguments (§5.2). The sovereign has been authorized to settle any conflicts over what exclusive liberty-rights in themselves citizens have contractually acquired. What counts as wrongful killing is determined by civil law: 'not every killing of a man is *Murder*, but only the killing of someone whom the *civil law* forbids us to kill' (DCv 6.16). Grounded in mutual promises of

---

[97] On the natural right of self-preservation as warranting defensive killing, see also EL 22.9; DCv 2.18; EW 5: 184–185; DPS 192.

[98] Samuel Pufendorf, *On the Natural State of Men*, ed. Michael Seidler (Lewiston, 1990) 129, objected against Hobbes: 'Who will deny the injustice, therefore, if one who lives in a natural state with us experiences a violation of something that nature alone has granted him?'

[99] Eleanor Curran, *Reclaiming the Rights of Hobbesian Subjects* (Basingstoke, 2007) 111, also 72–76, 100, 110, 165–168.

142   JUSTICE AND PROPERTY

non-interference, these personal rights are regulated by commutative justice: 'For what else is, *You shall not encroach on another's* but *You shall not encroach on that which has ceased to be yours by your own agreement*' (DCv 4.5).

I have argued that these arguments cannot be extended to rights in external things because, unlike other early modern theorists, Hobbes offered no account of how individuals can acquire private property through unilateral appropriation or division of common goods prior to the introduction of civil law. As a result, there are no uncontested provisional rights to external resources which individuals can agree to respect, by contractually alienating invasive rights to them. Some readers might disagree, objecting that the original covenant incorporates the rules of division propounded by subsequent natural laws.[100] That view is questionable. The laws of nature dictate how to procure peace in general, beyond the terms agreed to in the social contract. Granting the contention *arguendo*, the objection holds at most for the early works. Only those texts portray distributive justice, regulating the division of common resources, as a natural law duty of those who enter the original covenant. It commands private individuals to not 'take more rights' than they allow others to have on pain of *pleonexia* (EL 17.2; DCv 3.14). Perhaps the same requires enjoying non-divisible goods either in common or alternately by lot (EL 17.3–5; DCv 3.16–18). *Leviathan*, in any case, turns the same natural laws prescribing fair distributions into duties of arbitrators alone (§4.2). Distributing common goods has thus become the exclusive concern of the sovereign. This allowed Hobbes to argue that the sovereign creates private property rights in external things *ex nihilo* by enacting distributive laws (L 24.5).

Ex nihilo—with, perhaps, one exception. The inalienable natural rights of citizens include a right to unilaterally seize any goods needed to survive. Even within the state, 'it is permitted by the right of nature for people living in extreme need to take other people's things, even by force' (LL 30.18). Inalienable rights permit citizens to disobey civil laws 'without Injustice' (L 21.10). This so-called right of necessity morally entitles the destitute to set aside civil laws prohibiting theft.[101] Moreover, the rationale behind the retained right doubles as a legal justification. Anyone who 'destitute of food, or other things necessary for his life ... take the food' essential for self-preservation 'by force, or stealth' is 'totally Excused' (L 27.26). 'EXCUSE' Hobbes defined as that 'by which that which seemed a Crime, is proved

---

[100] EL 17.3–5; EL 18.7; DCv 3.16–18; DCv 4.14–15; L 15.25–28.

[101] On early modern rights of necessity, see Buckle, *Natural Law*, 45–48, 108–120, 160–161; S.G. Swanson, 'The Medieval Foundations of John Locke's Theory of Natural Rights', *History of Political Thought* 18 (1997) no. 3: 399–458; Siegfried Van Duffel and Dennis Yap, 'Distributive Justice before the Eighteenth Century: The Right of Necessity', *History of Political Thought* 32 (2011) no. 3: 449–464. *Leviathan*'s fifth law of nature forbids individuals to cling to resources that are to them 'superfluous, and to others necessary' (L 15.17). Rosamond Rhodes explores what this moral precept implies for Hobbes's theory of property in 'Hobbes's Fifth Law of Nature and Its Implications', *Hobbes Studies* 22 (2009) no. 2: 144–159.

to be none at all' (L 27.21).[102] To punish those forcibly taking victuals needed for survival equals punishing innocents. The right of necessity thus curtails what can count as distributive law to citizens: sovereign commands prohibiting the destitute to take direly needed resources cannot be law to them (L 27.22) (§6.2). Some might speculate further that distributive laws must, conversely, legally recognize the same inalienable rights to material necessities to be valid law. The right of necessity 'totally Excuseth' theft 'and takes away from it the nature of a Crime' (L 27.22). Does this make any goods forcibly taken by the starving legally belong to the starving (rather than to their initial proprietors)? Not necessarily. Hobbes may well have agreed with Grotius that rights of necessity merely give those in dire need the right to *use* resources that remain privately owned by others. As use-rights do not alter ownership status, the destitute can coherently have a duty to compensate owners afterwards for the rightful use of their goods.[103] The few lines on rights of necessity in Hobbes are too truncated to settle whether retained natural rights to seize material necessities have distributive implications, creating property rights.

CONCLUSION

This chapter has reconstructed Hobbes's developing views on property and distributive justice to see why and in what way private property presupposes a legal system. The two explanations derived from *Elements* and *De Cive* (the Security and the Precision Argument) rely on commutative justice (the justice of contractors). They assign a limited role to the state and presuppose provisional pre-political claims to property (*de facto* possessions). On *Leviathan*'s bolder Creation Argument, premised upon distributive justice, the task of the state goes beyond enforcing private contracts and arbitrating disputes. Distributive laws create private property rights *ex nihilo*: sovereigns literally 'distribute to every man his own' (L 15.15) so 'that each Man may know what is proper to him' (DPS 10).[104] My analysis corroborates Goldsmith's suggestion that Hobbes did not attain this

---

[102] Thus eliding the standard distinction between justification and excuse. A *prima facie* breach of the law is justified if one had a right so to act; excused if one cannot reasonably be held responsible for acting so. Andrew Botterell, 'A Primer on the Distinction between Justification and Excuse', *Philosophy Compass* 4 (2009) no. 1: 172–196.

[103] Grotius, *War and Peace*, 2.2.9, 3.12.1.1, 3.17.1. On rights of necessity in Grotius, see John Salter, 'Grotius and Pufendorf on the Right of Necessity', *History of Political Thought* 26 (2005) no. 2: 284–302; Dennis Klimchuk, 'Grotius on Property and the Right of Necessity', *Journal of the History of Philosophy* 56 (2018) no. 2: 239–260; Johan Olsthoorn, 'Two Ways of Theorizing Collective Ownership of the Earth' in James Penner and Michael Otsuka (eds), *Property Theory* (Cambridge, 2018) 196–199.

[104] My interpretation, if correct, disproves Fleischacker's thesis that no early modern philosopher 'put the justification of property rights under the heading of distributive justice'. Before the late eighteenth century, 'claims to property ... were matters for commutative justice; no one was given a right to claim property by distributive justice'. Samuel Fleischacker, *A Short History of Distributive Justice* (Cambridge, MA, 2004) 27.

144 JUSTICE AND PROPERTY

radically conventionalist position easily: it was not defended consistently until his redefinition of distributive justice in *Leviathan*. My reconstruction further revealed how elaborate and complex Hobbes's vindication of the sovereign's unbridled control over citizens' property is. Extensive theorizing was needed to show that rulers may by law and power 'deprive a good citizen of all his possessions' (LL 19.8; also L 19.8). Historical studies of ideas of property frequently omit Hobbes on the grounds that he had 'no place for a theory of property'.[105] A robust theory of *private* property is indeed absent in Hobbes. His is a different kind of property theory: one aiming not to delimit but to secure the sovereign's full rights over all that citizens have.

[105] Buckle, *Natural Law*, 3. Tully's *A Discourse on Property* and Waldron's *The Right to Private Property* mention Hobbes only in passing, while Garnsey summarizes his position in a single footnote. Peter Garnsey, *Thinking about Property: From Antiquity to the Age of Revolution* (Cambridge, 2007) 136n.

6
JUSTICE AND CIVIL LAW

INTRODUCTION

Rebels and other rabble-rousers, rued Hobbes, trumpet loudly that 'Kings need not be obeyed unless their commands are just' (DCv 12.1). To counter this seditious doctrine, he developed a two-pronged argument over time. The first prong warns citizens not to arrogate to themselves knowledge of what is just and unjust. To forestall internecine strife resulting from moral disagreement, citizens have agreed in the original covenant to henceforth take the civil law as the public measure of just and unjust, good and evil. For subjects, the sovereign's will ultimately determines the authoritative meaning and content of morality—even if some of his laws and decrees in fact materially contradict natural law. The second, more ambitious prong seeks to establish a key thesis of Hobbes's vindicatory project: civil laws cannot possibly be unjust or injurious to citizens. This chapter reconstructs and analyses this bold two-pronged argument.

Along the way, I provide new ammunition to a long-standing scholarly debate. Was Hobbes a legal positivist? Does he hold that whatever the sovereign commands to subjects is valid law, irrespective of its moral content? Many scholars answer in the affirmative, reasoning that his outspoken defence of political absolutism is bolstered by removing any moral constraints on civil law-making.[1] Analogously, we may think that legal positivism strengthens Hobbes's vindicatory project. After all, this vindication serves to morally empower absolute rulers. By showing that all-mighty sovereigns cannot possibly act unjustly towards their citizens, Hobbes demonstrated that rightful grievances justifying collective disobedience or rebellion cannot possibly arise. This chapter argues that Hobbes's vindicatory project is in fact incompatible with legal positivism. Insulating the sovereign from all taints of injustice required showing that civil laws cannot possibly be unjust or injurious to citizens. Hobbes's defence of that last thesis, I contend, makes his legal theory a non-positivist one.

Ongoing debates on the character of Hobbes's legal theory are marred by the common scholarly tendency to conflate justice with natural law. Against positivist readings, I contend that Hobbes rejects both constitutive tenets of legal

---

[1] Jean Hampton, *Hobbes and the Social Contract Tradition* (Cambridge, 1986) 107: 'his support for a positivist conception of law is derived from his support for absolute sovereignty. To say that instituting a state involves only instituting a ruler with absolute power is to say that the sole source of law in a state must be the sovereign's will.'

Hobbes on Justice. Johan Olsthoorn, Oxford University Press. © Johan Olsthoorn 2024.
DOI: 10.1093/9780191904585.003.0006

146   JUSTICE AND CIVIL LAW

positivism: the Sources Thesis and the Separability Thesis (§6.1 and §6.2). Against extant anti-positivist readings, I argue that a civil law's (non-)conformity with natural law does not affect its legal validity (§6.5). My reconstruction of the relation between civil law and justice proceeds by disentangling three conceptually distinct and non-tautological theses:

Sole Measure   Civil law is the sole authoritative measure of what is just and
                   unjust in the actions of citizens
All Laws Just   All civil laws are just
No Law Unjust   Civil laws cannot be unjust

These three claims are often ascribed indiscriminately to Hobbes, inadvisably. Hobbes espoused *Sole Measure* across his political works (§6.3). Despite having the theoretical resources needed to proclaim all distributive laws just, he expressly affirmed *All Laws Just* only twice, both times in minor works (EW 4: 252; EW 5: 182) (§6.4). *No Law Unjust* he defended vigorously from *De Cive* onwards (§6.6). That last doctrine, I argue, posits an ineliminable conceptual connection between civil law and justice, contrary to the Separability Thesis: for Hobbes, it is analytically true that whatever is civil law to citizens is neither unjust nor injurious to them. A crucial component of Hobbes's vindicatory project, this connection holds true in *Leviathan* in virtue of the Authorization Argument (replacing the earlier Consent Argument). Authorization precludes injustice—and citizens have individually authorized all the sovereign's actions, including immoral ones. Indeed, immoral laws and decrees are legally valid precisely because and insofar as they have been authorized by citizens. Peculiarly, existing positivist and anti-positivist interpretations of Hobbes's legal theory both go wrong on this exact point (§6.7).

6.1 LEGAL POSITIVISM

Legal positivism is a view on the conditions for legal validity. Amidst pervasive disagreement over its exact meaning, legal positivism is generally identified by the conjunction of two tenets: the Sources Thesis plus the Separability Thesis. The Sources Thesis states that as law is a human artefact, its existence and content depend on social facts and never solely on morality. 'In any legal system, whether a given norm is legally valid, and hence whether it forms part of the law of that system, depends on its sources, not its merits (where its merits, in the relevant sense, include the merits of its sources)'.[2] Law is something made ('posited') by

---

[2] John Gardner, 'Legal Positivism: 5½ Myths', *American Journal of Jurisprudence* 46 (2001) no. 1: 201. The Sources Thesis is sometimes called the Social Thesis. Joseph Raz, *The Authority of Law* (Oxford, 1979) 40–55.

humans, rather than something discovered through moral reasoning. However compelling the moral reasons are for making a particular law, those reasons do not themselves bring that law into being.

The Separability Thesis says that there is no necessary connection between law and morals.[3] Law and morality are analytically separable such that it is always conceptually open to ask substantive moral questions about law ('must this law be obeyed?', 'is this law just?'). The moralized conceptions of law prevalent in the natural law tradition conceptually foreclosed some of these questions. Take Francisco Suárez. He maintained that whenever a legislator 'prescribe[s] that which is unjust, such a precept <u>is not law</u>, inasmuch as it lacks the force or validity necessary to impose a binding obligation.'[4] John Austin (1790–1859), one of the founders of legal positivism, lambasted moralized conceptions of law. 'The existence of law is one thing; its merit or demerit another. Whether it be or be not is one enquiry; whether it be or be not conformable to an assumed standard, is a different enquiry.'[5] It must be possible, Austin insisted, to determine whether some norm is law without having to resort to moral argument. Justice and morality therefore cannot be validating conditions of law. In sum: 'Moral considerations do not form an essential part of the conditions of legal validity, and conceptually so.'[6]

The Separability Thesis implies that law is morally fallible.[7] It is a good thing generally to live under a system of law. But it is not true that any legally valid norm will, in virtue of being law, necessarily meet some moral standard. As Hart puts it: 'it is in no sense a necessary truth that laws reproduce or satisfy certain demands of morality, though in fact they have often done so.'[8] In other words, no necessary link obtains between law and morality such that we can deduce from L is existing law, that L has a particular moral quality.

Hobbes is traditionally read as a legal positivist.[9] Goldsmith regards him so since Hobbes 'denies that general principles of justice, morality, or rationality (as

---

[3] H.L.A. Hart, 'Positivism and the Separation of Law and Morals', *Harvard Law Review* 71 (1958) no. 4: 593–629. The label 'Separability Thesis' was coined by Jules L. Coleman, 'Negative and Positive Positivism', *Journal of Legal Studies* 11 (1982) no. 1: 141. Critics were quick to point out that there are many non-contingent links between law and morality—e.g. Tony Honoré, 'The Necessary Connection between Law and Morality', *Oxford Journal of Legal Studies* 22 (2002) no. 3: 489–495; Leslie Green, 'Positivism and the Inseparability of Law and Morals', 83 *New York University Law Review* (2008) 1035–1058. The debate now centres, more productively, on determining *which* kind of necessary relations between law and morality legal positivists must reject. E.g. Matthew Kramer, 'On the Separability of Law and Morality', *Canadian Journal of Law and Jurisprudence* 17 (2004) no. 2: 315–336; Giorgio Pino, 'Positivism, Legal Validity, and the Separation of Law and Morals', *Ratio Juris* 27 (2014) no. 2: 190–217.

[4] Suárez, *De Legibus*, 1.9.4, also 1.1.6. Also e.g. Aquinas, *Summa Theologica*, 1a.2ae.95.2.

[5] John Austin, *The Province of Jurisprudence Determined* (Indianapolis, 1998) 184n.

[6] Andrei Marmor, 'Legal Positivism: Still Descriptive and Morally Neutral', *Oxford Journal of Legal Studies* 26 (2006) no. 4: 689.

[7] Green, 'Positivism and the Inseparability', 1056–1058.

[8] H.L.A. Hart, *The Concept of Law*, second edition (Oxford, 1994) 185–186.

[9] For a brief overview of this evolving debate, see Anthony F. Lang and Gabriella Slomp, 'Thomas Hobbes: Theorist of Law', *Critical Review of International Social and Political Philosophy* 19 (2016) no. 1: 5–7.

148   JUSTICE AND CIVIL LAW

such) are criteria of the validity of law'.[10] Hampton concurs: 'law is understood to depend on the sovereign's will. No matter what a law's content, no matter how unjust it seems, if it has been commanded by the sovereign, then and only then is it law'.[11] Zagorin sees Hobbes as a legal positivist who converted 'natural law into a purely moral principle'.[12] Lloyd defends an intermediate position. She argues that Hobbes rejects the Separability Thesis: 'no command it would be immoral to obey could count as a law'. Yet as natural law enjoins us to treat as authoritative any sovereign determination of morality, 'no matter its substantive merits', Hobbes's theory is 'in practical terms indistinguishable from legal positivism'.[13] The traditional positivist interpretation has been rejected outright by Murphy. Hobbes's theory of law, he contends, is 'much more akin to earlier natural law accounts than to later positivist views'.[14] In a series of publications, Dyzenhaus has developed a complex anti-positivist interpretation. Subordinate judges, he points out, owe it to the sovereign to interpret civil law in their adjudication in line with natural law. In this way, 'unlike both the command theorists and contemporary legal positivists, Hobbes advances a theory of legal authority in which the "laws of nature" are given a prominent role in the determination of the content of the law'.[15]

This chapter joins sides with recent non- and anti-positivist readings of Hobbes. My grounds for doing so are novel. Previous attempts to distance Hobbes from legal positivism have focused overwhelmingly on the constraints natural law poses to valid legislative and judicial law-making.[16] I do not believe that there are any such constraints: for Hobbes, immorality does not invalidate civil law. Hobbes's legal theory is non-positivist for two other reasons. First, he spurns the Sources Thesis. Whether a sovereign command is law to a subject cannot be determined without resort to moral argument. Moral reasoning is required to ascertain whether the subject had previously obligated themselves to obey that particular command. Second, Hobbes denies the moral fallibility of law—and thus the

---

[10] M.M. Goldsmith, 'Hobbes on Law' in Tom Sorell (ed), *The Cambridge Companion to Hobbes* (Cambridge, 1996) 275. Also Philip Pettit, *Made with Words: Hobbes on Language, Mind, and Politics* (Princeton, 2008) 130.

[11] Hampton, *Hobbes and the Social Contract Tradition*, 107.

[12] Perez Zagorin, 'Hobbes as a Theorist of Natural Law', *Intellectual History Review* 17 (2007) no. 3: 253.

[13] S.A. Lloyd, 'Hobbes's Self-Effacing Natural Law Theory', *Pacific Philosophical Quarterly* 82 (2001) no. 3–4: 287, also 295. For another intermediate position, see George Duke, 'Hobbes on Political Authority, Practical Reason and Truth', *Law and Philosophy* 33 (2014) no. 5: 605–627.

[14] Mark Murphy, 'Was Hobbes a Legal Positivist?', *Ethics* 105 (1995) no. 4: 846, also 858. Also Claire Finkelstein, 'Hobbes and the Internal Point of View', *Fordham Law Review* 75, no. 3: 1223–1228.

[15] David Dyzenhaus, 'Hobbes on the Authority of Law' in David Dyzenhaus and Thomas Poole (eds), *Hobbes and the Law* (Cambridge, 2012) 188. See also Michael Cuffaro, 'On Thomas Hobbes's Fallible Natural Law Theory', *History of Philosophy Quarterly* 28 (2011) no. 2: 181–187; David Dyzenhaus, 'Hobbes's Constitutional Theory' in *Thomas Hobbes: Leviathan*, ed. Ian Shapiro (New Haven, 2010) 457, 464–471; David Dyzenhaus, *The Long Arc of Legality: Hobbes, Kelsen, Hart* (Cambridge, 2022) 88–148.

[16] E.g. Larry May, *Limiting Leviathan: Hobbes on Law and International Affairs* (Oxford, 2013) 41–42, 121.

6.2 CIVIL LAW AND SOVEREIGN PREROGATIVE

Separability Thesis—by postulating a necessary connection between law and injustice: 'no Law can be Unjust' (L 30.20).

Before we can reconstruct the relations between justice and civil law in Hobbes, the meaning of civil law must be clarified. Hobbes formally differentiates civil law from other traditional categories of law: natural law, moral law, divine law, common law, ecclesiastical law, martial law, and the law of nations. Yet he effectively reduced, in various ways, all those other types of law to civil law (the law of nations excepted). His legal reductionism served to ensure that the sovereign legislator—unbound by civil law—cannot be accused by subjects of violating any other kind of law either. By the time of *Leviathan*, Hobbes held that no norm is properly law among humans unless it has been promulgated so by the civil sovereign (§3.5). This allowed him to define law as such as civil law: 'A Law is the Command of him, or them that have the Soveraign Power, given to those that be his or their Subjects, declaring Publickly, and plainly what every of them may do, and what they must forbear to do' (DPS 32; also L 42.43). Any law proper has two essential characteristics: (1) it is freedom-depriving and (2) takes the form of commands. I discuss each mark in turn.

Law (*lex*) stands to right (*jus*) as obligation stands to liberty. 'LAW, determineth, and bindeth to one of them: so that Law, and Right, differ as much, as Obligation and Liberty' (L 14.3).[17] Freedom is the default position: persons are morally free in respect of φ unless some law prescribes or forbids φ. To be morally at liberty to φ is to have a right to φ. To lack that right is to be obligated *not* to φ.[18] Law essentially restricts rights/freedom by imposing obligations. As *Elements* puts it: 'right is that liberty which law leaveth us; and laws those restraints by which we agree mutually to abridge one another's liberty' (EL 29.5). 'Indeed the end of making civil laws was to restrict natural right, or the right of all men to all things, since, while that right stayed in place, there could be no peace' (LL 26.7). 'Law obligeth me to do, or forbear the doing of something; and therefore it lies upon me an Obligation' (DPS 37). More succinctly: '*Civill Law* is an *Obligation*' (L 26.43). Law differs from counsel in being obligatory. 'To do what one is instructed by *law* is a matter of *duty*; to take *advice* is *discretionary*' (DCv 14.1; also L 25.4; L 42.36). A person is free to disregard counsel 'at his owne perill, without injustice' (L 42.43). Flouting law proper,

---

[17] Also DCv 14.1, 3; L 26.43; DPS 37. On changing interpretations of the relation between *jus* and *lex* as culminating in Hobbes, see Michael J. White, 'How *Ius* (Right) Became Distinguished from *Lex* (Law): Two Early Episodes in the Story', *History of Political Thought* 40 (2019) no. 4: 583–606.

[18] On liberty as absence of obligation, see Robin Douglass, 'Thomas Hobbes's Changing Account of Liberty and Challenge to Republicanism', *History of Political Thought* 36 (2015) no. 2: 281–309.

150　JUSTICE AND CIVIL LAW

on the other hand, always involves an unjust violation of one's obligations—or so I will argue.

Only superiors can issue laws and thereby restrict subjects' liberty. Laws take the form of commands by a superior. 'Law, properly is the word of him, that by right hath command over others' (L 15.41). This claim has invited the misunderstanding that Hobbes has a command theory of law.[19] Command theorists hold that law obliges because and insofar as disobedience is punishable. As Austin wrote: 'Being liable to evil from you if I comply not with a wish which you signify, I am *bound* or *obliged* by your command, or I lie under a *duty* to obey it'.[20] Sanctions for non-compliance do not render law obligatory for Hobbes. Rather, a subject's prior obligation to obey the commander does so. 'Law in generall, is not Counsell, but Command; nor a Command of any man; but only of him, whose Command is addressed to one formerly obliged to obey him' (L 26.2; also DCv 14.1; L 42.36). Not every command qualifies as law: 'it is not the Imperative manner of speaking, but an absolute Subjection to a Person, that maketh his Precepts Laws' (L 42.104). Only commands addressed to persons previously bound to obey the commander are law and obligatory to them. This is so because 'a law obligeth no otherwise than by virtue of some covenant made by him who is subject thereunto' (EL 29.2).[21] Hence the assertion that 'the legislative power is from the assent of the subjects' (EW 5: 179; also L 42.123). While binding in virtue of subjects' prior obligation of simple obedience, any newly promulgated law further diminishes freedom by directly or indirectly prohibiting subjects from doing certain things. Thus, a law permitting subjects to trade consists in legal obligations imposed upon everyone else not to obstruct such trading (§5.4). In short, civil law *consists* in legal obligations imposed by the sovereign, diminishing citizens' liberties; yet civil law *is obligatory* in virtue of a prior contractual obligation to obey the commander.

Why do laws take the form of commands? Having previously covenanted to *simply* obey the lawgiver henceforth (i.e. irrespective of prescribed content), citizens are not owed any justification by the sovereign for new legislation imposed upon them. His mere say-so suffices. 'COMMAND is, where a man saith, *Doe this*, or *Doe not this*, without expecting other reason than the Will of him that sayes it' (L 25.2; also EL 29.2; DCv 14.1; EW 4: 343). Law and command differ in this respect from counsel. Counsel appeals to the addressee's interests and should be heeded

---

[19] E.g. Thomas Pink, 'Thomas Hobbes and the Ethics of Freedom', *Inquiry* 54 (2011) no. 5: 559; Ross Harrison, 'The Equal Extent of Natural and Civil Law' in David Dyzenhaus and Thomas Poole (eds), *Hobbes and the Law* (Cambridge, 2012) 25. Goldsmith, 'Hobbes on Law', 275–277, interprets Hobbes as a non-Austinian command theorist. For a correction, see Mark Murphy, 'Hobbes (and Austin, and Aquinas) on Law as Command of the Sovereign' in A.P. Martinich and Kinch Hoekstra (eds), *The Oxford Handbook of Hobbes* (Oxford, 2016) 339–358.

[20] Austin, *The Province of Jurisprudence*, 14. Hart, *The Concept of Law*, 6–7, 18–19, 82–85, objects that the command theory of law cannot adequately distinguish legislators from gunmen.

[21] On the distinction between law and covenant, see EL 29.2; DCv 14.2: 'We are obliged by an *agreement*; we are kept to our obligation by a *law*. An *agreement* obligates of itself; a *law* keeps one to one's obligations in virtue of the universal *agreement* to render obedience'.

CIVIL LAW AND SOVEREIGN PREROGATIVE   151

for this reason alone (L 25.3). By contrast, 'he that Commandeth, pretendeth thereby <u>his own Benefit</u>' (L 25.2; also L 42.101). Incidentally, this gloss on commands (and consequently on laws) jars with the received Aristotelian distinction between political and despotic rule. For Aristotle, government is despotic if it attends only to the ruler's interests. The rule of slaveholders over enslaved subjects is 'exercised primarily with a view to the interest of the master' and therefore despotic.[22] By contrast, government over free people is exercised 'essentially for the good of the governed'.[23] So is (male) rule over spouses and offspring. Hobbes, by contrast, defines civil law as binding commands issued by the sovereign *for his own benefit*. This definition holds true even if subjects have reason to obey the civil law only insofar as doing so is in *their* overall interest.[24]

Above, I suggested that any violation of a law proper (i.e. of civil law) involves a violation of pre-existing contractual obligations to obey. How to reconcile this claim with the inalienable natural rights of citizens? *Leviathan* includes a lengthy list of commands which citizens may disobey 'without injustice'.[25] All are commands which they could not rationally have promised to follow. Citizens have retained their natural right to resist sovereign commands to kill, maim, and accuse themselves, as well as commands to perform dangerous or dishonourable actions unnecessary for peace and public security (L 21.10–17). Following Murphy, I argue that any sovereign decree contravening a citizen's retained natural rights is *no law to* that citizen.[26] Only those sovereign commands which subjects had previously promised to obey can be law to them. 'And it is certain that men are obliged to the observation of all positive precepts, though with the loss of their lives, unless the right that a man hath to preserve himself make it, in case of a just fear, <u>to be no law</u>' (EW 5: 291). The same precept may be law to others, differently positioned such that the command does not infringe their inalienable rights. Civil laws need not be universal in scope—they can address only a subset of subjects (L 26.4). Court rulings, for instance, are law only to plaintiffs: 'every particular Judgement, is a Law to him, whose case is Judged' (L 26.38; also L 26.23). Laws being essentially fetters, commands that do not curtail a citizen's liberty are no law to her. Citizens who, without fault, are incapable of observing a particular law are fully excused from doing so. 'And to speak properly, that Law is no Law to him' (L 26.12). For that 'which totally Excuseth a Fact, and takes away from it the nature of a Crime, can

---

[22] Aristotle, *Politics*, 1278b34–35.

[23] Aristotle, *Politics*, 1278b40–1279a1. On the early modern uptake of Aristotle's distinction between political and despotic rule, see J.S. Maloy, 'The Aristotelianism of Locke's Politics', *Journal of the History of Ideas* 70 (2009) no. 2: 235–257.

[24] For further analysis, see Luciano Venezia, 'Hobbes' Two Accounts of Law and the Structure of Reasons for Political Obedience', *European Journal of Political Theory* 13 (2014) no. 3: 282–298.

[25] Hobbes was slow to endorse extensive individual rights of resistance. *Elements* had still maintained 'that the command of him, whose command is a law in one thing, is a law in every thing. For seeing a man is obliged to obedience before what he is to do be known, he is obliged to obey in general, that is to say, in every thing' (EL 29.3).

[26] Murphy, 'Was Hobbes a Legal Positivist?', 849–854.

152   JUSTICE AND CIVIL LAW

be none but that, which at the same time, taketh away the obligation of the Law' (L 27.22).

Incidentally, convicts' retained right to resist their own punishment provides another reason why Hobbes had to revise the distinction between distributive and penal laws in *Leviathan* (§5.4). Recall that *De Cive* had portrayed distributive and penal law as two '*parts* of the same law' (DCv 14.7). In *Leviathan*, the two become distinct *kinds* of laws: 'of Humane positive lawes, some are *Distributive*, some *Penal*'. Penal laws, we read, 'are those, which declare, what Penalty shall be inflicted on those that violate the Law; and speak to the Ministers and Officers ordained for execution' (L 26.38). Speak to them 'only', adds the Latin *Leviathan* (LL 26.38). To the person convicted, penal laws cannot possibly be law. After all, inalienable rights to self-preservation entitle all to forcibly resist even justly imposed punishment (L 14.29; L 21.12; L 28.2).[27]

For Hobbes, I have argued, a sovereign order lacks the status of law to a subject if that same subject may rightfully disobey it. That startling thesis holds true conceptually, in virtue of the meanings of law ('freedom-depriving commands from a superior') and right ('liberty of action'). Justice enjoins subjects to obey any valid law issued to them because they had previously covenanted to do so, and because breaking faith is unjust. The upshot is significant: Hobbes's conception of civil law is itself already incompatible with legal positivism.[28] His insistence that *all* laws proper are posited by the civil sovereign is often mistaken for endorsement of the Sources Thesis ('the existence and content of law depends on and can be ascertained by social facts'). In fact, the question 'which commands are law?' cannot be resolved without resort to moral argument. Whether a particular order is law to its addressee is determined by Hobbes's contractarian theory of political obligation. That theory determines which sovereign commands can be disobeyed without injustice and which ones subjects are obligated to obey. In sum, the *pactum generale obedientiae* sets the confines of civil law.

Though determining which sovereign commands count as law to individual subjects, the original covenant does not delimit what the sovereign may permissibly do or command. His authority extends well beyond the rule of law (§10.3). In his *Verse Life*, Hobbes boasted of having always defended the 'Kings Prerogative' (VL 260). The royal prerogative is a legal power which English monarchs possessed until 1689. It entitled them to rule arbitrarily, 'extra et contra legem' (up to a point).[29] According to Hobbes, the sovereign may legitimately issue binding

---

[27] Green denies that civil law defines what justice requires of citizens, on the grounds that it then 'would be unjust to run away when the sovereign commands me to stop and accept my punishment'— contrary to the inalienable right to resist punishment. The objection dissolves once we realize that penal sentences cannot possibly be law to subjects. Michael J. Green, 'Justice and Law in Hobbes', *Oxford Studies in Early Modern Philosophy* 1 (2003) 128.

[28] As pointed out by Murphy, 'Was Hobbes a Legal Positivist?'.

[29] Pasquale Pasquino, 'Locke on King's Prerogative', *Political Theory* 26 (1998) no. 2: 205. Also Thomas Poole, 'Hobbes on Law and Prerogative' in David Dyzenhaus and Thomas Poole (eds), *Hobbes and the Law* (Cambridge, 2012) 85–90. We should thus reject the claim by David Dyzenhaus, 'Hobbes

commands 'by force of a former Law' as well as 'by virtue of his Power' (L 21.19). Both laws and extra-legal orders have been authorized by each citizen singly: 'all that is done by him in Vertue of his Power, is done by the Authority of every Subject' (L 21.19). Subjects have 'authorised all his actions' (L 24.7)—'without exception' (L 21.10) and 'without stint' (L 16.14). '[W]hatsoever is commanded by the Soveraign Power, is as to the Subject (though not so allwayes in the sight of God) justified by the Command; for of such command every Subject is the Author' (L 22.15). Citizens have individually authorized even those sovereign commands which are no law to them and which they may rightfully resist. Thus, convicted criminals may justly resist their punishment, even though all punishment has 'for Author, the person condemned' (L 28.6; also L 20.13). Hobbes could coherently say this because authorization involves no diminishment of liberty: 'in these words, *I Authorise, or take upon me, all his actions*; in which there is no restriction at all, of his own former naturall Liberty: For by allowing him to *kill me*, I am not bound to kill my selfe when he commands me' (L 21.14; also L 14.29; LL 21.7).[30]

In sum, civil law conceptually presupposes a prior obligation to obey the lawgiver. Only contractual alienation of right can create that obligation. Authorization justifies whatever the sovereign commands to subjects (L 22.15). Yet it does not render these commands obligatory ('law'). Section 6.6 examines in depth how Hobbes invoked individual authorization to morally vindicate the sovereign within and beyond the rule of law. To anticipate, nothing the sovereign says or does, whether through law or otherwise, can be unjust to citizens. But first I will explain in what sense civil laws are the sole authoritative rules of just and unjust, right and wrong, in the actions of citizens—a thesis dubbed *Sole Measure*.

6.3 CIVIL LAW AS THE PUBLIC MEASURE OF JUSTICE OF ACTIONS

Clashing private value judgements figure centrally in Hobbes's explanation of the causes of conflict inside and outside the state.[31] Disagreements over good and evil reliably lead to 'Disputes, Controversies, and at last War' (L 15.40). Humans make

on the International Rule of Law', *Ethics and International Affairs* 28 (2014) no. 1: 55: 'Submission to sovereignty is thus ultimately submission to the rule of law'. Also David Dyzenhaus, 'Thomas Hobbes and the Rule by Law Tradition' in Jens Meierhenrich and Martin Loughlin (eds), *The Cambridge Companion to the Rule of Law* (Cambridge, 2021) 261–277.

[30] David Heyd altogether overlooks the role of individual authorization in justifying the sovereign's power to (capitally) punish wrongdoers in 'Hobbes on Capital Punishment', *History of Philosophy Quarterly* 8 (1991) no. 2: 119–134.

[31] S.A. Lloyd, *Ideals as Interests in Hobbes's Leviathan* (Cambridge, 1992) 260–265; Richard Tuck, 'Hobbes's Moral Philosophy' in Tom Sorell (ed), *The Cambridge Companion to Hobbes* (Cambridge, 1996) 184–193; Arash Abizadeh, 'Hobbes on the Causes of War: A Disagreement Theory', *American Political Science Review* 105 (2011) no. 2: 298–315.

154   JUSTICE AND CIVIL LAW

evaluative and normative judgements according to their shifting desires and aversions. Since desires differ both inter- and intra-personally (i.e. over time), humans are prone to disagree about almost everything. Amidst pervasive moral disagreement, peace remains out of reach as long as people follow their own judgements about right and wrong. Indeed, the state of nature *is* the condition in which humans, born free and equal, are entitled to follow their private value judgements: 'so long a man is in the condition of meer Nature, (which is a condition of War,) as private Appetite is the measure of Good, and Evill' (L 15.40; also DCv 3.31). Enduring peace and social stability requires people to forgo their natural right of self-government.

No common measure of right and wrong is found in nature itself (EL 29.8; L 5.3) (§3.4). To forestall hazardous conflict, 'men disagreeing shall by consent set up' a common 'Arbitrator or Judge' (L 6.7). His legislative will constitutes a common rule of good and evil within the state. Civil law replaces private appetite to become the 'common measure of all things that might fall in controversy' (EL 29.8). The common belief that judgements of good and evil belong to citizens 'without question' disposes them to rebellion (DCv 12.1; also DCv P.5; L 29.6; L 46.11). Anyone proudly laying claim to knowledge of good and evil risks inciting civil war.[32]

> all disputes arise from the fact that men's opinions differ about *mine* and *yours*, *just* and *unjust*, *useful* and *useless*, *good* and *bad*, *honourable* and *dishonourable*, and so on, and everyone decides them by his own judgement. Consequently, it is the responsibility of the same *Sovereign power* to come up with rules or measures that will be common to all, and to publish them openly, so that each man may know by them what he should call *his own* and what *another's*, what he should call *just* and *unjust*, *honourable* and *dishonourable*, *good* and *bad*; in summary, what he should *do* and what he should *avoid doing* in social life. These rules or measures are normally called the *civil laws*. (DCv 6.9)

For the sake of peace, citizens have obligated themselves to accept the civil laws as the sole authoritative measure of justice and injustice of actions. Call this doctrine *Sole Measure*:

> there are no authentic doctrines of just and unjust, good and evil, except the laws established in each commonwealth ... questions as to whether an action will be

---

[32] Adam and Eve were cast out of paradise for eating from the fruit of the Tree of Knowledge—a metaphor, in Hobbes's view, for 'the Cognisance or Judicature of *Good* and *Evill*' according to private judgement. Having 'acquired no new ability to distinguish between them aright', their descendants are compelled to institute a sovereign to make his sentence the common evaluative standard (L 20.17; also DCv 12.1; DCv 16.2; L 35.3).

just or unjust, good or evil, should be addressed only to those mandated by the commonwealth to interpret its laws. (DCv P.8)[33]

We can distinguish two different versions of *Sole Measure*, each with independent textual support. Some passages portray civil law as the public measure of justice since its laws first spell out which actions citizens are to perform or omit on pain of violating the original covenant (which justice dictates subjects to keep). On this version, civil law is logically prior to justice of actions. Other passages, found predominantly in *Elements* and *De Cive*, suggest the opposite. Both texts subsume 'just' and 'unjust', 'right' and 'wrong', among the terms liable to controversy (EL 29.8; DCv P.8; DCv 6.9; L 46.11). They have the sovereign adjudicate the meaning of 'just' and 'unjust' in the same way as he settles the meaning of weight measures ('quart', 'pound'—EL 29.8). This tacitly assumes that individuals can have conflicts over what is just and unjust prior to the introduction of civil law. Indeed, civil law serves in part to forestall such conflicts.

The last version is most prominent in *Elements*. Some government decrees, Hobbes conceded there, are 'unjust' for 'contrary to the law of God or nature' (EL 21.4; also EL 28.1). However, the sovereign did not 'covenant so much, as that his sentence shall be just'. Such a promise would call for a further act of judgement, to decide on the justice of the decision. And 'that were to make the parties judges of the sentence, whereby the controversy would remain undecided' (EL 17.7). Peace requires appointing an arbitrator to resolve all disputes, making his decision the final word on what is just and unjust, right and wrong. From *Leviathan* onwards, Hobbes settled on the term 'iniquitous' to capture general moral wrongdoing.[34] *Elements* still called transgressions of natural and divine law 'unjust'. For this reason, it does not contain *No Law Unjust*. *Elements* did already distinguish the wider sense of injustice as immorality, from injustice as injury/breach of covenant. The sovereign can be guilty of the former but not of the latter. 'For first, injury (by the definition [in EL 16.2]) is breach of covenant; but covenants . . . there passed none from the [sovereign] to any private man; and consequently it (viz. the people) can do him no injury' (EL 21.3). In *Elements*, civil laws can be unjust only by dint of violating natural law generally, not by breaking faith and wronging citizens.

I contend that Hobbes enduringly endorsed *both* versions of *Sole Measure*. The two versions capture two distinct roles of the sovereign. Qua lawmaker, the sovereign declares which actions shall henceforth be just and which unjust (i.e. civil liberties and felonies). This makes legislators 'not onely <u>Declarers</u>, but also <u>Makers</u> of the justice, and injustice of actions; there being nothing in mens Manners that

---

[33] Also EL 29.8; DCv 6.9; DCv 12.1; DCv 17.10, 14; L 18.10; L 20.16; L 26.3–4; L 29.6; L 42.96; L 46.11; L 46.32; DH 13.9; DPS 30; EW 4: 369–370.

[34] Daniel Eggers, 'Injury, Injustice, Iniquity: The Evolution of Hobbes's Theory of Justice', *Intellectual History Review* 24 (2014) no. 2: 178.

156   JUSTICE AND CIVIL LAW

makes them righteous, or unrighteous, but their conformity with the Law of the Soveraign' (L 42.96).[35] Qua highest judge, the sovereign authoritatively determines post hoc which actions citizens, charged with crime, were duty-bound to undertake or omit. Both civil laws and judicial rulings can be morally flawed ('iniquitous'). For instance, they can distribute property unfairly; deny the accused a fair trial; or knowingly condemn someone for a crime they didn't commit (L 24.7; L 26.24).

Citizens lack access to an independent authoritative standard to assess whether the sovereign's verdicts are morally sound. It does not follow that either civil laws or court rulings are *true* declarations of the meanings of controversial terms.[36] Authoritative adjudication does not establish truth. 'For the interpretation, though it be made by just authority, must not therefore always be true' (EW 4: 340; also LL 26.21; EW 7: 351). Several scholars overlook this *non sequitur*. Peters, for instance, attributes a 'conventionist' and 'bizarre and authoritarian theory of truth' to Hobbes in matters politic.[37] On the conventionalist interpretation of Hobbes on justice, '"just" has no inherent meaning apart from the sovereign's stipulations not only because that is convenient and peace-promoting, but also because it is true' (§1.1).[38] Hobbes's argument about the rationality to consent to arbitration is perfectly sound, however, without adding the 'bizarre' assumption that in adjudicating conflicts judges establish the true meaning of contested terms.

Commentators can seek to buttress the conventionalist interpretation in two ways. Either the sovereign is infallible or arbitration is a truth-maker. The first claim is both implausible and textually unsupported. Just before arguing for the need to install a sovereign arbitrator, Hobbes portrays human reasoning as inherently fallible. 'Reason it selfe is always Right Reason, as well as Arithmetique is a certain and infallible Art: But no one mans Reason, nor the Reason of any one number of men, makes the certaintie' (L 5.3). Arbitration is a truth-maker when a term's true meaning simply is what it is authoritatively stipulated to mean. Some passages about justice appear to support this view:

> *Just* and *unjust* did not exist until commands were given; hence their nature is relative to a command; and every action in its own nature is indifferent. What is *just* or *unjust* derives from the right of the ruler. Legitimate kings therefore make [faciunt] what they order just by ordering it, and make what they forbid unjust by forbidding it. (DCv 12.1)

---

[35] Also DCv 17.10; EW 4: 252–253; DH 10.5; DPS 31.

[36] As duly pointed out by James Bernard Murphy, *The Philosophy of Positive Law: Foundations of Jurisprudence* (New Haven, 2005) 117–142.

[37] Richard Peters, *Hobbes* (Harmondsworth, 1967) 57, also 54–58.

[38] Jeremy Waldron, 'Hobbes and the Principle of Publicity', *Pacific Philosophical Quarterly* 82 (2001) no. 3/4: 467. Also J.W.N. Watkins, *Hobbes's System of Ideas* (London, 1973) 109–114; Pettit, *Made with Words*, 127, 131, 152.

Commenting on these passages, Watkins likens Hobbes's sovereign to a 'Humpty-Dumpty . . . who determines what moral words shall denote'.[39] Consequently, 'it is not only iniquitous but *absurd* to dispute the rightness of the sovereign's commandments'.[40]

This seriously misconstrues Hobbes's position. Far from claiming that the sovereign, like some speaking egg, stipulates the true meaning of contested terms, Hobbes held that justice has a settled definition to begin with. Sovereign lawgivers are 'Makers of the justice, and injustice of actions' for citizens in virtue of that definition. When applied to their actions, justice *means* conduct in conformity with law: 'a just action . . . is that which is not against the law' (DPS 36). For subjects, just actions are by definition law-abiding; unjust ones by definition crimes. 'Lawes are the Rules of Just, and Unjust; nothing being reputed Unjust, that is not contrary to some Law' (L 26.4). 'What is unjust, but the transgression of a law?' (EW 4: 369).[41] Observe that citizens' law-abiding conduct is 'just' *derivatively*, in virtue of being performances of the original covenant of obedience. In turn, 'every crime is unjust' by dint of breaching that pact (LL 27.15) (§3.6).

6.4 ARE ALL CIVIL LAWS JUST?

Hobbes is frequently said to espouse *All Laws Just*. Take May: 'all laws, properly propounded, are just'.[42] 'Although all laws are just', Hampton avers, 'not all laws are good'.[43] On Dyzenhaus's reading, 'all the sovereign's laws are by definition just'.[44] Holden concurs: 'all laws are just simply in virtue of being laws'.[45] And Bobbio writes: 'the law is just merely because it is the law'.[46] Bobbio believes that *All Laws Just* follows from *Sole Measure*: 'it pertains to the sovereign to establish what is good and what is evil, so that what is commanded is just, and what is prohibited is unjust. Therefore the law is just'.[47] The inference is invalid. Declaring some action

---

[39] Watkins, *Hobbes's System of Ideas*, 110. Also Terence Ball, 'Hobbes's Linguistic Turn' in idem (ed), *Reappraising Political Theory* (Oxford, 1995) 94, 105. F.G. Whelan argues that Hobbes's legal theory is shaped by linguistic conventionalism in 'Language and Its Abuses in Hobbes' Political Philosophy', *American Political Science Review* 75 (1981) no. 1: 59–75.

[40] Watkins, *Hobbes's System of Ideas*, 111, also 3, 129–130. Also Ball, 'Hobbes's Linguistic Turn', 102. Thomas Holden criticizes such 'Humpty Dumpty semantics' in 'Hobbes on the Function of Evaluative Speech', *Canadian Journal of Philosophy* 46 (2016) no. 1: 138, also 128–129.

[41] Also L 27.21; L 46.31; EW 1: 74; DPS 31.

[42] May, *Limiting Leviathan*, 82, also 74–75.

[43] Hampton, *Hobbes and the Social Contract Tradition*, 241.

[44] Dyzenhaus, *The Long Arc*, 140; also Dyzenhaus, 'Authority of Law', 206.

[45] Holden, 'Function of Evaluative Speech', 129.

[46] Norberto Bobbio, *Thomas Hobbes and the Natural Law Tradition*, trans. Daniela Gobetti (Chicago, 1993) 161.

[47] Bobbio, *Thomas Hobbes*, 164. On Bobbio's reading, all crimes are what jurists call *mala prohibita*: 'the conduct proscribed is not wrongful prior to or independent of the law that defined it as criminal'. Douglas Husak, 'Malum Prohibitum and Retributivism' in idem, *The Philosophy of Criminal Law: Selected Essays* (Oxford, 2010) 411.

158 JUSTICE AND CIVIL LAW

A to be just does not make the declaration itself just. Correctly declaring *A* to be just at most makes it a good declaration. Even legally requiring citizens to call all statutes 'just' would not make those laws themselves so. *Sole Measure*, I conclude, does not entail *All Laws Just*.[48]

Commentators more typically treat *All Laws Just* as the logical inverse of *No Law Unjust*. Hobbes regularly claimed that civil laws cannot be unjust.[49] It has generally gone unnoticed that he rarely affirmed the apparent converse: that every civil law is just. In fact, he tacitly spurned *All Laws Just* in the *Dialogue*. There, Hobbes's spokesperson opposed Edward Coke's view that 'Law is a just Statute' on the grounds 'that it supposes that a Statute made by the Sovereign Power of a Nation may be unjust' (DPS 31). *Leviathan* makes the same point more succinctly: 'By a Good Law, I mean not a Just Law: for no Law can be Unjust' (L 30.20). If only just statutes are valid laws, Hobbes worried, then public officers and citizens will probe the moral quality of any sovereign decree to determine whether it is truly law. That would effectively reintroduce private judgements about right and wrong, inviting dispute and violent conflict. Notice that these seditious implications follow only if we assume that civil laws and statutes *can* fail to be just. Hobbes could have adopted Coke's definition while twisting its meaning: *whatever* the sovereign legislator commands to citizens is law and just. Why did he not do so? What stopped him from proclaiming *All Laws Just*?

As it happens, Hobbes unequivocally endorsed *All Laws Just* twice—both times in exchanges with Bramhall. 'Of Liberty and Necessity' from 1645 remarks: 'no *law* can possibly be *unjust*, inasmuch as every man maketh, by his consent, the law he is bound to keep, and which consequently <u>must be just</u>, unless a man can be unjust to himself' (EW 4: 252–253/EW 5: 151). Hobbes then adds, oddly: 'To make the *law*, is therefore to make a *cause* of *justice*, and to *necessitate* justice; and consequently, it is no injustice to make such a law' (EW 4: 253/EW 5: 152). Commenting on these passages a decade later, he concludes: 'But I have shown that <u>all laws are just, as laws</u>, and therefore not to be accused of injustice by those that owe subjection to them; and a just law is always justly executed' (EW 5: 182). What are we to make of these passages, the only two expressly upholding *All Laws Just*?

The last suggestion—that legislators fulfil justice by providing the norms that enable citizens to act justly—lacks theoretical support. Why would creating 'a *cause* of *justice*' render law-giving itself just? To citizens, congruence with civil law is what 'causes' their actions to be just, while deviance from the same standard

---

[48] Some may object that, civil law being the measure of justice, civil law is just when it conforms to itself (whatever that means). Some *p* (measures for *q*) are self-referentially *q*. Think of the prototype metre bar in Sèvres, France: that bar is exactly a metre long (as it itself attests). In reply: civil laws cannot be self-referentially just on Hobbes's conception of justice. Civil laws are the measure of justice of actions of citizens only, spelling out which actions they have covenanted to perform or omit. This measure is inapplicable to the commands of the non-covenanting sovereign legislator.

[49] E.g. EW 5: 151; EW 5: 175; EW 5: 234.

makes their actions unjust crimes (as per *Sole Measure*) (DH 10.5). That doctrine, I have argued, does not however entail *All Laws Just*. What about the remark about consent? Does prior consent to government make civil law just? Bramhall denied this. He accused Hobbes of conflating injustice with injury: 'if this [argument from consent] were true, it would preserve [laws], if not from being unjust, yet from being injurious' (EW 5: 158). The objection has some force. To see why, consider an interpretive puzzle raised by May.

Hobbes, May maintains, had the conceptual resources to proclaim all the sovereign's commands to be just. Actions do not need to have positive moral value to qualify as just. Not being unjust suffices: 'when a Covenant is made, then to break it is *Unjust* . . . And whatsoever is not Unjust, is *Just*' (L 15.2; also LL 15.2). Add the No Pact Argument: as sovereigns on their part never covenant with citizens, so they cannot unjustly break pact with them either. 'Since whatsoever is not unjust is just, it would seem that all the sovereign's actions, no matter how unfair, should always be called just. But Hobbes does not make this claim.'[50] What stopped him? May's own explanation has its shortcomings. Justice and injustice, he submits, presuppose subjection to 'some coercive power'. The sovereign is by definition free from human subjection. His actions are therefore not 'justice-apt'. This explanation misconstrues why justice and injustice are inapplicable beyond the state. Prevailing insecurity explains why all may permissibly forgo practising the natural law duty to perform covenants (§7.1). Coercive power, in turn, is merely an enabling condition for security. In conditions of peace, when we cannot reasonably cite danger as a pretext for shelving covenants, the sovereign *is* duty-bound to keep any covenants made on pain of injustice—should he have made any. *Contra* May, norms of justice in principle also apply to persons not subject to coercive power. Whence, then, Hobbes's reluctance to affirm *All Laws Just*?

My alternative explanation is speculative. The nub, I believe, lies in *Leviathan*'s redefinition of justice. Recall that in *Elements* and *De Cive* '*Just* means the same as done with right [*jure factum*], and *Unjust*, done without right [*Injuriâ*]' (DCv 3.5; also EL 16.4) (§2.2). Every action without right is an unjust breach of covenant because each person by nature has right to everything (EL 16.2; DCv 3.3). *Leviathan*, by contrast, defines commutative justice directly in terms of keeping faith: 'the nature of Justice, consisteth in keeping of valid Covenants' (L 15.3). On that mature definition, 'just action' is no longer identical to 'no injury'. Only actions that perform valid covenants are now just.[51] *Leviathan* thus (intentionally) introduces an asymmetry. No longer is every action done with right *ipso facto* just—even if every action without right remains unjust. If only instances of covenant-keeping are

---

[50] Larry May, 'Hobbes on Equity and Justice' in Craig Walton and Paul Johnston (eds), *Hobbes's Science of Natural Justice* (Dordrecht, 1987) 243; also May, *Limiting Leviathan*, 70.

[51] Glossing L 15.2, Brian Barry differentiates between the same two senses of 'just action' (covenant-keeping vs. action with right) in 'Warrender and His Critics', *Philosophy* 43 (1968) no. 164: 119–120.

160   JUSTICE AND CIVIL LAW

just, then this explains why Hobbes did not proclaim the sovereign's commands so. It explains why his vindication was negative (ruling out sovereign injustice) rather than positive (the sovereign as paragon of justice). Hobbes safeguarded the sovereign from accusations of injustice by insisting that he had made no covenants with anyone. That very claim made it impossible for civil law-making to be just (i.e. instances of covenant-keeping). Bramhall was thus on to something. On *Leviathan*'s novel definition of commutative justice, subjects' consent precludes civil laws from being injurious (to them). It does not render them just—instances of covenant-keeping by the legislator. Ditto for citizens' unconditional authorization. Authorization ensures that whatever the sovereign does is done in name and by right of every subject. Again, being done with right no longer renders actions just in *Leviathan*.

The phrase 'whatsoever is not Unjust, is *Just*' clashes with this reconstruction (L 15.2). Two reasons favour discounting the passage as a fluke, inconsistent with Hobbes's considered views on justice in *Leviathan*. First, if any not-unjust action is just, then citizens act *justly* when exercising their retained natural rights to resist state orders to kill, wound, or accuse themselves. Hobbes clearly had reason to avoid that riotous adjective. By redefining justice as performances of covenant, he ensured that justified acts of civic resistance no longer qualify as just. Second, if any action with right is just, then Hobbes contradicted himself when declaring from *Leviathan* onwards that justice and injustice are non-existent beyond the state (L 13.13; L 15.3; LL 27.3; DH 10.5). After all, before the natural right to everything is renounced, *whatsoever* is done is done with right (and thus justly). In sum, *Leviathan*'s introduction of both the state-dependency of justice and injustice and the 'true liberties of subjects' relied on discarding the older view that any action with right is just. It mandated redefining justice (§7.2). On *Leviathan*'s asymmetrical conceptualizations of justice and injustice, I propose, *No Law Unjust* does not entail *All Laws Just*. Further argument is required to establish that last doctrine.

My contention is that Hobbes did eventually develop sufficient theoretical resources to establish *All Laws Just*. So far my analysis has centred on commutative justice, commanding people to perform their covenants (L 15.14). From *Leviathan* onwards, Hobbes is entitled to say that (almost) all civil laws are just, and necessarily so, in virtue of another principle of justice—distributive justice. Recall that *Leviathan* equates distributive justice as equity with the Roman law definition of justice ('the constant will to give each their own') (§4.5; §5.5). That redefinition, I have argued, was accompanied by a reconceptualization of merit in distributive justice (§4.4). In *Leviathan*, merit is no longer a standard of worth tracked by distributive norms. Rather, distributive civil laws first create merit by instituting exclusive personal rights. These twin reconceptualizations permit the claim that all distributive laws are necessarily just, by dint of giving each their due. By bringing into existence the very rights justice orders respect for, distributive laws fulfil justice: 'to distribute to every man his own . . . is indeed Just Distribution' (L 15.15).

'This distribution is Justice, and this properly is the same which we say is ones own' (DPS 10).

It may seem that this argument for *All Laws Just*, grounded in distributive justice, does not apply to the second category of civil law: penal laws. The very distinction between the two seems to imply that penal laws do *not* distribute to each their own. The objection is too quick. The reason Hobbes divorces distributive from penal laws, I have suggested, lies in the forged conceptual tie between law and obligation. Since we cannot take on the obligation to punish ourselves, penal laws cannot be law 'to the Delinquent, (who cannot be supposed will faithfully punish himselfe)'. To count as law, penal laws must be addressed to some other party previously obligated to carry out these orders—namely, 'to publique Ministers appointed to see the Penalty executed' (L 26.38). By dictating to officials what punishments to inflict on malefactors, penal laws indirectly give the convicted their legal due. Not *all* penal laws are just, however. As §4.6 argued, various passages imply that legal sentences can be unjust by failing to give the accused what they deserve (punishment or absolution) (L 26.24). I conclude that Hobbes's subversive reinterpretation of the Roman law definition of justice does not entitle him to uphold *All Laws Just* without qualification. This may explain why he conspicuously failed to do so. Another possible explanation is that moralized definitions of law had historically been used to *restrict* sovereign authority: unjust legislative orders, it was held, are not valid law.[52] Hobbes, I surmise, stayed clear from *All Laws Just* to avoid the impression that justice and morality are conditions of legal validity—also because he roundly agreed that civil laws *can* be morally flawed.

6.5 CAN CIVIL LAWS CONTRADICT NATURAL LAW?

The sovereign—be it a single individual or a collective—is subject to natural law (and to natural law alone).[53] Supreme rulers assuredly can and do contravene natural law (i.e. the laws commanded by God through reason). *Elements* states that 'divers actions done by the people, may be unjust before God Almighty, as breaches of some of the laws of nature' (EL 21.3). While the sovereign 'can sin against natural laws' in sundry ways, such vices 'do not come under the strict and accurate signification of *wrong*'. For 'a *Wrong* is simply the violation of an agreement', and the sovereign made no binding agreements to anyone (DCv 7.14). As *Leviathan* puts it: 'It is true that they that have Soveraigne power, may commit Iniquity; but not Injustice, or Injury in the proper signification' (L 18.6). The sovereign act of issuing certain civil laws can be immoral as well. Laws 'ordained out of wantonnes, or cruelty, or envy, or for the pleasing of a favourite, or out of any other sinister

---

[52] E.g. Samuel Rutherford, *Lex, Rex: The Law and the Prince* (London, 1644) 254–255.
[53] L 29.9; L 30.30; LL 21.10; EW 4: 371; EW 5: 178; DPS 26, 39, 41.

162 JUSTICE AND CIVIL LAW

end ... the making of those laws was unjust' (EW 5: 178; also L 24.7).[54] Natural law forbids the sovereign from making laws out of vicious dispositions—dispositions at odds with its central moral command to 'seek peace, and follow it'. Think of a civil decree deliberately made to take vengeance on a romantic rival, or of a property law enacted to enrich favourites. Conversely, as natural law primarily binds in conscience, the act of making objectively immoral civil laws is justified in the eyes of God if sincerely done for the sake of peace.

A further question is whether civil laws *themselves* can be iniquitous or immoral (independent of the motives behind legislation). Can legally valid laws prescribe content contrary to natural law? Material contradictions arise when civil law commands what natural law forbids or vice versa. Various passages attest to this possibility. 'There may indeed in a Statute Law, made by Men be found Iniquity, but not Injustice' (DPS 31). The sovereign can interpret civil law iniquitously when adjudicating criminal or civil lawsuits: 'there is no Judge Subordinate, nor Soveraign, but may erre in a judgement of Equity' (L 26.24). Surely civil legislation can similarly misinterpret what natural law demands, for example by placing partial arbitrators in charge of conflict resolution or by requiring judges to disregard exonerating evidence. Perhaps, though, valid laws can be immoral only up to a point: fiendish inequity may be an invalidating condition. Some have argued that sovereign orders that negate the 'determinate content' of natural law cannot be legally valid.[55] Call this thesis *No Wicked Laws*. Think of a sovereign who, misled by flawed reasoning about what promotes international peace, issues in good faith a civil law ordering that all ambassadors of peace must be killed—a patent violation of *Leviathan*'s fifteenth law of nature (L 15.29).[56] Hobbes's own example comes from Coke. Coke had advocated confiscating goods of in absentia acquitted people who had fled the country in fear of arrest. That law, Hobbes claims, flatly opposes the natural law of equity—and yet it legally binds plaintiffs (L 26.24; DPS 177–178).

No Wicked Laws is not without textual support. We read that 'whatsoever is not against the Law of Nature, may be made Law in the name of them that have the Soveraign Power' (L 26.40). The line conversationally implies that orders contradicting natural law cannot be made law to subjects. *De Cive* considerably weakens that clause. It all but rules out the possibility of immoral civil laws: 'no civil law can be contrary to natural law (except a law which has been framed as a blasphemy against God; for in relation to Him commonwealths themselves are not *sui juris*,

---

[54] On sovereign moral wrongdoing, see EL 28.1; DCv 6.13n; DCv 7.14; DCv 15.18; L 18.6; L 21.7; L 22.15; L 24.7; EW 5: 178.

[55] David Dyzenhaus, 'Hobbes and the Legitimacy of Law', *Law and Philosophy* 20 (2001) no. 5: 479. Dyzenhaus has since amended his position. He now holds that the sovereign 'may explicitly override a law of nature', for instance by ordering 'that all mediators should be killed on sight' or 'that judges should act partially'. Dyzenhaus, *The Long Arc*, 136–137.

[56] An example taken from Murphy, 'Was Hobbes a Legal Positivist?', 857.

and are not said to make laws)' (DCv 14.10). Its supporting argument runs as follows:

P1: 'natural law commands that all civil laws be observed in virtue of the natural law which forbids the violation of agreements'

P2: 'For when we are obligated to obey before we know what orders will be given, then we are obligated to obey universally and in all things'

P3: Citizens have promised to obey the sovereign in all things (*suppressed premise*)

C1: 'it follows that no civil law can be contrary to natural law'[57]

The passage does not specify what it means for a 'civil law to be contrary to natural law'. Logical analysis suggests the following. The collective promise of simple obedience cannot guarantee the moral perfection of civil law *itself*. It cannot morally justify a civil law ordering, say, the killing of mediators of peace—unless we think that citizens can through mutual agreement make right what is wrong by nature. What the argument rather establishes is that *from the viewpoint of citizens*, natural law duties cannot conflict with the sovereign's binding commands (on the assumption that the natural law prohibiting violating of faith overrides all other natural law duties in case of conflict).[58] Citizens have conclusive moral reason to follow the sovereign's verdicts on what is right and wrong, regardless of their accuracy. That interpretation leaves open that civil law itself can have content materially contradicting natural law. The same explains why vicious civil laws are legally valid and binding to subjects all the same, contrary to *No Wicked Laws*. Indeed, citizens sin by disobeying civil laws that they consider sinful—even if those laws truly are wicked (DCv 15.18; L 16.7; DH 15.2).[59]

Leviathan's Mutual Containment Thesis likewise reconciles the demands of natural law and civil law only from the viewpoint of citizens.[60] Natural law and civil law 'contain each other, and are of equall extent'. Hobbes offers a two-pronged argument in support. First, 'every subject in a Common-wealth, hath covenanted to obey the Civill Law ... And therefore Obedience to the Civill Law is part also of the Law of Nature' (L 26.8). The natural law of justice requires citizens to simply obey the civil law as promised, irrespective of the moral quality of its content. Second,

---

[57] DCv 14.10: 'virtute legis naturalis quae prohibit violari pacta, lex naturalis omnes leges civiles jubet observari. Nam ubi obligamur ad obedientiam antequam sciamus quid imperabitur, ibi universalitur et in omnibus obedire obligamur. Ex quo sequitur legem civilem nullam ... contra legem naturalem esse posse.'

[58] Lloyd, 'Hobbes's Self-Effacing Natural Law Theory', 295.

[59] S.A. Lloyd, 'Hobbes on the Duty Not to Act on Conscience' in Robin Douglass and Laurens van Apeldoorn (eds), *Hobbes on Politics and Religion* (Oxford, 2018) 256–272.

[60] A moniker coined by G.S. Kavka, *Hobbesian Moral and Political Philosophy* (Princeton, 1986) 248. For discussion, see Duke, 'Hobbes on Political Authority', 610–614; Perez Zagorin, *Hobbes and the Law of Nature* (Princeton, 2009) 52–54, 90; Luciano Venezia, *Hobbes on Legal Authority and Political Obligation* (New York, 2015) 84–91.

164 JUSTICE AND CIVIL LAW

'the Lawes of Nature ... are not properly Lawes' outside the state (§3.5). To become truly law, natural law requires authoritative specification and legal sanctions. Only the sovereign can append these.

> When a Common-wealth is once settled, then are they actually Lawes, and not before; as being then the commands of the Common-wealth; and therefore also Civill Lawes: For it is the Soveraign Power that obliges men to obey them ... to make them binding, there is need of the Ordinances of Sovereign Power, and Punishments to be ordained for such as shall break them; which Ordinances are therefore part of the Civill Law. The Law of Nature therefore is a part of the Civill Law in all Common-wealths of the world. (L 26.8; also DH 13.9)

In *every* state, *all* natural law precepts are elevated to the status of civil law through addition of legal sanctions, by tacit or express consent of the sovereign. As the 1643 *Anti-White* states: 'The whole of the natural law is contained within the civil, however. This is because the state demands not only that what has been written be performed *as* written, but also that what is unwritten be done as natural reason dictates' (AW 38.4; also L 43.22). What guarantees that every sovereign turns the entire moral law into civil law? Hobbes offers no justification for this sweeping claim.[61] Citizens' collective renunciation of their rights of war upon joining the commonwealth, it is true, makes the precepts of natural law a mandatory standard of action for all (§3.6). The same does not convert natural law into civil law. Only sovereign legislation can do so. 'For though it be naturally reasonable; yet it is by the Soveraigne Power that it is Law' (L 26.22). As it happens, legislating morality is not as practically demanding as it may seem. Civil promulgation is not needed, natural law being already knowable through reason (DCv 14.14; L 26.13). Moreover, the sovereign can add penal sanctions to natural law without spelling out specific punishments for their violation. Any law, written or unwritten, that prohibits conduct without stating a corresponding penalty renders those who act contrariwise 'subject to Arbitrary punishment' (L 27.7; also DCv 13.16; LL 27.9; L 28.10). Punishment is after all a universally known consequence of law-breaking. The unwritten laws of nature, I conclude, need no codification to become civil law.

The Mutual Containment Thesis does not entail *No Wicked Laws*. For the thesis does not rule out the possibility of legally valid laws prescribing deeply immoral content to citizens. Natural law is incorporated wholesale within every legal system. But it does not morally restrict what counts as civil law to subjects. Indeed, a natural law proscribing φ can exist within the same legal system alongside a legally valid decree prescribing φ. Hobbes made this surprising claim when scolding

---

[61] Hampton, *Hobbes and the Social Contract Tradition*, 244; Arash Abizadeh, *Hobbes and the Two Faces of Ethics* (Cambridge, 2018) 236–241.

Coke's confiscation law, authorizing seizure of the property of persons 'judicially acquitted of the *Felony*' in absentia (DPS 178).[62] Coke's norm, he wrote, is 'no Law of *England*' (L 26.24). The norm is not invalidated by its inequity, however. Rather, Hobbes challenged Coke's claim that the common law of England includes this confiscation law. The common law *is* natural law—and Coke's norm contradicts natural law. If, however, an English judge misinterprets natural/common law and orders confiscation of the goods of someone legally acquitted for having fled in fear of charges, then this 'perverted . . . Sentence of the Judge, <u>be a Law to the party pleading</u>'. As inequitable sentences set no legal precedent, 'it is no Law to any Judge, that shall succeed him in that Office' (L 26.24). Hobbes, I conclude, unreservedly accepted that court sentences materially contradicting natural law are binding law to plaintiffs. The same holds true for immoral civil laws. The sovereign sometimes issues bills 'which he ought not to command; and yet when they are commanded, <u>they are Laws</u>' (L 42.106; also L 22.15; DPS 31).

Civil law is hence not morally flawless for Hobbes. Both the act of legislation and civil law itself can contravene natural law. Immorality is no invalidating condition of civil law. Immoral civil laws are legally binding to subjects all the same. There is thus no necessary connection between civil law and *natural law*. There *is* a necessary connection between civil law and *injustice*, however. The next section analyses Hobbes's arguments for *No Law Unjust*. This doctrine should likewise be understood in a viewpoint-relative manner. Civil law cannot possibly be unjust or injurious in relation to citizens. Sovereign law-making can, however, contravene natural law and thereby injure God (L 21.7; L 22.15; EW 5: 178). Citizens have no standing to accuse the sovereign of immoral conduct or law-giving. As per *Sole Measure*, they are duty-bound to take his verdicts as authoritative and obligatory.

6.6 WHY AND IN WHAT SENSE CIVIL LAW CANNOT BE UNJUST

Hobbes advanced two layers of arguments in defence of *No Law Unjust*. The first-order arguments are negative: the sovereign cannot possibly wrong his citizens. The same holds true for his binding commands—the civil laws. The second-order argument seeks to show, positively, that whatever the sovereign does or legislates is done with right (i.e. by authority of his subjects). That second-order argument is the Authorization Argument, new to *Leviathan*. It replaces the earlier Consent Argument (a first-order argument).

First-order arguments for *No Law Unjust* trade on the claim that the sovereign has made no covenant with anyone, thereby forestalling the possibility of

---

[62] For discussion, see Dyzenhaus, 'Hobbes and the Rule by Law Tradition', 264–267; Dyzenhaus, *The Long Arc*, 114, 127–128.

166   JUSTICE AND CIVIL LAW

sovereign injustice (defined as breaking faith) (EL 21.3; DCv 7.14; L 18.3–4). The non-covenanting claim was controversial at the time. In their oath of coronation, English monarchs commonly promised to protect the people; to rule justly; and to uphold all fundamental laws. King James VI and I expressly affirmed 'my promise and Oath made at my Coronation concerning Justice, and the promise therein for maintenance of the Law of the Land'.[63] He added though, 'that it is better for a King to maintaine an unjust Decree, then [for subjects] to question every Decree and Judgement, after the giving of a sentence, for then Suites shall never have end'.[64] Hobbes offered no less than five counter-arguments to dismiss royal covenants with the people, perhaps in recognition of his heterodoxy.[65] None of his arguments, it bears stressing, denies that sovereigns are obliged to keep their covenants—testament that the principles of justice are the same for all (§1.2).[66]

The first argument avers that citizens are not entitled to complain about sovereign injustice. The argument is concessive. It grants premises *arguendo* which Hobbes in fact repudiated—namely, that the sovereign *had* made covenants with his subjects. This makes it the last line of defence.

Argument 1:

Subjects should not accuse the sovereign of suspected breach of covenant, as this leaves 'no Judge to decide the controversie: it returns therefore to the Sword again....contrary to the designe they had in the Institution' (L 18.4; also DCv 12.4).

Accusations of sovereign injustice effectively reintroduce private judgement about right and wrong—and thereby the disagreement, conflict, and war that the original covenant was meant to end. To grant citizens standing to hold the sovereign morally accountable thus defeats their original aim in establishing a commonwealth.

Argument 2:

The sovereign could not have made a single covenant with the people as such, since 'the people' did not exist before the sovereign united the multitude into a people by becoming their common representative (L 18.4; cf. DCv 7.9, 12).

---

[63] King James VI and I, *Political Writings*, ed. J.P. Sommerville (Cambridge, 1995) 208. By 'justice', the King explained, is meant *unicuique suum tribuere*; by 'law', the common law.

[64] King James VI and I, *Political Writings*, 218. King James VI and I regarded the coronation promises as 'binding', albeit unenforceable by arms or resistance (as per his doctrine of passive obedience). Sybil M. Jack, ' "A Pattern for a King's Inauguration": The Coronation of James I in England', *Parergon* 21 (2004) no. 2: 77–78, 87.

[65] Howard Warrender, *The Political Philosophy of Hobbes* (Oxford, 1957) 125–126: 'On this subject more than any other, perhaps, Hobbes's writings take on an appearance of a tract for the times'. On Hobbes's use of argumentative overdetermination, see Alison McQueen, 'Hobbes's Strategy of Convergence', *Hobbes Studies* 33 (2020) no. 2: 135–152.

[66] Contemporary political absolutists agreed that supreme rulers are bound to keep any contracts they make with their subjects—despite being above the law. E.g. Bodin, *Six Books*, 92–93; Grotius, *War and Peace*, 1.3.16.

Hobbes deemed the parliamentarian claim that rulers have entered a pact with the people incoherent. The people as such does not exist before government is set up. Instituting a common representative *is* what first turns the pre-political 'multitude' into a single person endowed with one will, capable of speaking and acting as one—via their representative (L 16.13; L 26.5).[67] *De Cive* conceives of the commonwealth as the union forged through joint submission of private wills to the single will of the sovereign (DCv 5.6–9). That thought informs the next argument:

Argument 3:
The sovereign cannot have any directed obligations owed to citizens as a conceptual matter, 'because the individual wills of citizens are contained in the will of the commonwealth in such a way that if the commonwealth wills to release itself from such an obligation, the citizens also will to do so, and it is accordingly free'. (DCv 12.4; also DCv 6.14)

This argument is cagey. The sovereign, Hobbes reasons, can indirectly release himself from any obligations owed to citizens. For as the sovereign 'absorbs into its own will the will of the citizen', *citizens* annul all obligations their leader owes them whenever *their sovereign* wills so (DCv 7.7).

Argument 4 ('Consent Argument'):
In the original covenant citizens have consented to let the sovereign do whatever he judges necessary to secure peace, promising to abide by his every judgement. One cannot injure the willing. *Ergo*, the sovereign cannot injure his citizens.

Argument 5 ('Authorization Argument'):
Even if, counterfactually, the sovereign had made 'so many severall Covenants as there be men, those Covenants after he hath the Soveraignty are voyd, because what act soever can be pretended by any one of them for breach thereof, is the act both of himself, and of all the rest, because done in the Person, and by the Right of every one of them in particular'. (L 18.4)

What follows is an analysis and comparison of the last two arguments.

The Consent Argument appeals to the Roman law maxim 'volenti non fit injuria'.[68] *Elements* faulted civic complaints of sovereign injustice as 'implying this contradiction, that whereas he first ratified the [sovereign's] acts in general, he

---

[67] Quentin Skinner, *From Humanism to Hobbes* (Cambridge, 2018) 211–215.

[68] *Digest* 39.3.9. Cf. Aristotle, *Nicomachean Ethics*, 5.11 (1138a). On the history of the maxim, see T. Ingman, 'A History of the Defence of Volenti Non Fit Injuria', *Juridical Review* 26 (1981): 1–29. Kant glossed the maxim yet differently, arguing that the law cannot wrong citizens insofar as it expresses 'the general united will of the people'. Immanuel Kant, *Practical Philosophy*, ed. M.J. Gregor (Cambridge, 1996) 457.

168 JUSTICE AND CIVIL LAW

now disalloweth some of them in particular. It is therefore said truly, volenti non
fit injuria'. To complain of a law you have ratified through consent is absurd: 'it is
against reason for the same man, both to do and complain' (EL 21.3). *De Cive* and
Leviathan gloss the formula differently. They invoke it to explain why any former
covenant between the ruler and particular citizens becomes void through the establishment of sovereignty. 'Whatsoever is done to a man, conformable to his own
Will signified to the doer, is no Injury to him'. Even if the action done to the *volenti*
is a breach of covenant, and thus an injury, the fact that the person undergoes the
action willingly tacitly signifies 'a release of that Covenant' (L 15.13; also LL 15.11).
'Hence the thing is done with right [*jure*], and is therefore not a *wrong* [*injuria* non
est]' (DCv 3.7; also DCv 8.7). For this reason, too, civil law cannot be injurious to
the governed.

Bramhall denounced the Consent Argument as plain sophistry. Subjects have
not consented to sovereign injustice.[69] Hobbes countered that they had done so.
Any limitation on what the sovereign is legally permitted to do, he reasoned, re-
introduces disagreement, disorder, and ultimately civil war. A higher power in-
stalled to orderly adjudicate such disputes would by definition itself have legally
unlimited sovereignty (DCv 6.18; L 20.18).[70] Moreover, *Sole Measure* effectively
rules out any contractual conditions on the legitimate exercise of sovereign power.
After all, the sole authoritative standard of justice and morality within the state is
the civil law (which includes binding interpretations of natural law). The sovereign
cannot be kept to this standard since he can change the law at will—including what
counts as the authoritative interpretation of natural law (L 26.6). It follows once
more that the sovereign 'cannot be Accused by any of his Subjects, of Injury' (L
20.3; also L 20.13).

Citizens' consent morally transforms the sovereign's commands. Yet not in any
ordinary way. It is a truism today that issuing and revoking consent alters what
others may permissibly do (to us): 'consent turns a trespass into a dinner party; a
battery into a handshake; a theft into a gift; an invasion of privacy into an intimate
moment'.[71] We can waive directed obligations others have to us by giving our consent, thus creating new rights for them. Curiously, for Hobbes political consent
does not render permissible what was previously impermissible. After all, the sovereign never contractually alienated his natural right of private judgement, leaving
him entitled to follow his own interpretation of what is right and wrong regardless of anyone's consent. On Hobbes's idiosyncratic conception of 'injury', retained
rights of private judgement suffice to qualify sovereign conduct non-injurious

---

[69] John Bramhall, *Castigations of Mr. Hobbes* (London, 1657) 164.

[70] On Hobbes's regress argument for absolute sovereignty, see Hampton, *Hobbes and the Social
Contract Tradition*, 98–105.

[71] Heidi M. Hurd, 'The Moral Magic of Consent', *Legal Theory* 2 (1996) no. 2: 123. See also Larry
Alexander, 'The Moral Magic of Consent (II)', *Legal Theory* 2 (1996) no. 2: 165–174.

('with right'). Rather than granting new permissions, citizens' consent to be ruled merely 'strengthned' the supreme ruler's original right by removing as many hindrances to it (L 28.2; also EW 5: 153). Hobbes instead invokes political consent to restrict the rights *of consenters*: it altogether disentitles them from accusing the sovereign of moral wrongdoing.[72]

Leviathan's Authorization Argument is superior to the Consent Argument in two ways. It explains more powerfully why the sovereign cannot wrong citizens (a first-order argument). And it doubles as a second-order argument, ensuring that the sovereign cannot possibly lack right. I discuss each improvement in turn. On the Consent Argument, sovereign injury is inconceivable because *the willing* cannot be wronged. But in what sense subjects are 'willingly' mistreated by their sovereign remains obscure.[73] The Authorization Argument declares the same impossible for a more compelling reason: you cannot wrong *yourself*. Every citizen has individually authorized the sovereign (their common representative) to speak and act in their names. Authorization has an idiosyncratic meaning for Hobbes. It does not involve any delegation or transfer of rights, as some commentators mistakenly think.[74] Authorization involves no alienation of right (L 21.14; LL 21.7).[75] It consists instead in making another person's words or actions your own (L 16.14).

> For that which in speaking of goods and possessions, is called an *Owner* . . . speaking of Actions, is called an Author. And as the Right of possession, is called Dominion; so the Right of doing any Action, is called AUTHORITY . . . By Authority, is alwayes understood a Right of doing any act: and *done by Authority*, done by Commission, or Licence from him whose right it is. (L 16.4; also DH 15.2)[76]

For S to authorize K to φ means licencing K to φ in the name of S. Henceforth, whenever K φs their action should be regarded as S's and as performed by authority of S.

---

[72] Ramelet overlooks this key point in her otherwise insightful analysis of what moral difference political consent makes in Hobbes. Laetitia Ramelet, 'Hobbes and the Indirect Workings of Political Consent', *Hobbes Studies* 35 (2022) no. 2: 155–175.

[73] Michael Green, 'Authorization and Political Authority in Hobbes', *Journal of the History of Philosophy* 53 (2015) no. 1: 45–46.

[74] *Contra* David Gauthier, *The Logic of Leviathan* (Oxford, 1969) 124; Hampton, *Hobbes and the Social Contract Tradition*, 114–129. For a correction, see Green, 'Authorization and Political Authority', 26–37.

[75] With perhaps one exception. The sovereign is given the formal right to represent all and sundry: 'the Right of bearing the Person of them all, is given to him they make Soveraigne' (L 18.4). That right arguably originated in acts of authorization, being non-derivable from the natural right of self-preservation that grounds the right to everything.

[76] On the Roman law origins of this doctrine, see Daniel Lee, 'Hobbes and the Civil Law: The Use of Roman Law in Hobbes's Civil Science' in David Dyzenhaus and Thomas Poole (eds), *Hobbes and the Law* (Cambridge, 2012) 223–227.

170   JUSTICE AND CIVIL LAW

The significance of individual authorization lies largely in the immunities it provides to the sovereign.[77] Authorization makes it impossible for the sovereign to wrong his subjects, however morally outrageous his conduct.

> because every Subject is by this Institution Author of all the Actions, and Judgments of the Soveraigne Instituted; it followes, that whatsoever he doth, it can be no injury to any of his Subjects; nor ought he to be by any of them accused of Injustice. For he that doth any thing by authority from another, doth therein no injury to him by whose authority he acteth. (L 18.6; also L 24.7)

Each citizen singly is author of everything their sovereign representative says or does. And since 'to do injury to ones self, is impossible', it follows that the sovereign cannot possibly injure his subjects (L 18.6). '[H]e may take away from us, not only our Lands, Goods, and Liberties, but our Lives also if he will' (DPS 42). All without injustice. Unconditional authorization of unbridled power ensures that 'no Law can be Unjust':

> The Law is made by the Soveraign Power, and all that is done by such Power, is warranted, and owned by every one of the people; and that which every man will have so, no man can say is unjust. It is in the Lawes of a Common-wealth, as in the Lawes of Gaming: whatsoever the Gamesters all agree on, is Injustice to none of them. (L 30.20; also EW 5: 151; DH 15.3)

Incidentally, S's authorization of K does not curtail any liberties of S. For this reason, even sovereign commands which citizens never consented to obey (such as punitive orders) can be issued in their name and by their authority. The Authorization Argument thus renders non-injurious even government orders which individuals may resist without injustice. That conclusion had remained out of reach on the earlier Consent Argument.[78]

Citizens do not divest all their natural rights in *Leviathan's* social contract. Yet all do authorize their sovereign representative unconditionally, 'without exception' (L 21.10). Each subject singly declares 'to owne, and acknowledge himself to be Author of whatsoever he that so beareth their Person, shall Act, or cause to be Acted, in those things which concerne the Common Peace and Safetie' (L 17.13). The last clause, I propose, is no material restriction of sovereign power but

---

[77] Green, 'Authorization and Political Authority', 37–46.

[78] While capacious, the Authorization Argument arguably cannot preclude *all* sovereign injury. The argument comes with scope limits: not all denizens are capable of authorizing the sovereign. Devoid of reason, 'naturall fooles, children, or mad-men' lack the 'power to make any covenant . . . and consequently never took upon them to authorise the actions of any Soveraign' (L 26.12). The Authorization Argument cannot deny non-rational subjects the standing to complain about sovereign wrongdoing— unless perhaps non-circular reasoning can show that state-appointed guardians can authorize the sovereign on their wardens' behalf (L 16.10).

a formal one. After all, citizens have empowered the sovereign to decide (beholden to none but God) which issues affect domestic peace and security. He thus himself determines which of his legal and extra-legal acts are political ones—owned by every subject singly.[79]

Have subjects indeed 'authorised all the actions' of their sovereign—immoral ones included? (L 20.1) Lloyd deems this impossible: 'subjects *cannot* authorize the sovereign to violate the Laws of Nature because *they have themselves no right to violate the Laws of Nature*'.[80] After all, 'unless he that is the author hath the right of acting himself, the actor hath no authority to act' (DH 15.2; also EL 20.18). On the other hand, Hobbes insists repeatedly that subjects cannot be wronged by the sovereign's immoral conduct by dint of their authorization (L 22.15; L 24.7). Even innocent subjects killed inequitably out of spite are done no wrong. For the sovereign received 'the right to doe what he pleased' from each subject (L 21.7). What entitled him to say this? How can subjects have authorized brazen sins of their representative when they had no right to contravene natural law themselves? The answer, I propose, lies in the reason for why humans truly have right to everything outside the state. That all-encompassing right, I have argued, ultimately derives from the natural right all have to make their own judgements about right and wrong—including about what natural law means and in practice requires (§3.3 and §3.4). *This* right the sovereign exercises on his subjects' behalf. Like them before covenanting, the sovereign is accountable to God alone for sinning against natural law, not owing any justification to fellow humans. I conclude, *contra* Lloyd, that citizens *can* have authorized immoral conduct of the sovereign—and have actually done so unreservedly.

If the above reconstruction is correct, then the Authorization Argument positively ensures that the sovereign cannot lack right. It thus doubles as a second-order argument. Whatever he says or does is '*done by Authority*', that is, by right, of his subjects (L 16.4). Does Hobbes need authorization as an additional source of sovereign right—over and above his undiminished natural right? Unlikely. As a second-order argument the Authorization Argument seems superfluous—an instance of argumentative overdetermination. The sovereign certainly has not alienated any rights to citizens in the original covenant of government. Some might conjecture, tentatively, that he has like everyone else laid down his invasive rights

---

[79] According to Van Apeldoorn, citizens have even authorized everything their supreme ruler does in his private capacities, 'at home'. The sovereign's natural and political capacities, he claims, are analytically distinct but practically inseparable. Laurens van Apeldoorn, 'On the Person and Office of the Sovereign in Hobbes' *Leviathan*', *British Journal for the History of Philosophy* 28 (2020) no. 1: 62–63.

[80] S.A. Lloyd, *Morality in the Philosophy of Thomas Hobbes* (Cambridge, 2009) 284. Also S.A. Lloyd, 'Authorization and Moral Responsibility in the Philosophy of Hobbes', *Hobbes Studies* 29 (2016) no. 2: 169–188; S.A. Lloyd, 'Natural Law' in A.P. Martinich and Kinch Hoekstra (eds), *The Oxford Handbook of Hobbes* (Oxford, 2016) 279–280; Lloyd, 'Duty Not to Act', 266. For critical discussion of Lloyd's view, see Paul Weithman, 'Hobbes on Persons and Authorization' in S.A. Lloyd (ed), *Interpreting Hobbes's Political Philosophy* (Cambridge, 2019) 187–190.

172 JUSTICE AND CIVIL LAW

of war upon joining the commonwealth, by signing the logically prior covenant of peace dictated by the second law of nature—even as he retains his natural right of self-government. If so, then the sovereign may regain rights, contractually forsworn before, through citizens' unlimited authorization: namely, rights vis-à-vis citizens to act contrary to the terms of the covenant of peace. This intriguing but highly speculative proposal lacks textual support. Worse, it fits badly with Hobbes's claim that the sovereign's right to punish is grounded in his unabridged natural right (L 28.2). Even if authorization in no way materially augments the sovereign's rights, it still makes a difference formally. In the early works, the sovereign rules solely by exercising his natural right, unhindered by collective promises of non-resistance. In *Leviathan*, by contrast, he governs in addition in the name and by right of each of his subjects singly. They have individually authorized him to do as he pleases, to establish and maintain domestic peace and protection against foreign enemies.

6.7 WHY HOBBES WAS NO LEGAL POSITIVIST

Hobbes's disentanglement of justice from natural law complicates assessment of his relation to legal positivism. To examine whether Hobbes endorses the Separability Thesis, two questions need addressing. Does immorality legally invalidate sovereign decrees? And does injustice do so? The first question should be answered in the negative. The second cannot be answered straightforwardly for lack of evidence. After all, Hobbes strenuously ruled out the existence of unjust laws. This section argues that *No Law Unjust* nevertheless matters greatly for the proper characterization of Hobbes's legal theory, in two ways: (i) it directly contradicts a key tenet of legal positivism; and (ii) brings him closer to traditional natural law views on legal validity. I handle each point in turn, before ending by contextualizing *No Law Unjust* within seventeenth-century English constitutional thought.

No Law Unjust is plainly incompatible with legal positivism: it negates the Separability Thesis. In line with legal positivists' dismissal of moralized conceptions of law, the Separability Thesis requires that any connections between justice and law be contingent: they must not hold for all possible legal systems. Hobbes's doctrine that 'no law can be possibly unjust' is inimical to that thesis (EW 5: 151). *No Law Unjust* posits an ineliminable conceptual link between civil law and justice—or, more precisely, between law and *in*justice. It states that: if L is law to S, then L cannot be unjust towards S. Unjust actions being coextensive with injuries, it follows that if L is law to S, then L cannot injure S either. For Hobbes, these two conceptual claims hold true in virtue of either of the following arguments:

Consent Argument:

If L is a law to S, then S has willingly consented to be governed by the law-making authority that issued L. Since one cannot injure the willing, L cannot injure S.

Authorization Argument:
If L is a law to S, then S has authorized and hence owns every action of the law-making authority that issued L. Since one cannot injure oneself, L cannot injure S.

Both arguments can be formulated in terms of injustice as well. Legal positivists commonly take their hallmark Separability Thesis to mean that civil laws need not have positive moral value to be legally valid.[81] Hobbes, by contrast, argues that civil law cannot have *negative* moral value: 'no law can be unjust' (EW 5: 234).

Hobbes's forceful endorsement of *No Law Unjust* bears on his stance towards the traditional natural law view on legal validity. Augustine captured that position succinctly: 'a law that is not just does not seem to me to be a law'.[82] As it happens, Hobbes nowhere denies that *injustice* is an invalidating condition of law. He never gainsaid that unjust laws, were they to exist, are legally invalid, leaving subjects free to act contrariwise. To sidestep the seditious implications of the classic natural law doctrine, Hobbes adopted a different argumentative strategy—one that arguably keeps him closer to the legal framework of Augustine and later natural law theorists than commonly recognized. Rather than repudiating their criterion for legal validity, he rendered it practically meaningless by arguing that unjust laws simply cannot exist. That strategy is compatible with holding that, in principle, injustice would disqualify sovereign's orders from being law. Hobbes, I surmise, may well have endorsed the natural law account of legal validity in principle, while maintaining that it cannot possibly have legal effects in practice (because of *No Law Unjust*). Commentators have generally overlooked this point, I believe, because of their failure to adequately distinguish immorality (which does not affect legal validity) from injustice (which, I venture, might).[83] If my interpretive conjecture is correct, then Hobbes truly had much at stake in proving *No Law Unjust*.

That doctrine should be understood relationally. No civil law can be unjust or injurious *to citizens*. While civil legislation cannot wrong consenting subjects, the sovereign can through law-giving violate natural law and thereby injure God. Hobbes presses this 'subtile' point in reply to Bramhall.

> The laws of these kings, as they were laws, have relation only to the men that were their subjects; and the *making* of them, which was the action of every one of those kings, who were subjects to another king, namely, to God Almighty, had relation to the law of God. In the first relation, there could be no injustice in them; because

---

[81] E.g. James Morauta, 'Three Separation Theses', *Law and Philosophy* 23 (2004) no. 2: 124–127.
[82] Augustine, *On the Free Choice of the Will*, ed. Peter King (Cambridge, 2010) 1.5.11.
[83] E.g. Hampton, *Hobbes and the Social Contract Tradition*, 107; Goldsmith, 'Hobbes on Law', 286.

174   JUSTICE AND CIVIL LAW

> all laws made by him to whom the people had given the legislative power, are the acts of every one of that people; and no man can do injustice to himself. But in relation to God, if God have by a law forbidden it, <u>the making of such laws is injustice</u> ... Nevertheless, as it was a law to their subjects ... the law was not unjust. (EW 5: 177–178)

Violations of natural law are here called 'injustices' rather than 'iniquities'—the term Hobbes came to prefer later. That change of labels, incidentally, served to accentuate the very point made in the above quote. Hobbes's conceptions of injustice and injury are relational ones (§2.3). Sovereigns can do wrong only in relation to God, to whom alone they are morally accountable. By contrast, 'nothing the Sovereign Representative can doe to a Subject, on what pretence soever, can properly be called Injustice, or Injury' (L 21.7). Unconditional and unlimited authorization explains why immoral civil laws affronting God are nevertheless legally valid, rightful, and binding in relation to citizens. The Consent and Authorization Arguments thus ultimately render Hobbes's legal theory non-positivistic: they establish that no civil law, not even a wicked one, can be unjust or injurious to citizens.

In closing, let me elaborate on the legal status of that extraordinary view. *No Law Unjust* nominally resembles the classic constitutional maxim that 'the king can do no wrong'. In Bodin's words: 'a prince can do nothing that is foul or unjust'.[84] The dictum's meaning was highly contested in seventeenth-century England—eventually becoming central to legal justifications for beheading Charles I in 1649.[85] Incidentally, the maxim had originally buttressed sovereign legal unaccountability. As the representative of God on earth, the monarch was assumed to be guided by justice alone.[86] Unjust orders issued by him therefore had no legal import. If promulgated nevertheless, they became the legal responsibility of ministers, who alone could be held accountable for the king's unjust decrees. Parliamentarians later came to argue that the king can do no wrong *as king*. In his natural capacity, as a private individual, the king was deemed capable of wrongdoing—and potentially liable to (capital) punishment.[87] Hobbes rendered the sovereign's natural and political capacity practically inseparable to thwart this major threat to peace.[88] Reverting to the maxim's earlier interpretation was not appealing to him. That gloss had bought the sovereign legal impunity at the cost of greatly restricting his legislative powers: only his just decrees had the status of law.

---

[84] Bodin, *Six Books*, 109.

[85] Janelle Greenberg, 'Our Grand Maxim of State, "The King Can Do No Wrong"', *History of Political Thought* 12 (1991) no. 2: 209–228.

[86] Greenberg, 'Our Grand Maxim', 212–213. On the maxim's relation to early modern ideas of moral kingship, see David Chan Smith, *Sir Edward Coke and the Reformation of the Laws* (Cambridge, 2014) 267, 277.

[87] Greenberg, 'Our Grand Maxim', 219–220.

[88] Van Apeldoorn, 'On the Person and Office'.

'The maxim that apparently freed the king by asserting he could do no wrong was paradoxically one of the major constraints that kept him within the law'.[89] Hobbes's bold version of political absolutism required an innovative, limitless take on the maxim. For him, kings truly can do no wrong. Literally nothing the sovereign does in his natural or political capacity, however heinous, can be unjust or injurious to citizens. Hobbes designed his civil theodicy for legally untrammelled, all-powerful rulers—whose words and actions cannot lack authority vis-à-vis their citizens.

CONCLUSION

This chapter has outlined a new and encompassing non-positivist interpretation of Hobbes's legal theory. I have argued that Hobbes's conception of civil law is moralized in two ways. Each rejects a constitutive precept of legal positivism. First, Hobbes disavows the Sources Thesis. Since all human law conceptually presupposes a prior obligation of justice on the part of the governed, moral analysis is needed to establish whether a particular command by the sovereign is binding law to some citizen. Is the subject supposed to have obligated herself to obey that particular decree in the original pact of subjection? The terms of absolute subjection being always and everywhere the same, right reason ultimately answers this question.[90] Second, Hobbes repudiates the Separability Thesis by positing an ineliminable connection between law and injustice. If *L* is law to S, then *L* cannot be unjust to S—and necessarily so.

The position I ascribe to Hobbes seems practically contradictory. *No Law Unjust* assures citizens and public officials that probing the moral quality of civil law is pointless: civil laws cannot possibly be unjust. Yet to determine whether some sovereign decree is law to them to begin with, subjects must reflect on the conditions and limits of political subjection. The spotted tension is real but minor: subjects have after all promised 'the greatest obedience that can be given' (DCv 6.13). Still, the tension evinces, significantly, that Hobbes is less troubled by individual disobedience than by cracks in his civil theodicy. In the eyes of citizens, he stresses, all government conduct is morally impeccable—even those violent orders which are no law to them and which they may rightfully resist. Citizens are in no position to morally condemn civil legislation, for two reasons. First, they lack access to a public *standard* of morality distinct from civil law. To forestall all disputes and conflicts, subjects have agreed to treat the sovereign's will as the authoritative

---

[89] Joyce Lee Malcolm, 'Doing No Wrong: Law, Liberty, and the Constraint of Kings', *Journal of British Studies* 38 (1999) no. 2: 162.
[90] Deborah Baumgold, *Contract Theory in Historical Context* (Leiden, 2010) 96.

176 JUSTICE AND CIVIL LAW

interpretation of the laws of nature within the state—the sole measure of just and unjust, good and evil. Second, even had an independent standard been available, subjects would still have no *standing* 'to speak evill of their Soveraign; because they have authorised all his actions, and in bestowing the Soveraign Power, made them their own' (L 24.7).

PART IV
JUSTICE OUTSIDE THE STATE

7

NO PEACE, NO JUSTICE

INTRODUCTION*

> To this warre of every man against every man, this also is consequent;
> that nothing can be Unjust. The notions of Right and Wrong, Justice
> and Injustice have there no place. Where there is no common Power,
> there is no Law: where no Law, no Injustice. (L 13.13)

In these memorable and oft-quoted lines from *Leviathan*, Hobbes defends the doctrine that the existence of a state is necessary for norms of justice to arise or become effective. In other words, justice does not regulate human interactions outside the commonwealth (the norms of justice can in practice neither be followed nor flouted). Call this doctrine *Statism about Justice*.

Hobbes embraces *Statism about Justice* unreservedly: 'justice and injustice did not exist [nihil erat] before the commonwealth was set up' (LL 18.6; also L 15.3; LL 27.3; DH 10.5). This stunning position has made him a popular reference point in both realist theories of international relations and debates about global justice. Realists like Carr and Morgenthau draw on Hobbes's thought. Morgenthau even spots 'a profound and neglected truth' in Hobbes's dictum that justice has no place in the international sphere.[1] Beitz devotes more than thirty pages challenging what he calls 'the Hobbesian conception of international relations'.[2] Nagel defends a position on global justice that is self-proclaimed 'Hobbesian in spirit': interpersonal justice would require 'government as an enabling condition'.[3] And James

---

* This chapter reworks material from Johan Olsthoorn, 'Why Justice and Injustice Have no Place outside the Hobbesian State', *European Journal of Political Theory* 14 (2015) no. 1: 19–36. Only after publication of that article did I encounter Michael J. Green, 'Justice and Law in Hobbes', *Oxford Studies in Early Modern Philosophy* 1 (2003) 111–138. Some interpretive claims presented as original in my article had in fact already been made by Green. I appreciate having the opportunity here to acknowledge Green's original contributions.

[1] H.J. Morgenthau, *American Foreign Policy: A Critical Examination* (London, 1952) 34; E.H. Carr, *The Twenty Year's Crisis 1919–1939* (London, 2001) 63, 140. On Hobbes's legacy in thinking about international relations, see David Armitage, *The Foundations of Modern International Thought* (Cambridge, 2013) 59–74.

[2] C.R. Beitz, *Political Theory and International Relations* (Princeton, 1999) 14, 27–59.

[3] Thomas Nagel, 'The Problem of Global Justice', *Philosophy and Public Affairs* 33 (2005) no. 2: 147, 114. For critical analysis of Nagel's statism about justice, see Joshua Cohen and Charles Sabel, 'Extram Rempublicam Nulla Justitia?', *Philosophy and Public Affairs* 34 (2006) no. 2: 147–175; Arash Abizadeh, 'Cooperation, Pervasive Impact, and Coercion: On the Scope (not Site) of Distributive Justice', *Philosophy and Public Affairs* 35 (2007) no. 4: 318–358.

Hobbes on Justice. Johan Olsthoorn, Oxford University Press. © Johan Olsthoorn 2024.
DOI: 10.1093/9780191904585.003.0007

emphasizes the importance at the global level of Hobbes's 'basic insight' that assurance is key to questions of justice.[4]

In light of Hobbes's signpost prominence in these debates, the meaning and grounds of his doctrine that justice and injustice have no place beyond the commonwealth are surprisingly poorly understood. Some commentators even deny that Hobbes is truly wedded to *Statism about Justice*. Byron, for instance, thinks that persons commit injustice outside the state whenever they violate obligations imposed by the divinely dictated laws of nature.[5] In reply: *Statism about Justice* is a thesis about when norms of justice obtain between humans. In the state of nature, humans can sin against God's law without committing any 'injustice against men' [injustitia erga homines] (DCv 1.10n) (§3.2). It has not helped either that scholars have generally overlooked that Hobbes does not defend *Statism about Justice* prior to *Leviathan*. Both *Elements* and *De Cive* lack anything resembling the opening quotation. Reconstructions of the doctrine should draw on ideas new to *Leviathan*—unless an explanation can be given for why, all necessary premises present, Hobbes failed in his early works to draw statist conclusions, so congenial to his political project.

This chapter provides a comprehensive reconstruction of Hobbes's arguments for *Statism about Justice* and their various theoretical presuppositions and implications. Two distinct arguments for the doctrine can be gleaned from Hobbes's works: the so-called Revised Covenant Argument and the Propriety Argument. Both first appear in full-fledged form in *Leviathan*. As its name suggests, the Revised Covenant Argument is my improved take on the well-known Covenant Argument.

Commentators have discussed the Covenant Argument at great length. Injustice, the argument goes, consists in breaking valid covenants. Warranted assurance that the other party will perform is a validating condition of covenants. The sovereign alone can provide the security that makes it sufficiently safe, and hence morally mandatory, for all to perform their covenants. Outside the state, there are hence no valid covenants—making it impossible for people to act either justly or unjustly (by keeping or breaking faith). The argument, consensus has it, is both textually and philosophically problematic. Green's verdict is representative: 'there <u>can</u> be such a thing as a valid covenant in the state of nature and injustice . . . can exist in the absence of law and a common power'.[6] 'Hobbes', he concludes, 'has a marked tendency to exaggerate the civil sovereign's role in making justice possible.'[7] I fully agree that fear of default by other contractors cannot forestall injustice by invalidating all state-of-nature-covenants. Against

---

[4] Aaron James, 'Hobbesian Assurance Problems and Global Justice' in S.A. Lloyd (ed), *Hobbes Today* (Cambridge, 2013) 264–287.

[5] Michael Byron, *Submission and Subjection in Leviathan* (New York, 2015) 12–25.

[6] Green, 'Justice and Law in Hobbes', 119.

[7] Green, 'Justice and Law in Hobbes', 135.

INTRODUCTION   181

the grain, I hold that there are compelling interpretive reasons against ascribing the Covenant Argument to Hobbes. A textually better-grounded rival reconstruction is available that partially corroborates *Statism about Justice*: the Revised Covenant Argument (§7.1).

Hobbes no doubt accepts that valid covenants exist in the war-torn interpersonal and international states of nature. What he denies is that extra-statist actors can be appropriately accused by others of wrongfully breaking valid covenants. The Revised Covenant Argument outlines the rationale behind that paradoxical thesis. It being irrational and self-defeating to act morally amidst hostility, in the state of nature the mere will to keep covenants suffices to observe justice. Since humans cannot possibly know whether those reneging on covenants in war have made a *bona fide* assessment of present danger, warranted accusations of pact-breaking are non-existent outside the state. Universal rights of private judgement endow every pre-statist action with right vis-à-vis other humans, precluding all interpersonal injustice and injury (i.e. actions without right). The same holds true, *mutatis mutandis*, for conduct within the international state of nature (§9.5).[8] Unlike the Covenant Argument, the Revised Covenant Argument does successfully explain why *unjust* actions are non-existent in the state of nature. It does not show the same for *just* actions—though it comes close to this on *Leviathan*'s novel definition of justice as keeping faith (§7.2).

New to *Leviathan*, the Propriety Argument does establish *Statism about Justice* in full (§7.3). The argument builds upon Hobbes's various arguments for the state-dependency of private property (reconstructed in Chapter 5). Property has a broad meaning for Hobbes, covering all exclusive rights persons have vis-à-vis one another (including rights to their body and person). Across his works, Hobbes maintains that humans cannot have exclusive rights to anything in conditions of war. The Propriety Argument defines justice in terms of giving each their own—where 'own' denotes exclusive personal rights. The argument declares norms of justice to be inapplicable beyond the state on the grounds that justice, so understood, lacks content outside a legal system. The Revised Covenant Argument and the Propriety Argument, my analysis shows, are irreducibly distinct. Each presupposes a different conception of justice and each emphasizes different implications of the natural right to all things. Moreover, only on the Propriety Argument is it impossible for people to possess the virtue of justice outside the state.

---

[8] On the international arena being a warlike state of nature, see DCv ED.2; DCv 10.17; DCv 13.7; L 13.12; L 21.8; L 30.30; DPS 7–8.

7.1 THE (REVISED) COVENANT ARGUMENT

When asked why justice and injustice have no place outside the Hobbesian commonwealth, scholars commonly respond along the lines of the Covenant Argument. The argument can be formally written out as follows:

P1: Injustice consists in breaking valid covenants;
P2: Warranted assurance that the other party will perform is a validating condition of covenants;
P3: No such assurance is possible until a coercive power is set up to 'constrain those that would otherwise violate their faith' (L 14.19);
C1: No valid covenant exists outside the state;
C2: Unjust actions, understood as breaches of valid covenants, are likewise non-existent beyond the state.

Leviathan contains clear textual support for ascribing the argument to Hobbes:

> But because Covenants of mutuall trust, where there is a feare of not perform-ance on either part ... are invalid; though the Originall of Justice be the making of Covenants; yet Injustice actually there can be none, till the cause of such feare be taken away; which while men are in the naturall condition of Warre, cannot be done. Therefore <u>before the names of Just, and Unjust can have place</u>, <u>there must be some coërcive Power</u>, to compel men equally to the performance of their Covenants, by the terrour of some punishment, greater than the benefit they ex-pect by the breach of their Covenant ... and such power there is none before the erection of a Common-wealth. (L 15.3)

The Covenant Argument has received much scholarly criticism. The conclusion that valid covenants are non-existent beyond the commonwealth seems too strong for both textual and philosophical reasons. Commentators have identified at least three major problems with Hobbes's argument.[9] First, various passages suggest that valid covenants *are* possible outside the state. 'Covenants entred into by fear, in the condition of meer Nature, are obligatory', we read, at least until 'there ariseth some new, and just cause of feare, to renew the war' (L 14.27).[10] Likewise, coven-ants between states remain 'valid' until a novel 'just cause of distrust' crops up (L 22.29; also DCv 13.7). Those who break covenants without just grounds for dis-trust, Hobbes implies, do so wrongly. Second, if the existence of a coercive power

---

[9] E.g. Beitz, *Political Theory and International Relations*, 30; David Boonin-Vail, *Thomas Hobbes and the Science of Moral Virtue* (Cambridge, 1994) 74–76, 80; Green, 'Justice and Law in Hobbes', 115–119; Kinch Hoekstra, 'Hobbes on the Natural Condition of Mankind' in Patricia Springborg (ed), *The Cambridge Companion to Hobbes's Leviathan* (Cambridge, 2007) 120.

[10] Also EL 15.10, 13; DCv 2.4, 11, 13, 18; L 14.18–20, 30.

THE (REVISED) COVENANT ARGUMENT   183

really is a validating condition of covenants, then it seems that Hobbes's social contract of government cannot get off the ground. If a sovereign has to exist for covenants to be valid, then we cannot institute a sovereign by mutual covenant on pain of circularity—leaving us trapped in the state of nature.[11]

Third, the argument contains two enormous loopholes. It applies only to one kind of contract: 'Covenants of mutuall trust'. And only to a subset of those covenants: those where both parties have yet to perform.[12] Contracts are essentially mutual transfers of rights. In all contracts, rights are transferred the moment the agreement is signed. In some contracts, both parties perform immediately by delivering to one another 'the Thing contracted for' (i.e. the object of the transferred right) (L 14.11). In other contracts, one or more parties are trusted to perform their part at a future time. Contracts involving trust are called 'PACT, or COVENANT'. In covenants of *mutual* trust, all parties agree to perform later on. In covenants of *single* trust, one party performs instantly, while the other contractors are trusted to act later (EL 15.8–9; DCv 2.9–10; L 14.11). As rights are always transferred at the moment of contracting, if the trusted party inexcusably fails to do as promised then they act without right. Not-performing valid covenants is by definition unjust and injurious (DCv 3.3; L 14.7). Covenants are the only kind of contracts that can be broken, and conceptually so.

Only a new and reasonable fear that the other party will renege can invalidate covenants (DCv 2.11n; L 14.20, 27).

> If a Covenant be made, wherein neither of the parties performe presently, but trust one another; in the condition of meer Nature, (which is a condition of Warre of every man against every man,) upon any reasonable suspition, it is Voyd: But if there be a common Power set over them both, with right and force sufficient to compell performance; it is not Voyd. For he that performeth first, has no assurance the other will performe after . . . And therfore he which performeth first, does but betray himselfe to his enemy; contrary to the Right (he can never abandon) of defending his life, and means of living. (L 14.18; also EL 15.10; DCv 2.11)

Reasonable fears of betrayal cannot arise when the other party had performed right away. Covenants of single trust therefore *are* valid in the state of nature. The same is true for covenants of mutual trust 'where one of the parties has performed already' (L 15.5). According to Kavka, Hobbes is 'therefore totally wrong' in denying the

---

[11] Leslie Stephen, *Hobbes* (Cambridge, 1904) 194; Jean Hampton, *Hobbes and the Social Contract Tradition* (Cambridge, 1986) 134–136; J.P. Sommerville, *Thomas Hobbes: Political Ideas in Historical Context* (London, 1992) 54; A.P. Martinich, *The Two Gods of Leviathan* (Cambridge, 1992) 82–83; Alan Ryan, 'Hobbes's Political Philosophy' in Tom Sorell (ed), *The Cambridge Companion to Hobbes* (Cambridge, 1996) 226. For a possible way out, see Howard Warrender, *The Political Philosophy of Hobbes* (Oxford, 1957) 142.

[12] Brian Barry, 'Warrender and His Critics', *Philosophy* 43 (1968) no. 164: 123–124.

184 NO PEACE, NO JUSTICE

possibility of 'state-of-nature injustice'. As first-party performance annuls fears of sudden retraction, 'an injustice is done if... the second party, fails to reciprocate'.[13]

Kavka's conclusion is too quick. The sketched line of reasoning, it is true, shows that covenants of mutual trust can become void only when both parties have yet to perform—and only when a new cause for just fear arises. Critics have universally overlooked, however, that covenants can be rightfully set aside for reasons other than well-grounded fear that the other contracting party will default. General fear of *third* parties can justify the same. Vulnerability to third-party violence can make it irrational to perform one's promise even if the other contractors pose no danger whatsoever. Hobbes insists that prisoners of war freed in return for promised ransom are bound to pay their captors (EL 15.13; DCv 2.16; L 14.27). Such agreements are covenants of single trust: captors immediately perform their part by releasing their captives in exchange for future payment. Still, if freed captives judge that escalating hostilities make it impossible to safely discharge their debt, then the obligation to pay is suspended.[14]

Hobbes provides a general justification for this—valid objectively, in the eyes of God. Since the laws of nature are valued instrumentally, as 'a means of the conservation of men in multitudes', it would be irrational and self-defeating ('contrary to the ground of all Lawes of Nature') to practice morality when others pursue their self-preservation through violence instead (L 15.34, 36). In times of war, the laws of nature therefore do not always bind '*in foro externo*; that is, to the putting them in act' (L 15.36; also EL 17.10; DCv 3.27). This makes the laws of nature exceedingly 'easie to be observed' in perilous circumstances: all that is needed is a steady desire to keep these laws (L 15.39; also DCv 3.30). The same safety rider applies to the natural law duty of justice. To 'performe all he promises' amidst hostility 'should but make himself a prey to others, and procure his own certain ruine' (L 15.36). An unfeigned desire to keep covenants, Hobbes claims, in war suffices to observe justice, leaving belligerents in practice free to undo their every promise (L 15.39). God graciously takes the willingness to keep faith for the deed. The general dispensation to practice natural law in war is a key premise of the Revised Covenant Argument. It explains why pre-statist individuals can fulfil all that justice requires without actually ever doing what they promised.

According to Hobbes, people cannot possibly covenant away their natural right to refrain from practising morality in great danger. We cannot do so for the same reason that we retain certain inalienable natural rights within the state: such covenants can neither be rationally made nor reasonably upheld by others

---

[13] G.S. Kavka, *Hobbesian Moral and Political Theory* (Princeton, 1986) 351–352. Also Warrender, *The Political Philosophy of Hobbes*, 42–47, 64–65; Martinich, *Two Gods*, 82–87.

[14] This point has gone unmentioned in existing analyses of Hobbes's views on promises to kidnappers and thieves. They mostly focus on what such binding promises tell us about the character of his moral theory. E.g. Luciano Venezia, *Hobbes on Legal Authority and Political Obligation* (New York, 2015) 120–125.

(L 14.29–30; L 21.11–17).[15] The general point of entering pacts 'is nothing else but the security of a mans person, in his life, and in the means of so preserving life, as not to be weary of it' (L 14.8). It would be self-defeating to enter state-of-nature covenants that strictly require performance as this leaves one defenceless against enemies. Covenants must be performed only when 'keeping them seems likely to achieve the end for which they were made' (DCv 3.27). No covenant binds further 'than to our best endeavour' (EL 15.18; also DCv 2.14; L 14.25). As we can 'never abandon' the right of defending life and limb, every pact is presumed to contain this caveat (L 14.18).

The general dispensation clause to practice morality in war is not, I think, an *invalidating* condition of covenants. Rather, the dispensation is best seen as a permission to set aside principles of justice and morality as standards of action (§3.3). Recall that the right of nature entitles each individual to decide for themselves which course of action best promotes their self-preservation at present—be it acting peacefully or unleashing war (EL 14.8; DCv 1.9; L 14.1). Sometimes persons will judge external conditions to be such that practising the moral virtues is most conducive to their survival. At other times, the situation may be such as to render virtuous conduct highly risky if not plain stupid. Benevolence towards malicious enemies, for instance, only opens the doors to their violent attack. If danger is seen to beckon, individuals may at all times decide to omit or undo whatever they had promised, opting for the safety of self-protection by force of arms. Any new just fear again triggers the right to shelve performance. Which fears are just, each person is entitled to decide for themselves (L 14.18) (§8.5). If theirs is a good faith judgement, then subsequent resort to war is objectively justified (DCv 1.10n). By thus reigniting war, people do not *break* their covenants. They rather shove them aside as non-operative in present conditions. The dispensation clause, attached to any covenant, neither implies nor requires that the thus-suspended covenant is annulled. People fulfil all that justice requires in war by being genuinely willing to keep faith; it would be odd if covenants can be voided by the actions of those who fully comply with justice. I therefore take the validity of suspended covenants to persist: if the obligee believes the danger has subsided, then they become *in foro externo* obligated again to perform their part (if still contractually possible).

The safety rider applies not just to covenants but also to free gifts, that is, to *unilateral* alienation of right to someone else. For all sorts of reasons, extra-statist actors may decide to freely give up some rights to another party without receiving anything from them in turn. Such 'GIFT, FREE-GIFT, GRACE' is no form of contract (L 14.12; also EL 15.7; DCv 2.8). Within the state, reneging on one's gift (by taking back what you had freely given to another) is an injury/act without right since 'the Right passeth' (L 14.15). Yet in conditions of war, the right of nature entitles all to

---

[15] On Hobbes's account of when consent can be reasonably imputed to others, see Arash Abizadeh, *Hobbes and the Two Faces of Ethics* (Cambridge, 2018) 232–235.

186 NO PEACE, NO JUSTICE

claw back every donation whenever they sincerely judge that their preservation requires as much.

Hobbes adds a second, subjective justification that renders reneging on gifts or pledged faith *always* permissible vis-à-vis other humans in times of war. All have by nature in effect a right to do as they please: even if they wilfully act contrary to the dictates of reason, then still their equals cannot appropriately accuse them of wrongdoing. Chapter 3 outlined two arguments for why extra-statist actors have, as it were, a right to sin. First, as per *Untraceable Intentions*, during war people cannot possibly tell whether others resort to violence with sound intentions or foul ones—that is, whether warmongers had fulfilled their natural law duties by sincerely having willed peace before attacking. For epistemic reasons, pre-statist individuals cannot legitimately accuse others of having unjustly refused to carry out their agreements. Beyond human inspection, the safety rider attached to any state-of-nature covenant is in effect always met at the interpersonal level (§3.3). Had evidence of malice been available, *No Accusation without Law* states, equals could still not legitimately accuse their fellows of unlawful pact-breaking absent a common legal framework. For any such accusation would inadmissibly impose their private interpretation of what justice means and requires upon their equals. As long as natural equality reigns, people may rightfully ignore the moral censure of their fellows as mere expressions of their private opinion (§3.4). For all these reasons, covenants effectively pose no limits whatsoever on what individuals can rightfully do in war. As Hobbes's critic Tyrrell concluded: 'he who will not keep Faith any longer, may when he pleases pretend to be afraid, lest the other should break his Faith with him, and that very justly, whilst he himself is the only Judge of it'.[16] Where all are equal, only God can hold people morally accountable for perfidy.

We can now formally spell out the Revised Covenant Argument:

> P1: Unjust actions are actions without right;
> P2: Breaking valid covenants is unjust 'inasmuch as the party which acted or failed to act had already transferred the right to someone else' (DCv 3.3);
> P3: In war, persons have the right to forgo practising any law of nature whenever they themselves judge the situation to be too unsafe for this;
> P4: In war, the mere desire to keep covenants counts as observing them;
> P5: Pre-statist individuals lack the moral and epistemic standing to appropriately accuse others of having set aside their covenants for the wrong reasons;
> P6: All therefore have a natural right vis-à-vis others to do as they wish;

---

[16] [James Tyrrell], *A Brief Disquisition of the Law of Nature* (London, 1692) 363–364.

C1: Unjust actions, understood as actions without right, are non-existent beyond the state.

The Revised Covenant Argument holds only at the human level. Within the state of nature, persons sin against the laws of nature and wrong God by breaking covenants for no good reason. Yet vis-à-vis humans, all enjoy an unqualified right to everything in conditions of war.[17] They may even reclaim rights previously contractually alienated to someone else. Right reason entitles all to shelve any pact in case of just fear, appending this clause to every covenant. For both practical and principled reasons, people cannot admissibly accuse their equals of deviously breaking faith. Endowed with the natural right to follow their own judgement in all things, humans do not owe their peers any justification for their choices. In the state of nature, we therefore cannot lack right in relation to fellow humans: we may if we want undo all that we promised. Unjust actions being by definition actions without right, it follows that injustice against humans presupposes civil law—and renunciation of the natural right to everything.

The reason Hobbes stresses that 'Covenants of mutuall trust' become void 'upon any reasonable suspition', I surmise, is that any covenant of peace takes this form (L 14.18). The passage serves to underline the need for an additional pact of subjection. Outside the state, humans will forge truces to end incessant warfare. Some of these armistices create alliances between former belligerents, joining strengths against common enemies. In all truces, covenantees renounce their invasive rights of war by promising their allies to henceforth comply with the 'Articles of Peace' outlined by natural law (L 13.14). Hobbes is adamant that covenants of peace, preserving equality, will be short-lived unless contractors in addition form a social contract of government. 'Peace without subjection' is impossible for prickly creatures like us. We cannot reasonably 'suppose a great Multitude of men to consent in the observation of Justice, and other Lawes of Nature, without a common Power to keep them all in awe' (L 17.4).[18] Absent a supreme decider, people will pursue their private interests instead of the common good; ensuing disagreements will quickly come to blows. Moreover, all may resume the war by right at will. After all, rights of self-government are retained in covenants of peace; what is mutually alienated is instead the natural right to everything (EL 15.2; DCv 2.3; L 14.5). All hence remain entitled to end the ceasefire whenever rekindling the war *in their eyes* best promotes their self-preservation at that moment. A poor recipe for peace!

Summing up, previous attempts to explain why there is no justice and injustice outside Hobbes's commonwealth have been hampered by an inordinate focus upon the validity of state-of-nature covenants. This focus is a red herring. Their validity is ultimately irrelevant for the question of why there is no injustice outside

---

[17] EL 14.10; EL 20.5; EL 20.18; DCv 11.4; L 14.5; L 15.22.
[18] Also EL 19.4; EL 20.6; DCv 5.4; DCv 6.13n; L 14.31; DH 15.4.

188 NO PEACE, NO JUSTICE

the state. There are without doubt valid covenants in Hobbes's state of nature. And yet there can be no injustice—breaking of valid covenants. I have offered a new explanation for this paradox. Covenants come with massive loopholes outside legal systems. The mere will to keep these covenants counts as observing them, leaving agents free to pursue their self-preservation in whatever way they judge best (i.e. by peaceful or bellicose means). The general right to suspend actual implementation of obligations of justice when doing so is deemed dangerous is no invalidating condition of covenants. Still, being beyond interpersonal evaluation, it effectively leaves people free to ignore any agreement made at will. The Revised Covenant Argument, I conclude, successfully explains why in war nothing is unjust vis-à-vis other humans. It cannot prove the same for justice: the argument does not rule out that people occasionally carry out state-of-nature covenants when hazards abate. Besides, anyone who sincerely wills to keep faith thereby already fulfils all that justice requires outside the commonwealth.

7.2 JUSTICE BEFORE *LEVIATHAN*

Neither *Elements* nor *De Cive* defends *Statism about Justice*. Recognizing this further problematizes the standard explanation for this doctrine (i.e. the Covenant Argument). Both early works deny that binding covenants exist in the state of nature on the grounds that valid covenants presuppose some coercive power to punish pact breakers. Yet they conspicuously fail to draw the conclusion that just and unjust therefore have no place outside the commonwealth (EL 15.10; EL 20.5; DCv 2.11).[19] On the contrary, *Elements* positively affirms the existence of extra-statist justice and injustice. It denounces 'the unjust man' for declaring 'plainly that the justice of his actions dependeth upon civil constitution, from whence punishments proceeds'. The unjust man has no qualms about acting unjustly 'in the estate of nature' where no threat of civil punishment exists to deter him (EL 16.4). *De Cive* omits this claim.[20] Yet it does not avow *Statism about Justice* anywhere either. It comes closest in stating: 'No accord, therefore, or association based on agreement can give the security required for the practice of *natural justice*, without some common power to control individuals by instilling a fear of punishment' (DCv 5.5). The 1647 edition adds that 'injustice against men presupposes Human Laws, and there are none in the natural state' (DCv 1.10n). This passage denies only the existence of injustice outside the state. It does not say the same about justice.

When we read Hobbes's earlier works, we tend to fill in the blanks with lines of reasoning found in the all-too-familiar *Leviathan*. This is a habit we should resist. It

---

[19] Deborah Baumgold (ed), *Three-Text Edition of Thomas Hobbes's Political Theory* (Cambridge, 2017) 166.

[20] Baumgold (ed), *Three-Text Edition*, 170.

prevents us from recognizing developments in Hobbes's thought, thereby withholding an important heuristic for uncovering the arguments behind his doctrines (§1.4). Instead of blending *Elements* and *De Cive* with *Leviathan*, we should ask: why don't the early works explicitly endorse *Statism about Justice*? The answer is that the best argument then available—the Revised Covenant Argument—does not fully establish the thesis. While the argument proves injustice to have no place in war, it does not show the same for justice. What's more, on the conception of justice found in *Elements/De Cive*, just actions are not just *possible* in the state of nature—they are *omnipresent*.

Recall that the early works define 'just actions' as 'actions with right' (i.e. 'no injury') (§2.2). As *Elements* declares: 'justice and injustice, when they be attributed to actions, signify the same thing with no injury, and injury' (EL 16.4). *De Cive* concurs: 'When applied to actions, *Just* means the same as done with right [jure factum]' (DCv 3.5). In the early works, Hobbes conceives of justice primarily as a norm forbidding injury/wrongdoing. Breaking covenants is unjust only derivatively, in virtue of being 'without jus, or right; which was transferred or relinquished before' (EL 16.2). On this definition, just actions are ubiquitous in the state of nature. After all, the universal natural right to everything renders *all* actions 'just' (for: with right) before binding covenants were made. For the exact same reason, unjust actions (injuries) have no place outside the state. Hobbes could not coherently uphold *Statism of Justice* in any of the early works, I conclude, since on their accounts of justice, every extra-statist action is just. As long as just actions were defined as actions with right, justice has a place outside the state—regardless of whether there are any binding state-of-nature covenants.

Leviathan turns justice into the natural law duty to keep faith: 'the nature of Justice <u>consisteth</u> in keeping of valid Covenants' (L 15.3). Performance of covenants is now called the 'essence' of justice (LL 15.3). In *Leviathan*, violating covenants is axiomatically unjust, rather than derivatively so (i.e. because justice forbids injury; and any action breaking covenant is without right, previously renounced in said covenant). On its revised definition, actions done by natural right are no longer *ipso facto* just. Put differently: 'just' no longer means 'not being unjust'. In *Leviathan*, only those actions qualify as just that are instances of covenant-keeping. Few, if any, extra-statist actions are so. Every injustice continues to be an injury/action without right, since anyone who violates a covenant does what they had previously contractually obligated themselves to not do (L 14.7; L 15.12) (§2.2).

After defining injustice as '*the not Performance of Covenant*', *Leviathan* adds: 'whatsoever is not Unjust, is *Just*' (L 15.2; also LL 15.2). As Hoekstra observes, 'according to this definition, *everything* in the natural condition is just (unless there can be covenants therein, in which case there can also be injustices)'.[21]

---

[21] Hoekstra, 'Natural Condition of Mankind', 120. Also R.M. Lemos, *Hobbes and Locke: Power and Consent* (Athens, 1978) 22; Green, 'Justice and Law in Hobbes', 113; Bernard Gert, *Hobbes: Prince of Peace* (Malden, MA, 2010) 91.

190 NO PEACE, NO JUSTICE

Either way, the claim contradicts *Statism about Justice*. The claim amounts to a reversal to Hobbes's initial view, according to which all pre-civil actions alike are 'just' if done by natural right—peaceful as well as violent ones (§6.4). It implies that killing in self-defence is always just (for: 'with right')—and not only if the killer is a hired assassin. Later works express this controversial view several times. In the 1656 *Questions Concerning Liberty, Necessity, and Chance*, for instance, Hobbes asserts that outside the commonwealth:

> men are justly killed . . . for where there is no law, there no killing, nor any thing else can be unjust. And by the right of nature we destroy, without being unjust, all that is noxious, both beasts and men. And for beasts, we kill them justly, when we do it in order to our own preservation. (EW 5: 152)

Elsewhere in *Leviathan*, we read that enslaved people 'have no obligation at all; but may break their bonds, or the prison; and kill, or carry away captive their Master, justly [*jure*]' (L 20.10; also L R&C.7). Sovereigns in search of national security wage war on other countries 'justly' [*juste*] (L 17.2). All these lines reflect Hobbes's earlier conception of just action as acts done with right.

Such passages, I contend, are best regarded as remnants of a view which Hobbes by then had compelling reason to discard. Had he stuck to his initial definition of justice in *Leviathan*, then this would have rhetorically most inconvenient implications, given his new doctrine of 'the true Liberty of a Subject' (L 21.10). Consider: citizens have mutually promised to obey the sovereign as much as is rationally possible for them. Certain legitimate orders, Hobbes now realizes, they could not rationally have promised to obey—including orders to kill, wound, accuse, endanger, or defame themselves (L 21.10–17). With respect to all such orders, citizens have kept their natural right (i.e. liberty of action). Consequently, all subjects may refuse to obey those commands 'without Injustice' (L 21.10). If justice and injustice are mutually exhaustive, such that 'whatsoever is not Unjust, is *Just*', then citizens act justly whenever they rightfully refuse to obey dangerous or dishonourable commands (L 21.15). Hobbes had reason to distance himself from that unruly conclusion—to not further invite criticisms of having written a rebels' catechism.[22] He did so by redefining just actions narrowly as covenant-keeping acts. My conjecture is that *Leviathan*'s reconceptualization of justice serves to render his new doctrine of inalienable rights of resistance politically safe. The same was necessary (but not sufficient) for showing that justice presupposes the commonwealth. It is no coincidence, therefore, that both *Statism about Justice* and the doctrine of the true liberties of subjects first occur in *Leviathan*.

---

[22] John Bramhall, 'The Catching of Leviathan' in G.A.J. Rogers (ed), *Leviathan: Contemporary Responses to the Political Theory of Thomas Hobbes* (Bristol, 1995) 145.

7.3 THE PROPRIETY ARGUMENT

Leviathan contains a second, superior argument for *Statism about Justice*: the Propriety Argument. Preoccupied as scholars have been with the shaky Covenant Argument, scant attention has been paid to the Propriety Argument.[23] Both arguments for *Statism about Justice* are premised upon the natural right to everything: 'when the Soveraign Power ceaseth, Crime also ceaseth: there is no just and unjust, because of the right of all people to all things' (LL 27.3). Yet both arguments rely on different interpretations of the *jus in omnia*. The Revised Covenant Argument invokes the right to everything to show that vis-à-vis humans, no extra-statist action—however unreasonable—can be unjust/injurious/without right. The Propriety Argument, by contrast, points out that nothing is exclusively one's own as long as all retain their natural right to everything. Defining justice as the constant will to give each their own, the argument holds that justice presupposes exclusive personal rights—and therefore abandonment of the right to everything:

P1: Justice consists in the constant will to give each their own;
P2: One's 'own' consists of exclusive personal rights ('propriety');
P3: Propriety is non-existent outside the commonwealth due to each person's natural right to everything;
P4: All exclusive personal rights are legal property titles, created *ex nihilo* by distributive civil laws;
C1: Civil law is prior to justice.

Hobbes explicitly links the *jus omnium in omnia* to the commonplace claim that private property is of conventional origin.[24] At least since Cicero, it had been a commonplace that the world originally belonged to humanity as a whole. To increase efficiency, avoid conflict, and make charity possible, humans eventually decided to set up some scheme of private property. Hobbes, too, asserts that 'Nature has given all things to all men' (EL 14.10; DCv 1.10). Yet he radicalizes the dictum in three ways: (i) people can without injustice invade each other's natural rights to use common resources; (ii) regimes of private property are impossible outside the state; (iii) and nothing is properly one's own before civil law distinguishes *mine* from *thine* (§5.1).

---

[23] The most extensive discussion of the Propriety Argument to date is in Green, 'Justice and Law in Hobbes', 119–126. The argument is mentioned in passing by D.D. Raphael, 'Hobbes on Justice' in G.A.J. Rogers and Alan Ryan (eds), *Perspectives on Thomas Hobbes* (Oxford, 1988) 155; Hoekstra, 'Natural Condition of Mankind', 120; Daniel Eggers, 'Injury, Injustice, Iniquity', *Intellectual History Review* 24 (2014) no. 2: 175.

[24] E.g. EL 14.10; EL 20.2; EL 24.2; EL 27.8; DCv 6.1, 15; DCv 12.7; DCv 14.7, 9; L 18.10.

192　NO PEACE, NO JUSTICE

> Until a commonwealth is instituted, *all things belong to all men* [omnia omnium sunt] and there is nothing a man can call *his own* that any other man cannot claim by the same right as *his* (for where all things are *common*, nothing can be *proper* to any one man). (DCv 6.15)

Theft is impossible in the state of nature: 'nothing was another's (because nature gave all things to all men), and it was consequently not possible to encroach on what was another's' (DCv 14.9). So are wrongful assaults upon another's life, body, and person. 'Without Law every thing is in such sort every Mans, as he may take, possess, and enjoy without wrong to any Man, every thing, Lands, Beasts, Fruits, and <u>even the bodies of other Men</u>' (DPS 9). For Hobbes, all exclusive personal rights presuppose a legal system. Humans have no violable natural rights at all. This position was historically unprecedented. Rebuking him, Pufendorf denounced:

> the absurdity of saying that there is no injustice in the state of nature. For since injustice occurs through an act by which the right of others is violated, and since every person has in fact a natural and not merely conventional right to preserve his own life, limbs, and liberty against an illegitimate attack of others, it is clearly unjust to threaten an evil against another's life, members, and liberty for which that person has provided no demonstrable cause.[25]

Chapter 5 has shown that Hobbes developed over time three distinct arguments for the state dependency of private property (*Statism about Property*). The Security and Precision Argument are both found in *Elements/De Cive*. These arguments maintain that a legal system is needed to render pre-legal claims to property secure and determinate. Both arguments presume that 'each man has his own *right* and *property* by particular contracts, so that one man may say of *one thing* and another of *another thing* that it is his own' (DCv 6.1). The task of the state is to protect these private contracts, by prosecuting theft and fraud and by legally settling disputes over their contents (§5.2). Both arguments for why the existence of private property presupposes a legal system gel with the Revised Covenant Argument: the state's coercive power provides the safety needed to render private contracts establishing private property binding and secure.

The Propriety Argument relies on *Leviathan*'s bolder argument for *Statism about Property*: the Creation Argument (§5.5). Exclusive rights to external resources, this argument states, require more than legal protection to arise. Property rights are legal artefacts, created *ex nihilo* by distributive civil laws. The *mine* and *thine* that form the subject matter of justice are first brought into being by

---

[25] Samuel Pufendorf, *On the Natural State of Men*, ed. Michael Seidler (Lewiston, 1990) 122.

THE PROPRIETY ARGUMENT   193

distributive laws, allocating to each their own (L 24.5; DPS 35). For this reason, the Propriety Argument concludes, justice presupposes civil law:

> And therefore where there is no *Own*, that is, no Propriety, there is no Injustice; and where there is no coërcive Power erected, that is, where there is no Commonwealth, there is no Propriety; all men having Right to all things; Therefore where there is no Common-Wealth, there nothing is Unjust. (L 15.3)

The Latin *Leviathan* sums it up succinctly: 'Civitas, Proprietas Bonorum, & Justitia simul nata sunt' (LL 15.3; also LL 18.6). Conversely, once 'the distinction of propriety is taken away ... Justice becomes of no effect' (L 30.12).[26]

The Propriety Argument is premised upon the Roman law definition of justice, associated with Ulpian: '*Justice is the constant Will of Giving to every man his own*' (L 15.3).[27] As previous chapters have shown, Hobbes twisted the meaning of this maxim. *Leviathan* identified the formula with distributive justice as equity—the justice of arbitrators:

> Distributive Justice, the Justice of an Arbitrator; that is to say, the act of defining what is Just. Wherein, (being trusted by them that make him Arbitrator,) if he performe his Trust, he is said to distributive to every man his own: and this is indeed Just Distribution. (L 15.15)

The sovereign arbitrator gives each citizen their own by issuing distributive civil laws, obligating them to steer clear from what the law says belongs to others (§5.4). In distributing property rights to each subject, the sovereign creates rather than tracks rights/merit. Distributive justice is not a norm external and prior to the legal allocation of rights and goods. It is that division itself: 'This distribution is Justice' (DPS 10) (§4.5). This makes civil law logically prior to justice:

> it is Manifest that before there was a Law, there could be no Injustice, and therefore Laws are in their Nature antecedent to Justice and Injustice, and you cannot deny but there must be Law-makers, before there were any Laws, and Consequently

---

[26] The non-existence of justice and property outside the Hobbesian commonwealth is no consequence of scarcity. Hobbes's argument differs in this respect from that of Hume—who likewise made justice conditional on the existence of private property. According to Hume, justice and private property exist only in conditions of mitigated scarcity. We have no reason to treat objects as exclusively yours or mine amidst extreme scarcity or utmost abundance, 'rendering justice totally *useless*'. Extreme scarcity suspends the rules of property—allowing all to violently fend for themselves 'by all the means which prudence can dictate, or humanity permit'. The same explains why justice is suspended 'among the warring parties'. David Hume, *Enquiry Concerning the Principles of Morals*, ed. Tom L. Beauchamp (Oxford, 1998) 3.1.2–5, 8–13.

[27] *Institutes*, 1.1; *Digest*, 1.1.10. For discussion, see Dieter Hüning, 'From the Virtue of Justice to the Concept of Legal Order' in Ian Hunter and David Saunders (eds), *Natural Law and Civil Sovereignty* (London, 2002) 139–152.

194 NO PEACE, NO JUSTICE

before there was any Justice, I speak of Humane Justice; and that Law-makers were before that which you call Own, or property of Goods, or Lands distinguished by *Meum, Tuum, Alienum.* (DPS 36)

In sum, on the Propriety Argument, justice and injustice have no place outside the commonwealth since the exclusive rights that justice regulates originate in civil law.[28]

The Propriety Argument is new to *Leviathan. De Cive* thrice cites Ulpian's definition to demonstrate the conventional origin of private property rights.[29] But it contains no trace yet of the Propriety Argument. Several key premises were still missing. The Propriety Argument (an argument for *Statism about Justice*) is based on the Creation Argument (one for *Statism about Property*). Like that last argument, the Propriety Argument assumes that distributive justice as equity is a virtue of arbitrators, who legally demarcate *mine* from *thine*. That notion, in turn, relies on an anti-Aristotelian conception of merit. Both ideas first appear in *Leviathan* (§4.5; §5.5).

The Revised Covenant and the Propriety Arguments provide rival explanations for how certain actions (contractual rights-divestment) or laws (legal allocation of exclusive rights) can bring it about that norms of justice become applicable in practice. Moreover, the two arguments gloss *Statism about Justice* in diverging ways. The Revised Covenant Argument holds that the state, with its coercive power to punish pact breakers, needs to exist for norms of justice to *become effective.* Grounded in commutative justice, the argument understands unjust actions as violations of covenant. The Propriety Argument, premised upon distributive justice, assumes that justice consists in rendering to each their own. It makes the stronger claim that the commonwealth is needed for norms of justice to *arise*: justice is posterior to the institution of exclusive personal rights by civil legislation. The two arguments for *Statism about Justice* are therefore irreducibly distinct.

So far, I have written primarily about the justice and injustice of *actions*. Whether justice of *persons* (i.e. the virtue of justice) has place in the state of nature is another question. Recall that the virtue of justice (in its narrow sense) consists in the steady disposition to observe the natural law precept of justice (EL 16.4; DCv 3.5; L 15.10) (§3.7). Hobbes describes the virtue of justice in two ways, each corresponding to a distinct principle of justice. The virtue of *commutative* justice consists in 'that habit by which we stand to covenants' (EL 17.14). Elsewhere, he writes that 'men are counted and termed rightly just and unjust' insofar as they are

---

[28] Spinoza takes over the Propriety Argument from Hobbes, while modifying two of its premises. Baruch Spinoza, 'Political Treatise' in *The Collected Works of Spinoza*, vol. 2, ed. Edwin Curley (Princeton, 2016) 2.23. For discussion, see Johan Olsthoorn, 'Spinoza on Human and Divine Justice', *History of Philosophy Quarterly* 33 (2016) no. 1: 29–31.

[29] DCv ED.9; DCv 17.10; DCv 18.3. Ulpian's definition is further mentioned or hinted at in L 15.22; L 18.3; L 24.5; L 26.8; L 30.12; L 43.4; DPS 8–10; DPS 35.

disposed to abide by 'that which men make among themselves here by pacts and covenants' (EW 5: 115). The virtue of *distributive* justice, by contrast, consists in 'a constant will of giving to every man his own' (LL 15.9; also L 43.4). For arbitrators, distributive justice reduces to the virtue of equity (requiring impartial and even-handed adjudication) (§4.3). For citizens, it requires non-intrusion upon what civil law says belongs to others. Observe that for citizens 'all failures to give each his own are ultimately instances of breaking a covenant' since their original promise of simple obedience renders distributive laws obligatory to them.[30] Outside the state, I submit, humans can possess the virtue of commutative justice—but not that of distributive justice.

Ample textual evidence attests that humans can and do make valid covenants in the state of nature. Some may even occasionally keep their word. Doing so is not generally morally required, however. Justice is a most undemanding virtue in war. Sincerely willing to keep faith suffices to fulfil our duties—we do not actually need to stick to our agreements amidst hostility (which, Hobbes says, is usually plain foolishness). In other words, pre-statist individuals can fulfil justice merely by having good intentions (i.e. by back-pedalling on their word reluctantly). Conceivably, some are even steadily disposed to act justly—even if they never in fact keep faith in practice. While the demands of justice are easily met in war, people are not just by default. We have to be steadily disposed to do what justice requires—even if justice asks nothing more of us outside the state.[31]

By contrast, pre-statist individuals cannot possibly will to give each their own. Since absolutely nothing belongs exclusively to anyone in the state of nature, it is impossible for its inhabitants to even contemplate acting justly by giving each their own. 'The principles that each man has *his own* right proper to him and distinct from *another*'s, and that he is forbidden to violate the rights *of others*, have their source in the civil laws' (DCv 14.9). As per the Propriety Argument, a system of law is needed to first give justice its content. In this sense, we can say that justice and injustice 'are Qualities, that relate to men in Society, not in Solitude'—that is, to 'citizens' (LL 13.11). Incidentally, distributive justice is not the only moral norm devoid of content before civil laws are introduced. Where all things are common, Hobbes claims, norms forbidding adultery or murder are likewise meaningless (DCv 14.9).

---

[30] Green, 'Justice and Law in Hobbes', 114, also 123.

[31] Martinich, *Two Gods*, 76, writes that Hobbes 'leaves it open that everyone is just in the state of nature, because no one can break a law in a condition in which there are no laws'. I accept the conclusion yet reject his explanation: being just requires more than abstaining from injustice.

196 NO PEACE, NO JUSTICE

CONCLUSION

'Before covenants and laws were drawn up, neither justice nor injustice, neither public good nor public evil, was natural among men any more than it was among beasts' (DH 10.5). This chapter has dissected two Hobbesian arguments for this thesis, dubbed *Statism about Justice*. I have argued that only the Propriety Argument fully establishes it. Justice presupposes civil law since the content matter of justice ('propriety') is first created by the sovereign's distributive laws. The Revised Covenant Argument rules out all extra-statist *injustices*, yet leaves open the possibility of extra-statist *justice*.

Hobbes's defence of *Statism about Justice* has made him canonical in theories of international relations and global justice. The argumentative grounds of the doctrine are nevertheless squarely rooted in domestic concerns. *Statism about Justice*, I have shown, follows directly from *Statism about Property*. The Propriety Argument is the upshot of *Leviathan's* thesis that private property rights originate in civil legislation. That thesis, in turn, served to invalidate popular gripes about sovereign maldistribution, expropriation, and taxation without consent. Hobbes's struggle to develop a theory of property congenial to absolute rulers thus helps explain his belated endorsement of the state-dependency of justice and injustice. *Statism about Justice* does provide additional support for Hobbes's vindicatory agenda, by proving that the sovereign's foreign policy cannot possibly be unjust vis-à-vis other countries. The doctrine as a whole is not essential to his civil theodicy however. After all, the latter does not require showing that rulers cannot *act justly* within the international arena. The Revised Covenant Argument—which precludes extra-statist injustices only and thus fails to prove *Statism about Justice* in its entirety—served Hobbes's negative civil theodicy equally well.

Let me spell out, in closing, how the Revised Covenant and Propriety Arguments help forestall sovereign injustice in world affairs. Hobbes no doubt considers international truces and treaties valid and potentially beneficial.[32] Yet in line with the Revised Covenant Argument, sovereigns may rightfully withdraw from any international treaty whenever they judge doing so necessary for national safety: 'every Common-wealth . . . has an absolute Libertie, to doe what it shall judge . . . most conducive to their benefit' (L 21.8). Foreign contracting parties cannot possibly tell whether pacts are sidelined with fair or malign motives. Sovereigns therefore have *de facto* right to do as they please, keeping or undoing treaties at will. Duly perceiving where such reasoning leads to, Pufendorf scolded Hobbes for holding that '*Soveraign Princes* now, who are still with respect to one another in a *State of Nature*, should not be thought Guilty of Injustice, when they break their Compacts.'[33] To be sure, wanton breach of covenant brings war closer and is as

---

[32] E.g. DCv 2.18; L 20.4; L 21.24; L 22.29; LL 28.23; B 301.
[33] Pufendorf, *Nature and Nations*, 8.1.5.

CONCLUSION 197

such always forbidden by natural law. Yet, as we have seen, extra-statist sins against natural law are no injustices or injuries against human actors. It follows that any sovereign arbitrarily 'putting to death, or making Slaves of Embassadors' commits thereby no injustice to either the diplomat or their employer—even if such acts are blatant violations of natural law and injuries to God.[34] An in-depth analysis of morality among states follows in Chapter 9.

The Propriety Argument, in turn, implies that states have no exclusive territorial rights vis-à-vis one another. Territorial rights are commonly understood to consist of rights of jurisdiction within the territory; rights over the natural resources in it; and rights to control its borders.[35] Abizadeh has argued that 'the Hobbesian commonwealth has no essentially territorial jurisdictional boundaries'.[36] Hobbes views state authority primarily in terms of jurisdictional rights over persons, rather than as rights over territory.[37] Territory does not figure in his conception of the state: the commonwealth is defined as the multitude united as one person, by having jointly authorized a common representative to speak and act on their behalf.[38] The Propriety Argument further buttresses Abizadeh's argument. Exclusive rights over territory are non-existent in the international state of nature for the same reason that private property is so: neither is possible as long as extra-statist actors retain their universal right to everything. Hobbes, we shall see, attributes the same unlimited rights to any state-of-nature actor—be they individuals, states, or sovereigns: 'that which every man could do before the institution of commonwealths, every commonwealth can do by the law of nations' (LL 30.30). If the sovereign's duty to protect the people against foreign enemies indeed generates a veritable right to everything, debarring all exclusive rights of others, then the sovereign cannot wrong/injure other states by invading the lands they control (no matter how imprudent such aggression is). The next two chapters further examine the mutual rights and duties of international actors through the lens of just war theory.

[34] Following Tyrrell, *Brief Disquisition*, 245, also 360–363.
[35] David Miller, 'Territorial Rights: Concept and Justification', *Political Studies* 60 (2012) no. 2: 253.
[36] Arash Abizadeh, 'Sovereign Jurisdiction, Territorial Rights, and Membership in Hobbes' in A.P. Martinich and Kinch Hoekstra (eds), *The Oxford Handbook of Hobbes* (Oxford, 2016) 420.
[37] Abizadeh, 'Sovereign Jurisdiction', 424.
[38] Johan Olsthoorn, '*Leviathan* Inc.: Hobbes on the Nature and Person of the Commonwealth', *History of European Ideas* 47 (2021) no. 1: 22, 28.

8

RIGHTS OF WAR

INTRODUCTION

Hobbes's theory of justice is premised upon the natural right to everything. That postulate allowed him to claim, *inter alia*, that injury and injustice consist in breaking valid covenants (§2.1 and §2.2); that private property rights are created by and remain dependent on civil law (§5.4); and that justice and injustice are non-existent outside the state (§7.3). How did Hobbes justify his outlandish and unprecedented right to everything? What makes it the case that, absent binding covenants, 'every man was permitted to do anything to anybody, and to possess, use and enjoy whatever he wanted and could get' (DCv 1.10)? Various arguments for the doctrine can be gleaned from Hobbes's works. The absence of pre-political exclusive rights—even in one's own body and person—informs a negative justification: outside the state, nobody has claims on anyone else that they abstain from doing or taking certain things (§5.1). This chapter contends that Hobbes developed a positive justification for the natural right to everything by radicalizing received doctrines of just war and self-defence.

This is arguably the first study to take seriously Hobbes's contention that 'the right of all men to all things . . . is the right of War' (DCv P.15). I reconstruct the normative and conceptual presuppositions of the individual natural right to everything against the background of just war theory. My reconstruction has two parts. First, I show that Hobbesian natural rights of self-defence are exceptionally vast. They even encompass the right to conquer and enslave innocents (i.e. those who intend no harm). Hobbes was able to portray aggressive war as essentially defensive in character by reconceptualizing defensive force. Not only armed responses to immediate and present threats, but any war waged with the intention of heightening personal security is defensive and justified—including first strikes against innocents. Second, I show how Hobbes subverted various received just war principles to sanction individual use of violence in the state of nature. By reinterpreting the natural law duties of trust and charity, he rendered obsolete all received just war requirements bar the right-intention condition. Outside the state, the laws of nature cannot moderate or restrain rights of war since these norms bind *in foro externo* only when the agent judges their preservation secure. The result is an exceedingly lenient just war theory. My analysis explains why and in what sense Hobbesian agents are by nature enemies of one another: they have no presumptive duty to actively trust or aid one another absent agreements to the contrary.

Hobbes on Justice. Johan Olsthoorn, Oxford University Press. © Johan Olsthoorn 2024.
DOI: 10.1093/9780191904585.003.0008

My thesis that Hobbes's natural right to everything is normatively underpinned by a just war theory may seem surprising. Hobbes is commonly portrayed as a main exemplar of the so-called realist take on war.[1] Realists about war maintain that moral categories have no place in armed conflict.[2] The realm of war is beyond morality. As the proverb has it: all is fair in love and war. Realism is commonly positioned against two theoretical rivals: pacifism and just war theory.[3] Both realists and pacifists declare 'just war' to be a concept without real-world application—albeit for opposite reasons. While pacifists decry warfare as an unjustifiable evil,[4] realists disparage those 'kind-hearted people' who refuse to see 'what war really is'. 'To introduce the principle of moderation into the theory of war itself', the Prussian general Carl von Clausewitz (1780–1831) continued, 'would always lead to logical absurdity'.[5] When violently defending 'the safety of one's country', Niccolò Machiavelli (1469–1527) contended, 'there must be no consideration of just or unjust, of merciful or cruel, of praiseworthy or disgraceful'.[6] For Hobbes, too, justice of actions is inapplicable in conditions of violent conflict. In war, 'nothing can be Unjust. The notions of Right and Wrong, Justice and Injustice have there no place' (L 13.13).

This chapter follows recent revisionist interpretations in contending that Hobbes did have an ethical theory of war—the above quotation notwithstanding. Existing revisionist readings emphasize *moral limits* natural law places upon permissible defensive killing.[7] I will instead concentrate on Hobbesian rights of war—on *moral justifications* for using armed force. For Hobbes, 'rights of war' signify both individual and collective rights to resort to armed force. The same set of moral principles regulate interactions between any agent in the state of nature,

---

[1] E.g. Michael Walzer, *Just and Unjust Wars* (New York, 2015) 10–13; Carl Schmitt, *The Leviathan in the State Theory of Thomas Hobbes*, transl. George Schwab (Westport, 1996) 47–48.

[2] Realism *about war* should not be conflated with realism *about international relations*. The realist tradition in international relations is an approach to the study of international politics characterized by a number of distinctive methodological assumptions: (1) the international system is anarchic; (2) self-interest is of overriding explanatory value for political conduct; (3) politics always takes place within and between groups; (4) questions of power predominate in international affairs. Emphasizing the special character of politics within international affairs, the conjunction of these tenets gels with realism about war. The two realisms remain however analytically and practically separable. On the distinctive tenets of realism about international relations, see Jack Donnelly, *Realism and International Relations* (Cambridge, 2000) 9–13; William C. Wohlforth, 'Realism' in Christian Reus-Smit and Duncan Snidal (eds), *The Oxford Handbook of International Relations* (Oxford, 2008) 131–149.

[3] E.g. Nicholas Fotion, 'Reactions to War: Pacifism, Realism, and Just War Theory' in Andrew Valls (ed), *Ethics in International Affairs: Theories and Cases* (Lanham, 2000) 15–32.

[4] Absolute pacifists hold that waging war is unjustifiable in principle. Contingent pacifists acknowledge that warfare can be justified in theory while insisting that in the real world, waging war is (nearly) always unjustified.

[5] Carl von Clausewitz, *On War*, ed. Beatrice Heuser (Oxford, 2007) 14.

[6] Machiavelli, 'Discorsi' in *The Chief Works and Others*, vol. 1, ed. Allan Gilbert (Durham, 1989) 3.41.

[7] E.g. Delphine Thivet, 'Thomas Hobbes: A Philosopher of War or Peace?', *British Journal for the History of Philosophy* 16 (2008) no. 4: 701–721; S.A. Lloyd, 'International Relations, World Government, and the Ethics of War: A Hobbesian Perspective' in idem (ed), *Hobbes Today* (Cambridge, 2013) 291–301; Jeff McMahan, 'Hobbesian Defenses of Orthodox Just War Theory' in S.A. Lloyd (ed), *Hobbes Today*, 304–319.

200   RIGHTS OF WAR

be they individuals, sovereigns, or commonwealths. The laws of nations (*jus gentium*) governing international affairs are identical in substance to the laws of nature prescribing to each individual the socially necessary means to peace and self-preservation (EL 29.10; DCv 14.4). Moreover, 'every Soveraign hath the same Right, in procuring the safety of his People, that any particular man can have, in procuring the safety of his own Body' (L 30.30). For empirical reasons, however, these principles apply differently to extra-statist individuals as to international actors. This chapter explores the conditions for morally permissible resort to armed force within the *interpersonal* state of nature. Chapter 9 turns to the norms governing *international* war and peace. Jointly, the two chapters will provide an encompassing new interpretation of Hobbes's just war theory.

At this point, some readers may object that subsuming self-defence under 'war' is linguistically misplaced. Wars are temporally and spatially protracted conditions of hostility between political groups, rather than lethal skirmishes between private individuals. Hobbes's colourful invocation of a 'warre of every man against every man' should be seen as a dramatic metaphor, the objection goes, rather than as a condition governed by *jus belli* (L 13.13). The analysis provided in this chapter should quell this concern. Furthermore, Hobbes was not alone in conceptualizing rights of self-defence under the heading of war. According to Francisco de Vitoria (1485–1546), 'any person, even a private citizen, may declare and wage defensive war . . . not only for self-defence but also for the defence of their property and goods'.[8] Grotius subsumed under 'war' any condition of hostility, 'not even excluding single Combats'.[9] Locke agreed: 'force, or a declared design of force upon the Person of another, where there is no common Superior on Earth to appeal to for relief, *is the State of War*'.[10] Hobbesian individual rights of war should be understood in light of this wider tradition of thought.

8.1 JUSTIFYING VIOLENCE

The popular realist reading of Hobbes on war finds textual support in passages stating that the laws of nature are silent in war: '*inter arma silent leges*. There is little therefore to be said concerning the laws that men are to observe one towards another in time of war, wherein every mans' being and well-being is the rule of his actions' (EL 19.2; also DCv 5.2; DPS 36, 189). Natural law, prescribing the

---

[8] Francisco de Vitoria, *Political Writings*, ed. Anthony Pagden and Jeremy Lawrance (Cambridge, 1991) 299. Departing from Aquinas, Suárez similarly regarded the difference between 'wars' (armed contests between states) and 'duels' (armed contests between private individuals) to be 'material rather than formal'. Francisco Suárez, 'On Charity' in *Suárez: Selections from Three Works*, ed. Thomas Pink (Indianapolis, 2015) 13pr. Gentili, *De Jure Belli*, 12, dissented, insisting that 'the strife must be public; for war is not a broil, a fight, the hostility of individuals'.

[9] Grotius, *War and Peace*, 1.1.2.1.

[10] Locke, *Second Treatise*, 3.19.

social means to self-preservation, ceaselessly binds in conscience (*in foro interno*). However, agents are morally required to act on these norms only if they deem doing so safe (EL 17.10; DCv 3.27; L 15.36). When peace is out of reach, reason dictates: '*By all means we can, to defend our selves*' (L 14.4). The general non-observance of natural law in war augments personal danger, delimiting further the degree to which these norms should be practised. The main normative restraints on actions effective in war are laws of honour.[11] Their violation does not, however, amount to injustice: 'there be in war no law, the breach whereof is injury' (EL 19.2). *Leviathan*'s claim that nothing is unjust in war captures the same idea: belligerents cannot wrong their enemies (L 13.13).[12] Some vices forbidden by natural law, including intemperateness and wanton cruelty, are hard to conceive as means of self-defence, suggesting that some laws of nature continue to bind in practice even amidst widespread violence (EL 16.10; DCv 3.27n). Following this lead, revisionist readings of Hobbes on war have focused on moral norms governing actions, including prohibitions on cruelty, that are operative within war.[13]

This chapter reassesses Hobbes's views on war from the opposite direction. I focus on the moral authorization of individual armed force, rather than on moral restrictions on such force. What morally justifies using violence against other people in the natural condition? The exegetical significance of this question is reinforced by Hobbes's equation of the right of war with the right to everything.

as long as a person has no guarantee of security from attack, his primeval *Right* remains in force to look out for himself in whatever ways he will and can, i.e. a *Right to all things*, or a *Right of war* [*Jus in omnia*, sive *Jus belli*]. (DCv 5.1)

The right to all things is, in part, an unlimited right of war, derived from supposedly uncontroversial rights of self-defence: 'before the Institution of Common-wealth, every man had a right to every thing, and to do whatsoever he thought necessary to his own preservation; subduing, hurting, or killing any man in order thereunto' (L 28.2).[14]

How did Hobbes deduce rights to wage total war from rights of self-defence? It is not unreasonable, he posited first, for humans to defend themselves with all their might to avoid death and pain. Whatever is not unreasonable for us to do,

---

[11] EL 19.2; DCv 5.2; L 17.2. On plunder and piracy ('making war with small forces') as previously honourable vocations, see also EW 8: 5–6; DCv 13.14; L 10.49; LL 17.2.

[12] Also EW 5: 152; DPS 9; L R&C.7: '... Injustice, (for acts of open Hostility bear not that name)'.

[13] Thivet, 'Thomas Hobbes', 713–721; Larry May, 'A Hobbesian Approach to Cruelty and the Rules of War', *Leiden Journal of International Law* 26 (2013) no. 2: 293–313; Larry May, *Limiting Leviathan* (Oxford, 2013) 195–223; McMahan, 'Hobbesian Defenses'.

[14] On the natural right of self-preservation as warranting defensive killing, see also EL 22.9; DCv 2.18; DCv 8.10; EW 5: 152, 184–185; DPS 192. *Leviathan* contains no explicit identification of the right to everything with the right of war. This is due, I conjecture, to its new distinction between harming people by right of punishment vs. by right of war (L 28.13, 23). Both are grounded in the natural right to pursue self-preservation by all means necessary.

202 RIGHTS OF WAR

we have a right or liberty to. *Ergo*, each person has a natural right to seek to 'preserve his own life and limbs, with all the power he hath' (EL 14.6; also DCv 1.7; L 14.1; L 14.4). In what ways may we defend ourselves? By all *necessary* means, Hobbes replied—else the right is in vain (EL 14.7; DCv 1.8–10; DCv 1.10n). This line of argument establishes a natural right to do whatever is necessary to preserve ourselves. At this point, a quintessentially Hobbesian question is raised: who determines which actions are necessary to protect life and limb? Characteristic of the state of nature is human equality of right—the absolute absence of status hierarchies (L 31.1). In such a condition, each person has the right to judge for themselves what their self-preservation requires (EL 14.8–9; DCv 1.9). For anyone else to have the authority to make that judgement for us contravenes human natural equality of right. Evidently, we can make mistakes, misjudging a helping hand for a clenched fist. Error does not curb natural right though because each person is by right their own judge: 'In the judgment of the person actually doing it, what is done is rightly done, even if it is a wrong, and so is rightly done' (DCv 1.10n). The absence of human judges turns each person's natural right of self-preservation into a 'right to do and to possess everything that he shall judge to be necessary for his self-preservation' (DCv 1.10n; also EL 19.1). Hence, 'if you wish to kill, you have the right to do so' (DCv 2.18).[15]

Natural rights of self-defence, in conjunction with individual rights to judge, legitimate violence that falls well beyond the remit of self-defence proper. They allow each person to preventively attack others for reasons of self-protection.

> there is no way for any man to secure himselfe, so reasonable, as Anticipation; that is, by force, or wiles, to master the persons of all men he can, so long, till he see no other power great enough to endanger him: And this is no more than his own conservation requireth, and is generally allowed. (L 13.4)

Notice Hobbes's normative language: pre-statist individuals are morally allowed to resort to preventive war when they deem this necessary for self-preservation. Not only to forestall imminent attacks, but also to heighten their personal security more generally: 'And as their preservation, so also is their security a just pretence of invading those whom they have just cause to fear' (DPS 192). Indeed, Hobbes even morally sanctioned wars of conquest that are waged to increase personal protection: 'such augmentation of dominion over men, being necessary to a mans conservation, it ought to be allowed him' (L 13.4). In conditions of war, self-preservation generates rights 'even to one anothers body' (L 14.4); 'to one another's persons'

---

[15] Cumberland, *Treatise*, 359, spelled out Hobbes's conclusion: 'by the Name of *Right*, is to be understood, not the Liberty of acting according to *right Reason*, or any Law of Nature; but of acting any thing, *as he will himself*. For critical discussion of Hobbes's argument, see Daniel Eggers, 'Hobbes, Kant, and the Universal "Right to All Things"', *Hobbes Studies* 32 (2019) no. 1: 55–56.

(EL 15.2); and to 'their lives' (L 21.6). The subsequent analysis will reveal that such wars were certainly not 'generally allowed' at the time. The scope of Hobbes's 'right of nature in making War' was historically unprecedented (DPS 192).[16]

Philosophers today distinguish between two sets of just war requirements: norms determining permissible resort to armed force (*jus ad bellum*); and those specifying permissible conduct within war (*jus in bello*).[17] That distinction cannot easily be made with respect to Hobbesian rights of war due to his signature doctrine that the natural human condition is conflict-ridden.[18] Hobbes enumerated several causes of conflict (competition, diffidence, glory) prior to introducing rights of war.[19] Yet what makes life outside the state a war *of all against all* is each person's natural right to everything. 'The right of all men to all things, by which one man *rightly* attacks and the other *rightly* resists (an unfailing spring of suspicion and mutual resentment)' makes 'men's natural state . . . a war of every man against every man' (DCv 1.12; also EL 14.11).[20] Hobbes thus spelled out *jus belli* against a pre-existing condition of war (even if the introduction of rights of war further exacerbates conflict). The same is true for the international state of nature, which too is by default a condition of war (§9.1).

This complicates determining what Hobbes's view is on the causes that justify reverting to armed force. Classical just war theories recognized several just causes for war. To mention some of the more influential, Cicero maintained that no war is just unless fought to recover usurped property or to ward off enemies.[21] The canon lawyer Gratian recognized the same two just causes for war: 'to regain what has been stolen or to repel the attack of enemies'.[22] Aquinas, citing Augustine, insisted that war may only be waged to avenge culpable wrongdoing.[23] Grotius identified three just causes for war: '*Defence*, the *Recovery* of what's our own, and *Punishment*'.[24] Rejecting the category of punitive war, Pufendorf proposed three

[16] Similar expressions are used at DCv 6.2; L 28.23. See also DCv 12.2; B 279. L 24.4 mentions 'just Warre' in passing, depicting it as a means of acquiring foreign resources.

[17] Two other sets of just war requirements, bracketed here, are *jus ex bello* (determining how wars may permissibly be ended) and *jus post bellum* (spelling out post-war moral requirements).

[18] Stephen C. Neff emphasizes how path-breaking Hobbes's insistence on the naturalness of war is in *War and the Law of Nations: A General History* (Cambridge, 2005) 135–137.

[19] EL 14.3–5; DCv 1.4–6; L 13.6–7. On Hobbes on the causes of war, see Jean Hampton, 'Hobbes's State of War', *Topoi* 4 (1985) no. 1: 47–60; G.S. Kavka, *Hobbesian Moral and Political Theory* (Princeton, 1986) 83–125; Arash Abizadeh, 'Hobbes on the Causes of War: A Disagreement Theory', *American Political Science Review* 105 (2011) no. 2: 298–315; Arash Abizadeh, 'Glory and the Evolution of Hobbes's Disagreement Theory of War: From *Elements* to *Leviathan*', *History of Political Thought* 41 (2020) no. 2: 265–298. The *trivium* of causes is reminiscent of Thucydides, *The Peloponnesian War*, 1.75; in Hobbes's translation: 'we were forced to advance our dominion to what it is, out of the nature of the thing itself; as chiefly for fear, next for honour, and lastly for profit' (EW 8: 81).

[20] Rousseau derided Hobbes's 'sophist' reasoning that 'this mutual enmity is not innate and immediate, but founded on the inevitable competition of the right of each to all things' in 'The State of War' in *The Collected Writings of Rousseau*, vol. 11, ed. Christopher Kelly (Hanover, NH, 2005) 63.

[21] Cicero, *The Republic and the Laws*, ed. Jonathan Powell, transl. Niall Rudd (Oxford, 1998) 69.

[22] Gratian, *Decretum*, II causa 23.2.1 in Gregory M. Reichberg, Henrik Syse, and Endre Begby (eds), *The Ethics of War: Classic and Contemporary Readings* (Malden, MA, 2006) 113.

[23] Aquinas, *Summa Theologica*, 2a.2ae.40.1.

[24] Grotius, *War and Peace*, 2.1.2.2.

204   RIGHTS OF WAR

rival *casus belli*: (i) self-defence; (ii) repairing injuries and recovering what is due; and (iii) securing protection against future injuries.[25]

Punishment is no ground for just war on Hobbes's account either—at least not in *Leviathan*. There, punishment presupposes by definition public authority over those punished (L 28.1; L 28.5–6). 'Harme inflicted upon one that is a declared enemy, fals not under the name of Punishment' since enemies—including rebels— are not subject to public authority (L 28.13) (§10.3).[26] It seems that Hobbes cannot recognize recovery of property as a just ground for war either. After all, he denied the persistence of private property rights in conditions of war, insisting more generally that exclusive rights are first brought into existence by civil law (*Statism about Property*) (§5.5; §7.3). Observe, though, that private property is non-existent outside the state in part *because* war reigns there. Hobbes developed his account of the permissible use of violence against a bellicose background in which 'there be no Propriety, no Dominion, no *Mine* and *Thine* distinct; but onely that to be every mans, that he can get; and for so long, as he can keep it' (L 13.13; also L 24.5; L 29.10). Small wonder that he omitted recovery of property as a just cause of war. The *Dialogue* does explicitly mention justifications for initiating warfare. 'Necessity, and Security are the principle justifications, before God, of beginning War. Injuries receiv'd justifie a War defensive; but for reparable injuries, if Reparation be tendred, all invasion upon that Title is Iniquity' (DPS 192; also L 42.127). This suggests that Hobbes in principle accepted avenging injuries as just causes for war once the commonwealth is instituted—a finding possibly relevant for just wars between states.[27] While it might therefore not be entirely correct to say that 'only war undertaken for motives of self-preservation is fully legitimate',[28] self-defence is for Hobbes the sole just cause for war applicable in the *interpersonal* state of nature. The next sections show that Hobbes enlarged the category of permissible defensive violence to include self-defence proper as well as overall

---

[25] Samuel Pufendorf, *The Whole Duty of Man*, ed. Ian Hunter and David Saunders (Indianapolis, 2003) 2.16.2.

[26] This argument for restricting punishment to the civil domain rests on Hobbes's doctrine of authorization, first developed in *Leviathan*. His earlier works ground rights of punishment not in superior *authority*, but in eminent physical *power*: 'For a greater power is always required to punish . . . than theirs who are punished' (EL 20.19). As humans, by nature roughly equal in power, can team up to combine their force, punishment is on that earlier account conceivable in the state of nature. Various passages in *De Cive* attest to the existence of pre-political rights of punishment (DCv 6.5; DCv 6.12; DCv 16.15).

[27] It is unclear how this passage squares with the view, reiterated in the *Dialogue*, that neither property nor injury exists beyond the state (DPS 9). Pufendorf, *Nature and Nations*, 8.1.3, dismissed Hobbes's doctrine 'that there was no Property before the Institution of Civil Government' on the grounds that 'all Sovereign Princes and Commonwealths are now actually in a State of Nature, and their Properties are not determin'd by any common Law or Judge, but solely by Compact, and the natural means of Acquisition; and yet I believe no Body ever imagin'd that Princes might ravage, or steal from one another, without incurring the Guilt of Rapine or Theft'.

[28] Thivet, 'Thomas Hobbes', 706, also 713.

security, while simultaneously eliminating nearly all moral restrictions on legitimate defence.

8.2 RADICALIZING RIGHTS OF SELF-DEFENCE

Tuck has argued at length that the modern natural law tradition, initiated by Grotius and Hobbes, is characterized by the attempt to derive a set of universally acceptable moral norms from the natural right of self-preservation.[29] Their minimalist natural law theories putatively served to counter a form of moral scepticism revived by Charron and Montaigne. 'Fully conscious of the salience of the principle of self-preservation in the sceptics' account of how man should actually live', both thinkers would have erected a moral theory on the back of this principle to beat the sceptics at their own game.[30] Various commentators have criticized Tuck's reconstruction of Grotius's and Hobbes's natural law theories on both textual and contextual grounds.[31] His claim that natural rights of self-preservation served as a sure and uncontested foundation for morality has not hitherto been questioned. The claim is not implausible. Gentili called the right to repel force by force, a Roman law maxim, 'the most generally accepted of all rights'.[32] Moreover, Hobbes buttressed his self-defence doctrine with arguments from authority—a most unusual move for him. Cicero's oration *For Milo* proves, according to Hobbes, 'that it is and hath been always lawful for one private man to kill another for his own preservation' (EW 5: 184; also EW 5: 53).[33] Such ostensible agreement with received views is misleading. No one before or after Hobbes set so few limits on legitimate self-defence.[34]

Consider *For Milo*. Hobbes's appeal to Cicero's authority was triply disingenuous. First, on Cicero's retelling of the episode, the slain Clodius attacked Milo

---

[29] Richard Tuck, 'Grotius, Carneades and Hobbes', *Grotiana* 4 (1983) no. 1: 43–62; Tuck, 'The "Modern" Theory of Natural Law' in Anthony Pagden (ed), *The Languages of Political Theory in Early-Modern Europe* (Cambridge, 1987) 99–120; Tuck, *Hobbes* (Oxford, 1989) 68–74; Tuck, *Philosophy and Government, 1572–1651* (Cambridge, 1993) xv–xvi, 173–176, 196–199, 347–348; Tuck, 'Hobbes's Moral Philosophy' in Tom Sorell (ed), *The Cambridge Companion to Hobbes* (Cambridge, 1996) 187–189.

[30] Tuck, *Philosophy and Government*, 173.

[31] E.g. Robert Shaver, 'Grotius on Scepticism and Self-Interest', *Archiv für Geschichte der Philosophie* 78 (1996) no. 1: 27–47; Perez Zagorin, 'Hobbes without Grotius', *History of Political Thought* 21 (2000) no. 1: 16–40; Thomas Mautner, 'Grotius and the Skeptics', *Journal of the History of Ideas* 66 (2005) no. 4: 577–601; Benjamin Straumann, *Roman Law in the State of Nature*, trans. Belinda Cooper (Cambridge, 2015) 51–61, 97.

[32] Gentili, *De Jure Belli*, 59. Also Thucydides, *The Peloponnesian War*, 3.56; in Hobbes's translation: 'by the law of all nations it is lawful to repel an assailing enemy' (EW 8: 322).

[33] The references are presumably to §30 (cf. §§6–11). Marcus Tullius Cicero, 'Pro Milone' in *Cicero: Defence Speeches*, ed. D.H. Berry (Oxford, 2000) 183–223. On the historical background to Cicero's speech, see A.W. Lintott, 'Cicero and Milo', *Journal of Roman Studies* 64 (1974) 62–78.

[34] Suzanne Uniacke, *Permissible Killing: The Self-Defence Justification of Homicide* (Cambridge, 1994) 61–63.

206   RIGHTS OF WAR

first: Milo's attack was justified by the present and immediate danger he faced. Nothing in *For Milo* suggests that Cicero deemed preventive attacks justified. Second, Cicero emphasized that Clodius was morally liable to be killed. Both for plotting to kill Milo (§§25–30) and as a tyrant and enemy of the state (§§75–91).[35] Third, while glossing the passage, Hobbes interpreted the right of self-defence in an increasingly expansive sense. Individuals do not just have the right to kill in extreme danger, they have a general 'right to destroy whatsoever he thinketh <u>can</u> annoy him' (EW 5: 185). For Hobbes, killing counts as defensive even if it serves to avert *possible* threats.

In what follows, I argue that Hobbes rendered rights of self-defence uniquely capacious by stripping them of at least five traditional moral restrictions. First, he rejected the traditional just war tenet that defensive killing is legitimate only in response to wrongdoing. Second, he unreservedly accepted the permissibility of preventive war. Third, anticipatory violence may be used not only to avert possible attacks but also to conquer innocents, to augment security against third parties. Fourth, rights to engage in defensive violence are no longer moderated by charity or any other principle of natural law. Fifth, the right-intention condition becomes the sole criterion determining what counts as lawful defensive force. The first two features have been recognized by scholars before and are not unique to Hobbes; the last three have hitherto gone unnoticed and are as far as I know without historical precedent.

Hobbes's encompassing understanding of legitimate self-defence was far from uncontroversial. The church fathers Ambrose (c.340–397) and Augustine (354–430) had even denied the lawfulness of killing in self-defence, on the ground that it displays an undue clinging to mundane affairs (such as bodily preservation). Killing aggressors is permitted only in defence of others.[36] In maxims that would become proverbial, Roman jurists had maintained that by nature, individuals may kill others in defence both of themselves and of their goods: 'it is permissible to repel force by force [*vim vi repellere*], and this right is conferred by nature.'[37] For 'whatever a person does for his bodily security, he can be held to have done rightfully.'[38] However, defensive killing is lawful only in response to *immediate* threats: 'Anyone who comes with arms we may repel with arms. But this must be at once and not after an interval.'[39]

---

[35] For Cicero's defence of tyrannicide by private individuals, denounced by Hobbes (EL 27.10; DCv P.5; DCv 12.3; L 29.14), see also his *On Duties*, 3.31; *The Republic*, 2.46–48. On Hobbes on tyranny, see Kinch Hoekstra, 'Tyrannus Rex vs. *Leviathan*', *Pacific Philosophical Quarterly* 82 (2001) no. 3: 420–446.

[36] Rory Cox, 'The Ethics of War up to Thomas Aquinas' in Seth Lazar and Helen Frowe (eds), *The Oxford Handbook of Ethics of War* (Oxford, 2018) 105–108. Augustine, *On the Free Choice of the Will*, ed. Peter King (Cambridge, 2010) 1.4.9.22–1.5.13.40. Also Augustine, Letter 47 to Publicola: 'As to killing others in order to defend one's own life, I do not approve of this, unless one happens to be a soldier or public functionary acting, not for himself, but in defense of others or of the city in which he resides.'

[37] *Digest* 43.16.1.27.

[38] *Digest* 1.1.3; also *Digest* 9.2.4–5.

[39] *Digest* 43.16.3.9.

A framing commitment of scholastic just war theory was the distinction between defensive and offensive force. Defensive force is a response to ongoing harm. Force is offensive if it seeks to punish or avenge injuries that are past and done. The immediacy condition was thus built into the very concept of defensive force. Scholastic just war theorists typically made the possession of legitimate authority a precondition for just offensive wars only. Citing the *vim vi repellere* maxim, Vitoria held that 'any person, even a private citizen, may declare and wage defensive war'.[40] Suárez agreed: 'the power of defending oneself against an unjust aggressor is conceded to all'.[41] Both added that only legitimate rulers have the right to wage offensive wars—to punish wrongs or redress injuries. Aquinas had likewise allowed private individuals to kill in self-defence, provided this was done not vindictively but for the sake of self-preservation.[42] Yet for him, self-defence was essentially distinct from war, which only legitimate authorities are entitled to wage.[43]

Grotius expanded the set of wrongs that allow individuals to resort to armed force in two ways. First, he broke new ground by denying that the right of punishment is essentially political in origin, presupposing jurisdictional authority over the wrongdoer.[44] According to the Dutchman, everyone is morally authorized to punish wrongdoers for the public good. For such private punishment upholds society and does not violate the (forfeited) rights of wrongdoers.[45] This position informs his expansive conception of war as signifying *any* condition of violent conflict. Indeed, for Grotius (as for Hobbes and Locke), the same principles regulate wars between states and armed conflict between private individuals, thus collapsing any categorical distinction between war and self-defence.[46]

Second, Grotius reinterpreted the classical doctrine that war is justified only in response to wrongdoing in a rather bellicose way. Citing Augustine, he wrote: 'There is no other *reasonable* Cause of making War, but an *Injury* received'.[47] Yet his gloss on this commonplace departed markedly from tradition. Medieval scholastics had depicted just war as essentially penal in character, waged to punish culpable enemies: 'namely, that those who are attacked should deserve

---

[40] Vitoria, *Political Writings*, 299.

[41] Suárez, 'On Charity', 13.2.1.

[42] On Aquinas on justified self-defence, compare the contrasting readings of Gregory M. Reichberg, *Thomas Aquinas on War and Peace* (Cambridge, 2017) 173–200; Daniel Schwartz, 'Thomas Aquinas and Antonio de Córdoba on Self-Defence: Saving Yourself as a Private End', *British Journal for the History of Philosophy* 26 (2018) no. 6: 1045–1063.

[43] Aquinas discussed warfare in *Summa Theologica*, 2a.2ae.40, and individual self-defence in *Summa Theologica*, 2a.2ae.67.7.

[44] The orthodox view was defended by e.g. Aquinas, *Summa Theologica*, 2a.2ae.40.1; Vitoria, *Political Writings*, 300; Gentili, *De Jure Belli*, 41. Suárez agreed, adding that foreigners make themselves subject to another state or ruler by committing wrongs against them. Suárez, 'On Charity', 13.2.1.

[45] Grotius, *War and Peace*, 2.20.8–9, 2.20.40.4.

[46] Locke, *Second Treatise*, 2.7–3.21. For Grotius, 'there is no significant moral difference between [pre-statist] individuals and states . . . both may use violence in the same way and for the same ends'. Richard Tuck, *The Rights of War and Peace* (Oxford, 1999) 85.

[47] Grotius, *War and Peace*, 2.1.1.4.

208 RIGHTS OF WAR

the attack on account of some offence [*culpam*].[48] Sixteenth-century Spanish scholastics gradually shifted from a punitive to a liability model of war, waged against liable enemies in order to redress grave injuries (wrongs).[49] As Vitoria contended, 'the sole and only just cause for waging war is when a wrong [*injuria*] has been inflicted', adding that 'all the doctors' agreed on this.[50] Suárez concurred: a 'just and sufficient reason for war is the infliction of a grave injustice which cannot be avenged or repaired in any other way'.[51] Liability requires wrongdoing but not culpability (being morally at fault). It thus covers those who act wrongly out of ignorance (such as, it was alleged, indigenous peoples in the Americas). Grotius went further, conceptualizing injuries as (threatened) rights-violations.[52] Not all injuries, so understood, are acts without right. Rights of self-defence, Grotius explained, are not remedial (arising from another person's wrongdoing) but morally bedrock: 'this Right of Self-Defence, arises directly and immediately from the Care of our own Preservation, which Nature recommends to every one, and not from the Injustice or Crime of the Aggressor'.[53] Natural law allows us to defensively kill innocent threats: persons who have done nothing wrong (e.g. well-intentioned enemy soldiers, deluded persons, innocent obstacles).[54] Being innocent, people who pose such threats retain their right to resist in self-defence in turn. This opens up the possibility of true bilateral justice: where both belligerent parties fight each other by right.[55]

Hobbes agreed with Grotius that rights to kill in self-defence derive from natural rights of self-preservation rather than from another's injustice. He went further still by denying that legitimate self-defence can ever injure others. In the bellicose state of nature, people do not wrong others by defensively killing them. 'Without Law every thing is in such sort every Mans, as he may take, possess, and enjoy <u>without wrong to any Man</u>, every thing, Lands, Beasts, Fruits, and even the

---

[48] Aquinas, *Summa Theologica*, 2a.2ae.40.1.

[49] Reichberg, *Thomas Aquinas on War and Peace*, 142–172; Pärtel Piirimäe, 'Alberico Gentili's Doctrine of Defensive War and Its Impact on Seventeenth-Century Normative Views' in Benedict Kingsbury and Benjamin Straumann (eds), *The Roman Foundations of the Law of Nations* (Oxford, 2010) 191–192. The punitive conception of war dovetailed particularly well with the legitimate authority requirement: only sovereign rulers, endowed with due jurisdictional authority, are entitled to wage war. The liability model begun to loosen that link.

[50] Vitoria, *Political Writings*, 303.

[51] Suárez, 'On Charity', 13.4.1.

[52] Grotius, *War and Peace*, 2.1.2.1, 3.11.2.

[53] Grotius, *War and Peace*, 2.1.3; also 3.1.2.1.

[54] Grotius, *War and Peace*, 2.1.3–4.

[55] Cases of invincible ignorance excepted, classical just war theorists generally considered this impossible. At most one of the contending parties can be 'truly' or 'objectively' right. Both sides can, however, be epistemically justified in believing in the rightness of their cause, rendering their use of force morally blameless. Epistemic justification does not imply moral justification. It merely excuses an otherwise wrong action. E.g. Vitoria, *Political Writings*, 282, 312–313; Suárez, 'On Charity', 13.4.1; Gentili, *De Jure Belli*, 32; cf. Grotius, *War and Peace*, 2.23.13.3. For an overview of late scholastic debates over ostensible bilateral justice, see Daniel Schwartz, 'Late Scholastic Just War Theory' in Seth Lazar and Helen Frowe (eds), *The Oxford Handbook of Ethics of War* (Oxford, 2018) 125–131.

bodies of other Men, if his Reason tell him he cannot otherwise live securely' (DPS 9). Why are innocents not wronged when others kill them for personal security? The answer lies partly in his idiosyncratic conception of injury, partly in the natural right to everything. For Hobbes, injury/wrong denotes the missing rights of the wrongdoer. It does not mean violating the rights of others (§2.1). His equation of injury and injustice with breach of covenant, in turn, assumes a natural right to everything. Acts without right *must* be breaches of agreement since humans cannot lack right except after its contractual divestment: 'where no Covenant hath preceded, there hath no Right been transferred, and every man has right to every thing; and consequently, no action can be Unjust' (L 15.2). Since the *jus in omnia* precludes injury, Hobbes needed a non-remedial account of rights of violent self-defence to get the natural right to everything off the ground in the first place. This non-remedial authorization is the right of nature, permitting each to do whatever they judge best protects themselves—including killing and enslaving innocents to enhance personal security.

In Hobbes's war of all against all, each person—attackers and defenders alike—wages a just war. Given the '*right to all things*, it necessarily follows that some men would be attacking and other defending themselves, and both by *right*' (DCv 2.3; also EL 14.11; DCv 1.12). Classical just war theorists allowed lethal force only in response to grave wrongdoing. Hobbes jettisoned that requirement, maintaining even that rights to wage war *never* arise from wrongdoing outside the state (due to the omnipresent right to all things). Even culpable and convicted wrongdoers retain rights of self-defence. 'For they but defend their lives, which the Guilty man may as well do, as the Innocent' (L 21.17).[56] Hobbesian natural rights of self-preservation are morally basic and never lost. That unprecedented view underpins his infamous doctrine: 'To this warre of every man against every man, this also is consequent; that nothing can be Unjust' (L 13.13). In extra-statist conditions, all conflicts are just ('with right') on both sides. Not for epistemic reasons, but because each individual has the inalienable and non-forfeitable right to defend their life and limbs.[57]

---

[56] Grotius, *War and Peace*, 2.1.18.1, had gainsaid unjust aggressors a right of self-defence, 'no more than a Criminal can plead a Right of defending himself against the publick Officers of Justice'. Rodin underlines the counter-intuitiveness of Hobbes's view: 'With the exception of Hobbes, almost no commentator believes that it is permissible to employ force against such threats to save one's own life'. David Rodin, *War and Self-Defense* (Oxford, 2002) 83.

[57] For a contemporary critique of Hobbes's doctrine that all wars are 'just and lawful on both sides', see James Tyrrell, *A Brief Disquisition of the Law of Nature* (London, 1692) 317–319.

8.3 (BEYOND) PREVENTIVE WAR

Philosophers today distinguish between two forms of anticipatory strikes/wars: *pre-emption* and *prevention*. Pre-emptive attacks can be defined as first strikes on an imminent and direct threat; preventive ones as first strikes on a distant threat (where 'distant' is best understood probabilistically rather than temporally).[58] Scholastic just war theorists generally allowed pre-emptive strikes against immediate threats, provided they are necessary.[59] Grotius concurred. The right of self-defence justifies anticipatory attacks only in case of 'present' and 'inevitable' danger to one's life, limb, or chastity.[60] Fear of one's neighbour's strength, however reasonable, is not a just cause for war.[61]

Alberico Gentili (1552–1608) has been credited with providing the first sustained defence of preventive war—half a century before Hobbes.[62] Gentili insisted that waging war is justified only out of necessity.[63] But what counts as necessity? The Italian jurist conceded that his criteria for 'necessity' are rather undemanding.[64] Killing in self-defence can be lawful even if other life-saving options are available.[65] And preventive wars fought out of just fear count as 'necessary' and 'defensive' as well ('a defence dictated by expediency'). For 'no one ought to expose himself to danger. No one ought to wait to be struck, unless he is a fool'.[66] It is hence often lawful 'to injure others to avoid an injury to yourself'.[67] After all, 'we kill a snake as soon as we see one, even though it has not injured us and will perhaps not harm us. For thus we protect ourselves before it attacks us'.[68] His justification of preventive strikes against any 'probable and possible' attack makes Gentili's theory truly ground-breaking—and unambiguously a theory of *preventive* war.[69] Grotius roundly rejected his predecessor's views: 'to pretend to have a Right to

---

[58] David Luban, 'Preventive War', *Philosophy and Public Affairs* 32 (2004) no. 3: 213, 230. For general discussion, see Walzer, *Just and Unjust Wars*, 74–85; Henry Shue and David Rodin (eds), *Preemption: Military Action and Moral Justification* (Oxford, 2007).

[59] On scholastic thinking about anticipatory warfare, see Kinga Tibori Szabó, *Anticipatory Action in Self-Defence* (The Hague, 2011) 31–58; Reichberg, *Thomas Aquinas on War and Peace*, 201–222.

[60] Grotius, *War and Peace*, 2.1.3–7.

[61] Grotius, *War and Peace*, 2.2.13.4, 2.22.5.1.

[62] Gregory M. Reichberg calls Gentili 'one of the first authors in the Christian West openly to endorse the idea of preventive war' in 'Preventive War in Classical Just War Theory', *Journal of the History of International Law* 9 (2007) no. 1: 15. Also Benedict Kingsbury and Benjamin Straumann, 'Introduction' in idem (eds), *Alberico Gentili: The Wars of the Romans*, transl. David Lupher (Oxford, 2011) xxiii.

[63] Gentili, *De Jure Belli*, 20.

[64] Gentili, *De Jure Belli*, 58: 'Thus in speaking of necessity we are not speaking with absolute accuracy'.

[65] Gentili, *De Jure Belli*, 58–59.

[66] Gentili, *De Jure Belli*, 61, 62.

[67] Gentili, *De Jure Belli*, 73.

[68] Gentili, *De Jure Belli*, 61.

[69] Gentili, *De Jure Belli*, 66.

injure another, merely from a Possibility that he may injure me, is repugnant to all the Justice in the World'.[70]

Hobbes's one-time employer Francis Bacon (1561–1626) sided with Gentili. Bacon dismissed 'the opinion of some of the schoolmen ... that a war cannot justly be made but upon a precedent injury or provocation. For there is no question but a just fear of an imminent danger, though there be no blow given, is a lawful cause of war'.[71] Preventive wars waged out of just fear, he insisted, are really defensive and legitimate.[72] Not all early modern defences of preventive war hinged on a re-definition of 'defensive war'. Invoking the dictum 'necessity ... breaks every law', the Flemish humanist Justus Lipsius (1547–1606) declared offensive wars justified when they are necessary and done for the right reasons ('to preserve his position, never to extend it').[73]

Tuck duly positions Hobbes within the bellicose humanist tradition of Gentili and Bacon.[74] Distinctive of these thinkers is their recasting of certain forms of an-ticipatory violence as essentially defensive. This was achieved, in part, by concep-tualizing defensive force not as a response to an immediate and present threat, but as war waged in order to heighten security against known enemies. Hobbes devel-oped the same line of thought: 'Nature gave a Right to every man to secure himselfe by his own strength, and to invade a suspected neighbour, by way of prevention' (L 26.43; also DCv 1.14; L 22.31; DPS 192). 'With his concept of "preventive war"', Thivet observes, 'Hobbes distances himself from the Just War tradition by at-tempting to define a war of aggression ... as a kind of defensive war'.[75]

Commentators have however overlooked a key difference between the pre-ventive war doctrines of Gentili and Bacon, and that of Hobbes. His two predeces-sors sanctioned anticipatory force to forestall plotting enemies: 'It is lawful for me to attack a man who is making ready to attack me'.[76] Hobbes, much more radically, legitimated waging war to augment personal security against innocents posing no threat and intending no harm. Belligerents justly fight not merely over control over external resources, but also over control over other persons:

---

[70] Grotius, *War and Peace*, 2.1.17. Grotius refers to Gentili in the marginalia. On Grotius on pre-ventive war, see Reichberg, 'Preventive War', 19–25.

[71] Francis Bacon, 'Of Empire' in *The Essays or Counsels, Civil and Moral*, ed. Brian Vickers (Oxford, 1999) 44.

[72] Francis Bacon, *Considerations Touching a Warre with Spaine* (London, 1629) 15.

[73] Justus Lipsius, *Politica*, ed. Jan Waszink (Assen, 2004) 4.14.8–9.

[74] Tuck, *The Rights of War and Peace*, 126–139. On the intellectual links between Gentili, Bacon, and Hobbes, see also Kinch Hoekstra, 'Thucydides and the Bellicose Beginnings of Modern Political Theory' in Katherine Harloe and Neville Morley (eds), *Thucydides and the Modern World* (Cambridge, 2012) 25–54; Kinch Hoekstra, 'Hobbes's Thucydides' in A.P. Martinich and Kinch Hoekstra (eds), *The Oxford Handbook of Hobbes* (Oxford, 2016) 552–557, 563–572.

[75] Thivet, 'Thomas Hobbes', 710.

[76] Gentili, *De Jure Belli*, 62. Gentili proceeded to quote Thucydides, *The Peloponnesian War*, 3.12; in Hobbes's translation: 'seeing it is in their hands to invade at pleasure, it ought to be in ours to anticipate' (EW 8: 279).

212 RIGHTS OF WAR

> there is no way for any man to secure himselfe, so reasonable, as Anticipation; that is, by force, or wiles, to master the persons of all men he can, so long, till he see no other power great enough to endanger him: And this is no more than his own conservation requireth, and is generally allowed. (L 13.4)

There being strength in numbers, individuals have a natural right to engage in anticipatory warfare to coerce others to join their sides (their personal slave army, if you will), thus amplifying their power. Natural right permits conquering other people not just to thwart *their* future attacks, but also to acquire dominion and so fortify oneself against future third-party threats. After all, if they 'should not by invasion increase their power, they would not be able, long time, by standing only on their defence, to subsist. And by consequence, such augmentation of dominion over men, being necessary to a mans conservation, it ought to be allowed him' (L 13.4).

Hobbes's conception of power as eminence reinforces competition over external resources (human and non-human). For Hobbes, power is essentially relative and positional: 'power simply is no more, but the excess of the power of one above that of another. For equal powers opposed, destroy one another' (EL 8.4).[77] People are after eminence—having more power than others. Personal security is heightened, not by acquiring external resources as such, but by acquiring more resources than one's enemies (L 17.3). Conquering and forcibly subduing a hundred people is of little help in shoring up my position if my nemesis violently obtains dominion over a thousand men. Her surplus power cancels out mine. Power being relative, as long as all must rely on their own power for self-protection, humans will search restlessly for ever more resources as means for personal security (L 11.2). Only when the state steps in, providing protection to all, does this volatile dynamic end.

Hobbes's radical extension of the domain of legitimate anticipatory force explains why the natural condition is a war of all against all. People may lawfully strike first not only to neutralize possible threats but also to improve their defensive position generally. This is no longer a doctrine of preventive war—permitting first strikes against possible threats to prevent them from harming you. It is a theory of total defensive war, against all and sundry: 'in declared Hostility, all infliction of evil is lawfull' (L 28.13; also EL 19.1; DCv 2.18). Hobbes, remarkably, portrayed such imperialist warfare as essentially defensive in character.

---

[77] On the positionality of power amidst Hobbes's changing views on power, see Sandra Field, 'Hobbes and the Question of Power', *Journal of the History of Philosophy* 52 (2014) no. 1: 64–65, 74.

8.4 CHARITY AND THE RIGHT-INTENTION REQUIREMENT

Revisionist readings of Hobbes on war have highlighted his condemnation of wars for glory.[78] 'In the state of nature there is in all men a will to do harm', we read, 'but not for the same reason or with equal culpability' (DCv 1.4). Vain-glorious persons, overestimating their own worth, seek to harm others because they deem themselves—unreasonably—entitled to superior goods and honour (L 13.4). Hobbes condemned aggression undertaken for glory: 'nothing but fear can justify the taking away of another's life' (EL 19.2). National wars of aggrandizement, waged 'out of ambition, or of vain-glory', he likewise declared irrational and immoral (EL 28.9; also DCv 13.14; L 29.22; DPS 13). Justified use of violence requires a right intention. This section reveals that the right-intention condition is the only traditional just war requirement recognized by Hobbes, and the sole criterion for determining what counts as defensive force.

In classical just war theory, the right-intention clause spells out a necessary condition for *jus ad bellum*. A wrong intention—the particular end adopted by the agent—suffices to render unjust the infliction of proportionate violence on a liable offender. Vengeance done to see another suffer is morally prohibited, while harming a wrongdoer for reasons of deterrence or correction may be justified.[79] Some might think that Hobbes denounces aggression for glory not because it falls short of some right-intention condition but because it endangers self-preservation. Natural law prohibits cruelty, defined as wanton infliction of harm, because 'to hurt without reason, tendeth to the introduction of Warre' (L 15.19). The wrong-making feature of cruelty would thus lie in its expected bellicose consequences. This interpretive suggestion should be rejected. Hobbes indeed insisted that moral vices are bad because and insofar as they hamper peace. Yet in conditions of war, irenic tendencies should be assessed at the level of intention, not that of action (DCv 3.27n). Thus, if the agent truly was afraid, their ensuing resort to violence is no sin. Even if, misjudging present dangers, their chosen course of action foreseeably escalates conflict—thus deviating from what sound reasoning enjoins (DCv 1.10n).

For Hobbes, there is no interpersonally binding standard of right conduct other than the civil law (DH 13.8). This is so because by nature all agents—be they individuals or sovereigns—are entitled to judge for themselves what conduct most conduces to their security. Human natural equality of right implies that each is accountable to God alone—who 'taketh the will for the deed, both in good and evil actions' (EL 18.10; also EL 25.10; L 43.20). Outside the state, any action performed with a right intention is justified, regardless of its moral qualities or consequences: 'every man being his own Judge, and accused onely by his own

---

[78] E.g. Thivet, 'Thomas Hobbes', 705–707.
[79] Aquinas, *Summa Theologica*, 2a.2ae.108.1.

214   RIGHTS OF WAR

Conscience, and cleared by the Uprightnesse of his own Intention' (L 27.3). The same principle extends to individual rights to wage war: 'if a man in the state of nature, be in hostility with men, and thereby have lawful title to subdue or kill, according <u>as his own conscience and discretion shall suggest unto him</u> for his safety and benefit' (EL 22.9). The right-intention requirement prohibits waging war for mere glory; it permits any war waged out of due fear.

Hobbes was able to make the right-intention criterion the sole criterion for just defensive killing because of a remarkable feature of his moral theory: whether natural law ought to be practised is conditional on the agent's preservation being deemed secure. Right reason dictates that '*every man, ought to endeavour Peace, as farre as he has hope of obtaining it; and when he cannot obtain it, that he may seek, and use, all helps, and advantages of Warre*' (L 14.4; also EL 14.14; DCv 2.2). Hobbesian agents are bound in conscience to seek peace and follow it. Yet anyone who sincerely judges that behaving peacefully is in present circumstances unsafe may by natural right avail themselves of the full means of war for self-protection (DCv 3.27; DCv 5.1; L 15.36). Reason enjoins as much because, Hobbes claimed, the moral virtues are merely instrumentally good, as the socially necessary means to achieve felicity and self-preservation (DCv 3.31; L 15.40).[80] Pre-statist individuals fulfil all that morality demands of them by attacking, enslaving, and killing their fellows reluctantly. Hobbes thus ruled out the possibility of conflict between what morality demands and what is required for each person's principal natural good (i.e. self-preservation). The *jus in omnia*, we have discovered, presupposes the conditionality of the duty to practice natural law upon the agent's preservation not being considered imperilled.

Along the way Hobbes transformed the meaning of the right-intention criterion. The criterion traditionally required those initiating war 'to have a rightful intention, so that they intend the advancement of good, or the avoidance of evil'.[81] On Hobbes's account, war should intend to promote *one's own* good (i.e. self-preservation). It need not be pursued as a means for furthering the *common* good. On the contrary: initiating war is morally permissible whenever the common good ('peace') cannot safely be pursued in practice (in the agent's opinion). If the *in foro interno* requirement of natural law is met, then anything goes.

The theoretical implications become clear by looking at charity (*caritas*). Classical just war theorists generally discussed war under this heading.[82] The biblical duty to love your neighbour as yourself determined when, how, and to what end armed force is permissibly used. For Grotius, charity constrains the lawful exercise of rights of individual and collective self-defence. 'Circumstances too may

---

[80] On Hobbes's theory of the good and its place within his ethics, see Arash Abizadeh, *Hobbes and the Two Faces of Ethics* (Cambridge, 2018) 139–179; Johan Olsthoorn, 'On the Absence of Moral Goodness in Hobbes's Ethics', *The Journal of Ethics* 24 (2020) no. 2: 241–266.

[81] Aquinas, *Summa Theologica*, 2a.2ae.40.1.

[82] E.g. Aquinas, *Summa Theologica*, 2a.2ae.40.1; Suárez, 'On Charity'.

sometimes fall out so, that it may not only be laudable, but an Obligation in us to forbear claiming our Right, on account of that Charity which we owe to all Men, even tho' our Enemies.[83] Paradoxically, charity may order us to refrain from exercising our rights: 'every Thing that is conformable to Right properly so called, is not always absolutely lawful; for sometimes our Charity to our Neighbour will not suffer us to use this rigorous Right.'[84]

In *Elements*, Hobbes included charity as a specific natural law duty, ordering agents to '*help and endeavour to accommodate each other, as far as may be without danger of their persons, and loss of their means, to maintain and defend themselves*' (EL 16.8). Charitable persons 'desire to assist and advance others' (EL 9.17; L 6.22).[85] The phrasing emphasizes the conditionality of the moral duty to help others. Self-preservation comes first, mutual aid being morally required merely as a necessary social means to preservation. Acting charitably is therefore imperative only when self-preservation is not considered imperilled. Otherwise, each may avail themselves of all the rights of war (thus rendering natural law, prescribing the means of peace, inoperative as standards of action). It follows that the laws of nature are incapable of constraining rights of war. Hobbesian rights of war are morally bounded only by the right-intention criterion. The same places the due exercise of these rights beyond human scrutiny. In war, it is epistemically impossible for humans to accuse vain-glorious warmongers of wrongdoing: to outsiders, their aggressive conduct could just as well be driven by sound intentions of self-defence (as per *Untraceable Intentions*).

8.5 JUST FEAR, DISTRUST, AND NATURAL ENMITY

According to Gentili, agents may engage in anticipatory warfare to thwart any 'probable and possible' attack.[86] But he added a qualifying rider: 'A just cause for fear is demanded; suspicion is not enough'. The Italian jurist provided a non-subjective standard for this requirement: 'a just fear is defined as the fear of a greater evil, a fear which might properly be felt even by a man of great courage'.[87] Bacon similarly held that 'a just feare (without an actuall invasion or offence) is a sufficient ground of a Warre, and in the nature of a true defensive'. A fear is just when prompted by 'cleare foresight of imminent danger'.[88] Hobbes contended that a 'just

---

[83] Grotius, *War and Peace*, 2.24.2.3; also 2.1.9.1.

[84] Grotius, *War and Peace*, 3.1.4.2; also 3.2.6.

[85] Parallel passages in later texts omit the term 'charity' when canvassing the same natural law enjoining individuals to be accommodating and considerate to others (DCv 3.9; DCv 4.7; L 15.17). This allowed Hobbes to recast charity as the sum of the laws of nature (L 26.36; L 30.13; DH 13.9; cf. EL 18.8). Deborah Baumgold (ed), *Three-Text Edition of Thomas Hobbes's Political Theory* (Cambridge, 2017) 173–174.

[86] Gentili, *De Jure Belli*, 66.

[87] Gentili, *De Jure Belli*, 62.

[88] Bacon, *Considerations Touching a Warre*, 8. Cf. Vattel, *Law of Nations*, 3.3.44.

216   RIGHTS OF WAR

fear' stops the precepts of natural law from binding in practice. Indeed, citizens are not even bound to obey the civil laws 'in case of a just fear' to their self-preservation (EW 5: 291; also L 27.20; EW 4: 322). The dispensation clause that moral laws oblige in practice only if the agent judges behaving morally safe, allows all to shelve any state-of-nature covenant at will (§7.1). Conquest of innocents being a permissible means of self-defence, persons may forcibly subdue contracting parties keeping their part of the deal to fortify themselves against perceived third-party threats. State-of-nature covenants, this logic suggests, fail to end open enmity.

While Gentili's and Bacon's just-fear requirements effectively restrict permissible resort to war, the same cannot be said of Hobbes's. He depleted the criterion of its critical edge in two ways. First, by setting an impossibly high bar on security. 'And as their preservation, so also is their security a just pretence of invading those whom they have just cause to fear, unless sufficient caution be given to take away their fear, which Caution (for any thing I can yet conceive) is utterly impossible' (DPS 192). Grotius had earlier declared such a high standard of security utterly unreasonable: 'such is the Condition of the present Life, that we can never be in perfect Security. It is not in the way of Force, but in the Protection of Providence, and in innocent Precautions, that we are to seek for Relief against uncertain Fear.'[89] Hobbes conceded as much in *De Cive*: 'It is in fact impossible to secure people from harm from each other, so that they cannot be wrongly hurt or killed; and so this is not for discussion.' Security is rather the condition of having no 'reasonable cause to fear other men as long as [one] refrains from wronging them' (DCv 6.3).[90] However, absent a functioning system of law enforcement, each person has reason to fear all others and hence 'may lawfully rely on his own strength and art, for caution against all other men' (L 17.2).

Second, by subjectivizing the just-fear criterion through his postulate of human natural equality of right: 'in the condition of meer Nature, where all men are equall, and judges of the justnesse of their own fears' (L 14.18).[91] Whether a covenant of mutual trust can safely be kept hence 'is for the fearful party to decide' (DCv 2.11). Outside the state, each person reneging on their covenants out of fear does so rightfully, since they themselves are by natural right the judge of the justness of their fears. Only God can judge whether an agent breaks faith viciously (i.e. in violation of the right-intention criterion). Humans lack the epistemic capacity and moral standing to accuse their equals of acting against conscience (§3.3 and §3.4; §7.1).[92] In the state of nature, humans are in no position to denounce another's

---

[89] Grotius, *War and Peace*, 2.1.17; also Pufendorf, *Nature and Nations*, 3.6.9, likewise objected: 'the fear that men will break faith, based only on the general depravity of men's nature, is not enough to justify refusal to fulfil a pact'.

[90] Hobbes is guilty of inconsistency for setting lower standards of security within the state than outside it, impugns Tyrrell, *Brief Disquisition*, 376–384.

[91] As noted by Hoekstra, 'Hobbes's Thucydides', 564.

[92] E.g. EL 25.3; L 27.2; L 30.30; L 42.80.

breach of covenant as unwarranted. Unjust breaches of agreement being undetectable in war, all may with impunity do as they please.

We might think that even on a thus-weakened criterion of just fear, considerations of security do not justify preventively attacking all and sundry. Surely someone showing no intent to harm us cannot reasonably be deemed a threat to our personal security. As Pufendorf wrote: 'For as long as my Neighbour doth me no Injury, and I do not apparently take him in any Preparation for such a Design... I ought to presume, he will always continue in the same Mind'.[93] For Grotius, permissible defensive war requires 'moral Certainty' that the enemy 'has not only Forces sufficient, but a full Intention to injure us'.[94] Walzer likewise argues that legitimate anticipatory strikes require 'a manifest intent to injure' and 'a degree of active preparation that makes that intent a positive danger'.[95] Why didn't Hobbes recognize a similar moral restriction on preventive violence?

Hobbes's doctrines of the right to everything and of natural enmity are both premised, I contend, upon natural distrust.[96] Trust, for Hobbes, is something that needs to be *earned* through positive signs of good will, rather than something one has by default but *loses* by displaying malicious intent. The state of nature is empirically a condition of war in which all fear all. Countries guard their borders and wall their cities. 'Can men express their universal distrust of one another more openly? All commonwealths and individuals behave in this way, and thus admit their fear and distrust of each other' (DCv P.11; also DCv 17.27). Moreover, people have a *right* to be distrustful of one another absent a functioning government: 'there is no need to trust first and kill later when he lets you down' (DCv 2.18). Hobbesian agents are under no natural duty to presumptively trust and think well of others absent countervailing evidence (a duty delimiting rights to engage in anticipatory violence). Anyone may by right be attacked preventively: signs of maliciousness are not needed. The knowledge that all can rightfully attack all reinforces general fear and suspicion, creating a vicious cycle. Each person has both reason and right to distrust and preventively attack all others to heighten personal security (DCv 1.12). Add Hobbes's sanctioning of imperialist warfare—conquering and enslaving innocent people to enlarge one's power is permissible if done to augment protection—and we truly get a war of all against all.

---

[93] Pufendorf, *Nature and Nations*, 8.6.5; also Samuel Pufendorf, *On the Natural State of Men*, ed. Michael Seidler (Lewiston, 1990) 128; Tyrrell, *Brief Disquisition*, 326–327; Aquinas, *Summa Theologica*, 2a.2ae.60.4: 'unless we have evident indications of a person's wickedness, we ought to deem him good, by interpreting for the best whatever is doubtful about him'.

[94] Grotius, *War and Peace*, 2.22.5.1.

[95] Walzer, *Just and Unjust Wars*, 81.

[96] The concept of trust has received considerable attention in Hobbes scholarship lately. E.g. Deborah Baumgold, 'Trust in Hobbes's Political Thought', *Political Theory* 41 (2013) no. 6: 838–855; Eva Odzuck, 'The Concept of Trust in Hobbes's Political Philosophy' in Laszlo Kontler and Mark Somos (eds), *Trust and Happiness in the History of European Political Thought* (Leiden, 2017) 118–141; Peter Schröder, *Trust in Early Modern International Political Thought, 1598–1713* (Cambridge, 2017) 104–119.

218 RIGHTS OF WAR

Natural enmity is one of Hobbes's most innovative and controversial doctrines: 'men are enemies [*hostes*] to each other when they are not subject one to the other or to any common ruler' (DCv 14.19; also DCv 9.3; DCv 17.27; L 28.23). The doctrine was explicitly rejected by Gentili. 'Men are not foes of one another by nature . . . No war is natural'.[97] Peace being the default condition, war commences only when others 'act as our enemies, plot against us, and threaten us'.[98] As argued in §8.3, Hobbes departed from Gentili in permitting preventive attacks even on those who threaten no harm. By natural right, pre-statist individuals may resort to armed force to obtain control over innocent others in order to amplify personal security. This unprecedented doctrine of legitimate anticipatory force, I contend, underpins Hobbes's doctrine of natural enmity. In the state of nature, people do not have to pose a threat for others to be allowed to attack them. Their natural right of self-preservation suffices to entitle individuals to wage a just war against anyone else.

One theoretical precursor of Hobbes's doctrine of natural enmity is found in Bacon. Citing Clinias in Plato's *Laws* (626a), the statesman had argued that the international arena is a condition of universal hostility: 'there is ever between all Estates a secret Warre'.[99] Hobbes generalized this claim to hold wherever, and because, there is no sovereign capable of providing security—including among extra-statist individuals. A second precursor is found in the works of another English statesman, Sir Walter Raleigh (1552–1618). Overpopulation might lead to a 'remedilesse or necessary Warre', fought over scarce resources: 'Suffice it that when any Country is overlaid by the multitude which live upon it, there is a naturall necessity compelling it to disburthen it self and lay the Load upon others, by right or wrong'.[100] Hobbes twice mentioned wars of survival due to overpopulation: 'And when all the world is overcharged with Inhabitants, then the last remedy of all is Warre; which provideth for every man, by Victory, or Death' (L 30.19; also DCv ED.6). Fought for the sake of self-preservation, expansionary wars of survival are presumably initiated with right.[101]

Hobbes's dismissal of a natural duty to trust has two further theoretical implications. First, it reinforces the moral importance of gratitude. War ends only when general distrust ceases. Trust, I have argued, must be earned by displaying

---

[97] Gentili, *De Jure Belli*, 55–56.

[98] Gentili, *De Jure Belli*, 56. Pufendorf, *Nature and Nations*, 2.2.7, appealed to 'Holy Scripture; which represent the Natural State of Man, not Hostile, but Peaceful'. The laws of nature, bidding each person to be sociable and to abstain from hurting without provocation, render the natural condition of humanity peaceful (2.2.9). Locke, *Second Treatise*, 3.19, likewise urged us not to confound the state of war with the state of nature—'a State of Peace, Good Will, Mutual Assistance, and Preservation'.

[99] Bacon, *Considerations Touching a Warre*, 11. The same passage is cited in Pufendorf, *Nature and Nations*, 2.2.5. For discussion, see Hoekstra, 'Thucydides and the Beginnings', 51–54.

[100] Walter Rawleigh [sic], *A Discourse of the Originall and Fundamentall Cause of Naturall, Customary, Arbitrary, Voluntary and Necessary Warre* (London, 1650) 9–10.

[101] Paolo Pasqualucci, 'Hobbes and the Myth of "Final War"', *Journal of the History of Ideas* 51 (1990) no. 4: 647–657.

positive signs of good will. At the same time, those manifesting good will to their enemies, by freely conferring some benefit to them, are trusting them to be charitable in turn. For people, being naturally selfish, help others only in order to procure greater favours or assistance for themselves in return (EL 16.6). People are not morally obliged to trust their benefactors, as even benefactors might later prove treacherous. Yet natural law does command each to act such that others are not made worse off for displaying good will. Otherwise 'there will be no beginning of benevolence, or trust; nor consequently of mutuall help; nor of reconciliation between enemies' (LL 15.14; also EL 16.6; DCv 3.8).[102]

Second, while any reasonable fear voids covenants made, agreements should in principle be kept with everyone—even with thieves and robbers (EL 15.13; DCv 2.16; L 14.27). In this respect, Hobbes departed from a long tradition inspired by Cicero:

> if an agreement is made with pirates in return for your life, and you do not pay the price, there is no deceit, not even if you swore to do so and did not. For a pirate is not counted as an enemy proper, but is the common foe of all. There ought to be no faith with him.[103]

Cicero's claim reflected the Roman law distinction between lawful/public enemies and unlawful/private ones. 'Enemies are those who have publicly declared war on us or on whom we have publicly declared war; others are "brigands" or "pirates".[104] War, properly understood, is a formally declared violent conflict between political communities. The laws of war (*jus belli*) were traditionally deemed inapplicable in conflicts with pirates, rebels, brigands, and other private belligerents. For hostilities with such common foes of humanity are endless. In the early modern period, this idea was taken up and further developed in the so-called regular war tradition, exemplified by Balthazar Ayala (1548–1584), Gentili, and Emer de Vattel (1714–1767).[105] Citing the *Digest*, Gentili declared that lawful enemies are those

---

[102] Reconciliation for Hobbes means 'the propitiation of enemies in orders to win their favour'. Maximilian Jaede, 'Forgiveness and Reconciliation in Hobbes's Natural Law Theory', *History of European Ideas* 43 (2017) no. 8: 842.

[103] Cicero, *On Duties*, 3.107. Balthazar Ayala, *Three Books on the Law of War*, ed. John Westlake (Washington, 1912) 59-61, 64, followed Cicero on faith with pirates. Bodin, *Six Books*, 1-2, likewise denied that justice requires repaying 'ransom promised unto robbers for a mans redemption'. On Bodin on robbers, pirates, and other common enemies of humanity, see Daniel Lee, *The Right of Sovereignty* (Oxford, 2021) 182-184, 193-201.

[104] *Digest*, 50.16.118; also *Digest*, 49.15.24. Frederick H. Russell, *The Just War in the Middle Ages* (Cambridge, 1975) 4-8, 49-54.

[105] Peter Haggenmacher, 'Just War and Regular War in Sixteenth-Century Spanish Doctrine', *International Review of the Red Cross* 32 (1992) no. 290: 434-445; Neff, *War and the Law of Nations*, 95-130; Gregory M. Reichberg, 'Just War and Regular War: Competing Paradigms' in David Rodin and Henry Shue (eds), *Just and Unjust Warriors* (Oxford, 2008) 193-213; Pablo Kalmanovitz, 'Early Modern Sources of the Regular War Tradition' in Seth Lazar and Helen Frowe (eds), *The Oxford Handbook of Ethics of War* (Oxford, 2018) 145-164.

220 RIGHTS OF WAR

who have 'officially declared war upon us, or upon whom we have officially declared war'.[106] A lawful enemy is 'the equal of his opponent'.[107] By contrast, 'it is not obligatory to keep faith, or even one's oaths, with pirates and brigands, for such men are not included in the number of the enemy [*hostis*]'.[108] Pirates, having placed themselves outside of human society altogether, could lawfully be killed by all and sundry: 'Piracy is contrary to the law of nations and the league of human society. Therefore war should be made against pirates by all men, because in the violation of that law we are all injured'.[109]

Hobbes's insistence that agreements made with thieves should in principle be kept aligned him with the just war views of Grotius—but from opposite starting points. The Dutch philosopher was adamant that promises made with robbers, rebels, and other 'perfidious' enemies are morally binding.[110] The law of nature governs interactions with everyone, malefactors included: 'their being Enemies, does not make them cease to be Men'.[111] While Grotius had insisted, against Gentili, that pirates remain part of human society and within the remit of natural law, Hobbes deemed agreements potentially valid with everyone precisely because he rejected their Stoic idea of a global human community.[112] Gentili had denied natural enmity: pirates *become* foes of humanity by breaking natural law. For Hobbes, the natural human condition is warlike. Friendship, like trust, is hence something that needs to be earned, rather than something that is foregone by contravening natural law or *jus gentium*. Agreements are necessary to first establish peace and to transform enemies into allies: 'For all men that are not Subjects, are either Enemies, or else they have ceased from being so, by some precedent covenants' (L 28.23). Natural enmity allowed Hobbes to jettison the category of unlawful enemies.[113] All enemies are lawful ones: each is by nature endowed with the same rights of war, grounded in the inalienable right of self-preservation. Moreover, natural law

---

[106] Gentili, *De Jure Belli*, 15.

[107] Gentili, *De Jure Belli*, 12.

[108] Gentili, *De Jure Belli*, 144, also 22–26.

[109] Gentili, *De Jure Belli*, 124.

[110] Grotius, *War and Peace*, 3.19.13.1; also 2.13.15, 3.19.2. Wolff would later concur: 'things which are promised to an enemy as an enemy, nay, even to a robber and a brigand as robber and brigand, must be observed'. Altering the significance of this contention, for Wolff anyone waging an unjust war is a robber or brigand. Wolff, *Jus Gentium*, 413, 493, also 515.

[111] Grotius, *War and Peace*, 3.19.1.2. Grotius recognized a range of normative differences between irregular wars and formally declared wars between political communities, as the voluntary law of nations applies only to the latter. Johan Olsthoorn, 'Grotius and the Early Modern Tradition' in Larry May (ed), *The Cambridge Handbook of the Just War* (Cambridge, 2018) 35–42.

[112] On the place of the Stoic idea that 'the whole world was, as it were, one commonwealth' in early modern international thought, see Ursula Vollerthun, *The Idea of International Society: Erasmus, Vitoria, Gentili and Grotius*, ed. James L. Richardson (Cambridge, 2017).

[113] Maximilian Jaede, 'Hobbes on the Making and Unmaking of Citizens', *Critical Review of International Social and Political Philosophy* 19 (2016) no. 1: 90.

orders us to seek peace with everyone—thieves and robbers included. Natural enmity thus radically recast the background conditions against which Hobbes shaped his just war theory.

CONCLUSION

This chapter has excavated the logical structure of Hobbes's unusually lenient account of the conditions of permissible armed force within the interpersonal state of nature. That structure is two-pronged. It includes, first, a radicalization of the just-war model associated with Thucydides, Gentili, and Bacon. That model characteristically depicts just wars as essentially defensive, while being notably liberal about what counts as 'defensive'. It thus sidelines the punitive conception of war, long dominant in the just war tradition. Out-throwing his intellectual predecessors, Hobbes declared all force defensive that aims to fortify one's power (qua means of self-preservation). The second prong eliminates nearly all remaining moral restrictions on the permissible use of defensive force. Agents may rightfully resort to war if and when they sincerely desire that peace obtains while judging that peace-promoting conduct (i.e. *acting* morally) is in present conditions perilous. Human natural equality of right subjectivizes natural law absent civil law. Even objectively disastrous actions are performed rightfully if done for the sake of self-protection. The right-intention requirement is thus the only remaining moral principle restricting rights of war.

Untraceable intentions and natural equality of right, in turn, render the right-intention clause toothless in interpersonal relations. Amidst hostility, humans cannot possibly tell on what grounds their fellows resort to armed force. Extra-statist violence could have equally been prompted by just fear or by sheer wickedness. Besides, humans lack the standing to duly accuse their free and independent equals of having foul intentions. All are morally accountable to God alone for living up to natural law. In the state of nature, all belligerents therefore have a practically unlimited right of war, grounded in morally basic rights of self-defence. Leibniz succinctly captured Hobbes's position:

> And, since you assumed that each person has the right to do whatever may seem necessary for the preservation of his own safety, and as you decided that everyone must be the judge of his own needs, it was easy for you to conclude that in that state of affairs <u>a just war would be waged by all against all</u>.[114]

---

[114] Leibniz to Hobbes in *The Correspondence of Thomas Hobbes*, vol. 2, ed. Noel Malcolm (Oxford, 1994) 734. Also Cumberland, *Treatise*, 350.

Chapter 9 shows that the same feeble just war principles govern wars between states. As the laws of nature cannot constrain *individual* rights of war, neither can justice and the law of nations constrain *international* rights of war. By naturalizing and internalizing *jus gentium*, Hobbes ensured that neither subjects nor foreign enemies can appropriately accuse sovereigns of waging unjust wars.

9

MORALITY AMONG STATES

INTRODUCTION*

Establishing full sovereign immunity from taints of injustice requires insulating him from moral criticisms of international policy. Having shown that domestic laws cannot possibly be unjust (to those subjected to them), further argument is needed to prove that sovereign conduct cannot possibly stand in breach of international laws and agreements (including the natural and positive law of nations). International norms of armed conflict formed especially combustible material. Controversy raged among early modern philosophers over whether subjects are bound in conscience to refuse to fight plainly unjust wars. Vitoria, Suárez, and Grotius were among those endorsing conscientious objection in principle. All three held that 'if the war seems patently unjust to the subject, he must not fight, even if he is ordered to do so by the prince'.[1] Subjects, Grotius insisted, face no conflict of duties in this respect: 'if the War be unjust it is no Disobedience to decline it'.[2] Norms of international justice could thus delimit duties of political obedience and determine the moral quality of sovereign rule more generally. How did Hobbes neutralize this challenge to his vindicatory project?

The early modern period witnessed a surge in theorizing about international ethics. This chapter explores the character and normative foundations of Hobbes's international ethics by thinly contextualizing it within that blossoming intellectual field. By international ethics, I mean all moral norms applying to international actors, both those authorizing and restraining conduct.[3] In Hobbes's case, international ethics is composed of three distinct sets of moral principles: (i) natural rights; (ii) the laws of nature; and (iii) justice. His account of international ethics

---

* This chapter is based on Johan Olsthoorn, 'Hobbes on International Ethics' in Marcus Adams (ed), *A Companion to Hobbes* (Blackwell-Wiley, 2021) 252–267.

[1] Francisco de Vitoria, *Political Writings*, ed. Anthony Pagden and Jeremy Lawrance (Cambridge, 1991) 307. Francisco Suárez, 'On Charity' in *Suárez: Selections from Three Works*, ed. Thomas Pink (Indianapolis, 2015) 13.6.8: 'common soldiers . . . may go to war when summoned to do so, provided it is not clear to them that the war is unjust'. Grotius, *War and Peace*, 2.26.3.1: 'if it plainly appears [to subjects ordered to fight] that the War is unlawful, it is their Duty not to meddle in it.'

[2] Grotius, *War and Peace*, 2.26.4.5.

[3] The chapter makes no inroads otherwise into the province of international relations theory. Hobbes's theoretical conjectures on the empirical conditions of and constraints on interactions between states are left undiscussed, as are considerations of mere prudence in international affairs. On Hobbes on international relations, compare the contrasting readings of Charles Beitz, *Political Theory and International Relations* (Princeton, 1999) 27–59; Noel Malcolm, 'Hobbes's Theory of International Relations' in idem, *Aspects of Hobbes* (Oxford, 2002) 432–456; David Boucher, *Appropriating Hobbes: Legacies in Political, Legal, and International Thought* (Oxford, 2018) 186–219.

Hobbes on Justice. Johan Olsthoorn, Oxford University Press. © Johan Olsthoorn 2024.
DOI: 10.1093/9780191904585.003.0009

224 MORALITY AMONG STATES

is reductionist in this respect: he had no place for a separate law of nations and subsumed all rights of war under natural rights. Hobbes's international ethics is reductionist in a second respect as well: the exact same norms nominally apply to any agent in the state of nature, be they individuals, states, or sovereigns—even if these norms differ in their application and normative grounding. As DCv 14.4 states: 'the Elements of *natural law* and *natural right* ... may, when transferred to whole *commonwealths* and *nations*, be regarded as the Elements of the *laws* and of the *right of Nations* [*legum* et *juris gentium*]'.

This chapter offers a novel reconstruction of the arguments behind both reductionist moves. The explanation predominant in the existing literature, I contend, is inapplicable to *Leviathan*. To buttress the claim that *jus gentium* (the moral principles regulating interactions between states) is identical to the laws of nature (dictating to individuals the necessary means for peace and self-preservation), commentators have argued that in the international state of nature commonwealths occupy a normative position analogous to individuals in the interpersonal one. As Boucher writes, Hobbes's reductionism about international ethics 'requir[ed] the state to be viewed as an artificial person if it was to be subject in a similar way to the law of nations as individuals are to its exact equivalent the law of nature'.[4] Call this the Assimilation Argument. The argument has clear textual support in *De Cive* 14.4. Yet it is dropped from *Leviathan* onwards. With reason: natural law, binding in conscience alone (the sole court of natural justice), loses its prescriptive force when applied to states. Neither the prospect of this-worldly preservation nor that of otherworldly bliss is capable of explaining why *jus gentium* is normative for states.

As reflected by their new textual location, *Leviathan* applies norms of international ethics directly to sovereigns (rather than to commonwealths). While in substance the same as those of interpersonal ethics, these principles consequently come to differ, I maintain, in their normative grounds. The sovereign's duty to seek peace with foreign enemies and the concomitant right to resort to armed force when peace cannot be had are not morally foundational (as individual rights of self-defence are). Rather, rights and duties of international ethics are normatively underpinned by the natural law duty of gratitude. That duty morally requires the sovereign to duly discharge his role-specific duties, including providing defence against external enemies. In *Leviathan*, Hobbes's international ethics are thus informed by sovereign duties of care to national subjects—not unlike the tacit ethical assumptions of some modern realist theories of international relations. In the same move, *Leviathan* foregrounds that the principles of international ethics bind the sovereign in conscience alone. As in interpersonal conflict, a right intention is all that is required for resort to international war to be permissible. By naturalizing

---

[4] Boucher, *Appropriating Hobbes*, 152.

and internalizing the principles of international ethics, Hobbes insulated the sovereign from civic and foreign accusations of flouting norms of international law and justice.

9.1 STATES OF WAR

Hobbes's state of nature is by default a state of war. This holds true for both the pre-statist interpersonal state of nature (inhabited by individuals) and the extra-statist international one (inhabited by commonwealths). 'For the state of commonwealths towards each other is a *natural* state, i.e. a state of hostility. Even when the fighting between them stops, it should not be called Peace, but an intermission' in fighting (DCv 13.7).[5] Hobbes's bellicose portrayal of the international arena resembles that by his erstwhile employer Francis Bacon: 'there is ever between all Estates a secret Warre.'[6] Enduring peace requires a common power capable of providing security and of punishing injustices. Such a common power is by definition absent outside the state.

Cruder interpretations consider the Hobbesian natural condition to be entirely void of morality. Morgenthau, for instance, attributes to Hobbes the 'extreme dictum' that 'the state creates morality as well as law and that there is neither morality nor law outside the state.'[7] In fact, Hobbes recognized three distinct sets of deontic principles operative in the state of nature: the laws of nature, natural rights, and justice. The natural condition being a state of war, agents are not morally required to *act* upon the norms of justice and natural law if they judge that doing so would render them vulnerable to death and invasion (defeating the purpose of moral conduct) (EL 17.10; DCv 3.27; L 15.36). When peace is deemed out of reach, each may avail themselves of blanket natural rights of self-defence: '*By all means we can, to defend our selves*' (L 14.4) (§3.3). Moral laws are in this sense silent 'in time of war, wherein every mans' being and well-being is the rule of his actions' (EL 19.2; also DCv 5.2; DPS 36, 189). The laws of nature, prescribing the socially necessary means to establish peace, nevertheless ceaselessly bind in conscience and are, to that extent, operative even in conditions of war. The dispensation clause of the duty to practice justice and natural law—each agent equally

---

[5] For further depictions of the internal arena as a state of war, see e.g. DCv ED.2; DCv 10.17; L 13.12; L 21.8; DPS 7–8. On Hobbes's idiosyncratic conception of peace, see DCv 1.12; L 13.8; L 18.9.

[6] Francis Bacon, *Considerations Touching a Warre with Spaine* (London, 1629) 11. Richard Tuck ventures to speculate that 'Hobbes actually drafted the treatise for his master [Bacon]' in *The Rights of War and Peace* (Oxford, 1999) 127. Kinch Hoekstra offers some considerations against Tuck's hypothesis in 'Hobbes's Thucydides' in A.P. Martinich and Kinch Hoekstra (eds), *The Oxford Handbook of Hobbes* (Oxford, 2016) 565–566.

[7] H.J. Morgenthau, *American Foreign Policy: A Critical Examination* (London, 1952) 34. For an elaborate critique of the moral relativist reading of Hobbes found in the older realist literature, see Malcolm, *Aspects of Hobbes*, 433–440.

226 MORALITY AMONG STATES

having the right to assess for themselves whether present conditions permit harm-free performance—applies to international actors as well: 'against Enemies, whom the Common-wealth judgeth capable to do them hurt, it is lawfull by the originall Right of Nature to make warre' (L 28.23; also DCv 6.2; DCv 14.22).

Commonwealths and pre-statist individuals face different *empirical* conditions, making the international state of war a less wretched condition for subjects than the pre-statist war of all against all. The latter dramatically immiserates individuals, precluding all industry, agriculture, and trade. International hostility, on the other hand, stimulates arms production and military employment, thereby upholding 'the Industry of their Subjects' (L 13.12). Humans are by nature both highly vulnerable and roughly equal in power—the weakest being able to kill the strongest (DCv 1.3; L 13.1).[8] Neither postulate holds true for states, rendering international war less existential. The *normative* positions of commonwealths and pre-statist individuals appear at first sight structurally identical: both are endowed with the same right of nature and governed by the same laws of nature. However, what these principles in practice permit, require, and prohibit is contingent on the empirical situation agents are in. All agents must seek peace yet may avail themselves of armed force when deemed imperilled. But the prescribed means for establishing security differ for nations and pre-statist individuals.[9]

Consider wars of conquest. The right of nature allows each individual to preventively attack everyone else—not only to thwart *their* future attacks, but also to fortify themselves against possible third-party threats (§8.3). There being strength in numbers, natural right sanctions waging unprovoked war upon innocents in order to subdue and forcibly incorporate them into one's personal slave army. Rights of self-preservation allow everyone 'by force, or wiles, to master the persons of all men he can' to enhance personal security. 'Such augmentation of dominion over men, being necessary to a mans conservation, it ought to be allowed him' (L 13.4). While imperialist strategies are both permissible and reasonable at the individual level, at the international level they are generally less so. In internally stable and peaceful commonwealths, sovereigns can heighten external security by encouraging industry and commerce and by investing in public defence—options not available to individuals in the state of nature (DCv 13.7–8; L 29.18). Sovereigns do have the right to attack and conquer other states if they judge this necessary

---

[8] Hobbes's argument for natural equality of power alludes to the received doctrine that the highest legal power is that of life and death (*jus vitae necisque*). Possession of that legal power was commonly seen as a mark of sovereignty. E.g. Jean Bodin, *Method for the Easy Comprehension of History*, transl. Beatrice Reynolds (New York, 1969) 169. Hobbes naturalized this power, in order to subversively attribute it to pre-statist individuals.

[9] Vattel was hence uncharitable when accusing Hobbes of failing to realize that natural law changes its requirements when applied to nations. '[T]he *law of nations* is originally no other than the *law of nations applied* to nations. But as the application of a rule cannot be just and reasonable unless it be made in a manner suitable to the subject, we are not to imagine that the law of nations is precisely and in every case the same as the law of nature . . . the same general rule, applied to two subjects, cannot produce exactly the same decisions, when the subjects are different'. Vattel, *Law of Nations*, prol. §6.

for national security (DPS 191–192). Yet military adventurism is a risky strategy and therefore generally imprudent (DCv 13.14).[10] In sum: among nations, wars of conquest do not generally promote security—unlike in the all-out war among individuals. This helps explain why 'in wars between nations a degree of restraint has normally been observed' (DCv 5.2).

Informing another moral dissimilarity, some laws of nature arguably apply only to individuals, others only to states. Only individuals are by the second law of nature obliged to be willing to renounce their right to everything and submit themselves to a common sovereign. There is no textual evidence that Hobbes expected the same of states.[11] *Elements* includes a specific law of nature forbidding discrimination in passage and trade, akin to the WTO's most-favoured-nation principle.

> It is also a law of nature, *That men allow commerce and traffic* [i.e. trade] *indifferently to one another.* For he that alloweth that to one man, what he denieth to another, declareth his hatred to him, to whom he denied; and to declare hatred is war. And upon this title was grounded the great war between the Athenians and the Peloponnesians. For would the Athenians have condescended to suffer the Megareans, their neighbours, to traffic in their ports and markets, that war had not begun. (EL 16.12)[12]

This law will in practice apply to states alone. It has little purchase in the interpersonal state of nature, where the *bellum omnium contra omnes* precludes trade (L 13.9). Hobbes's inclusion under natural law of a principle sanctioning free trade is indicative of his attempt to naturalize the law of nations, to which I turn now.

9.2 NATURALIZING THE LAW OF NATIONS

Hobbes's reduction of *jus gentium* to natural law is one of his signature contributions to modern international thought.[13] Earlier theorists had made *jus gentium*

---

[10] While Hobbes's imperialism about private warfare is generally overlooked, anti-imperialist readings of Hobbes on international affairs proliferate. E.g. Malcolm, *Aspects of Hobbes*, 441–443; Richard Tuck, 'Grotius, Hobbes, and Pufendorf on Humanitarian Intervention' in Stefano Recchia and J.M. Welsh (eds), *Just and Unjust Military Intervention* (Cambridge, 2013) 107–110; Patricia Springborg, 'Hobbes, Donne and the Virginia Company: *Terra Nullius* and "The Bulimia of Dominium"', *History of Political Thought* 36 (2015) no. 1: 113–164; Theodore Christov, *Before Anarchy: Hobbes and His Critics in Modern International Thought* (Cambridge, 2015) 128–135; Hoekstra, 'Hobbes's Thucydides', 563–569.

[11] Gauthier argues that the second law of nature, as applied to nations, requires pursuing mutual disarmament. David Gauthier, *The Logic of Leviathan* (Oxford, 1969) 207–212.

[12] Cf. Thucydides, *The Peloponnesian War*, 1.67 (= EW 8: 71). Gentili had condemned the Athenians for closing their ports to the Megareans as contravening the law of nations in *De Jure Belli*, 88. On duties of non-discrimination in international trade, see also Vitoria, *Political Writings*, 279–280; Grotius, *War and Peace*, 2.2.22.

[13] David Armitage, *The Foundations of Modern International Thought* (Cambridge, 2013) 67–69; Boucher, *Appropriating Hobbes*, 141–148.

228   MORALITY AMONG STATES

partly or wholly a matter of tacit international agreement (i.e. of positive/voluntary/customary law). Positive international law—being morally arbitrary, mutable, and of conventional origin—was regarded as categorically distinct from natural law. For Suárez, the law of nations was entirely a matter of human agreement: '*jus gentium* properly so called ... differs from the natural law because it is based upon custom rather than upon nature'.[14] Grotius concurred.[15] Sharply as it breaks with this tradition, Hobbes's naturalistic conception of *jus gentium* is curiously undermotivated. *Elements* simply ends with the assertion: 'As for the law of nations, it is the same with the law of nature. For that which is the law of nature between man and man, before the constitution of commonwealth, is the law of nations between sovereign and sovereign, after' (EL 29.10). Can we derive any arguments from Hobbes's works to justify this equation?

One implicit argument can be drawn from Hobbes's conception of law. Law, properly understood, are commands addressed to someone previously bound to obey the commander (EL 29.2–4; DCv 14.1; L 26.2; DPS 32) (§6.2). Natural law counts as law proper qua authoritative commands issued by a superior to subjects bound to obedience (DCv 3.33; L 15.41; L 26.8). Equals (i.e. people who are not subordinated to each other) are not bound to accept another's judgement of what is natural or divine law. For this reason, naturally binding precepts are law among humans only *qua* civil law. The same reasoning applies to divine law. *Jus gentium* can be truly law only qua divine decrees (i.e. as natural law) (L 30.30). But amidst deep disagreement over what God in fact commanded, all pre-statist individuals equally are entitled to follow their own interpretation of divine law. Civil legislation is therefore needed to make God's eternal and revealed word law among humans (§3.5). Agreements are not laws (EL 29.2; DCv 14.2). Customary law is law only by tacit consent of the civil sovereign (L 26.7; DPS 162). Hobbes's conception of law as binding commands issued by a sovereign precludes the existence of customary international law. He nowhere explicitly called the positive law of nations an oxymoron.[16] Yet he strongly implied the same:

All *human law* is *civil law*. For the state of man outside the commonwealth is a state of enmity; and because in that state no one is subject to anyone else, there are no laws beyond the dictates of right reason, which is divine law. (DCv 14.5)

Hidden within Hobbes's texts is another set of moves to support his antipositivist conception of *jus gentium*. Hobbes silently subsumed under natural law various principles previously associated with the voluntary law of nations. Take

[14]   Suárez, *De Legibus*, 2.19.6, also 2.17.9; 2.19.4.

[15]   E.g. Grotius, *War and Peace*, prol. 41–42, 47.

[16]   Cf. Pufendorf, *Nature and Nations*, 2.3.23: 'Nor do we conceive, that there is any other Voluntary or Positive Law of Nations, properly invested with a true and legal Force, and obliging as the Ordinance of a Superior Power'.

the inviolability of ambassadors of peace (EL 16.13; DCv 3.19; L 15.39; cf. L 23.11–12). Many early modern thinkers maintained, with Grotius, that all 'the Rights of Embassy' fall under 'that Law of Nations which we call voluntary'.[17] These include that 'Law of Nations, which renders the Persons of Embassadors sacred and inviolable'.[18] As Samuel Rachel (1628–1691) argued: 'that Ambassadors who come even from enemies, and may be bringing a declaration of war from a quarter already guilty of wrongdoing, should be entitled to security so unique and solemn ... this must unquestionably be attributed not to the Law of Nature, but to the deliberate choice of Nations'.[19] Tellingly, some of Hobbes's scathing criticisms of received criteria for transgressions of natural law (whatever 'is against the consent of all nations, or the wisest and most civil nations') typically concerned *jus gentium* (EL 15.1; also DCv 2.1).[20]

To support his naturalization of the law of nations, Hobbes could also have categorized some of its received elements under civil law. Clear examples of this are lacking. Most principles standardly subsumed under the positive law of nations he rather dispenses with by silence (e.g. rights of hospitality and of postliminy). Some may think of the institution of private property, which Hobbes insists is an effect of civil law. Yet this institution was only considered part of the law of nations in its loose sense ('non-morally required widely observed human practices'); not in the strict sense central in this chapter ('moral norms governing international relations').[21]

Scholars have hitherto overlooked Hobbes's concomitant naturalistic conception of rights of war (*jus belli*)—justifying preventive attacks and outright conquest. *De Cive* calls the natural right to everything a right of war: 'as long as a person has no guarantee of security from attack, his primeval *Right* remains in force to look out for himself in whatever ways he will and can, i.e. a *Right to all things*, or a *Right of war* [*Ius in omnia, sive Ius belli*]' (DCv 5.1; also DCv P.15). Hobbes accorded pre-statist individuals and commonwealths virtually unrestrained rights to wage

---

[17] Grotius, *War and Peace*, 2.18.1. Also Vitoria, *Political Writings*, 281; Suárez, *De Legibus*, 2.19.7; John Locke, 'Essays on the Law of Nature' in *Locke: Political Essays*, ed. Mark Goldie (Cambridge, 1997) 107. Wolff, *Jus Gentium*, 536, contends that the inviolability of ambassadors is established neither by natural nor by customary law. It holds by bilateral pacts alone.

[18] Grotius, *War and Peace*, 2.18.4.6.

[19] Samuel Rachel, *Dissertations on the Law of Nature and of Nations*, ed. Ludwig von Bar (Washington, 1916) 215. Pufendorf, *Nature and Nations*, 2.3.23, followed Hobbes in subsuming the law of embassies under natural law. Velthuysen distinguished between a natural and customary law of nations, while likewise following Hobbes in subsuming the law of ambassadors under the former. Lambert van Velthuysen, *A Letter on the Principles of Justness and Decency*, ed. Malcolm de Mowbray (Leiden, 2013) 72. For an overview of early modern ideas on diplomatic immunity, see Eileen Young, 'The Development of the Law of Diplomatic Relations', *British Yearbook of International Law* 40 (1964) 148–167.

[20] *Digest* 1.1.4: '*Jus gentium*, the law of nations, is that which all human peoples observe.'

[21] The last was labelled '*jus inter gentes*' by Richard Zouche, *An Exposition of Fecial Law and Procedure, or of Law between Nations*, ed. J.L. Brierly (Washington, 1911) 1. For different takes on this classic distinction, see Suárez, *De Legibus*, 2.19.8; Nathaniel Culverwell, *An Elegant and Learned Discourse of the Light of Nature*, ed. R.A. Greene and H. MacCullum (Indianapolis, 2001) 63.

230   MORALITY AMONG STATES

war: 'for where there is no law, there no killing, nor any thing else can be unjust. And by the right of nature we destroy, without being unjust, all that is noxious, both beasts and men' (EW 5: 152). Any actor in the state of nature may by natural right defend themselves in any way they deem useful. Rights to wage defensive wars were commonly regarded as due by nature and held by pre-statist individuals.[22] Hobbes substantially enlarged these natural rights of war by granting individuals a natural right to enslave the vanquished (aggressors and innocents alike). Previous thinkers had maintained that rights to enslave and govern those conquered in war were introduced by common usage of humanity, placing them under the positive law of nations.[23] Hobbes, by contrast, argued that rights of self-defence grant each 'lawful title to subdue or kill, according as his own conscience and discretion shall suggest unto him for his safety and benefit' (EL 22.9). Each human by nature has right to rule all others (DCv 15.5; L 31.5). Consequently, he could claim that '*slaves* are acquired by war just like other things' (DCv 9.9). Natural rights being mere liberty-rights, dominion arises only when subjects covenant to submit themselves to another (L 20.11). All sovereign rule, whether obtained by institution or by conquest, involves natural rights to rule rendered effective by subjects' pacts of submission.

9.3 THE ASSIMILATION ARGUMENT

Only one explicit argument for reducing *jus gentium* to natural law is found in Hobbes's works—the Assimilation Argument in *De Cive*: 'because commonwealths once instituted take on the personal qualities of men, what we call *natural law* in speaking of the duties of individual men is called the *law of nations* [*jus gentium*], when applied to whole commonwealths, peoples, or nations' (DCv 14.4). Armitage calls this 'the clearest statement Hobbes would ever give of his rationale for identifying the law of nations with the law of nature.'[24] Tuck glosses the same passage as attesting that Hobbes morally assimilated pre-statist individuals to sovereign states.[25] Boucher agrees: 'In order to establish the efficacy of the equation of the law of nature and the law of nations, which differ only in the subjects they regulate, it is necessary that individuals and states somehow be equated.'[26] The

---

[22] E.g. Vitoria, *Political Writings*, 299; Suárez, 'On Charity', 13.2.1.

[23] E.g. Vitoria, *Political Writings*, 281; Suárez, *De Legibus*, 2.17.2, 2.19.8; Gentili, *De Jure Belli*, 332; Grotius, *War and Peace*, 3.7–3.8.

[24] Armitage, *Foundations of Modern International Thought*, 64.

[25] Hobbes 'accepted . . . the Grotian assimilation of individuals to sovereign states'. Tuck, *The Rights of War and Peace*, 129. Tuck's book traces the legacy of Grotius's putative moral identification of pre-statist individuals with sovereign states: 'Grotius had thus made the claim that an individual in nature (that is, before transferring any rights to a civil society) was morally identical to a state, and that there were no powers possessed by a state which an individual could not possess in nature'. Tuck, *The Rights of War and Peace*, 82; also 85, 95, 108, 228.

[26] Boucher, *Appropriating Hobbes*, 149; also Dieter Hüning, 'Inter Arma Silent Leges: Naturrecht, Staat und Völkerrecht bei Thomas Hobbes' in Rüdiger Voigt (ed), *Der Leviathan* (Baden-Baden, 2000) 135; Georg Cavallar, *The Rights of Strangers* (Aldershot, 2002) 179–180. *De Cive's* Assimilation

Assimilation Argument for identifying the law of nations with natural law does not require independent states to be like pre-statist individuals in all respects; nor does it rule out character differences between the international and interpersonal states of nature. The argument merely has states somehow 'take on' the moral rights and duties individuals possess by nature. The Assimilation Argument thus captures only part of the 'domestic analogy' ascribed to Hobbes by international relations scholars.[27] (Modelling international relations on the interpersonal state of nature, the analogy denies the uniqueness of international society.)

The Assimilation Argument gains plausibility from other passages morally likening states to pre-statist individuals. In the natural condition 'of Absolute Liberty, such as is theirs, that neither are Soveraigns, nor Subjects' (L 31.1), each agent equally has the right to follow their own judgement, beholden to none but God. 'So in States, and Common-wealths not dependent on one another, every Common-wealth ... has an absolute Libertie, to doe what it [i.e. its sovereign representative] shall judge ... most conducing to their benefit' (L 21.8; also EL 20.18). More succinctly, 'sovereign power [is] no less absolute in the commonwealth, than before commonwealth every man was absolute in himself to do, or not to do, what he thought good' (EL 20.13; also DCv 6.18).

Upon reflection, the Assimilation Argument proves problematic: the reasons for why natural law is normative for individuals do not straightforwardly hold for commonwealths. Hobbes's interpersonal ethics is standardly regarded as being normatively grounded in the value of self-preservation.[28] The right of nature allows individuals to use their powers and abilities in whatever way they deem fit to preserve their lives; while the law of nature prohibits self-destructive acts and requires each to adopt the surest means to self-preservation (L 14.1–3). Does natural law

---

Argument left a long legacy in international thought. E.g. Baruch Spinoza, 'Political Treatise' in *The Collected Works of Spinoza*, vol. 2, ed. Edwin Curley (Princeton, 2016) 3.11: 'since the Right of the supreme power is nothing more than the Right itself of nature, it follows that two states are related to one another as two men are in the state of nature'. Later theorists—including Wolff, Vattel, and Reid—combined a similar line of reasoning with Pufendorf's notion of the state as a moral person, endowed with capacities of reason and will. That conception of the moral person of the state differs from Hobbesian state personality. Ben Holland, *The Moral Person of the State: Pufendorf, Sovereignty and Composite Polities* (Cambridge, 2017) 91, 210–212; Wolff, *Jus Gentium*, 9, 84; Vattel, *Law of Nations*, prol. §11; Thomas Reid, *On Practical Ethics*, ed. Knud Haakonssen (Edinburgh, 2007) 95.

[27] Beitz, *Political Theory*, 36–50; Cavallar, *The Rights of Strangers*, 179–189; Chiara Bottici, *Men and States: Rethinking the Domestic Analogy in a Global Age*, transl. Karen Whittle (New York, 2009) 39–51; Hedley Bull, *The Anarchical Society*, 4th ed. (New York, 2012) 44–49. Noel Malcolm has criticized realist interpretations of Hobbes for advancing a 'complete parallelism between individuals and states, so that anything he said about the psychology and the predicament of the former in the state of nature must equally apply to the latter'. Malcolm challenges both empirical and normative parallels between states and individuals, arguing that the parallelism holds true only partially, namely at the 'jural level' of interpersonal rights and duties. Malcolm highlights Hobbes's reduction of *jus gentium* to natural law without explaining it. Malcolm, *Aspects of Hobbes*, 443, 446; also Noel Malcolm, 'What Hobbes *Really* Said', *The National Interest* 81 (2005) 122–128.

[28] The main rival to the standard prudentialist reading of Hobbes's moral philosophy is Lloyd's reciprocity interpretation. S.A. Lloyd, *Morality in the Philosophy of Thomas Hobbes* (Cambridge, 2009).

232   MORALITY AMONG STATES

likewise dictate commonwealths (the multitude incorporated into one body politic) to pursue self-preservation, either of itself or of its composite members? Why would states have self-preservation-based rights and duties?[29] Further argument is needed to account for the normativity of natural law as applied to commonwealths.

Compounding the quandary, Hobbesian laws of nature are idiosyncratic in binding in conditions of war in conscience alone (DCv 3.27; DCv 4.21; L 15.36). In the bellicose natural condition, each person equally is beyond moral reproach by anyone but God, having a natural right to determine for themselves how best to seek personal security: 'there being no other Law remaining, but that of Nature, there is no place for Accusation; every man being his own Judge, and accused onely by his own Conscience' (L 27.3; also L 14.30). As God alone can know our conscience, only he can hold us accountable for abiding by natural law outside the state (EL 25.3; L 42.80) (§3.3). Commonwealths have no inner consciences and are not the kind of entities God can keep in line by threats of otherworldly torment. In what way, then, is natural law normative for states?

Other early modern theorists maintained that the law of nations is at least in part enforceable by international society. Vattel held that many duties imposed by the law of nations are binding in conscience alone, on the Hobbesian grounds that 'every nation [is] free, independent, and sole arbitress of her own actions'.[30] Other nations can have no enforceable right 'when the correspondent obligation depends on the judgement of the party in whose breast it exists'—each state being free to determine themselves what 'the dictates of his own conscience' require.[31] However, states can enforce their perfect rights not to be injured and to protect themselves from blatant injustice.[32] Vattel's intellectual predecessor, Christian Wolff (1679–1754), had likewise insisted that many things are due to nations by enforceable right. *Inter alia*, each nation has a perfect right to resist being injured/wronged ('security');[33] that pacts made with them are kept inviolate;[34] and that other nations abstain from interfering in their government.[35] When faced with (threatened) injury, Wolff maintained, each commonwealth has a right to unilaterally initiate war if the enemy refuses to accept third-party arbitration and peaceful negotiation to settle the conflict.[36]

Hobbes's laws of nature are exceptional in being *entirely* unenforceable by humans outside the state. Anyone is entitled to abide by their own interpretation of

---

[29] Beitz, *Political Theory*, 52.
[30] Vattel, *Law of Nations*, 2.1.8.
[31] Vattel, *Law of Nations*, prol. §17.
[32] Vattel, *Law of Nations*, 2.5.70.
[33] Wolff, *Jus Gentium*, 130.
[34] Wolff, *Jus Gentium*, 195.
[35] Wolff, *Jus Gentium*, 130–131, 137–138.
[36] Wolff, *Jus Gentium*, 292–293. By definition, 'whatever is done contrary to the perfect right of another is a wrong' (528, also 90). Justice imposes 'a perfect obligation of nations for each to allow the other its right' (135).

morality in the natural condition (DCv 2.1n; DH 13.8). For this reason, 'the Lawes of Nature . . . in the condition of meer Nature . . . are not properly Lawes, but qualities that dispose men to peace, and to obedience' (L 26.8) (§3.5). Beyond moral reproach by their equals, pre-statist individuals are instead motivated to abide by natural law in order to secure self-preservation and heavenly bliss. Neither rationale can be ascribed unproblematically to states. How then can states be bound by the same moral principles? How to render intelligible the assertion that commonwealths 'take on' the rights and duties of pre-statist individuals? Perhaps readers can come up with creative solutions, in line with Hobbes's principles. Significantly, Hobbes made no such explanatory attempts himself. On the contrary, perhaps in recognition of these difficulties, he abandoned the Assimilation Argument altogether in *Leviathan*, altering the normative underpinnings of *jus gentium* along the way.

9.4 THE OFFICE OF THE SOVEREIGN

Both the English and Latin *Leviathan* reiterate the equation of *jus gentium* with natural law. It has hitherto gone unnoticed, however, that the discussion of international law is moved from the chapter on laws to that on the sovereign's duties (cf. EL 29.10; DCv 14.4; L 30.30). This shift, I contend, is highly significant. Amending his earlier view, Hobbes now emphasizes that the duties of *jus gentium* really apply to sovereigns (bearing the person of the commonwealth). As the laws of nations bind in conscience only outside the state, they should be understood to apply 'to Common-wealths, that is, to the Consciences of Soveraign Princes, and Soveraign Assemblies; there being no Court of Naturall Justice, but in the Conscience onely; where not Man, but God raigneth' (L 30.30). One commentator has remarked that this passage 'left implicit what Hobbes had made explicit in *De Cive*: that the commonwealth once constituted as an artificial person took on the characteristics and the capacities of the fearful, self-defensive individuals who fabricated it'.[37] I disagree. As signalled by its new textual location, Hobbes turned abiding by international ethics into a role-specific duty of sovereigns, for which they are accountable to God alone. That role-specific duty, I contend, undergirds and alters the normativity of Hobbes's international ethics from *Leviathan* onwards.

Commonwealths are as free and equal vis-à-vis other commonwealths as individuals are vis-à-vis each other in the state of nature. Yet sovereigns are normatively positioned differently in relation to one another than pre-statist individuals are. Sovereigns have been contractually entrusted with a distinct set of duties, owed to God alone.

---

[37] Armitage, *Foundations of Modern International Thought*, 64.

The OFFICE of the Sovereign ... consisteth in the end, for which he was trusted with the Soveraign Power, namely the procuration of *the safety of the people*; to which he is obliged by the Law of Nature, and to render an account thereof to God, the Author of that Law, and to none but him. (L 30.1; also EL 28.1; DCv 13.2)

Pre-statist individuals lack such role-specific duties of care. One of the sovereign's main tasks is to protect the people against foreign enemies. Defence against external enemies is a prime good of citizens (EL 28.3; EL 28.9; DCv 13.6–7) and a key reason for instituting the commonwealth (EL 20.2; L 18.1; L 25.13). Indeed, the right to decide on war and peace with other nations is an essential mark of sovereignty (DCv 6.7; L 18.12). My contention is that the law of nations dictates to sovereigns *how* they should procure the people's safety against foreign enemies: 'the people's safety dictates the law by which Princes come to know their *duty*' (DCv 13.2). For instance, its principles prohibit national wars of aggrandizement, waged 'out of ambition, or of vain-glory' (EL 28.9; also DCv 13.14; L 29.22; DPS 13). A sovereign initiating war for glory flouts his role-specific duties by contravening the moral duty to seek external peace.

The sovereign is obliged by natural law to fulfil his role-specific duties to his best endeavour. Which law(s) of nature underpins these duties? Some specific sovereign duties track separate laws of nature (such as moral duties of equity and mercy); others do not.[38] Following suggestions by Murphy and Malcolm, I argue that the natural law of gratitude enjoins the sovereign to fulfil role-specific duties in general.[39] Sovereigns are duty-bound to do their utmost to provide external defence on pain of acting 'in contravention of the trust of those who put the sovereign power in their hands' (DCv 13.4).[40] Duties of gratitude spring from free gifts, as duties of justice arise from covenants. The sovereign's duties are not assigned to him by the people. Rather, these duties are the moral upshot resulting from having freely received supreme power from them. (Recall that sovereigns-by-institution are third-party beneficiaries in the original covenant, receiving the benefit of the mutual exchange between citizens in the form of supreme power.[41]) Sovereigns are morally obliged to give subjects 'no reasonable cause to repent' their good will by

---

[38] Curran argues rightly that at least some office-specific duties of sovereigns are irreducible to natural law duties. Their violation is hence not wrong in itself. Curran leaves unexplained what makes performance of such morally arbitrary offices morally binding. She overlooks that the sovereign is obliged by the natural law of gratitude to abide by the entire set of duties. Eleanor Curran, *Reclaiming the Rights of Hobbesian Subjects* (New York, 2007) 113–116.

[39] Mark Murphy, 'Deviant Uses of "Obligation" in Hobbes' *Leviathan*', *History of Philosophy Quarterly* 11 (1994) no. 3: 284; Malcolm, *Aspects of Hobbes*, 447; Malcolm, 'What Hobbes *Really* Said', 126.

[40] According to DCv 13.4, only sovereigns-by-institution are bound by this duty of trust; sovereigns-by-acquisition—who have contracted with each subject separately—are not. *Leviathan* lacks a statement to this effect. Deborah Baumgold (ed), *Three-Text Edition of Thomas Hobbes's Political Theory* (Cambridge, 2017) 340–341.

[41] Larry May, *Limiting Leviathan: Hobbes on Law and International Affairs* (Oxford, 2013) 48–66.

discharging their office well (L 15.16; also L 28.22). Should they breach the trust, then this is 'not to be called injury; it hath another name (viz.) INGRATITUDE' (EL 16.7; also DCv 3.8; L 15.16; L 24.7). Again, sovereigns owe this natural law duty to God alone.

Closely connected as sovereign and state are in Hobbes's political theory, some might think that I am exaggerating the shift between *De Cive* and *Leviathan*. *De Cive* defines the commonwealth as a civil person created by having each member of the multitude subject their will to a common sovereign (DCv 5.6–9). As a social construct, the commonwealth is incapable of unmediated action. It can will and do things only through the sovereign (whose will stands for the will of all).[42] Commonwealths can thus only conform to the principles of international ethics indirectly, through the sovereign's will, even in the early works. Doesn't this mean that these principles apply to the sovereign in *De Cive* as well? Well, not in the sense that they oblige *him*. The Assimilation Argument leaves unexplained why the sovereign is morally bound to abide by *jus gentium*. In calling *jus gentium* the law of nature applied to nations, it indicates that these principles somehow bind the commonwealth itself (i.e. the collective body of the people). That 'commonwealths once instituted take on' the natural rights and duties of its members does not imply that the sovereign thereby becomes morally obligated to adhere to the law of nations (e.g. by having some of his own natural law duties be transformed into *jus gentium* duties). *Leviathan*, by contrast, does explain why abiding by the law of nations is part of the sovereign's duties. It declares that *jus gentium* binds the sovereign indirectly, through his natural law duty to show gratitude for having been entrusted by the people with supreme power.

Complicating matters, the sovereign also serves as representative of the commonwealth. In that capacity he interacts with representatives of other states. Thus, the sovereign signs treaties with foreign allies on behalf of the commonwealth. Any obligations vis-à-vis other states assumed in such pacts are attributed by fiction to the commonwealth (whose person the sovereign bears). Those treaty obligations, I have proposed, are not normative for commonwealths. How could they be? Commonwealths are corporate entities that cannot speak or act except via the sovereign (L 26.5; L 31.38). They are not the kind of entities capable of being bound by *jus gentium*. Perhaps in recognition of this, *Leviathan* makes duties of *jus gentium* incumbent upon the sovereign alone. He is obliged by justice to keep whatever international treaties he has made as head of state—provided, of course, that doing so in his view at present best promotes *salus populi*.

---

[42] On the meaning of civil person and the nature of the commonwealth in *De Cive*, see Johan Olsthoorn, 'Leviathan Inc.: Hobbes on the Nature and Person of the Commonwealth', *History of European Ideas* 47 (2021) no. 1: 19–22. The reconceptualization of *jus gentium* as applying to sovereigns, rather than to states, is arguably facilitated by *Leviathan*'s novel theory of representation. Clarifying the relation between sovereign and state as one of representation, the sovereign is now defined as he who acts on behalf of the commonwealth.

236 MORALITY AMONG STATES

Leviathan's novel foundation of the principles of international ethics entails two further revisions (compared to interpersonal morality). First, while individual rights to wage war are essentially rights of *self*-defence, the sovereign's rights to wage war against enemies of the commonwealth are at bottom rights of *other*-defence. Sovereigns by right wage war with external enemies, not to secure their own self-preservation but to protect their people from foreign aggression. 'And every Soveraign hath the same Right, in procuring the safety of his People, that any particular man can have, in procuring the safety of his own Body' (L 30.30).[43] Second, brazenly belligerent sovereigns do double wrong. They violate the laws of nations, dictating to rulers the surest means to international peace. And they violate the specific natural law commanding gratitude, imposing an additional duty on the sovereign. Empowered to protect the citizens against external enemies, the sovereign is morally obliged to deliver on their trust.[44]

Sovereigns are accountable to God alone for fulfilling these moral duties. The deity kindly takes the endeavour for the deed; meaning that objectively disastrous decisions—imprudently deviating from what natural law dictates are the surest means to achieve national security—are justified if done in good faith (DCv 1.10n; DCv 3.27n; DPS 192). To support his contention that the law of nations binds in conscience alone, I have suggested, *Leviathan* ditches the earlier Assimilation Argument. The common contention that *states* are bound by Hobbes's law of nations/nature should hence be rejected. In *Leviathan*, *jus gentium* binds the sovereign representative—not the commonwealth whose person he carries. The concluding section argues that international principles of justice and of just war are likewise matters of conscience alone.

9.5 INTERNALIZING THE LAW OF NATIONS

Rights to wage war, Chapter 8 has shown, are foundational to Hobbes's political theory. They provide a positive justification for the 'right of all men to all things . . . which is the right of War' (DCv P.15). Sovereigns wield the same right of war when defending their people against domestic and foreign enemies: 'the commonwealth retains its original Right against the dissenter, i.e. the *right of war*, as against an enemy' (DCv 6.2; also DCv 14.22; L 28.23). Just as individuals may by nature

---

[43] The parallel passage in the Latin *Leviathan* is more ambiguous: 'Nam *Ius Gentium & Ius Naturae* idem sunt. That which every man could do before the institution of commonwealths, every commonwealth can do by the law of nations [or right of nature: *jus gentium*]' (LL 30.30).

[44] One way to violate this duty of national protection, Pufendorf suggests, is by engaging in humanitarian intervention: 'the prime obligation of leaders to seek the preservation of their own states surely forbids them to endanger their own status for another's sake, except insofar as a coincident advantage permits'. Samuel Pufendorf, *On the Natural State of Men*, ed. Michael Seidler (Lewiston, 1990) 131.

determine at their own discretion when self-preservation requires using armed force, so sovereigns are entitled to make that call within the state.

In *De Cive*, Hobbes defused the potentially destabilizing role of ideological assessments of war by insisting that questions of just war are practically irrelevant to citizens. Subjects have, after all, promised simple obedience. 'I am not acting unjustly if I go to war at the order of my commonwealth though I believe that it is an unjust war; rather I act unjustly if I refuse to go to war, claiming for myself the knowledge of what is just and unjust which belongs to the commonwealth' (DCv 12.2).[45] This neutralizing strategy holds regardless of whether some wars are in fact unjust. Hobbes's later works, I submit, more boldly question the very possibility of unjust wars.

The *Dialogue* contains Hobbes's most extensive engagement with received just war doctrines. It stresses that decisions about war and peace are a sovereign prerogative, morally restrained only by the positional requirement to protect the people in any way deemed effective. Consider the passage on the lawfulness of armed intervention in foreign conflicts. 'If the War upon our Neighbours [by a third country] be Just, it may be question'd whether it be Equity or no to Assist them against the Right'. In response, the philosopher—supposedly Hobbes's spokesperson—tersely waives away any moral qualms about assisting unjust belligerents.

> For my part I make no Question of that at all, unless the Invader will, and can put me in security, that neither he, nor his Successors shall make any Advantage of the Conquest of my Neighbour, to do the same to me in time to come; but there is no Common Power to bind them to the Peace. (DPS 23)

For the sovereign, it does not matter morally whether enemies have just cause for war. When dealing with 'Enemies, whom the Common-wealth judgeth capable to do them hurt . . . the Sword Judgeth not, nor doth the Victor make distinction of Nocent, and Innocent, as to the time past; nor has other respect of mercy, than as it conduceth to the good of his own People' (L 28.23). Like all other natural law requirements, duties of mercy need not be practised in times of war (L 30.23). Whatever policy the sovereign judges best protects the people he may permissibly adopt.

Chapter 8 argued that in morally endorsing preventive wars aimed at security and in portraying them as essentially defensive in character, Hobbes followed Gentili and Bacon (§8.3). His two combative forerunners deemed preventive war permissible against any threat one has reason to fear. More lenient than them still, Hobbes held that aiming to generally augment security is sufficient to render

---

[45] Pufendorf, *Nature and Nations*, 8.1.8, agreed, insisting that a subject should simply 'obey, and leave his *Sovereign* to answer for the *Justice* of the War before GOD'.

238   MORALITY AMONG STATES

anticipatory force permissible. Conquering those who intend no harm is allowed if done to promote self-preservation (L 13.4). 'And as their preservation, so also is their security a just pretence of invading those whom they have just cause to fear ... Necessity, and Security are the principle justifications, before God, of beginning War' (DPS 192). Any international war is defensive (and hence *ad bellum* just) if motivated by considerations of national security. Sovereigns may, 'upon injury done him, or upon want of caution that injury be not done him in time to come, repaire, and secure himself by Warre; which is in summe, deposing, killing, or sub-duing, or doing any act of Hostility' (L 42.127).

Hobbes further departed from Gentili and Bacon by subjectivizing the just-fear criterion through his postulate of natural equality of right (§8.5).[46] Within condi-tions of war, each agent equally rightfully relies on their own strength and judge-ment to determine how best to preserve themselves. Only God is able and entitled to judge whether agents sincerely endeavour to abide by the natural law duty to pursue peace. Hobbes thereby effectively made having a right intention the sole criterion for permissible resort to armed force:

> to make War upon another like Soveraign Lord, and dispossess him of his Lands ... is Lawful, or not Lawful according to the intention of him that does it. For, First, being a Soveraign Ruler, he is not subject to any Law of Man; and as to the Law of God, where the intention is justifiable, the action is so also. (DPS 191–192)

The laws of nations, prescribing the means to international peace, are consequently duties of conscience alone. Each sovereign equally has the right to follow their own judgement as to which foreign policies at present best protect their people—irenic or belligerent ones.

The same holds true for obligations of justice to keep international pacts and truces. Commentators have rightly pointed out that Hobbes denied neither the possibility nor the benefits of international cooperation.[47] 'Leagues between Common-wealths, over whom there is no humane Power established, to keep

---

[46] Cf. Gentili, *De Jure Belli*, 62: 'a just fear is defined as the fear of a greater evil, a fear which might properly be felt even by a man of great courage' [Jus autem metus definitur timor majoris malitatis; quiq; merito in homine constantissimo cadat]. Bacon, *Considerations Touching a Warre*, 8: 'I say just feare, for as the Civilians doe well define that the legall feare is *justus metus qui cadit in constantem virum*, in private cases, so there is *justus metus qui cadit in constantem Senatum in causa publica*, not out of umbrages, light jealousnesse, apprehensions a farre off, but out of cleare foresight of imminent danger'. Both were paraphrasing *Digest* 4.2.6: 'Metum autem non vani hominis, sed qui merito et in homine constantissimo cadat.'

[47] On the prospects of trust between nations, see Peter Schröder, *Trust in Early Modern International Political Thought, 1598–1713* (Cambridge, 2017) 104–119. For Hobbesian defences of an international legal order, see May, *Limiting Leviathan*, 173–223; David Dyzenhaus, 'Hobbes on the International Rule of Law', *Ethics and International Affairs* 28 (2014) no. 1: 53–64; Larry May, 'Limiting Leviathan: Reply to My Critics', *Hobbes Studies* 27 (2014) no. 2: 199–206.

them all in awe, are not onely lawfull, but also profitable for the time they last' (L 22.29).[48] However, such temporary leagues are by their very nature insufficient to guarantee enduring peace: 'an association formed only for mutual aid, does not afford to the parties ... the security which we are looking for, to practice, in their relations with each other, the *laws of nature*' (DCv 5.4). Lacking a common power to keep members' wills aligned amidst inevitable disagreements, associations are inherently unstable (DCv 5.6). The *Dialogue* voices scepticism about the viability of 'a constant Peace ... between two Nations, because there is no Common Power in this World to punish their Injustice: mutual fear may keep them quiet for a time, but upon every visible advantage they will invade one another' (DPS 7–8). Any newly arising just fear renders international pacts inoperative, retriggering hostilities (§7.1). 'And if a weaker Prince, make a disadvantageous peace with a stronger, for feare; he is bound to keep it; unless ... there ariseth some new, and just cause of feare, to renew the war' (L 14.27; also DCv 13.7).

International leagues by definition lack a common judge to settle conflicts and enforce rulings. They hence leave its members in a state of nature, where each party has right to judge for themselves the safety of continued cooperation. Whether a covenant can safely be kept 'is for the fearful party to decide' (DCv 2.11). Outside the state, each person reneging on their covenants out of fear does so rightfully since they themselves are by natural right the judge of the justness of their fears (L 14.18). Just as each individual 'may lawfully rely on his own strength and art, for caution against all other men' absent a functioning system of law enforcement, so may 'Cities and Kingdomes ... upon all pretences of danger, and fear of Invasion ... endeavour as much as they can, to subdue, or weaken their neighbours, by open force, and secret arts, for want of other Caution, justly' (L 17.2). Indeed, sovereigns are *ex officio* obliged to weaken enemies by any means possible: 'They may also do anything that seems likely to subvert, by force or by craft, the power of foreigners whom they fear; for the rulers of commonwealths are obliged to do all they can to ensure that the calamities they fear do not happen' (DCv 13.8).

I have argued that Hobbes internalized the principles of international ethics, including *jus belli*, through their dispensation clause. Binding primarily in conscience in the warlike international arena, these principles leave international actors beyond human reproach. Supreme rulers may make terrible foreign policy decisions, imprudently endangering the state. Whether such foolishness is prompted by foul intentions—and hence a sin—other international actors lack epistemic access and moral standing to determine. *Leviathan*'s Review and Conclusion contains a passage facially in tension with this reading. Hobbes there denounces as seditious the search to 'justifie the War by which their Power was at first gotten'. Any such attempt would be counterproductive since it would justify all 'successefull Rebellions'. Few

---

[48] For further evidence of international agreements and alliances, see DCv 2.18; L 20.4; L 21.24; LL 28.23; B 301. For discussion, see Gabriella Slomp, *Hobbes against Friendship* (Cham, 2022) 47–54.

240 MORALITY AMONG STATES

have obtained power fairly: 'there is scarce a Common-wealth in the world, whose beginnings can in conscience be justified' (L R&C.8). That sorry fact is irrelevant, though, for political legitimacy. Hobbes is a functionalist about political legitimacy: sovereigns possess the right to rule in virtue of providing protection to their subjects at present.[49] Hobbes's admission that kingdoms can be gotten by 'unjust violence' shows, the objection goes, that wars can be unjust in a humanly identifiable way (L 15.4). True enough. In reply: the objection only proves the truism that *civil wars*—rebellions and coups—can be unjust. Violently seizing power from one's sovereign lord is without doubt always unjust (L 18.3). That is compatible with my claim that humans cannot assess the justice or injustice of wars in the interpersonal and international states of nature, 'there being no Court of Naturall justice, but in the Conscience onely; where not Man, but God raigneth' (L 30.30). Provided, that is, that violent rebellions do not *ipso facto* amount to a return to the state of nature. Chapter 10 defends that last clause.

CONCLUSION

This chapter has analysed Hobbes's reductionism about the principles of international ethics. Across his works, Hobbes insists that the law of nations equals the law of nature, and *jus belli* the right of nature. These continuities in substance notwithstanding, I have argued that Hobbes significantly revised his account of international ethics in *Leviathan*. There, *jus gentium* directly applies to sovereigns (rather than to states), enjoining them how to fulfil their role-specific duties to safeguard the people from foreign threats. This revision allowed Hobbes to internalize the principles of international ethics: they bind the sovereign in conscience. This helped render the sovereign immune from human accusations of international injustice. Citizens have neither epistemic access nor the moral and political standing to second-guess the sovereign's intentions. The sovereign is morally accountable to God alone. In normatively grounding principles of international ethics in the sovereign's positional duties to promote *salus populi*, *Leviathan*'s theory resembles some modern realist theories of international relations. With this important qualification: Hobbes's principles of international ethics exclusively concern defence against external enemies, rather than pursuit of national interest generally.[50]

---

[49] On the theory of legitimate authority outlined in *Leviathan*'s Review and Conclusion and its consistency with views Hobbes advanced elsewhere, see Kinch Hoekstra, 'The *De Facto* Turn in Hobbes's Political Philosophy' in Tom Sorell and Luc Foisneau (eds), *Leviathan after 350 Years* (Oxford, 2004) 33–73.

[50] On the ethical commitments buried in realist theories of international relations, see Steven Forde, 'Classical Realism' in Terry Nardin and David R. Mapel (eds), *Traditions of International Ethics* (Cambridge, 1992) 62–84; C.A.J. Coady, 'The Moral Reality in Realism', *Journal of Applied Philosophy* 22 (2005) no. 2: 121–136; Jack Donnelly, 'The Ethics of Realism' in Christian Reus-Smit and Duncan Snidal (eds), *The Oxford Handbook of International Relations* (Oxford, 2008) 150–162.

CONCLUSION 241

We are now in a position to assess the general character of Hobbes's just war theory. I have been arguing that Hobbes radicalized the defensive war model associated with Thucydides, Gentili, and Bacon. That model depicts just wars as essentially defensive in character, while being notably liberal about what counts as defensive. Placing Hobbes within this intellectual tradition simultaneously distances him from the proto-realist reason-of-state tradition of Machiavelli and Lipsius.[51] Machiavelli, it is true, twice cited Livy's dictum that 'only those wars that are necessary are just'.[52] But unlike Hobbes, he made no attempt to back up that principle by engaging with traditional theories of just war and self-defence. On the contrary, Machiavelli's main contention is that rulers should be willing to sidestep binding moral norms for the sake of national interest. A prince should 'not deviate from right conduct if possible, but be capable of entering upon the path of wrong-doing when this becomes necessary'.[53] Rulers should do what national security requires, including through war, disregarding if necessary ordinary norms of justice (such as the duty to keep faith). Subsequent reason-of-state theorists concurred that the duty of princes to pursue the common good sometimes overrules requirements of justice.[54] Hobbes, by contrast, ruled out conflicts between pursuing *salus populi* and norms of international justice. Any obligation of justice to act in accordance with international agreements is voided once the sovereign spots a new cause for fear. Not faith and fidelity, but force and fraud are the main virtues in war. Machiavelli and Hobbes both developed realist theories of international relations: the international domain is anarchic, conflict-ridden, and dominated by questions of power and national security.[55] Yet while Machiavelli downplayed, if not ignored, the place of justice in war and international affairs, Hobbes managed to moralize reason-of-state positions, stressing the need for security, through his idiosyncratic just war theory.

---

[51] On Hobbes's relation to the reason-of-state tradition, see Noel Malcolm, *Reason of State, Propaganda, and the Thirty Year's War: An Unknown Translation by Thomas Hobbes* (Oxford, 2007) 92–123.

[52] Niccolò Machiavelli, 'Discorsi' in *The Chief Works and Others*, vol. 1, ed. Allan Gilbert (Durham, 1989) 3.12; Machiavelli, *The Prince*, ed. Quentin Skinner and Russell Price (Cambridge, 1988) 88.

[53] Machiavelli, *The Prince*, 62. For discussion, see Quentin Skinner, *Machiavelli* (Oxford, 1981) 38–53.

[54] E.g. Justus Lipsius, *Politica*, ed. Jan Waszink (Assen, 2004) 4.13–14.

[55] On Machiavelli on international affairs, compare Mikael Hörnqvist, *Machiavelli and Empire* (Cambridge, 2004) 81–97; Marco Cesa (ed), *Machiavelli on International Relations* (Oxford, 2014) 1–31; Erica Benner, *Machiavelli's Ethics* (Princeton, 2009) 451–483. Realism about international relations is hence compatible with diverse attitudes to war and justice, as argued by Steven Forde, 'Varieties of Realism: Thucydides and Machiavelli', *The Journal of Politics* 54 (1992) no. 2: 372–393.

10

REBELS, TRAITORS, ENEMIES, AND FOOLS

INTRODUCTION*

the nature of this offence, consisteth in the renouncing of subjection; which is a relapse into the condition of warre, commonly called Rebellion; and they that so offend, suffer not as Subjects, but as Enemies. For *Rebellion*, is but warre renewed. (L 28.23)

This chapter examines in what sense, if any, individuals must abide by justice to remain members of the commonwealth. It does so by analysing the juridical status of Hobbesian rebels. Are rebels still subjects? Do they still owe allegiance to their (erstwhile) sovereign? Plenty of passages suggest that rebels, by their act of rebellion, forfeit their citizenship. Citizens and subjects being synonyms for Hobbes, it seems that by renouncing subjection (the essence of rebellion) rebels *ipso facto* renounce their citizenship. Those who 'having been by their own act Subjects, deliberately revolting, deny the Soveraign Power' are enemies to the commonwealth (L 28.13). And according to the Latin *Leviathan*, 'hostes cives non sunt' (LL 28.13). Furthermore, rebels are punished 'not by *civil right*, but *by natural right*, i.e., not as *bad citizens*, but as *enemies of the commonwealth*, and not by the *right of government* or dominion, but by the *right of war*' (DCv 14.22). The *Citizenship Forfeiture* thesis imparts coherence on these claims: by denying the sovereign's authority rebels cease to be citizens, thus forgoing 'the privilege of being punished by a precedent law' (EW 4: 294). Rousseau would later defend the same idea: 'every malefactor who attacks the social right becomes through his transgressions a rebel and a traitor to the homeland; in violating its laws, he ceases to be a member, and he even wages war with it'.[1]

Citizenship Forfeiture faces philosophical and interpretive objections. The doctrine seems to imply a thoroughly voluntaristic account of political obligation that is both implausible and at odds with Hobbes's social contract theory. Citizenship and subjection being identical, if rebels forfeit their citizenship by unilaterally

---

* This chapter significantly revises and expands Johan Olsthoorn, 'Forfeiting Citizenship: Hobbes on Traitors, Rebels, and Enemies' in Paschalis M. Kitromilides (ed), *Athenian Legacies: European Debates on Citizenship* (Firenze, 2014) 237–252.

[1] J.J. Rousseau, 'The Social Contract' in *Jean-Jacques Rousseau: The Basic Political Writings*, ed. D.A. Cress (Indianapolis, 1987) 2.5.4.

Hobbes on Justice. Johan Olsthoorn, Oxford University Press. © Johan Olsthoorn 2024.
DOI: 10.1093/9780191904585.003.0010

and unjustly renouncing subjection, then it seems the same injustice frees them from subjection to the sovereign (i.e. from political obligation). But how can an unjust action dissolve one's political obligations? As Gentili wrote: 'One who is a subject does not by rebellion free himself from subjection to the law'.[2] *Citizenship Forfeiture* suggests that citizenship, the result of a voluntary act of submission, can be quit at will—albeit at the price of injustice. Yet Hobbes was adamant that natural rights are divested unconditionally and cannot be taken back. The power of releasing belongs exclusively to the sovereign. 'And consequently none of his Subjects, by any pretence of forfeiture, can be freed from his Subjection' (L 18.4). Can subjects not release themselves from subjection, period, or not without committing an injustice?

This chapter defends *Citizenship Forfeiture*. Hobbesian rebels indeed lose their citizenship through their act of rebellion.[3] Rebels, I argue, are no longer part of the body politic or commonwealth, the nature of which is said to consist in 'subjection' (DCv 6.3). Moreover, by disavowing the *pactum generale obedientiae*, rebels place themselves beyond the legal order. I deny, however, that rebellion voids the obligation to obey the sovereign, incurred in the original covenant. That obligation is not part of the legal order but is presupposed by it. By detaching political obligation from loss of citizenship, my reading can counter the objections raised above.

My argument is grounded in a detailed analysis of Hobbes's views on treason. For Hobbes, as for his contemporaries, rebellion is a form of treason (DPS 91).[4] Though generally considered one of the most important theorists of political obligation, what Hobbes says about treason has received little scrutiny.[5] This chapter takes some steps towards redressing this. I show that treason occupies a central

---

[2] Gentili, *De Jure Belli*, 22.

[3] *Citizenship Forfeiture* has previously been defended by Tommy L. Lott, 'Hobbes's Right of Nature', *History of Philosophy Quarterly* 9 (1992) no. 2: 175–176. Commentators dispute whether Hobbes's theory of inalienable rights of self-defence logically implies a right to rebel in extreme circumstances. Taking no stance in this debate, I maintain that *if* there is a right to rebel, *then* this right cannot be exercised without loss of citizenship. Defenders of a Hobbesian right to rebel include Jean Hampton, *Hobbes and the Social Contract Tradition* (Cambridge, 1986) 197–208; G.S. Kavka, 'Some Neglected Liberal Aspects of Hobbes's Philosophy', *Hobbes Studies* 1 (1988) no. 1: 102–105; Alan Ryan, 'Hobbes's Political Philosophy' in Tom Sorell (ed), *The Cambridge Companion to Hobbes* (Cambridge, 1996) 237–241; Susanne Sreedhar, *Hobbes on Resistance* (Cambridge, 2010) 132–167.

[4] Rebellion was legally classified as high treason in England from the early fourteenth century onwards. 'The Great Statute of Treason' (25 Edward III, st.5, c.2, from 1352) declares the following actions high treason: (1) plotting to kill the king, the queen, or eldest heir to the throne; (2) violating the chastity of the queen, the king's daughter, or the wife of the eldest heir; (3) levying wars against the king; (4) supporting the king's enemies, in his realm or elsewhere; (5) counterfeiting the royal seals; (6) counterfeiting money or bringing false money into the realm; (7) killing high magistrates, such as the chancellor or treasurer. J.G. Bellamy, *The Law of Treason in England in the Later Middle Ages* (Cambridge, 1970) 23; John Baker, *An Introduction to English Legal History* (Oxford, 2019) 568–570. Hobbes has the lawyer faithfully quote Edward's statute in its entirety in the *Dialogue* (DPS 87–88). The philosopher's subsequent summary adds as treasonous: (1) a soldier plotting to kill officers in times of war; (2) imprisoning the king; (3) plotting to raise rebellion (DPS 90–91; cf. DCv 14.20).

[5] But see Laurens van Apeldoorn, 'Hobbes on Treason and Fundamental Law', *Intellectual History Review* 33 (2023) no. 2: 183–203.

244 REBELS, TRAITORS, ENEMIES, AND FOOLS

place in Hobbes's social contract theory. Treason, for Hobbes, essentially consists in a disavowal of the original covenant, that is, of the mutual promise to obey the sovereign in all things. Treason differs from all other crimes in that it questions the authority of the legal system as such. This makes it 'the Highest Crime of all' (DPS 87). Strikingly, Hobbes contends that acts of treason (including rebellion) cannot be forbidden by civil law on pain of circularity. This helps explain why rebels and traitors cannot be punished by civil law, the authority of which they repudiate. Civil law applies only to those who consider themselves bound by the original covenant (citizens or *subditi*). I conclude by pointing out how my analysis elucidates his notorious 'Reply to the Foole' (L 15.4).

10.1 'THE HIGHEST CRIME OF ALL'

For Hobbes, treason (Latin: *crimen laesae majestatis*)[6] consists in the denial of legitimate sovereign authority. *De Cive*, the first of his works to discuss treason, defines *crimen laesae majestatis* as: 'A deed or word by the citizen or subject by which he reveals that he no longer intends to obey the man or council to whom the sovereign power in the commonwealth has been committed' (DCv 14.20).[7] *Leviathan* likewise accuses rebels of treason on the ground that they 'deliberatly deny the Authority of the Common-Wealth established' (L 28.23; also L 28.13; LL 28.13). The rejection of sovereign authority can be total ('no obedience is due to the king at all') or partial ('the king has no right to collect taxes without parliamentary representation') (DCv 14.20). Attempts by subjects to usurp supreme authority amount to a negation of sovereign's right to rule. Such attempts are hence treasonous: 'in any commonwealth it is the crime of treason for any individual citizen or any number of citizens together, to claim for themselves any authority whatever over the whole commonwealth' (DCv 17.26). By portraying seizure of essential rights of sovereignty as a denial of lawful authority, *De Cive* makes rebellion the paradigmatic form of treason.[8] The underlying conception of treason as the unlawful denial or usurpation of sovereign power was historically commonplace. One legal historian concludes that Hobbes's account of treason, unlike

---

[6] Hobbes's Latin works use *crimen laesae majestatis* throughout as translations of treason. Compare L 27.37 with LL 27.33; L 28.13 with LL 28.13. See also DCv 14.20–22; DPS 49.

[7] In line with *Untraceable Intentions* (§3.3), persons can only be condemned for treason when external signs ('a deed or word') reveal their malign intentions (DPS 97–98).

[8] 'Treason' stands for 'high treason' throughout this chapter. 25 Edward III had distinguished between high and petty treason. Petty treason consists in breaches of fealty owed to superiors other than the king. A servant slaying his master, a wife killing her husband, an ecclesiastic poisoning a superior— all were considered instances of petty treason. Hobbes accepted this traditional legal distinction (DPS 92–93, 107–108, 119, 121). On the legal status of petty treason in early modern England, see Bellamy, *The Law of Treason*, 87, 225–231; Matthew Lockwood, 'From Treason to Homicide: Changing Conceptions of the Law of Petty Treason in Early Modern England', *Journal of Legal History* 34 (2013) no. 1: 31–49.

his path-breaking accounts of sovereignty and political obligation, is unoriginal, 'very much a product of his time'.[9] Their verdict overlooks other original features of Hobbes's account, including his depiction of traitors as public enemies and his thesis that treason consists in a disavowal of the original covenant.

The original covenant grounds the authority of civil law. 'An *agreement* obligates of itself; a *law* keeps one to one's obligations in virtue of the universal *agreement* to render obedience' (DCv 14.2). In rejecting the sovereign's authority, rebels and other traitors declare themselves unbound by the mutual promise of simple obedience. Along the way, they reject *all* civil laws together, said to be 'contained' in it:

> The obligation to obey individual civil laws is derived from the force of the agreement by which individual citizens are obligated to each other to offer absolute and universal obedience . . . to the sovereign . . . so that that agreement contains within itself all the laws together; it is consequently evident that the citizen who renounces the general pact of obedience [pacto generali obedientiæ] is <u>renouncing all the laws together</u>. This evil is more serious than any single sin as constant sinning is more serious than a *single* sin. And this is the sin which is called the CRIME OF LÈSE-MAJESTÉ. (DCv 14.20)

Treason involves a rejection of the validity of the legal system as such.[10] By comparison, 'the greatest of other Crimes, for the most part; are breaches of one only, or at least of very few Laws' (DPS 92). The claim is not that treason alone breaches the original covenant. Every crime does so: 'by violating civil laws, we also violate the natural laws which command that civil laws be kept' (DCv 14.23).[11] Yet no other crime involves wholesale renunciation of the original covenant. The traitor finds herself here alongside the fool, who cares not a whim about observing justice but makes and breaks agreements as it suits their advantage (§10.5). Both the fool and the traitor deny that they are morally bound by the original covenant. In this respect, the two differ markedly from the common criminal who neither rejects the sovereign's authority nor the original covenant's validity as such.

Leviathan changes the definition—but not the substance—of treason by incorporating the additional layer of 'fundamental laws'.[12] Instead of a repudiation of the original covenant, Hobbes now calls the crime of lèse-majesté a 'designe, or act, contrary to a Fundamentall Law' (L 27.37). Fundamental laws were at the time seen as those laws the sovereign cannot change or revoke, since they are

---

[9] D. Alan Orr, *Treason and the State: Law, Politics, and Ideology in the English Civil War* (Cambridge, 2002) 56.

[10] Dieter Hüning, 'Hobbes on the Right to Punish' in Patricia Springborg (ed), *The Cambridge Companion to Hobbes's Leviathan* (Cambridge, 2007) 221.

[11] The same is implied by *Leviathan*'s claim that '[a]ll Crimes doe equally deserve the name of Injustice' (L 27.21). For any unjust action is a failure to perform a valid covenant (L 15.1).

[12] For a contextual analysis of the political significance of this redefinition, see Van Apeldoorn, 'Hobbes on Treason'.

constitutive of either the commonwealth or sovereignty.[13] Neither *Elements* nor *De Cive* mentions the term 'fundamental law'. *Leviathan* labels those laws fundamental 'which being taken away, the Common-wealth faileth, and is utterly dissolved; as a building whose Foundation is destroyed' (L 26.42). The laws indispensable to the commonwealth's preservation are for Hobbes those constitutive of sovereign power: 'a Fundamentall Law is that, by which Subjects are bound to uphold whatsoever power is given to the Soveraign . . . without which the Common-wealth cannot stand' (L 26.42). In other words, fundamental laws are the constitutional foundations of essential rights of sovereignty.[14] And that foundation, Hobbes claims, is the original pact of government. The sole fundamental law is therefore 'that Law of Nature that binds us all to obey him, whosoever he be, whom lawfully and for our own safety we have promised to obey' (B 195; also B 321). The fundamental law which traitors 'designe, or act, contrary to' is thus the third law of nature, ordering agents to perform valid covenants. I conclude that *Leviathan*'s redefinition of treason does not substantively change *De Cive*'s contractarian theory of treason. Its reference to fundamental laws is epiphenomenal, so to speak, added on top.

Another distinctive feature of treason are its bellicose consequences. Treason involves 'a relapse into the condition of warre, commonly called Rebellion. For *Rebellion*, is but warre renewed' (L 28.23).[15] 'Then for the Nature of Treason by Rebellion; is it not a return to Hostility? What else does Rebellion signifie?' (DPS 95). The term 'return' suggests that rebels revert to the natural condition of mankind—a state of war 'as is of every man, against every man' (L 13.8). By disavowing the original covenant, made to establish peace and security, the rebel apparently slides back into a hostile pre-political condition, beyond the legal order and outside the commonwealth. Worse, the rebel becomes an enemy not just to the sovereign but to all their erstwhile fellow citizens alike, breaking all ties with human society: 'men are enemies to each other when they are not subject one to the other or to any common ruler' (DCv 14.19; also DCv 9.3; DCv 17.27; L 28.23). Like the dissenter, the rebel 'must either submit to their decrees, or be left in the condition of warre he was in before; wherein he might without injustice be destroyed by any man whatsoever' (L 18.5; also DCv 6.2; DPS 142–143).

Hobbes was not the only early modern theorist holding that rebels and traitors can be justly killed by all and sundry. Grotius maintained the same: 'Against Traitors and publick Enemies every private Man . . . is a Soldier'.[16] According to

---

[13] Martyn P. Thompson, 'The History of Fundamental Law in Political Thought from the French Wars of Religion to the American Revolution', *American Historical Review* 91 (1986) no. 5: 1103–1128.

[14] L 26.41–42; L 30.6: 'the Essentiall Rights (which are the Naturall, and Fundamental Lawes) of Soveraignty'. L 18.17 spells out what the essential rights of sovereignty are.

[15] The same etymological link between rebellion and *rebellare* was highlighted (albeit with political motives opposite to Hobbes's) by Locke, *Second Treatise*, 19.226–227; Algernon Sidney, *Discourses Concerning Government*, ed. Thomas G. West (Indianapolis, 1996) 3.36.

[16] Grotius, *War and Peace*, 1.4.16.

Locke, unjust force in the absence of legal recourse '*puts* him that uses it *into a state of War*, and makes it lawful to resist him'.[17] Anyone unjustly initiating hostilities is properly styled a rebel—tyrants included.[18] For both Grotius and Locke, rebels launch an unjust war of aggression, in which they may be justly resisted by all. Hobbes's just war theory rules out any distinction between just and unjust enemies (§8.2; §8.5). This affects the normative status of rebels. What makes rebels liable to be killed is not the injustice of their aggression. Rather, rebellious traitors may 'be lawfully killed by any Man that would, as one might kill a Wolf', that is, in virtue of posing a threat to personal and collective security (DPS 142–143). Hence 'in a sudden Rebellion, any man that can suppresse it by his own Power in the Countrey where it begins, without expresse Law or Commission, may lawfully doe it' (L R&C.11).

Summing up, rebellion and treason generally differ from lesser crimes in four ways. They characteristically involve: (i) a denial of sovereign authority; (ii) a disavowal of the original pact of obedience; and (iii) a return to hostility. The next two sections discuss a fourth distinctive feature: (iv) rebels and traitors are punished not as 'bad citizens, but as enemies of the commonwealth', by the right of war (DCv 14.22).

10.2 REBELLIOUS SUBJECTS AND/OR ENEMIES?

Can rebels be simultaneously subject to and enemies of the commonwealth? Some commentators see no contradiction between rebellion and citizenship, citing in support two passages mentioning 'rebellious subjects' (DCv 17.26; L 40.10).[19] *Citizenship Forfeiture* refuses to make too much of such phrases. After all, 'rebellious' may well refer to a disposition to rebel rather than to active rebellion. This section collects evidence in favour of the thesis that engaging in rebellion *ipso facto* results in loss of citizenship for Hobbes.

Edward Coke (1552–1634) had distinguished 'disloyal traitors', who renounced their allegiance, from enemies who never were 'in the Protection and Ligeance of the King' (DPS 94).[20] Invoking a distinction originating in Roman law, he dubbed

---

[17] Locke, *Second Treatise*, 18.207, also 3.16–20, 19.232.

[18] Locke, *Second Treatise*, 19.226–227. The doctrine that usurpers initiate a war in which they can lawfully be killed by all naturally suited defenders of tyrannicide. E.g. Edward Sexby, 'Killing Noe Murder' [1657], reprinted in *Divine Right and Democracy*, ed. David Wootton (Harmondsworth, 1986) 374–375: 'every Thing is lawful against [a usurper] that is lawful against an open Enemy, whom every private Man hath a Right to kill'. Bodin had previously subsumed tyrants under the common foes of humanity, liable to be killed by all. Daniel Lee, *The Right of Sovereignty* (Oxford, 2021) 183, 201–212.

[19] Sreedhar, *Hobbes on Resistance*, 156–158. The Latin *Leviathan* deletes these words (LL 40.9).

[20] Edward Coke, *The Third Part of the Institutes of the Laws of England* (London, 1644) 11. On Coke on treason, see David Chan Smith, *Sir Edward Coke and the Reformation of the Laws* (Cambridge, 2014) 74–90.

248 REBELS, TRAITORS, ENEMIES, AND FOOLS

traitors and rebels private/unlawful enemies (instead of public/lawful enemies).[21] A lawful enemy, Gentili explained, is 'the equal of his opponent'.[22] Only in conflicts with lawful enemies, it was widely held, do the international laws of war apply. Hostilities with unlawful enemies (such as pirates, robbers, and rebels) are not wars proper, since they are either common foes of all humanity or still *de jure* subjects (§8.5). Typically, Ayala had refused to elevate rebels to the status of lawful enemies. In a work written while enlisted as a jurist in the Spanish army that was vainly trying to quell the Dutch rebellion, he wrote: 'rebels ought not to be classed as enemies [*hostis*], the two being quite distinct, and so it is more correct to term the armed contention with rebel subjects execution of legal process, or prosecution, and not war'.[23] A century and a half later, Wolff and Vattel likewise defined rebels as disloyal subjects rather than as lawful enemies; thereby denying that *jus gentium* regulates how governments should treat rebels.[24]

Hobbes derided the received distinction between disloyal traitors and lawful/public enemies: 'as if it could not be that one and the same Man should be both an Enemy, and a Traytor' (DPS 95; also DPS 20). If citizens 'renew the War against him' to whom they 'swore Allegiance', then 'are they not again open Enemies'? (DPS 95). Pressed by Bramhall on the same point, Hobbes reiterated that all enemies share the same normative status. 'An open enemy and a perfidious traitor are both enemies' (EW 4: 294). By repeatedly dismissing the distinction between public/lawful and private/unlawful enemies, Hobbes passed up on one salient theoretical explanation of how rebels can be enemies while remaining subject to the civil law.

Citizenship Forfeiture finds further support in Hobbes's conceptions of 'citizen' and 'commonwealth'. Skinner has shown in great detail how Hobbes challenged the republican idea of citizen as a person not in the power of someone else.[25] Hobbes declared, provocatively, that citizenship is compatible, nay even identical with subjection. *De Cive* (notice the title) consistently equates citizens with subjects: 'cives sive subditi'.[26] *Leviathan*, too, treats 'citizen' and 'subject' as synonyms. The English

---

[21] *Digest* 50.16.118: 'Enemies are those who have publicly declared war on us or on whom we have publicly declared war; others are "brigands" or "pirates".' On this distinction, see Carl Schmitt, *The Concept of the Political*, ed. George Schwab (Chicago, 2007) 28–29; Maximilian Jaede, 'Hobbes on the Making and Unmaking of Citizens', *Critical Review of International Social and Political Philosophy* 19 (2016) no. 1: 90–91.

[22] Gentili, *De Jure Belli*, 12.

[23] Balthazar Ayala, *Three Books on the Law of War*, ed. John Westlake (Washington, 1912) 2.14.

[24] Wolff, *Jus Gentium*, 513; Vattel, *Law of Nations*, 3.18.288, 291–292.

[25] Quentin Skinner, *Reason and Rhetoric in the Philosophy of Hobbes* (Cambridge, 1996) 284–293; Quentin Skinner, 'States and the Freedom of Citizens' in Quentin Skinner and Bo Stråth (eds), *States and Citizens: History, Theory, Prospects* (Cambridge, 2003) 11–27; Quentin Skinner, *Hobbes and Republican Liberty* (Cambridge, 2008). Also M.G. Dietz, 'Hobbes' Subject as Citizen' in idem (ed), *Thomas Hobbes and Political Theory* (Lawrence, 1990) 91–119; David Burchell, 'The Disciplined Citizen: Thomas Hobbes, Neostoicism and the Critique of Classical Citizenship', *Australian Journal of Politics and History* 45 (1999) no. 4: 506–524.

[26] DCv 6.20; DCv 12.8; DCv 14.20.

version mentions the term 'citizen' only three times (twice in relation to ancient societies).[27] 'Civis', by contrast, occurs dozens of times in the Latin *Leviathan*—translating 'subject'.[28] Subjects are called such because they subject themselves to the sovereign. 'Each of the *citizens*... is called a SUBJECT [subditis] of him who holds the *sovereign power*' (DCv 5.11). *Leviathan* likewise defines 'subject' in contradistinction with sovereignty: 'he that carryeth this Person [of the Commonwealth] is called SOVERAIGNE ... and every one besides, his SUBJECT' (L 17.14). As Zarka perceptively observes, 'Hobbes reduces the notion of citizen completely to that of subject'.[29] Paradoxically, for Hobbes citizenship presupposes subjection, not freedom. '*A free Subject*' is an oxymoron (L 5.5). The difference between a free person and an enslaved one lies not in the freedom of the former. After all, both enjoy corporeal liberty—liberty in the proper sense: 'in this sense all *slaves* and *subjects* are *free* who are not in bonds or in prison' (DCv 9.9; also L 21.6). Having been entrusted with their bodily freedom in exchange for simple obedience, citizens and non-enchained enslaved people are equally bound to obey their sovereign lord (EL 23.9). The difference between the two lies rather in whom else they serve: 'the FREE MAN is one who serves only the commonwealth, while the SLAVE serves also his fellow citizen' (DCv 9.9). Slaves as fellow citizens—Hobbes's republican adversaries will have recoiled in shock.[30]

The equation of citizenship with subjection to the sovereign helps explain why traitors are no longer subjects. It is tautologically true that anyone renouncing their subjection thereby renounces citizenship. Citizenship thus requires present rather than past submission to the sovereign. This idea finds support in Hobbes's definition of commonwealth. '[T]he nature of a commonwealth consists in that *union* or *subjection*' generated by the citizens' mutual agreement to authorize the sovereign to represent them (DCv 6.3).[31] Hobbes conceives of the commonwealth as an incorporation: a set of individuals bound together by a common power such that they are capable of speaking and acting as one person. This requires collective submission to—and, in *Leviathan*, universal authorization of—a common spokesperson. The commonwealth, then, is the multitude united as one person by having each constituent member promise simple obedience to a common authority (the sovereign). Since the commonwealth exists in virtue of the *pactum generale obedientiae*, the rebel's unilateral disavowal of allegiance jettisons her

---

[27] L 13.10; L 21.7; L 39.2.

[28] As noted by Y.C. Zarka, 'The Political Subject' in Tom Sorell and Luc Foisneau (eds), *Leviathan after 350 Years* (Oxford, 2004) 178. *Elements* mentions 'citizen' not once.

[29] Zarka, 'The Political Subject', 179.

[30] And not just republican critics. Pufendorf, *Nature and Nations*, 7.2.20, objected that by making 'Civis an equivalent Term with *Subditus*, a *Subject*' Hobbes turned 'Women, Children, and Servants' into citizens proper. This equalizing consequence showcases the liberal potential of Hobbes's illiberalism. Noel Malcolm, 'Thomas Hobbes: Liberal Illiberal', *Journal of the British Academy* 4 (2016) 113–136.

[31] Also e.g. DCv 5.9; L 17.13; L 20.18.

from the artificial unity that is the commonwealth. Refusing to be represented by the sovereign, rebels and traitors are no longer part of 'the Multitude so united in one Person' or 'COMMONWEALTH' (L 17.13).[32] This evinces that passages about 'rebellious subjects' notwithstanding, rebellion and citizenship are by definition incompatible. As the Latin *Leviathan* states in the context of rebellion: 'hostes cives non sunt' (LL 28.13). *Citizenship Forfeiture* explains, moreover, why rebels' future offspring are lawfully punished as well. Though themselves innocent of treason, their parents' loss of citizenship renders them stateless: 'the vengeance is lawfully extended, not onely to the Fathers, but also to the third and fourth generation not yet in being, and consequently innocent of the fact, for which they are afflicted'—to wit, their forefathers' deliberate denial of the 'Authority of the Common-wealth established' (L 28.23).

Ample supporting evidence notwithstanding, *Citizenship Forfeiture* faces two related objections. First, if rebellion—whether successful or not—indeed turns rebels into non-subjects, then this seems to imply that the rebel achieves through unjust means part of her aim—withdrawal of subjection. Cumberland already chided Hobbes for holding that 'any Member of the State, may, by Rebellion, free himself from the condition of a Subject, and transfer himself into a Hostile or Natural State'.[33] How can the crime of treason destroy the very political obligation it violates? Unjustly reneging on a promise does not usually cancel the obligations owed to the promisee. My stubborn refusal to pay taxes results in a failure to pay my due; few will think it also voids my obligation to pay. Second, the suggestion that political obligations can be quit at will (albeit at the price of injustice) contradicts Hobbes's claims about release from covenants. 'Men are freed of their Covenants two ways; by Performing; or by being Forgiven'—not by unilateral renunciation of subjection (L 14.26).[34]

A possible fix is found in Jaede's analysis of the conditions of Hobbesian citizenship. By formally declaring rebels enemies, he argues, the sovereign simultaneously strips them of their citizenship: 'sovereign authority generally extends to the question of whether individuals be admitted as legal subjects; those who defy the sovereign could, alternatively, be treated as public enemies'.[35] The sovereign's prerogative to decide on political membership is in Jaede's view a precondition for the rule of law.[36] Traitors would thus, like exiles, be legally banished from the

---

[32] Hobbes's accounts of authorization and personation are subject of intense scholarly debate. I have outlined my own interpretation in Johan Olsthoorn, '*Leviathan* Inc.: Hobbes on the Nature and Person of the Commonwealth', *History of European Ideas* 47 (2021) no. 1: 17–32. That article challenges the prevailing view that the sovereign brings the commonwealth into being by representing it as such.

[33] Cumberland, *Treatise*, 748–749.

[34] Subjects are released from their duty to obey in the following five ways: if the sovereign abdicates; is defeated; is unable to provide protection; appoints no successor; or banishes the subject (DCv 7.18; DCv 8.9; L 21.21–25).

[35] Jaede, 'Making and Unmaking', 98 (cf. 94–99).

[36] Jaede, 'Making and Unmaking', 95.

commonwealth by sovereign decree: 'a Banished man, is a lawfull enemy of the Common-Wealth that banished him; as being no more a Member of the same' (L 28.21).[37] Hobbesian sovereigns undeniably have the right to single-handedly release citizens from their subjection. They also have the exclusive authority to 'determine who is an ally [*amicus*] or public enemy [*hostis publicus*] of the commonwealth' and 'who are to be citizens' (DCv 17.11). Yet the sovereign's power to brandish citizens 'public enemies' and banish them from the commonwealth does not preclude the possibility that rebels unilaterally forfeit citizenship by engaging in rebellion. Nor does it explain away textual evidence indicative of that possibility: 'the nature of this offence, consisteth in the renouncing of subjection' (L 28.23). As the Latin *Leviathan* states: 'although they were citizens before, yet if they later declared themselves enemies, they suffer as enemies, not as citizens' (LL 28.13).

Hobbes's exchanges with Bramhall provide another potential solution to our riddle. Bramhall argued that 'a rebellious Subject is still a Subject, *de jure*, though not, *de facto*; by right, though not by deed'.[38] As the pact of obedience ought never to have been broken in the first place, traitors remain by right subjects. Hobbes grants him this point without really addressing the objection. 'But though the king loses none of his right by the traitor's act, yet the traitor loseth the privilege of being punished by a precedent law' (EW 4: 294). That the sovereign's right to rule 'cannot be extinguished by the act of another' is evident (L 29.23). After all, the sovereign did not receive any rights in the original covenant, having already had 'a right to all things *before the transfer of the right*' (DCv 2.4). The right to all things includes a natural right 'to reign over all the rest' (L 31.5; also DCv 15.5). Subjects really only promise the sovereign not to hinder him in the exercise of his natural right (EL 15.3; DCv 2.4; L 14.6; L 28.2). In other words, the right of dominion is not generated but rather becomes effective by covenants of subjection (§2.3). It follows that a retraction of allegiance does not diminish the sovereign's rights.

The present conundrum concerns the corresponding duty to obey. Do rebellious citizens still owe allegiance to the sovereign? The *de jure* vs. *de facto* distinction makes sense in this regard: although *de facto* enemies, rebels may *de jure* still owe obedience. However, Hobbes does not take up Bramhall's suggestion (the distinction is not employed anywhere else).[39] We should refrain, I submit, from letting our interpretation rest exclusively on a distinction endorsed only once—upon the instigation of a hostile critic.[40] Especially since the distinction fits badly with the

---

[37] On banishment and excommunication (a kind of exile), see DCv 7.18; DCv 17.26; L 42.20–31; L 42.103; LLA 2.38; DPS 142–143.

[38] John Bramhall, 'The Catching of Leviathan' in G.A.J. Rogers (ed), *Leviathan: Contemporary Responses to the Political Theory of Thomas Hobbes* (Bristol, 1995) 118. Cf. EW 4: 290.

[39] The only other instance of *de jure* vs. *de facto* appears in a discussion of the question whether witnesses are judges only of fact, or also of right (LL 26.25).

[40] At other places, too, Hobbes nominally accepts at Bramhall's urging terminology he dismisses elsewhere. Take his endorsement of Bramhall's distinction between natural and moral goodness (EW 5: 193–194). As Hobbes's theory of the good (as developed elsewhere) has no place for moral goodness,

252 REBELS, TRAITORS, ENEMIES, AND FOOLS

idea, defended above, that citizenship requires present submission. Fortunately, another interpretive solution is available.

10.3 BEYOND THE LEGAL ORDER...

According to Hobbes, the rebel's apparently successful renunciation of subjection results in loss of the 'the privilege of being punished by a precedent law'. Traitors are instead disciplined 'at the king's will' (EW 4: 294).[41] As self-proclaimed enemies of the state, rebels and traitors cannot be legally prosecuted as citizens. They must rather be crushed by the right of war. Why is it that 'such as are Traytors may by the Law of Reason be dealt withal, as Ignoble and Treacherous Enemies' (DPS 92)? Why does a citizen's rejection of the legal system result in expulsion from that same system? Surely the rule of law applies to criminal anarchists, too.

Several Hobbesian answers can be construed.[42] First, the rebel's open declaration of hostility arguably triggers rights of collective defence, and 'in declared Hostility, all infliction of evill is lawfull' (L 28.13; also DPS 92, 95). And the sovereign has been authorized to do whatever he deems necessary in defence against enemies (e.g. EL 20.8; DCv 6.7; L 18.12). Practice provides a second explanation. Traitors had historically been dealt with as enemies of the state—Hobbes himself cites the French regicide François Ravaillac (EW 4: 294; DPS 163). On the other hand, English law included detailed prescriptions of punishments due to traitors—as Hobbes knew (DPS 163–165; L 28.13).

A theoretically more fundamental argument draws on what is arguably Hobbes's most original claim concerning treason: rebellion cannot be forbidden by civil law on pain of circularity. The civil law obligates citizens in virtue of their allegiance proclaimed in the covenant of subjection. A civil law prohibiting rebellion would thus be ordering, vainly, the allegiance on which its own authority rests.

> If a sovereign prince made a civil law in the form: *do not rebel!*, he would achieve nothing. For unless the citizens are previously obligated to obedience, i.e., not to rebel, every law is invalid; and an obligation which binds one to do something which one is already obligated to do is superfluous. (DCv 14.21)

---

we should discount this passage as not being reflective of his authentic views. Johan Olsthoorn, 'On the Absence of Moral Goodness in Hobbes's Ethics', *The Journal of Ethics* 24 (2020) no. 2: 251–259.

[41] Also DCv 14.22; L 28.13, 23; L R&C.7. Analogously, children may be killed for rebellion by their parents (EL 23.8).

[42] Rosler's rival explanation ('it cuts . . . legal red tape') is unsatisfying in failing to engage with Hobbes's underlying theoretical commitments. Andrés Rosler, 'Odi et Amo? Hobbes on the State of Nature', *Hobbes Studies* 24 (2011) no. 1: 109.

Individuals who deny the authority of the legal order cannot be commanded by law to accept it. Any such command would be question-begging in presupposing the very authority the rebel disputes (LL 30.4). Logic requires that rebellion is forbidden by a more fundamental law.

> For a Civill Law, that shall forbid Rebellion, (and such is all resistance to the essentiall Rights of Soveraignty,) is not (as a Civill Law) any obligation, but by vertue onely of the Law of Nature, that forbiddeth the violation of Faith. (L 30.4)[43]

Treason is therefore a breach of natural law alone, not of civil law.

> The sin which is the crime of treason by natural law is a transgression of natural, not civil, law. For since the obligation to civil obedience, by force of which all civil laws are valid, is prior to every civil law, and the crime of treason is by nature simply violation of that obligation; it follows that it is the law which preceded civil law which is violated by the crime of treason; and that is the natural law, by which we are forbidden to break agreements and our pledged faith. (DCv 14.21)[44]

The obligation of simple obedience incurred in the original covenant is the functional equivalent of Kelsen's *Grundnorm*. This obligation has to be accepted for all other laws to be legally authoritative: 'which natural obligation, if men know not, they cannot know the right of any law the sovereign maketh' (L 30.4).

In *De Cive*, Hobbes maintained that there can be no punishment for rebellion because there can be no civil law forbidding rebellion. 'It follows from this that *rebels, traitors* and others convicted of *treason* are punished not by *civil right*, but by *natural right*, i.e. not as *bad citizens*, but as *enemies of the commonwealth* ... by the *right of war*' (DCv 14.22). The inference seems too quick. After all, the sovereign is authorized to punish violations of natural law in general. The civil law expressly introduces punishments for breaches of natural law. Indeed, the precepts of natural law first become law proper through 'the Ordinances of Soveraign Power',

---

[43] Warrender, quoting the same passages, altogether misses Hobbes's point. On his reading, civil laws cannot forbid rebellion 'unless there is a prior obligation to obey the sovereign'. Howard Warrender, *The Political Philosophy of Hobbes: His Theory of Obligation* (Oxford, 1957) 147–148.

[44] Hobbes in fact distinguished between two kinds of high treason. Some acts are crimes of high treason by common or natural law (the two are identical for Hobbes); others by civil law alone (i.e. by convention). Take 'the Killing of a Justice', for example, declared high treason by 25 Edward III. In Hobbes's view, this is 'not otherwise High Treason, but by the Statute' (DPS 91). Other examples of high treason by statute are forging money and counterfeiting seals, both ordained high treason by 25 Edward III (DCv 14.20; cf. L 27.40). The sovereign may decide to call 'something lèse majesté which in its own nature is not, rightly fix[ing] an invidious name, and perhaps a heavier penalty, on the sinner'. Yet he 'does not [thereby] make the sin itself more serious' (DCv 14.20). By contrast, plotting to kill the king, aiding his enemies, and all other things 'tending to the Kings Destruction, or Disherison' are 'High Treason before this Statute by the Common-Law' (DPS 90). In short, 'Treason is a Crime of it self, *Malum in se*, and therefore a Crime at the Common-Law, and High Treason the Highest Crime at the Common-Law that can be' (DPS 89).

254   REBELS, TRAITORS, ENEMIES, AND FOOLS

which specify their content and set punishments 'for such as shall break them' (L 26.8; also DH 15.4) (§3.5). Why, then, are violations of the *third* law of nature not legally punishable?

Leviathan completes the argument through its novel definition of punishment. Individual authorization, Hobbes now argues, is constitutive of punishment.[45] 'PUNISHMENT, *is an Evill inflicted by publique Authority, on him that hath done, or omitted that which is Judged by the same authority to be a Transgression of the Law*' (L 28.1). Punishment by definition has 'for Author, the person condemned' (L 28.6; also L 14.29). Ordinary criminals are knowingly punished by their own authority—even if they may rightfully resist their punishment: 'though the subject think the law just, as when a thief is by law condemned to die, yet he may lawfully oppose the execution ... any way he can' (EW 4: 373). Not so for rebels: 'all the Harmes that can be done them, must be taken as acts of Hostility' (L 28.13). Rejecting the authority of the sovereign, rebels take the state's coercive responses to their sedition for illegitimate acts of hostility—for violence without right. 'And for the Punishment, they take it but for an act of Hostility; which when they think they have strength enough, they will endeavour by acts of Hostility, to avoyd' (L 30.4). The distinction between punishment and hostility is absent from *Elements* and *De Cive*. *Leviathan*'s novel theory of authorization first allowed Hobbes to distinguish the two.

De Cive had suggested, curiously, that all transgressions of natural law are castigated extra-legally. *Leviathan* drops this claim. It states instead that these ordinances are binding law only to those who accept the sovereign's authority. Punishment for rebellion is conceptually impossible since punishment by definition presupposes the very recognition of sovereign authority rebels disavow. Public order must therefore be restored via the right of war (L 28.23). The civil law, Hobbes concludes, by definition applies only to subjects, and rebels are no longer subjects:

> For the Punishments set down in the Law, are to Subjects, not to Enemies; such as are they, that having been by their own act Subjects, deliberately revolting, deny the Soveraign Power. (L 28.13; also LL 28.13)

By 'professing to be no longer' subject to the law, rebels 'deny they can transgresse it' (L 28.13). Similarly, we read that divine harm inflicted upon atheists is not 'properly a punishment, as upon a subject that had broken the law, but a Revenge, as upon Enemy, or Revolter, that denyeth the Right of our Saviour to the Kingdome'

---

[45] On the place of authorization in *Leviathan*'s theory of punishment, see Arthur Yates, 'The Right to Punish in Thomas Hobbes's *Leviathan*', *Journal of the History of Philosophy* 52 (2014) no. 2: 233–254; Michael J. Green, 'Authorization and the Right to Punish', *Pacific Philosophical Quarterly* 97 (2016) no. 1: 113–139.

(L 42.103; also DCv 14.19).[46] These passages constitute strong evidence for *Citizenship Forfeiture.*

There is one complicating factor. The sovereign, Hobbes maintained, generally has the authority to govern extra-legally, by prerogative (§6.2). He can issue binding commands in the name of the commonwealth 'by force of a former Law' as well as 'by virtue of his Power' (L 21.19).[47] Both laws and extra-legal orders are issued by right and impose obligations of non-resistance upon citizens (unless they contravene their inalienable natural rights). For all sovereign commands, without exception, are commissioned by each citizen's authority: 'all that is done by him in Vertue of his Power, is done by the Authority of every Subject' (L 21.19).[48] Hobbes's legal system includes all authorized sovereign commands, whether promulgated on the basis of precedent law or exacted through power. It thus extends, paradoxically, beyond the rule of law. The sovereign is authorized to impose punishments not spelled out by precedent law. If a law declares φ-ing a crime without stating a corresponding penalty, then those who φ become 'subject to Arbitrary punishment' (L 27.7; also DCv 13.16; L 28.10). Punishment is, after all, a universally known consequence of law-breaking. The sovereign cannot however punish citizens for anything other than transgressions of civil law. *Nulla poena sine lege*—this maxim holds true in virtue of the meaning of punishment (L 28.1; L 28.11).

It does not follow that the sovereign therefore acts without right whenever he sanctions subjects arbitrarily or excessively (i.e. over and above legally stated penalties) (L 28.10). After all, citizens have authorized the sovereign unconditionally, 'without stint' (L 16.14) and 'without exception' (L 21.10). Even killing someone acknowledged innocent—a clear violation of the natural laws of equity and trust—is done by authority of each citizen, including the slain, as all have granted the sovereign 'the right to doe what he pleased' (L 21.7). Arbitrary public inflictions of harm, though no form of punishment, are nonetheless authorized by the person innocently stricken. This raises the question of why authorized impositions of non-penal harm upon the rebel are acts of war (rather than legal acts proper)? The answer must be that, distinctively, rebels and traitors refuse to recognize sovereign authority altogether—unlike citizens rightfully resisting either punishment or arbitrary public harm. That refusal *ipso facto* expels them from Hobbes's expansive legal system, turning them into public enemies and non-citizens.

---

[46] Atheism consists in the treasonous refusal to acknowledge God's majesty, providence, and power (DCv 15.19; DCv 16.18; DCv 18.11; EW 4: 291).

[47] Thomas Poole, 'Hobbes on Law and Prerogative' in David Dyzenhaus and Thomas Poole (eds), *Hobbes and the Law* (Cambridge, 2012) 85–90; Laurens van Apeldoorn, 'Hobbes on Property: Between Legal Certainty and Sovereign Discretion', *Hobbes Studies* 34 (2021) no. 1: 74.

[48] This passage (and others) proves Dyzenhaus's constitutionalist reading textually untenable. On his interpretation, only those decrees that citizens are obligated to obey are legally valid and issued by sovereign authority. Any command which a subject may rightfully resist, including punishment, lacks their authority and (he claims) places them back in a state-of-nature relationship with the ruler. David Dyzenhaus, *The Long Arc of Legality: Hobbes, Kelsen, Hart* (Cambridge, 2022) 121–123, 126.

Treason, I have argued, can neither be legally prohibited nor legally punished. For this reason, rebels forgo the privilege of being punished by law. That doctrine is reminiscent of Gentili's dictum that 'malefactors do not enjoy the privileges of a law to which they are foes'.[49] Significantly, the Italian jurist advanced this claim to explain why the laws of war, and the various rights and immunities they accord to belligerents, do not apply to pirates and robbers. Those common foes of humanity have rejected the law of nations (of which *jus belli* is a part) (§8.5). Hobbes, I conjecture, took over the principle Gentili had invoked to limit the scope of *jus gentium*, applying it to civil law.

The best way to make sense of Hobbes's discussions of treason and rebellion is by adopting *Citizenship Forfeiture*. Law's empire extends only over those within the commonwealth: the citizens or *subditi* who at present accept the sovereign's authority. By engaging in rebellion, rebels disavow the original covenant that grounds the normativity of the entire legal system. They thereby place themselves outside the legal order. This is why they are punished as enemies, by the right of war. I deny, however, that self-exclusion from the legal order entails a return to a state without obligations. Not all normative ties are cut. The obligation incurred in the mutual promise to obey the sovereign, which is not part of the legal order but rather upholds it, has not been erased.

10.4 ... YET WITHIN THE REALM OF JUSTICE

It is commonly thought that the state of rebellion is equivalent to or even identical with the state of nature.[50] This is a mistake. This section argues that 'the condition of warre, commonly called Rebellion' (L 28.23) differs from the state of nature in two crucial respects. In the natural condition (i) the 'notions of Right and Wrong, Justice and Injustice' have no place (L 13.13); and (ii) directed obligations, owed to other humans, are absent. Anyone 'without covenants or subjection one to another' inhabits a state of nature (EL 22.2) (§2.5).[51] (As Kavka notes, any individual agent may find herself in a state of nature; it need not refer to the state of a country at large.[52]) By contrast, both justice and obligations owed to others endure in the state of rebellion.

Behemoth textually supports my reading. Hobbes's history of the English Civil War singles out lack of knowledge about civil rights and duties as the main cause

---

[49] Gentili, *De Jure Belli*, 22.

[50] E.g. David Gauthier, 'Thomas Hobbes and the Contractarian Theory of Law', *Canadian Journal of Philosophy*, suppl. 16 (1990) 32–33; Kinch Hoekstra, 'Hobbes on the Natural Condition of Mankind' in Patricia Springborg (ed), *The Cambridge Companion to Hobbes's Leviathan* (Cambridge, 2007) 114; David Armitage, *Civil Wars: A History in Ideas* (New Haven, 2017) 111.

[51] Also EL 23.9, 12; DCv 15.1; L 31.1; EW 4: 287; EW 5: 184.

[52] G.S. Kavka, *Hobbesian Moral and Political Theory* (Princeton, 1986) 88.

of the rebellion. Clergy and universities are accused of having failed to teach citizens their duty.[53] We read about 'reducing' a rebellious Parliament 'to their duty' (B 194). Also mentioned are erstwhile rebels who 'were converted to their duty by their own natural reason' (B 294). Such passages indicate that rebellion does not annihilate political obligations owed to the sovereign. Political obligations can persist despite rebels' expulsion from the commonwealth, because subjects always owe obedience to the sovereign personally, in his natural capacity (rather than in his political capacity, as representative of the commonwealth). This must be so since the joint promise to obey a common ruler antedates the commonwealth (created by this mutual agreement).[54]

The inalienable right of self-defence complicates matters. *Inter arma silent leges* (EL 19.2; DCv 5.2; DPS 36). The right of self-defence cuts both ways. Rebels and the sovereign alike may lawfully defend themselves by all means. According to Hobbes, 'a great many men together, hav[ing] already resisted the Sovereign Power unjustly' may band together to defend their lives, 'which the Guilty man may as well do, as the Innocent' (L 21.17; cf. EL 27.2). 'There was indeed injustice in the first breach of their duty; Their bearing of Arms subsequent to it, though it be to maintain what they have done, is no new unjust act' (L 21.17). In other words, while the initial act of rebellion was unjust, subsequent acts of self-defence are not. When no protection is forthcoming, no obedience is due (L 21.21; L 29.23; L R&C.6). Yet crucially, an offer of amnesty eliminates any grounds for lawful resistance: 'the offer of pardon taketh from them, to whom it is offered, the plea of self-defence, and maketh their perseverance ... unlawfull [injusti]' (L 21.17; LL 21.15).

The term 'injusti' attests that the right of self-defence suspends, rather than destroys, the self-incurred obligation to simply obey the sovereign. The injustice in question is unlikely to refer to a violation of natural law duties (outlining general rules of reason on how to survive amidst others). For a start, by this time, Hobbes no longer called transgressions of natural law duties as such 'unjust'.[55] From *Leviathan* onwards, injustice is defined directly as breach of covenant (L 15.2). Second, to offer to pardon past offences is to make an offer of peace.[56] Yet pre-statist individuals, being subject to none, have a natural right to judge for themselves whether it is safe to enter conditions of peace. The duty to accept government pardons on pain of injustice is incompatible with this natural right of private judgement. The obligation rebels violate when they continue to fight despite being offered amnesty

---

[53] E.g. B 110, 158ff, 168ff, 302, 322–323.

[54] Laurens van Apeldoorn, 'On the Person and Office of the Sovereign in Hobbes' *Leviathan*', *British Journal for the History of Philosophy* 28 (2020) no. 1: 57–58, 65.

[55] DPS 31; LL 18.6: 'For what is done contrary to the law of nature is called inequitable [iniquum]; what is done contrary to the civil law, unjust [injustum]'.

[56] Natural law requires rulers to offer amnesty to penitent rebels to bring about domestic peace (EL 16.9; DCv 3.10; L 15.18). On the natural law duty to pardon enemies, see Maximilian Jaede, 'Forgiveness and Reconciliation in Hobbes's Natural Law Theory', *History of European Ideas* 43 (2017) no. 8: 834–836, 841–842.

must therefore be the directed obligation of justice incurred in the original covenant. This obligation to simply obey the sovereign is owed both to their former citizens and to their ruler (DCv 6.20; DCv 7.14; L 18.3). Natural law does not require agents to keep covenants in perilous conditions of hostility (L 15.36). While laws are silent in times of war, the self-incurred obligation of simple obedience persists (§7.2). As soon as peace can be had, rebels should end their uprising—on pain of committing a new injustice. That injustice consists in a refusal to accept the sovereign's authority over them when this can safely be done. Rebels thus still owe obedience to their sovereign.

Rebellion is therefore no relapse into the state of nature. Only the utter dissolution of the commonwealth brings about that state 'of absolute Liberty, such as is theirs, that neither are Soveraigns, nor Subjects' (L 31.1). The self-incurred obligation to obey the sovereign persists until the sovereign's power is critically undermined. Rebellion does not itself cancel political obligations. Successful rebellions do, however, erode the sovereign's capacity to provide protection, which conditions this duty (L 29.23; L 30.3).[57] Only in that sense do 'Rebellions . . . destroy Justice' (DPS 40). The civil war waged against King Charles I was a rebellion. Its success, rather than its beginning, generated a state of nature. Rebellion turns into a state of nature the moment the sovereign is no longer capable of protecting his subjects—when 'the enemies get a finall Victory' (L 29.23; also DCv 7.18; L 21.25; L R&C.6). At that moment, and not before, do obligations to others dissolve, and justice and injustice no longer have place.

The common bipartite division between the state of nature and the commonwealth, between natural liberty and civil subjection, is hence incomplete. Between the state of nature, devoid of obligations and justice, and the empire of law lies 'the condition of warre, commonly called Rebellion' (L 28.23). *Statism about Justice* may seem to imply that Hobbes confines the realm of justice to the commonwealth. My analysis of the juridical condition of rebellion tells against this inference. Rebellion consists in the bellicose limbo between subjection and anarchy where civil law no longer applies, but justice still does. The state of rebellion is beyond the legal order, yet within the realm of justice: the two domains are non-overlapping.

10.5 THE FOOL CONSIDERS COMMITTING TREASON

My analysis of treason and its place within Hobbes's constitutional theory sheds new light on his much-debated 'Reply to the Foole'. It explains why threats of

---

[57] Deborah Baumgold, 'When Hobbes Needed History' in G.A.J. Rogers and Tom Sorell (eds), *Hobbes and History* (London, 2000) 25–43; Kinch Hoekstra, 'The *De Facto* Turn in Hobbes's Political Philosophy' in Tom Sorell and Luc Foisneau (eds), *Leviathan after 350 Years* (Oxford, 2004) 33–73.

punishment are powerless against foolish reasoning. The fool doubts whether acting justly is always rational (i.e. in their enlightened self-interest):

> The Foole hath sayd in his heart, there is no such thing as Justice; and sometimes also with his tongue; seriously alleaging, that every mans conservation, and contentment, being committed to his own care, there could be no reason, why every man might not do what he thought conduced thereunto: and therefore also to make, or not make; keep, or not keep Covenants, was not against Reason, when it conduced to ones benefit. He does not therein deny, that there be Covenants; and that they are sometimes broken, sometimes kept; and that such breach of them may be called Injustice, and the observance of them Justice: but he questioneth, whether Injustice, taking away the feare of God, (for the same Foole hath sayd in his heart there is no God,) may not sometimes stand with that Reason, which dictateth to every man his own good . . . and if it be not against Reason, it is not against Justice: or else Justice is not to be approved for good. (L 15.4)[58]

Hobbes replies: 'This specious reasoning is neverthelesse false' (L 15.4). Two arguments lay bare the fool's irrationality. First, injustice generally 'tendeth to his own destruction'. Even if the fool's malicious plan succeeds through some unforeseeable turn of events, it will not have been 'reasonably or wisely done'. Second, he 'that breaketh his Covenant, and consequently declareth that he thinks he may with reason do so, cannot be received into any Society, that unite themselves for Peace and Defense, but by the errour of them that receive him'. If the fool is to live in society, 'it is by the errours of other men, which he could not foresee, nor reckon upon' (L 15.5).[59]

Hobbes's reply to the fool has been discussed extensively in the literature. The passage is commonly interpreted as an attempt to prove that acting morally/justly, or being disposed to so act, is always rational. 'The central substantive issue that Hobbes and the Foole disagree over', Kavka writes, 'is whether it is rational ex ante for an agent to violate core moral rules when doing so promises to benefit her'.[60] Commentators have long been vexed by the apparent inadequacy of Hobbes's rebuttal. Zaitchik, for instance, rails:

> The problems with this reply are so astoundingly obvious that one must wonder how Hobbes dared to give it . . . Hobbes seems to miss the point of the Fool's

---

[58] Compare DCv 14.19n; L 27.10; L 30.5; LL 15.4.

[59] Compare Thucydides, *The Peloponnesian War*, 1.84; in Hobbes's translation: 'For we are not to build our hopes upon the oversights of them, but upon the safe foresight of ourselves' (EW 8: 89).

[60] G.S. Kavka, 'The Rationality of Rule-Following: Hobbes's Dispute with the Foole', *Law and Philosophy* 14 (1995) no. 1: 9. Also e.g. David Gauthier, 'Thomas Hobbes: Moral Theorist', *The Journal of Philosophy* 76 (1979) no. 10: 553–558; Gregory J. Robson, 'Two Psychological Defenses of Hobbes's Claim against the "Fool"', *Hobbes Studies* 28 (2015) no. 2: 135; Roger Crisp, *Sacrifice Regained: Morality and Self-Interest in British Moral Philosophy from Hobbes to Bentham* (Oxford, 2019) 22–25.

objection, which was not that unilateral violation of covenant is *generally* advantageous or rational but rather that it might sometimes be.[61]

With such a conclusion, the chances are that the commentator is missing the point. The fool, I contend, is not pondering the rationality of breaking just any agreement. The covenant they consider breaking is the original covenant. In other words, the fool is considering committing treason.

Hobbesian citizens can violate norms of justice in two ways. Any crime is in breach of the original promise to simply obey the sovereign and therefore unjust. The fool contemplates another kind of injustice: disavowing the validity of the original covenant and hence of the legal system as such. The fool's treacherous disowning of their political obligation is worse than any ordinary law-breaking, just 'as *constant* sinning is more serious than a *single* sin' (DCv 14.20). Anyone so foolish may be inclined to commit petty crimes when deemed advantageous, observing the civil law only when crime is not expected to pay. Hobbes's rejoinder nevertheless primarily considers whether citizens can ever rationally pursue treason, not criminal behaviour generally.[62]

Once we interpret the fool as a traitor, Hobbes's reply starts to make sense. It explains why the fool is never reminded of the likelihood of civil punishment. Rather, the fool risks being 'cast out of Society', making his injustice 'tendeth to his own destruction' (L 15.5). Without downplaying the horrors of early modern prisons, this would be pretty dramatic a depiction of the fate felons face. The description is more apt if the fool is questioning the rationality of abstaining from treason. Further textual support for this reading is found in four examples Hobbes gives of foolish reasoning. 'The Kingdome of God is gotten by violence', we read, 'but what if it could be gotten by unjust violence?' The second example explicitly mentions treason. Coke had argued that legal accusations of treason levelled against a royal heir are annulled the moment they become King. 'If the right Heire of the Crown be attainted of Treason; yet the Crown shall descend to him, and *eo instante* the Atteynder be voyd' (L 15.4).[63] Such specious reasoning, Hobbes objected, makes regicide rational. Later on, the fool is twice explicitly portrayed as pondering rebellion. Any attempt at 'attaining Soveraignty by Rebellion' is foolish for two reasons. Success 'cannot reasonably be expected, but rather the contrary; and because by

---

[61] A. Zaitchik, 'Hobbes's Reply to the Fool: The Problem of Consent and Obligation', *Political Theory* 10 (1982) no. 2: 246–247. Also e.g. David Gauthier, *The Logic of Leviathan* (Oxford, 1969) 87–88; David Gauthier, *Morals by Agreement* (Oxford, 1986) 161–162; Michael LeBuffe, 'Hobbes's Reply to the Fool', *Philosophy Compass* 2 (2007) no. 1: 31–45.

[62] Lott, 'Hobbes's Right of Nature', 175–176, makes the same distinction between treason and ordinary crime. Yet he proceeds to argue that Hobbes's 'inadequate' reply to the fool meant to show the categorical irrationality of both.

[63] At L 15.4, Malcolm's Clarendon edition of *Leviathan* adds a footnote citing Edward Coke, *The First Part of the Institutes of the Laws of England* (London, 1628) 1.1.8: 'if the right heire of the Crowne be attainted of Treason, yet shall the Crowne descend to him, and *eo instante* (without any other reversall) the attainder is utterly avoided, as it fell out in the case of *Henrie* the seventh'.

gaining it so, others are taught to gain the same in like manner' (L 15.7). After declaring that rebellion is prohibited 'by virtue onely of the Law of Nature, that forbiddeth the violation of Faith' (L 30.4), Hobbes challenged those who hold that 'Justice is but a word, without substance; and that whatsoever a man can by force, or art, acquire to himselfe . . . is his own, which I have already shewed to be false' (L 30.5). There *is* such a thing as justice, Hobbes insists, and it requires keeping promises of simple obedience to the sovereign.

Several commentators have previously noted that in his reply to the fool, 'Hobbes is preoccupied with those who foment rebellion more than with ordinary criminals'.[64] Yet the significance of this point has not been fully grasped; perhaps because the same commentators continue to subsume 'flagrant' law-breakers among Hobbes's fools as well.[65] This chapter has shown that the choice situation rebels face differs qualitatively from that of common criminals. The criminally minded weigh potential illicit gains against the risk of being caught and punished. The traitorous fool ponders the profits of seizing political power against the hazards of being warred against. Rebellion, Hobbes avers, cannot possibly be curbed by 'terrour of legall punishment' (L 30.4). For in disputing sovereign authority, the rebel simultaneously disowns the penal status of coercive state responses. Insofar as the fool is considering treason, no legal sanction will deter her. Only the prospect of war could, potentially limitless in scope.[66]

In analysing treason and its place within Hobbes's social contract theory, this chapter has elucidated the theoretical distinction between rebels/traitors and criminals, and the distinct ways in which they violate justice; allowing me to render intelligible Hobbes's reply to the fool. Justice, I have shown, does not simply order citizens to refrain from crime. Its main demand is more basic. Justice enjoins citizens to refrain from treason and to accept and uphold the authority of the legal order, grounded in the original covenant. The norm of justice is not part of the legal system; rather it is its normative foundation.

CONCLUSION

This chapter has argued that Hobbes endorsed *Citizenship Forfeiture*: by treacherously renouncing their subjection, rebels become enemies and non-subjects.

---

[64] Kinch Hoekstra, 'Hobbes and the Foole', *Political Theory* 25 (1997) no. 5: 624. Also Patricia Springborg, 'Hobbes's Fool the *Insipiens*, and the Tyrant-King', *Political Theory* 39 (2011) no. 1: 96; S.A. Lloyd, 'Hobbes's Reply to the Foole', *Hobbes Studies* 18 (2005) 52, 58–61, 67: 'there is powerful textual support for the claim that Hobbes is primarily even if not exclusively concerned with claims that attempts at sedition may accord with reason'. Dyzenhaus, *The Long Arc*, 98, sees the fool as a 'self-declared outlaw'—'no ordinary criminal'.

[65] Hoekstra, 'Hobbes and the Foole', 624.

[66] We should thus dismiss Hoekstra's suggestion that the sovereign should set up proportionate punishments to deter the fool ('Hobbes and the Foole', 627).

Citizenship requires present submission to the sovereign, that is, enduring acknowledgement of his authority. Rebels expel themselves from the legal order by disavowing the original covenant. *Citizenship Forfeiture* does not entail that rebels are no longer bound by the original covenant. Subjects cannot unilaterally destroy the obligation created by the mutual agreement to obey the sovereign—not even by unjust means. That original pact should be kept as a matter of justice, the fundamental law that renders civil law morally binding. Rebellion does not annihilate the obligation to simply obey the sovereign. For that obligation is not part of the legal order; it rather upholds it. It is an obligation of justice at the level of natural, not civil law. For Hobbes, political obligation is not possessed as a citizen. Rather, recognition of one's political obligation is what makes one a citizen.

In closing, let me point out how my analysis of treason and rebellion helps clarify the relation between justice and the state. Justice was traditionally seen as essential to the commonwealth. From Cicero onwards, it was a commonplace that only those human collectives where justice is observed are truly states. 'For what is a state other than an equal partnership in justice?'[67] Augustine concurred: 'Justice removed, then, what are kingdoms but great band of robbers?'[68] The church father held that a multitude becomes a unified people through a common agreement on what justice requires. Absent such an agreement, there is no people and hence no commonwealth.[69] Hobbes, too, regarded justice as a precondition of the commonwealth. 'Justice it selfe' gives the commonwealth 'life' and sustains it (L 29.1). Yet in his view, the state existentially needs not so much just *government*, as just *citizens*. For the multitude to stay united as a single people and commonwealth, citizens must observe justice. Not in the sense of abstaining from crime. But in a more fundamental sense: as enduringly acknowledging the validity of the original covenant and the authority of the sovereign. Rebels' traitorous and unjust dismissal of these norms ruptures the commonwealth, expelling them from this 'real Unitie of them all' (L 17.13). By contrast, even the most outrageously sinful government preserves intact the unity of the commonwealth provided that all citizens continue to agree that its legislation, however immoral its content, are the authoritative measures of just and unjust actions. A failure to govern in line with natural law, Hobbes warned, will inevitably lead to civil unrest if not outright rebellion (L 31.40). But the commonwealth starts to shatter only when citizens, perhaps in response to government oppression, unjustly renege on their original covenant—and not before.

---

[67] Cicero, *The Republic*, 1.49, also 3.43.

[68] Augustine, *The City of God against the Pagans*, ed. R.W. Dyson (Cambridge, 1998) 147. Also Bodin, *Six Books*, 1–3.

[69] Augustine, *The City of God*, 78, 951–952.

PART V
A REVIEW AND CONCLUSION

11
THE 'MORTALL GOD' VINDICATED

My Life and Writings speak one Congruous Sense /
Justice I teach, and Justice Reverence (VL 264)

When the exercise of sovereign power 'hath the resemblance of an unjust act', Hobbes wrote dismally after the dark days of civil war, then it 'disposeth great numbers of citizens (when occasion is presented) to rebell' (LL 29.3). Aggrieved subjects will not revolt, he held, unless they 'believe that their rebellion is just, their discontents grounded upon great injuries' (EL 27.14). Remove civic gripes and grievances and peace and concord can reign. Hobbes took that insight to the letter. His civil theodicy boldly aimed to resolve the problem of human evil caused by absolute and arbitrary government. A life-long student of human nature, Hobbes knew political leaders warts and all: proud, prickly, and passion-driven like any of us. Yet however erratic and abusive their rule, he claimed stunningly, 'nothing the Soveraign Representative can doe to a Subject, on what pretence soever, can properly be called Injustice, or Injury' (L 21.7). Hobbes went through great lengths to prove that all-powerful sovereigns can do no wrong to their citizens—not even by arbitrarily despoiling them of their lives and goods. This brief review and conclusion traces the argumentative structure which he erected to absolve the '*Mortall God*' from all stains of injustice (L 17.13).

Remarkably, the very same principles of justice that chain subjects to simple obedience, free sovereigns from all moral allegations by mortals. Justice could play that dual role, I have intimated, because Hobbes conceives of deontic notions relationally. Take the concept of law. The eternal laws of nature, we read over and over, are divine commands issued through natural reason.[1] Commentators have long downplayed this textually unassailable doctrine because it facially contradicts Hobbes's later claim that natural law is truly law only as civil law (L 26.8; EW 4: 284–285). Perceived tensions vanish once we realize that the laws of nature can be divine law without being law *between* humans (§3.5). Partial and error-prone people deeply disagree over the meaning and content of the dictates of right reason—God's eternal moral law. In the state of nature, each person relies on their own interpretation of right reason to determine what morality permits, prohibits, and requires. Naturally free and equal, no one is obliged to 'take for Gods law'

---

[1] E.g. EL 17.12; EL 18.1; EL 29.7; DCv 3.33; L 15.41; L 29.9; L 30.30; L 42.37.

Hobbes on Justice. Johan Olsthoorn, Oxford University Press. © Johan Olsthoorn 2024.
DOI: 10.1093/9780191904585.003.0011

another's word (L 33.24). Even sound interpretations of the laws of nature are no law to those free to disobey the interpreter (L 26.22). Conversely, flagrantly wrong glosses on natural law are binding law to anyone contractually obligated to follow the expositor's judgement (§6.5).

This innovative account of when natural law is interpersonally binding underlies the sovereign's legal and moral unaccountability to his subjects. It unshackles him from all legal restraints while keeping him personally yoked to the precepts of natural law. Civil legislation, like legal adjudication, can contravene morality. If it does, 'as it was a law to their subjects . . . the law was not unjust. But the making of it was, of which they were to give account to none but God' (EW 5: 178). The same action, Hobbes claims here, can be unjust in relation to some party while being with right towards others. For Hobbes, φ-ing is unjust only towards those to whom the agent lacks the right to φ. Injustice towards humans must consist in breach of covenant because of each person's original natural right to everything. The sovereign does not owe it to his subjects to govern morally, having been granted 'the right to doe what he pleased' vis-à-vis them (L 21.7). Pre-statist individuals do not have any directed obligations to each other to comply with natural law either: 'in the absence of sovereign power . . . anyone may do whatever he pleases, or whatever seems right to him' (DCv 11.4).

Grasping the relational nature of law, right, obligation, justice, and injury is key to understanding Hobbes's ethics and politics. Consider the cornerstone of his theory of justice: the natural right to everything. Hobbes sometimes portrays this right as unlimited and unconditional, allowing each 'to do whatsoever he listeth to whom he listeth' (EL 14.10). Other passages restrict the right to whatever the agent sincerely believes promotes their preservation (DCv 1.10n; DCv 3.27n). Such apparent incongruities have long vexed commentators. The puzzle dissolves once we view the *jus omnium in omnia* relationally. All have by nature unlimited rights vis-à-vis fellow humans. Yet people are not fully free in relation to God: he demands *bona fide* pursuit of self-defence.

The relational nature of law, right, and injury also explains salient character differences between natural law duties vs. obligation of justice. Obligations of justice, created by contractual alienation of right, are always directed. They are owed to all other contractors and their violation wrongs those whose personal liberties it unjustly hinders. Natural law duties are non-directed outside the state. What explains this difference is not that obligations of justice are 'genuinely moral' and natural law duties are 'merely prudential'.[2] The reason pre-statist individuals do not wrong/injure the persons they harm by transgressing natural law is rather that in conditions of natural equality, each is entitled to judge for themselves what (if anything) morality demands in practice. Natural rights of private judgement shield

---

[2] *Contra* Arash Abizadeh, *Hobbes and the Two Faces of Ethics* (Cambridge, 2018) 21–22, 218.

sinners from moral accusation and ensure that trespasses can be injuries (i.e. acts without right) only vis-à-vis God (as per *Sinning with Right*). Only once civil legislation elevates the laws of nature into interpersonally binding laws do moral duties become owed to others. Like pre-statist individuals, the sovereign is bound by the laws of nature yet entirely free to adopt and follow his own interpretation of them. His retained right of private moral judgement renders him morally unaccountable to his subjects. It ensures that he can do wrong (i.e. lack right) against God alone.

Hobbes advances two powerful arguments to render supreme rulers immune to accusations of injustice and injury by their subjects. According to the Consent Argument, citizens' absolute subjection precludes sovereign injury. For 'whatever he does, is done with their consent, and no wrong can be done to one who consents to it' (DCv 8.7). Citizens' unconditional authorization achieves the same on *Leviathan*'s Authorization Argument. 'For he that doth any thing by authority from another, doth therein no injury to him by whose authority he acteth' (L 18.6). Both arguments vindicate sovereigns' conduct only in relation to their subjects. Citizens cannot with reason criticize their lord, no matter how morally flawed his rule: 'whatsoever is commanded by the Soveraign Power, is as to the Subject (though not so always in the sight of God) justified by the Command; for of such command every Subject is the Author' (L 22.15). Hobbes sometimes invokes these two arguments to prove that whatever the sovereign does to a subject can be no injury *to her*.[3] And sometimes to make the more general point that subjects lack the standing to call *any* government action 'unjust', regardless of who is harmed by it.[4]

Each argument goes a long way in establishing that citizens cannot possibly have justified grievances against the government. Let sovereigns commit injustice by knowingly punishing innocents or by wilfully reneging on government agreements. Even so, the arguments show, subjects cannot accuse them of injury/injustice on pain of absurdity: it being impossible to wrong oneself/the willing. No further vindicatory argument besides these two seems needed. Undeterred, Hobbes did advance many additional arguments: his civil theodicy is argumentatively overdetermined. Take his several arguments for why private property rights never exclude the sovereign. According to the Allotment Argument, government expropriation cannot possibly wrong/injure citizens since their belongings are from the outset owned by their sovereign *dominus* (§5.3). The Allotment Argument seems redundant. The Consent and Authorization Arguments already establish that the sovereign may rightfully take citizens' possessions whenever he judges it necessary: 'the Kings word, is sufficient to take any thing from any Subject, when there is need; and ... the King is Judge of that need' (L 20.16). What does Hobbes gain by adding that subjects never had full-fledged property rights

---

[3] The Consent Argument is used in this way in EL 28.1; DCv 3.7; DCv 8.7; L 15.13; EW 5: 152. The Authorization Argument in L 18.6; L 20.13; L 21.7; L 22.15.

[4] E.g. EL 21.3; L 24.7; L 30.20.

268   THE 'MORTALL GOD' VINDICATED

to begin with—that theirs are merely rights to enjoy resources owned by the sovereign? Similarly, if unconditional authorization anyway deprives citizens of the standing to condemn their ruler of wrongdoing, why bother showing that government handouts and legal sentences cannot possibly be unjust by failing to give each their due?

Hobbes's reasons for pursuing argumentative overdetermination are partly rhetorical, partly required by systematic considerations. His battery of arguments means to leave no room for the seditious thought that the sovereign can do wrong. Letting his entire vindication rest on one powerful line of argument—say, unlimited authorization—would have greatly reduced his critics' demolition work. Valuing multiple lines of defence, Hobbes systematically showed that the sovereign cannot possibly violate principles of justice *in any way*. Argumentative overdetermination also helped stop gaps in his conclusions. For instance, the Authorization Argument does not rule out sovereign injustice towards non-subjects—for example by waging unjust wars. Hobbes's account of interstate morality explains why non-divine agents are in no position to morally evaluate sovereign decisions to resort to war, leaving yet less place for conscientious refusals to fight in wars citizens perceive as unjust. Intertextual comparisons plainly evince his ambition to methodically erase all scope for sovereign injustice and injury. Think of his concessions in *Elements* and *De Cive* that excessive or unequal taxation can give rise to 'justified complaint' (DCv 13.10; also EL 24.2) (§4.4). *Leviathan's* reconceptualizations of distributive justice and merit closed that loophole.

Hobbes's bold thesis that sovereigns cannot possibly commit injustice or injury to their citizens has certainly not gone unnoticed in the literature. Yet its conceptual and argumentative foundations and wider theoretical implications have not been explored before in any great detail, perhaps because scholars tend to accept Hobbes's many definitional curiosities as holding true by stipulation. This book has reconstructed in full the chains of reasoning and tacit conceptual revisions that supported his many idiosyncratic definitions. Hobbes's civil theodicy rests on large-scale conceptual engineering: he systematically reinterpreted the meaning of basic moral and political terms and rearranged their conceptual interrelations. For instance, he reconceptualized injury as action without right (*sine jure*) (§2.1); rights as mere liberties (§2.1); justice as keeping faith (§2.2); consent as attributed consent (§2.5); merit as due by grace alone (§4.5); sovereign power as including *dominium* over subjects' lives and goods (§5.3); first attacks on innocents as lawful exercises of self-defence (§8.3); and rebels as non-subjects (§10.3).

A theory of just war and self-defence underlies Hobbes's theory of justice. His natural law doctrine is at its core an account of when and how agents may resort to armed force; and when and how they must seek peace with others. The natural right to everything *is* a right of war, the laws of nature *are* the rules of peace. The Hobbesian commonwealth is built upon an armistice, ending the natural condition of relentless war. Hobbes's social contract, I have argued, is composed of two analytically distinct covenants. In the 'the covenant of Subjection', persons give up their rights of self-government through joint submission to an absolute ruler (L 21.24). In the logically prior 'Covenant of Peace', individuals mutually renounce their bellicose right to everything (L 14.31). The resulting truce, ending the war of all against all, is coeval with the commonwealth since government power is needed to make people perform their pacts. Theoretically central as rights of war and peace are to his thinking, the popular belief that Hobbes was a realist about war is deeply mistaken.

Hobbes on Justice complicates Hobbes's relation to another form of realism as well. Political realists have claimed Hobbes as an intellectual predecessor on grounds of him prioritizing questions of legitimacy (authority to rule) over those of justice (moral principles governing the due exercise of that authority).[5] Political realists uphold two claims to establish the priority of legitimacy over justice. First, justice is not a ground of legitimate political authority—provision of peace, security, trust, and social stability are. Second, social order is the first and most basic demand of politics. No peace, no politics.[6] Both claims can with reason be ascribed to Hobbes. Individuals principally join political society to obtain protection against domestic and foreign enemies; peace being a precondition for self-preservation amidst others. Moreover, sovereigns possess the right to be obeyed because and insofar as they provide citizens with personal security; not because and insofar as they govern justly. As Pierre Bayle (1647–1706) observed long ago, Hobbes sees provision of social order not as a necessary but as a sufficient condition for legitimate political authority.[7] That said, for Hobbes justice nonetheless figures among the preconditions of legitimate authority. Not so much because civil peace and hence political legitimacy are at risk if sovereigns do not govern in line with natural law (a wider moral category than justice). But because disagreements over justice are politically destabilizing and need to be forestalled for sovereigns to realize enduring domestic peace. In short: while *just* government is no ground for political legitimacy, domestic peace is; and theoretically ruling out the possibility of *unjust* government promotes peace. In this way, Hobbes made justice an ideological problem for realist theories of political legitimacy.

As the opening vignette of Hans Kohlhase colourfully illustrated, unjust treatment by government officials can create deep and lasting grievances among citizens. Seeing others wrongfully suffer can trigger ire. '*Anger* for great hurt done to another, when we conceive the same to be done by Injury, INDIGNATION' (L 6.21). Resentment and indignation are potentially destabilizing passions, capable of spurring subjects to rebellion. This book has reconstructed in full Hobbes's theoretical

---

[5] Robin Douglass, 'Hobbes and Political Realism', *European Journal of Political Theory* 19 (2020) no. 2: 252–255.

[6] Bernard Williams, *In the Beginning Was the Deed*, ed. Geoffrey Hawthorn (Princeton, 2005) 3.

[7] Pierre Bayle, 'Hobbes' in *Bayle: Political Writings*, ed. S.L. Jenkinson (Cambridge, 2000) 79.

responses to this danger. His theory of justice aimed to systematically eliminate the possibility of justified grievances against government. The passion for justice itself does not need to be stamped out. It can be redirected. Justice differs in this respect from freedom. Since peace requires absolute subjection, humans' natural love for freedom and dominion is intrinsically hostile to social stability. Subjects' longing for liberty must be trimmed down for their own good. The passion for justice, by contrast, can be a positive source of political stability. Right reason teaches us that justice is essential to the commonwealth and a precondition for peace and self-preservation. Some rational folks recognize this, scorning all fraud and law-breaking as contrary to their enlightened self-interest. Such just persons are few and far between. For most mortals, the 'Passion to be reckoned upon, is Fear' (L 14.31). Threats of penal sanctions must dissuade them from law-breaking. And that is alright. Domestic peace does not require that subjects abstain from crime out of an urge to be just. It does forbid that they revolt, hurt and resentful, in response to felt injuries. By governing in line with the eternal laws of nature, rulers minimize the risk that citizens become irked and inclined to rebel. Yet even if they reign most irrationally and abusively, none of their suffering subjects can ever with reason feel aggrieved by their mortal God. That is the justice taught and revered by Thomas Hobbes of Malmesbury.

Bibliography

Abizadeh, Arash. 2007. 'Cooperation, Pervasive Impact, and Coercion: On the Scope (Not Site) of Distributive Justice', *Philosophy and Public Affairs* 35, no. 4: 318–358.

Abizadeh, Arash. 2011. 'Hobbes on the Causes of War: A Disagreement Theory', *American Political Science Review* 105, no. 2: 298–315.

Abizadeh, Arash. 2016. 'Sovereign Jurisdiction, Territorial Rights, and Membership in Hobbes' in A.P. Martinich and Kinch Hoekstra (eds), *The Oxford Handbook of Hobbes*, 397–431. Oxford: Oxford University Press.

Abizadeh, Arash. 2018. *Hobbes and the Two Faces of Ethics*. Cambridge: Cambridge University Press.

Abizadeh, Arash. 2020. 'Glory and the Evolution of Hobbes's Disagreement Theory of War: From *Elements* to *Leviathan*', *History of Political Thought* 41, no. 2: 265–298.

Adams, Marcus. 2019. 'Hobbes's Laws of Nature in *Leviathan* as a Synthetic Demonstration: Thought Experiments and Knowing the Cause', Philosophers' *Imprint* 19, no. 5: 1–23.

Alexander, Larry. 1996. 'The Moral Magic of Consent (II)', *Legal Theory* 2, no. 2: 165–174.

Aquinas, Thomas. 1912–1936 [1266–1273]. *Summa Theologica*, 22 vols, transl. Fathers of the English Dominican Province, second edition. London: Burns, Oates and Benziger.

Aristotle. 1996. *The Politics and the Constitution of Athens*, ed. Stephen Everson. Cambridge: Cambridge University Press.

Aristotle. 2000. *The Nicomachean Ethics*, ed. Roger Crisp. Cambridge: Cambridge University Press.

Armitage, David. 2013. *The Foundations of Modern International Thought.* Cambridge: Cambridge University Press.

Armitage, David. 2017. *Civil Wars: A History in Ideas*. New Haven: Yale University Press.

Armstrong, John M. 1997. 'Epicurean Justice', *Phronesis* 42, no. 3: 324–334.

Augustine. 1998 [426]. *The City of God against the Pagans*, ed. R.W. Dyson. Cambridge: Cambridge University Press.

Augustine. 2010 [c.395]. *On the Free Choice of the Will*, ed. Peter King. Cambridge: Cambridge University Press.

Austin, John. 1998 [1832]. *The Province of Jurisprudence Determined*. Indianapolis: Hackett.

Austin, Michael. 1999. 'The Genesis Narrative and the Primogeniture Debate in Seventeenth-Century England', *The Journal of English and Germanic Philology* 98, no. 1: 17–39.

Ayala, Balthazar. 1912 [1582]. *Three Books on the Law of War*, 2 vols, ed. John Westlake, transl. John Pawley Bate. Washington: Carnegie Institution.

Bacon, Francis. 1629. *Considerations Touching a Warre with Spaine*. London: n.p.

Bacon, Francis. 1999. *The Essays or Counsels Civil and Moral*, ed. Brian Vickers. Oxford: Oxford University Press.

Baker, John. 2019 [1971]. *An Introduction to English Legal History*, fifth edition. Oxford: Oxford University Press.

Ball, Terence. 1995. 'Hobbes's Linguistic Turn' in idem (ed), *Reappraising Political Theory: Revisionist Studies in the History of Political Thought*, 83–106. Oxford: Clarendon Press.

Barry, Brian. 1968. 'Warrender and His Critics', *Philosophy* 43, no. 164: 117–137.

Baumgold, Deborah. 2000. 'When Hobbes Needed History' in G.A.J. Rogers and Tom Sorell (eds), *Hobbes and History*, 25–43. London: Routledge.

Baumgold, Deborah. 2008.'The Difficulties of Hobbes Interpretation', *Political Theory* 36, no. 6: 827–855.

272 BIBLIOGRAPHY

Baumgold, Deborah. 2010. *Contract Theory in Historical Context: Essays on Grotius, Hobbes, and Locke*. Leiden: Brill.

Baumgold, Deborah. 2010. 'Slavery Discourse before the Restoration: The Barbary Coast, Justinian's *Digest*, and Hobbes's Political Theory', *History of European Ideas* 36, no. 4: 412–418.

Baumgold, Deborah. 2013. 'Trust in Hobbes's Political Thought', *Political Theory* 41, no. 6: 838–855.

Baumgold, Deborah (ed). 2017. *Three-Text Edition of Thomas Hobbes's Political Theory: The Elements of Law, De Cive and Leviathan*. Cambridge: Cambridge University Press.

Bayle, Pierre. 2000. 'Hobbes' in *Bayle: Political Writings*, ed. S.L. Jenkinson, 79–92. Cambridge: Cambridge University Press.

Beever, Allan. 2004. 'Aristotle on Equity, Law, and Justice', *Legal Theory* 10, no. 1: 33–50.

Beever, Allan. 2013. *Forgotten Justice: The Forms of Justice in the History of Legal and Political Theory*. Oxford: Oxford University Press.

Beitz, Charles R. 1999 [1979]. *Political Theory and International Relations* , revised edition. Princeton: Princeton University Press.

Bejan, Teresa. 2023. 'Hobbes and Hats', *American Political Science Review* 117, no. 4: 1188–1201.

Bellamy, J.G. 1970. *The Law of Treason in England in the Later Middle Ages*. Cambridge: Cambridge University Press.

Benner, Erica. 2009. *Machiavelli's Ethics*. Princeton: Princeton University Press.

Birks, Peter and Grant McLeod (eds). 1987. *Justinian's Institutes*. London: Duckworth.

Blau, Adrian. 2009. 'Hobbes on Corruption', *History of Political Thought* 30, no. 4: 596–616.

Blau, Adrian. 2011. 'Uncertainty and the History of Ideas', *History and Theory* 50, no. 3: 358–372.

Blau, Adrian. 2020. 'Meanings and Understandings in the History of Ideas', *Journal of the Philosophy of History* 14, no. 2: 232–256.

Bobbio, Norberto. 1993. *Thomas Hobbes and the Natural Law Tradition* , transl. Daniela Gobetti. Chicago: The University of Chicago Press.

Bodin, Jean. 1962 [1606]. *The Six Bookes of a Commonweale* , ed. Kenneth Douglas McRae. Cambridge, MA: Harvard University Press.

Bodin, Jean. 1969 [1566]. *Method for the Easy Comprehension of History* , transl. Beatrice Reynolds. New York: Columbia University Press.

Boonin-Vail, David. 1994. *Thomas Hobbes and the Science of Moral Virtue*. Cambridge: Cambridge University Press.

Botterell, Andrew. 2009. 'A Primer on the Distinction between Justification and Excuse', *Philosophy Compass* 4, no. 1: 172–196.

Bottici, Chiara. 2009 [2004]. *Men and States: Rethinking the Domestic Analogy in a Global Age* , transl. Karen Whittle. New York: Palgrave Macmillan.

Boucher, David. 2018. *Appropriating Hobbes: Legacies in Political, Legal, and International Thought*. Oxford: Oxford University Press.

Bramhall, John. 1657. *Castigations of Mr. Hobbes*. London: printed for J. Crook.

Bramhall, John. 1995 [1658]. 'The Catching of Leviathan, or the Great Whale' in G.A.J. Rogers (ed), *Leviathan: Contemporary Responses to the Political Theory of Thomas Hobbes*, 115–179. Bristol: Thoemess Press.

Brandom, Robert B. 2002. *Tales of the Mighty Dead: Historical Essays in the Metaphysics of Intentionality*. Cambridge, MA: Harvard University Press.

Brett, Annabel S. 2011. *Changes of State: Nature and the Limits of the City in Early Modern Natural Law*. Princeton: Princeton University Press.

Brunschwig, Jacques. 1996. 'The Aristotelian Theory of Equity' in Michael Frede and Gisela Striker (eds), *Rationality in Greek Thought*, 115–156. Oxford: Clarendon Press.

Buckland, W.W. 1970 [1908]. *The Roman Law of Slavery: The Condition of the Slave in Private Law from Augustus to Justinian*. Cambridge: Cambridge University Press.

Buckle, Stephen. 1991. *Natural Law and the Theory of Property: Grotius to Hume*. Oxford: Oxford University Press.

Bull, Hedley. 2012 [1977]. *The Anarchical Society: A Study of Order in World Politics*, fourth edition. New York: Palgrave Macmillan.

BIBLIOGRAPHY   273

Burchell, David. 1999. 'The Disciplined Citizen: Thomas Hobbes, Neostoicism and the Critique of Classical Citizenship', *Australian Journal of Politics and History* 45, no. 4: 506–524.

Byron, Michael. 2015. *Submission and Subjection in Leviathan: Good Subjects in the Hobbesian Commonwealth*. New York: Palgrave Macmillan.

Cappelen, Herman. 2020. 'Conceptual Engineering: The Master Argument' in Alexis Burgess, Herman Cappelen, and David Plunkett (eds), *Conceptual Engineering and Conceptual Ethics*, 132–151. Oxford: Oxford University Press.

Carr, E.H. 2001 [1939]. *The Twenty Year's Crisis 1919–1939: An Introduction to the Study of International Relations*. London: MacMillan.

Cavallar, Georg. 2002. *The Rights of Strangers: Theories of International Hospitality, the Global Community, and Political Justice since Vitoria*. Aldershot: Ashgate.

Cesa, Marco (ed). 2014. *Machiavelli on International Relations*. Oxford: Oxford University Press.

Christov, Theodore. 2015. *Before Anarchy: Hobbes and His Critics in Modern International Thought*. Cambridge: Cambridge University Press.

Cicero. 1949. *De Inventione*, ed. H.M. Hubbell. Cambridge, MA: Harvard University Press.

Cicero. 1991. *On Duties*, ed. M.T. Griffin and E.M. Atkins. Cambridge: Cambridge University Press.

Cicero. 1998. *The Republic and the Laws*, ed. Jonathan Powell, transl. Niall Rudd. Oxford: Oxford University Press.

Cicero. 2000. *Defence Speeches*, ed. D.H. Berry. Oxford: Oxford University Press.

Cicero. 2006. *Speech on Behalf of Publius Sestius*, ed. Robert A. Kaster. Oxford: Clarendon Press.

Clausewitz, Carl von. 2007 [1823]. *On War*, ed. Beatrice Heuser, transl. Michael Howard and Peter Paret. Oxford: Oxford University Press.

Coady, C.A.J. 2005. 'The Moral Reality in Realism', *Journal of Applied Philosophy* 22, no. 2: 121–136.

Cohen, Joshua and Charles Sabel. 2006. 'Extram Rempublicam Nulla Justitia?', *Philosophy and Public Affairs* 34, no. 2: 147–175.

Coke, Edward. 1628. *The First Part of the Institutes of the Laws of England. Or, a Commentarie upon Littleton*. London: printed for the Societie of Stationers.

Coke, Edward. 1644. *The Third Part of the Institutes of the Laws of England: Concerning High Treason, and other Pleas of the Crown, and Criminall Causes*. London: printed by M. Flesher.

Coke, Roger. 1660. *Elements of Power & Subjection: Or the Causes of All Humane, Christian, & Legal Society*, printed under the title *Justice Vindicated, from the False Fucus Put upon It, by Thomas White Gent, Mr Thomas Hobbs, and Hugo Grotius*. London: printed by Tho. Newcomb.

Coleman, Jules L. 1982. 'Negative and Positive Positivism', *Journal of Legal Studies* 11, no. 1: 139–164.

Corbin, Thomas A. 2022. 'On Equity and Inequity in Thomas Hobbes's *Dialogue*', *Southern Journal of Philosophy* 60, no. 4: 518–539.

Corsa, A.J. 2013. 'Thomas Hobbes: Magnanimity, Felicity and Justice', *Hobbes Studies* 26, no. 2: 130–151.

Courtland, Shane D. (ed). 2018. *Hobbesian Applied Ethics and Public Policy*. London: Routledge.

Cox, Rory. 2018. 'The Ethics of War up to Thomas Aquinas' in Seth Lazar and Helen Frowe (eds), *The Oxford Handbook of Ethics of War*, 99–121. Oxford: Oxford University Press.

Crisp, Roger. 2019. *Sacrifice Regained: Morality and Self-Interest in British Moral Philosophy from Hobbes to Bentham*. Oxford: Oxford University Press.

Cromartie, Alan. 2005. 'General Introduction' in Alan Cromartie and Quentin Skinner (eds), *Thomas Hobbes: A Dialogue between a Philosopher and a Student*, xiv–lxv. Oxford: Clarendon Press.

Cromartie, Alan. 2011. 'The *Elements* and Hobbesian Moral Thinking', *History of Political Thought* 32, no. 1: 21–47.

Cudworth, Ralph. 1996 [1731]. *A Treatise Concerning Eternal and Immutable Morality, with a Treatise of Freewill*, ed. Sarah Hutton. Cambridge: Cambridge University Press.

274 BIBLIOGRAPHY

Cuffaro, Michael. 2011. 'On Thomas Hobbes's Fallible Natural Law Theory', *History of Philosophy Quarterly* 28, no. 2: 175–190.

Culverwell, Nathaniel. 2001 [1652]. *An Elegant and Learned Discourse of the Light of Nature*, ed. R.A. Greene and H. MacCullum. Indianapolis: Liberty Fund.

Cumberland, Richard. 2005 [1672]. *A Treatise of the Laws of Nature*, ed. Jon Parkin. Indianapolis: Liberty Fund.

Curley, Edwin. 1992. '"I Durst Not Write so Boldly": Or How to Read Hobbes's Theological-Political Treatise' in Emilia Giancotti (ed), *Hobbes e Spinoza: Scienza e Politica*, 497–593. Naples: Bibliopolis.

Curran, Eleanor. 2006. 'Lost in Translation: Some Problems with a Hohfeldian Analysis of Hobbesian Rights', *Hobbes Studies* 19, no. 1: 58–76.

Curran, Eleanor. 2007. *Reclaiming the Rights of Hobbesian Subjects*. New York: Palgrave Macmillan.

Curran, Eleanor. 2010. 'Blinded by the Light of Hohfeld: Hobbes's Notion of Liberty', *Jurisprudence* 1, no. 1: 85–104.

Darwall, Stephen. 1995. *British Moralists and the Internal 'Ought', 1640–1740*. Cambridge: Cambridge University Press.

Darwall, Stephen. 2013. *Morality, Authority, and Law: Essays in Second-Personal Ethics I*. Oxford: Oxford University Press.

Darwall, Stephen. 2013. *Honor, History, and Relationship: Essays in Second-Personal Ethics II*. Oxford: Oxford University Press.

Darwall, Stephen. 2023. *Modern Moral Philosophy: From Grotius to Kant*. Cambridge: Cambridge University Press.

Dietz, M.G. 1990. 'Hobbes' Subject as Citizen' in idem (ed), *Thomas Hobbes and Political Theory*, 91–119. Lawrence: University Press of Kansas.

Donnelly, Jack. 2000. *Realism and International Relations*. Cambridge: Cambridge University Press.

Donnelly, Jack. 2008. 'The Ethics of Realism' in Christian Reus-Smit and Duncan Snidal (eds), *The Oxford Handbook of International Relations*, 150–162. Oxford: Oxford University Press.

Douglass, Robin. 2015. 'Thomas Hobbes's Changing Account of Liberty and Challenge to Republicanism', *History of Political Thought* 36, no. 2: 281–309.

Douglass, Robin. 2020. 'Hobbes and Political Realism', *European Journal of Political Theory* 19, no. 2: 250–269.

Duke, George. 2014. 'Hobbes on Political Authority, Practical Reason and Truth', *Law and Philosophy* 33, no. 5: 605–627.

Dyzenhaus, David. 2001. 'Hobbes and the Legitimacy of Law', *Law and Philosophy* 20, no. 5: 461–498.

Dyzenhaus, David. 2010. 'Hobbes's Constitutional Theory' in *Thomas Hobbes: Leviathan*, ed. Ian Shapiro, 453–480. New Haven: Yale University Press.

Dyzenhaus, David. 2012. 'Hobbes on the Authority of Law' in David Dyzenhaus and Thomas Poole (eds), *Hobbes and the Law*, 186–209. Cambridge: Cambridge University Press.

Dyzenhaus, David. 2014. 'Hobbes on the International Rule of Law', *Ethics and International Affairs* 28, no. 1: 53–64.

Dyzenhaus, David. 2021. 'Thomas Hobbes and the Rule by Law Tradition' in Jens Meierhenrich and Martin Loughlin (eds), *The Cambridge Companion to the Rule of Law*, 261–277. Cambridge: Cambridge University Press.

Dyzenhaus, David. 2022. *The Long Arc of Legality: Hobbes, Kelsen, Hart*. Cambridge: Cambridge University Press.

Edwards, John. 1699. *The Eternal and Intrinsick Reasons of Good and Evil: A Sermon*. Cambridge: printed at the University Press.

Eggers, Daniel. 2009. 'Liberty and Contractual Obligation in Hobbes', *Hobbes Studies* 22, no. 1: 70–103.

Eggers, Daniel. 2014. 'Injury, Injustice, Iniquity: The Evolution of Hobbes's Theory of Justice', *Intellectual History Review* 24, no. 2: 167–184.

BIBLIOGRAPHY 275

Eggers, Daniel. 2019. 'Hobbes, Kant, and the Universal "Right to All Things"', *Hobbes Studies* 32, no. 1: 46–70.

Englard, Izhak. 2009. *Corrective and Distributive Justice from Aristotle to Modern Times.* Oxford: Oxford University Press.

Evrigenis, Ioannis. 1999. 'The Doctrine of the Mean in Aristotle's Ethical and Political Theory', *History of Political Thought* 20, no. 3: 393–416.

Feinberg, Joel. 1970. 'The Nature and Value of Rights', *The Journal of Value Inquiry* 4, no. 4: 243–257.

Feinberg, Joel. 1974. 'Noncomparative Justice', *The Philosophical Review* 83, no. 3: 297–338.

Feinberg, Joel. 1984. *Harm to Others.* Oxford: Oxford University Press.

Field, Sandra. 2014. 'Hobbes and the Question of Power', *Journal of the History of Philosophy* 52, no. 1: 61–85.

Filmer, Robert. 1991. *Patriarcha and Other Writings*, ed. J.P. Sommerville. Cambridge: Cambridge University Press.

Finkelstein, Claire. 2006. 'Hobbes and the Internal Point of View', *Fordham Law Review* 75, no. 3: 1211–1228.

Fleischacker, Samuel. 2004. *A Short History of Distributive Justice.* Cambridge, MA: Harvard University Press.

Foisneau, Luc. 2004. '*Leviathan*'s Theory of Justice' in Tom Sorell and Luc Foisneau (eds), *Leviathan after 350 Years*, 105–122. Oxford: Clarendon Press.

Foisneau, Luc. 2007. 'Hobbes et les Limites de la Justice' in Jauffrey Berthier and Jean Terrel (eds), *Lumières 10: Hobbes: Nouvelles Lectures*, 187–202. Bordeaux: Université Presses de Bordeaux.

Foisneau, Luc. 2007. 'Omnipotence, Necessity, and Sovereignty: Hobbes and the Absolute and Ordinary Powers of God and King' in Patricia Springborg (ed), *The Cambridge Companion to Hobbes's Leviathan*, 271–290. Cambridge: Cambridge University Press.

Forde, Steven. 1992. 'Classical Realism' in Terry Nardin and David R. Mapel (eds), *Traditions of International Ethics*, 62–84. Cambridge: Cambridge University Press.

Forde, Steven. 1992. 'Varieties of Realism: Thucydides and Machiavelli', *The Journal of Politics* 54, no. 2: 372–393.

Forster, Greg. 2003. 'Divine Law and Human Law in Hobbes's *Leviathan*', *History of Political Thought* 24, no. 2: 189–217.

Fotion, Nicholas. 2000. 'Reactions to War: Pacifism, Realism, and Just War Theory' in Andrew Valls (ed), *Ethics in International Affairs: Theories and Cases*, 15–32. Lanham: Rowman & Littlefield.

Frazer, Michael. 2010. 'The Modest Professor: Interpretive Charity and Interpretive Humility in John Rawls's *Lectures on the History of Political Philosophy*', *European Journal of Political Theory* 9, no. 2: 218–226.

Gamauf, Richard. 2009. 'Slaves Doing Business: The Role of Roman Law in the Economy of a Roman Household', *European Review of History* 16, no. 3: 331–346.

Gardner, John. 2001. 'Legal Positivism: 5½ Myths', *American Journal of Jurisprudence* 46, no. 1: 199–227.

Garnsey, Peter. 2007. *Thinking about Property: From Antiquity to the Age of Revolution.* Cambridge: Cambridge University Press.

Gauthier, David. 1969. *The Logic of Leviathan: The Moral and Political Theory of Thomas Hobbes.* Oxford: Clarendon Press.

Gauthier, David. 1979. 'Thomas Hobbes: Moral Theorist', *The Journal of Philosophy* 76, no. 10: 547–559.

Gauthier, David. 1986. *Morals by Agreement.* Oxford: Clarendon Press.

Gauthier, David. 1990. 'Thomas Hobbes and the Contractarian Theory of Law', *Canadian Journal of Philosophy*, Suppl. 16: 5–34.

Gauthier, David. 2001. 'Hobbes: The Laws of Nature', *Pacific Philosophical Quarterly* 82, no. 3/4: 258–284.

Gentili, Alberico. 1933 [1588]. *De Jure Belli Libri Tres*, 2 vols, ed. John C. Rolfe. Oxford: Clarendon Press.

276 BIBLIOGRAPHY

Gert, Bernard. 2010. *Hobbes: Prince of Peace*. Malden, MA: Polity Press.

Giers, Joachim. 1958. *Die Gerechtigkeitslehre des jungen Suárez: Edition und Untersuchung seiner römischen Vorlesungen De justitia et jure*. Freiburg im Breisgau: Herder.

Gilbert, Margaret. 2004. 'Scanlon on Promissory Obligation: The Problem of Promisees' Rights', *The Journal of Philosophy* 101, no. 2: 83–109.

Goldsmith, M.M. 1966. *Hobbes's Science of Politics*. New York: Columbia University Press.

Goldsmith, M.M. 1969. 'Introduction' in Ferdinand Tönnies (ed), *Hobbes: The Elements of Law, Natural and Politic*, second edition, v–xxi. London: Frank Cass.

Goldsmith, M.M. 1996. 'Hobbes on Law' in Tom Sorell (ed), *The Cambridge Companion to Hobbes*, 274–304. Cambridge: Cambridge University Press.

Green, Leslie. 2008. 'Positivism and the Inseparability of Law and Morals', *New York University Law Review* 83: 1035–1058.

Green, Michael J. 2003. 'Justice and Law in Hobbes', *Oxford Studies in Early Modern Philosophy* 1: 111–138.

Green, Michael J. 2015. 'Authorization and Political Authority in Hobbes', *Journal of the History of Philosophy* 53, no. 1: 25–47.

Green, Michael J. 2016. 'Authorization and the Right to Punish', *Pacific Philosophical Quarterly* 97, no. 1: 113–139.

Green, Michael J. 2021. 'Hobbes's Minimalist Moral Theory' in Marcus Adams (ed), *A Companion to Hobbes*, 171–183. Malden, MA: Blackwell-Wiley.

Greenberg, Janelle. 1991. 'Our Grand Maxim of State, "The King Can Do No Wrong"', *History of Political Thought* 12, no. 2: 209–228.

Greene, Robert A. 2015. 'Thomas Hobbes and the Term "Right Reason": Participation to Calculation', *History of European Ideas* 41, no. 8: 997–1028.

Grotius, Hugo. 1926. *Introduction to the Jurisprudence of Holland*, ed. R. W. Lee. Oxford: Clarendon Press.

Grotius, Hugo. 2005 [1625]. *The Rights of War and Peace*, 3 vols, ed. Richard Tuck. Indianapolis: Liberty Fund.

Grotius, Hugo. 2006. *Commentary on the Law of Prize and Booty*, ed. M.J. van Ittersum. Indianapolis: Liberty Fund.

Haakonssen, Knud. 1996. *Natural Law and Moral Philosophy: From Grotius to the Scottish Enlightenment*. Cambridge: Cambridge University Press.

Haggenmacher, Peter. 1992. 'Just War and Regular War in Sixteenth-Century Spanish Doctrine', *International Review of the Red Cross* 32, no. 290: 434–445.

Hampton, Jean. 1985. 'Hobbes's State of War', *Topoi* 4, no. 1: 47–60.

Hampton, Jean. 1986. *Hobbes and the Social Contract Tradition*. Cambridge: Cambridge University Press.

Hampton, Jean. 1992. 'Hobbes and Ethical Naturalism', *Philosophical Perspectives* 6: 333–353.

Hanin, Mark. 2012. 'Thomas Hobbes's Theory of Conscience', *History of Political Thought* 33, no. 1: 55–85.

Harrington, James. 1992. *The Commonwealth of Oceana* and *A System of Politics*, ed. J.G.A. Pocock. Cambridge: Cambridge University Press.

Harris, James. 2011. 'The Pastness of Past Moral Philosophy', *British Journal for the History of Philosophy* 19, no. 2: 327–338.

Harrison, Ross. 2012. 'The Equal Extent of Natural and Civil Law' in David Dyzenhaus and Thomas Poole (eds), *Hobbes and the Law*, 22–38. Cambridge: Cambridge University Press.

Hart, H.L.A. 1958. 'Positivism and the Separation of Law and Morals', *Harvard Law Review* 71, no. 4: 593–629.

Hart, H.L.A. 1982. *Essays on Bentham: Studies in Jurisprudence and Political Theory*. Oxford: Clarendon Press.

Hart, H.L.A. 1994 [1961]. *The Concept of Law*, second edition. Oxford: Clarendon Press.

Harvey, Martin. 2002. 'A Defense of Hobbes's "Just Man"', *Hobbes Studies* 15, no. 1: 68–86.

Harvey, Martin. 2004. 'Teasing a Limited Deontological Theory of Morals out of Hobbes', *The Philosophical Forum* 35, no. 1: 35–50.

BIBLIOGRAPHY 277

Harvey, Martin. 2004. 'Hobbes and the Value of Justice', *The Southern Journal of Philosophy* 42, no. 4: 439–452.

Harvey, Martin. 2006. 'Grotius and Hobbes', *British Journal for the History of Philosophy* 14, no. 1: 27–50.

Harvey, Martin. 2009. 'Hobbes's Voluntarist Theory of Morals', *Hobbes Studies* 22, no. 1: 49–69.

Hewitt, Annie. 2008. 'Universal Justice and *Epieikeia* in Aristotle', *Polis* 25, no. 1: 115–130.

Heyd, David. 1991. 'Hobbes on Capital Punishment', *History of Philosophy Quarterly* 8, no. 2: 119–134.

Hinton, R.W.K. 1968. 'Husbands, Fathers and Conquerors', *Political Studies* 16, no. 1: 55–67.

Hobbes, Thomas. 1839–1845. *The English Works of Thomas Hobbes of Malmesbury*, 11 vols, ed. William Molesworth. London: John Bohn.

Hobbes, Thomas. 1839–1845. *Opera Philosophica quae Latine Scripsit*, 5 vols, ed. William Molesworth. London: John Bohn.

Hobbes, Thomas. 1969 [1640]. *The Elements of Law, Natural and Politic*, ed. Ferdinand Tönnies. London: Frank Cass, second edition.

Hobbes, Thomas. 1976 [c.1643]. *Thomas White's De Mundo Examined*, ed. H.W. Jones. London: Bradford University Press.

Hobbes, Thomas. 1991 [1658]. 'De Homine' in *Man and Citizen*, ed. Bernard Gert, 33–85. Indianapolis: Hackett.

Hobbes, Thomas. 1994 [1640]. *The Elements of Law, Natural and Politic*, ed. J.C.A. Gaskin. Oxford: Oxford University Press.

Hobbes, Thomas. 1994. *The Correspondence*, 2 vols, ed. Noel Malcolm. Oxford: Clarendon Press.

Hobbes, Thomas. 1998 [1642, 1647]. *On the Citizen*, ed. Richard Tuck, transl. Michael Silverthorne. Cambridge: Cambridge University Press.

Hobbes, Thomas. 2005 [1681]. 'A Dialogue between a Philosopher and a Student, of the Common Laws of England' in *Thomas Hobbes: Writings on Common Law and Hereditary Right*, ed. Alan Cromartie and Quentin Skinner, 1–146. Oxford: Clarendon Press.

Hobbes, Thomas. 2008 [1688]. *Historia Ecclesiastica*, ed. Patricia Springborg, Patricia Stablein, and Paul Wilson. Paris: Honoré Champion.

Hobbes, Thomas. 2009 [1679]. *Behemoth, or The Long Parliament*, ed. Paul Seaward. Oxford: Clarendon Press.

Hobbes, Thomas. 2012 [1651, 1668]. *Leviathan*, 3 vols, ed. Noel Malcolm. Oxford: Clarendon Press.

Hoekstra, Kinch. 1997. 'Hobbes and the Foole', *Political Theory* 25, no. 5: 620–654.

Hoekstra, Kinch. 1999. 'Nothing to Declare? Hobbes and the Advocate of Injustice', *Political Theory* 27, no. 2: 230–235.

Hoekstra, Kinch. 2001. 'Tyrannus Rex vs. *Leviathan*', *Pacific Philosophical Quarterly* 82, no. 3: 420–446.

Hoekstra, Kinch. 2003. 'Hobbes on Law, Nature and Reason', *Journal of the History of Philosophy* 41, no. 1: 111–120.

Hoekstra, Kinch. 2004. 'The *De Facto* Turn in Hobbes's Political Philosophy' in Tom Sorell and Luc Foisneau (eds), *Leviathan after 350 Years*, 33–73. Oxford: Clarendon Press.

Hoekstra, Kinch. 2006. 'The End of Philosophy (The Case of Hobbes)', *Proceedings of the Aristotelian Society* 106, no. 1: 25–62.

Hoekstra, Kinch. 2007. 'Hobbes on the Natural Condition of Mankind' in Patricia Springborg (ed), *The Cambridge Companion to Hobbes's Leviathan*, 109–127. Cambridge: Cambridge University Press.

Hoekstra, Kinch. 2012. 'Thucydides and the Bellicose Beginnings of Modern Political Theory' in Katherine Harloe and Neville Morley (eds), *Thucydides and the Modern World*, 25–54. Cambridge: Cambridge University Press.

Hoekstra, Kinch. 2013. 'Hobbesian Equality' in S.A. Lloyd (ed), *Hobbes Today: Insights for the 21st Century*, 76–112. Cambridge: Cambridge University Press.

Hoekstra, Kinch. 2016. 'Hobbes's Thucydides' in A.P. Martinich and Kinch Hoekstra (eds), *The Oxford Handbook of Hobbes*, 547–574. Oxford: Oxford University Press.

278 BIBLIOGRAPHY

Hohfeld, W.N. 1923. *Fundamental Legal Conceptions*, ed. W.W. Cook. New Haven: Yale University Press.

Holden, Thomas. 2016. 'Hobbes on the Function of Evaluative Speech', *Canadian Journal of Philosophy* 46, no. 1: 123–144.

Holland, Ben. 2017. *The Moral Person of the State: Pufendorf, Sovereignty and Composite Polities*. Cambridge: Cambridge University Press.

Honoré, Tony. 2002. 'The Necessary Connection between Law and Morality', *Oxford Journal of Legal Studies* 22, no. 3: 489–495.

Höpfl, Harro. 2004. *Jesuit Political Thought: The Society of Jesus and the State, c.1540–1640*. Cambridge: Cambridge University Press.

Hörnqvist, Mikael. 2004. *Machiavelli and Empire*. Cambridge: Cambridge University Press.

Hoye, J. Matthew. 2019. 'Natural Justice, Law, and Virtue in Hobbes's *Leviathan*', *Hobbes Studies* 32, no. 2: 179–208.

Hume, David. 1998 [1751]. *Enquiry Concerning the Principles of Morals*, ed. Tom L. Beauchamp. Oxford: Clarendon Press.

Hüning, Dieter. 2000. 'Inter Arma Silent Leges: Naturrecht, Staat und Völkerrecht bei Thomas Hobbes' in Rüdiger Voigt (ed), *Der Leviathan*, 129–164. Baden-Baden: Nomos.

Hüning, Dieter. 2002. 'From the Virtue of Justice to the Concept of Legal Order: The Significance of the *suum cuique tribuere* in Hobbes's Political Philosophy' in Ian Hunter and David Saunders (eds), *Natural Law and Civil Sovereignty*, 139–152. New York: Palgrave-Macmillan.

Hüning, Dieter. 2007. 'Hobbes on the Right to Punish' in Patricia Springborg (ed), *The Cambridge Companion to Hobbes's Leviathan*, 217–240. Cambridge: Cambridge University Press.

Hurd, Heidi M. 1996. 'The Moral Magic of Consent', *Legal Theory* 2, no. 2: 121–146.

Husak, Douglas. 2010. *The Philosophy of Criminal Law: Selected Essays*. Oxford: Oxford University Press.

Hutton, Sarah. 2014. 'Intellectual History and the History of Philosophy', *History of European Ideas* 40, no. 7: 925–937.

Ibbetson, David. 2013. '*Iniuria*, Roman and English' in Eric Descheemaeker and Helen Scott (eds), *Iniuria and the Common Law*, 33–48. Oxford: Hart.

Ingman, T. 1981. 'A History of the Defence of Volenti Non Fit Injuria', *Juridical Review* 26: 1–29.

Isidore of Seville. 2006. *The Etymologies*, ed. Stephen A. Barney et al. Cambridge: Cambridge University Press.

Jack, Sybil M. 2004. '"A Pattern for a King's Inauguration": The Coronation of James I in England', *Parergon* 21, no. 2: 67–91.

Jaede, Maximilian. 2016. 'Hobbes on the Making and Unmaking of Citizens', *Critical Review of International Social and Political Philosophy* 19, no. 1: 86–102.

Jaede, Maximilian. 2017. 'Forgiveness and Reconciliation in Hobbes's Natural Law Theory', *History of European Ideas* 43, no. 8: 831–842.

James, Aaron. 2012. *Fairness in Practice: A Social Contract for a Global Economy*. Oxford: Oxford University Press.

James, Aaron. 2013. 'Hobbesian Assurance Problems and Global Justice' in S.A. Lloyd (ed), *Hobbes Today: Insights for the 21st Century*, 264–287. Cambridge: Cambridge University Press.

Johnston, David. 2011. *A Brief History of Justice*. Malden, MA: Wiley-Blackwell.

Kalmanovitz, Pablo. 2018. 'Early Modern Sources of the Regular War Tradition' in Seth Lazar and Helen Frowe (eds), *The Oxford Handbook of Ethics of War*, 145–164. Oxford: Oxford University Press.

Kant, Immanuel. 1996. *Practical Philosophy*, ed. and transl. M.J. Gregor. Cambridge: Cambridge University Press.

Kavka, G.S. 1986. *Hobbesian Moral and Political Theory*. Princeton: Princeton University Press.

Kavka, G.S. 1988. 'Some Neglected Liberal Aspects of Hobbes's Philosophy', *Hobbes Studies* 1, no. 1: 89–108.

Kavka, G.S. 1995. 'The Rationality of Rule-Following: Hobbes's Dispute with the Foole', *Law and Philosophy* 14, no. 1: 5–34.

BIBLIOGRAPHY 279

Kelsen, Hans. 1971 [1957]. 'What Is Justice?' in idem, *What Is Justice? Justice, Law, and Politics in the Mirror of Science*, 1–24. Los Angeles: University of California Press.

Keyt, David. 1988. 'Injustice and Pleonexia in Aristotle', *Southern Journal of Philosophy* 27, suppl. 251–257.

Keyt, David. 1991. 'Aristotle's Theory of Distributive Justice' in David Keyt and F.D. Miller (eds), *A Companion to Aristotle's Politics*, 238–278. Oxford: Blackwell.

King James VI and I. 1995. *Political Writings*, ed. Johann P. Sommerville. Cambridge: Cambridge University Press.

Kingsbury, Benedict and Benjamin Straumann (eds). 2011. *Alberico Gentili: The Wars of the Romans*, transl. David Lupher. Oxford: Oxford University Press.

Kleist, Heinrich von. 2013. *Michael Kohlhaas*, ed. Axel Schmitt. Berlin: Suhrkamp.

Klimchuk, Dennis. 2012. 'Hobbes on Equity' in David Dyzenhaus and Thomas Poole (eds), *Hobbes and the Law*, 165–185. Cambridge: Cambridge University Press.

Klimchuk, Dennis. 2018. 'Grotius on Property and the Right of Necessity', *Journal of the History of Philosophy* 56, no. 2: 239–260.

Kramer, Matthew H. 2004. 'On the Separability of Law and Morality', *Canadian Journal of Law and Jurisprudence* 17, no. 2: 315–336.

Lærke, Mogens, J.E.H. Smith, and Eric Schliesser (eds). 2013. *Philosophy and Its History: Aims and Methods in the Study of Early Modern Philosophy*. Oxford: Oxford University Press.

Laird, John. 1934. *Hobbes*. London: E. Benn.

Lamprecht, S.P. 1940. 'Hobbes and Hobbism', *American Political Science Review* 34, no. 1: 31–53.

Lang, Anthony F. and Gabriella Slomp. 2016. 'Thomas Hobbes: Theorist of Law', *Critical Review of International Social and Political Philosophy* 19, no. 1: 1–11.

Lawson, George. 1992 [1660]. *Politica Sacra et Civilis*, ed. Conal Condran. Cambridge: Cambridge University Press.

LeBuffe, Michael. 2007. 'Hobbes's Reply to the Fool', *Philosophy Compass* 2, no. 1: 31–45.

Lee, Daniel. 2012. 'Hobbes and the Civil Law: The Use of Roman Law in Hobbes's Civil Science' in David Dyzenhaus and Thomas Poole (eds), *Hobbes and the Law*, 210–235. Cambridge: Cambridge University Press.

Lee, Daniel. 2013. '"Office Is a Thing Borrowed": Jean Bodin on Offices and Seigneurial Government', *Political Theory* 41, no. 3: 409–440.

Lee, Daniel. 2018. 'Unmaking Law: Jean Bodin on Law, Equity and Legal Change', *History of Political Thought* 39, no. 2: 269–296.

Lee, Daniel. 2020. 'Sovereignty and Dominium: The Foundations of Hobbesian Statehood' in Robin Douglass and Johan Olsthoorn (eds), *Hobbes's On the Citizen: A Critical Guide*, 126–144. Cambridge: Cambridge University Press.

Lee, Daniel. 2021. *The Right of Sovereignty: Jean Bodin on the Sovereign State and the Law of Nations*. Oxford: Oxford University Press.

Leibniz, G.W. 1985 [1710]. *Theodicy*, ed. Austin Farrer, transl. E.M. Huggard. La Salle, Illinois: Open Court.

Leibniz, G.W. 1988. *Political Writings*, ed. Patrick Riley. Cambridge: Cambridge University Press.

Lemos, R.M. 1978. *Hobbes and Locke: Power and Consent*. Athens: University of Georgia Press.

Lenhoff, Arthur. 1942. 'Development of the Concept of Eminent Domain', *Columbia Law Review* 42, no. 4: 596–638.

Lintott, A.W. 1974. 'Cicero and Milo', *The Journal of Roman Studies* 64: 62–78.

Lipsius, Justus. 2004 [1589]. *Politica*, ed. Jan Waszink. Assen: Van Gorcum.

Lloyd, S.A. 1992. *Ideals as Interests in Hobbes's Leviathan: The Power of Mind over Matter*. Cambridge: Cambridge University Press.

Lloyd, S.A. 1997. 'Coercion, Ideology, and Education in Hobbes's *Leviathan*' in Andrews Reath, Barbara Herman, and Christine Korsgaard (eds), *Reclaiming the History of Ethics: Essays for John Rawls*, 36–65. Cambridge: Cambridge University Press.

Lloyd, S.A. 2001. 'Hobbes's Self-Effacing Natural Law Theory', *Pacific Philosophical Quarterly* 82, no. 3–4: 285–308.

280 BIBLIOGRAPHY

Lloyd, S.A. 2005. 'Hobbes's Reply to the Foole: A Deflationary Definitional Interpretation', *Hobbes Studies* 18, no. 1: 50–73.

Lloyd, S.A. 2009. *Morality in the Philosophy of Thomas Hobbes: Cases in the Law of Nature.* Cambridge: Cambridge University Press.

Lloyd, S.A. 2013. 'International Relations, World Government, and the Ethics of War: A Hobbesian Perspective' in idem (ed), *Hobbes Today: Insights for the 21st Century*, 288–303. Cambridge: Cambridge University Press.

Lloyd, S.A. 2016. 'Authorization and Moral Responsibility in the Philosophy of Hobbes', *Hobbes Studies* 29, no. 2: 169–188.

Lloyd, S.A. 2016. 'Natural Law' in A.P. Martinich and Kinch Hoekstra (eds), *The Oxford Handbook of Hobbes*, 264–289. Oxford: Oxford University Press.

Lloyd, S.A. 2018. 'Hobbes on the Duty Not to Act on Conscience' in Robin Douglass and Laurens van Apeldoorn (eds), *Hobbes on Politics and Religion*, 256–272. Oxford: Oxford University Press.

Lloyd, S.A. 2021. 'The State of Nature as a Continuum Concept' in Marcus Adams (ed), *A Companion to Hobbes*, 156–170. Malden, MA: Blackwell-Wiley.

Lobban, Michael. 2007. *A Treatise of Legal Philosophy and General Jurisprudence. Vol. VIII: A History of the Philosophy of Law in the Common Law World, 1600–1900.* Dordrecht: Springer.

Lobban, Michael. 2012. 'Thomas Hobbes and the Common Law' in David Dyzenhaus and Thomas Poole (eds), *Hobbes and the Law*, 39–67. Cambridge: Cambridge University Press.

Locke, John. 1975 [1689]. *An Essay Concerning Human Understanding*, ed. P.H. Nidditch. Oxford: Oxford University Press.

Locke, John. 1988 [1690]. *Two Treatises of Government*, ed. Peter Laslett. Cambridge: Cambridge University Press.

Locke, John. 1997. *Locke: Political Essays*, ed. Mark Goldie. Cambridge: Cambridge University Press.

Lockwood, Matthew. 2013. 'From Treason to Homicide: Changing Conceptions of the Law of Petty Treason in Early Modern England', *Journal of Legal History* 34, no. 1: 31–49.

Long, A.A. and D.N. Sedley (eds). 1987. *The Hellenistic Philosophers*, vol. 1. Cambridge: Cambridge University Press.

Lopata, B.B. 1973. 'Property Theory in Hobbes', *Political Theory* 1, no. 2: 203–218.

Lott, Tommy L. 1992. 'Hobbes's Right of Nature', *History of Philosophy Quarterly* 9, no. 2: 159–180.

Luban, Daniel. 2018. 'Hobbesian Slavery', *Political Theory* 46, no. 5: 726–748.

Luban, David. 2004. 'Preventive War', *Philosophy and Public Affairs* 32, no. 3: 207–248.

Ludwig, Bernd. 1998. *Die Wiederentdeckung des Epikureischen Naturrechts. Zu Thomas Hobbes' philosophischer Entwicklung von 'De Cive' zum 'Leviathan' im Pariser Exil, 1640–1651.* Frankfurt a.M.: Klostermann.

Luther, Martin. 1991 [1523]. 'On Secular Authority' in *Luther and Calvin on Secular Authority*, ed. Harro Höpfl, 3–43. Cambridge: Cambridge University Press.

Machiavelli, Niccolò. 1988 [1532]. *The Prince*, ed. Quentin Skinner and Russell Price. Cambridge: Cambridge University Press.

Machiavelli, Niccolò. 1989. *The Chief Works and Others*, 3 vols, ed. Allan Gilbert. Durham: Duke University Press.

Macpherson, C.B. 1962. *The Political Theory of Possessive Individualism: Hobbes to Locke.* Oxford: Clarendon Press.

Macpherson, C.B. 1968. 'Introduction' in *Hobbes: Leviathan*, ed. C.B. Macpherson, 9–63. Baltimore: Penguin.

Malcolm, Joyce Lee. 1999. 'Doing No Wrong: Law, Liberty, and the Constraint of Kings', *Journal of British Studies* 38, no. 2: 161–186.

Malcolm, Noel. 2002. *Aspects of Hobbes*. Oxford: Oxford University Press.

Malcolm, Noel. 2005. 'What Hobbes *Really* Said', *The National Interest* 81: 122–128.

Malcolm, Noel. 2007. *Reason of State, Propaganda, and the Thirty Year's War: An Unknown Translation by Thomas Hobbes*. Oxford: Clarendon Press.

BIBLIOGRAPHY   281

Malcolm, Noel. 2016. 'Thomas Hobbes: Liberal Illiberal', *Journal of the British Academy* 4: 113–136.

Maloy, J.S. 2009. 'The Aristotelianism of Locke's Politics', *Journal of the History of Ideas* 70, no. 2: 235–257.

Mara, Gerald M. 1988. 'Hobbes's Counsel to Sovereigns', *The Journal of Politics* 50, no. 2: 390–411.

Marmor, Andrei. 2006. 'Legal Positivism: Still Descriptive and Morally Neutral', *Oxford Journal of Legal Studies* 26, no. 4: 683–704.

Martinich, A.P. 1992. *The Two Gods of Leviathan: Thomas Hobbes on Religion and Politics*. Cambridge: Cambridge University Press.

Martinich, A.P. 1995. *A Hobbes Dictionary*. Cambridge, MA: Blackwell.

Martinich, A.P. 2021. *Hobbes's Political Philosophy: Interpretation and Interpretations*. Oxford: Oxford University Press.

Mathie, William. 1987. 'Justice and Equity: An Inquiry into the Meaning and Role of Equity in the Hobbesian Account of Justice and Politics' in Craig Walton and Paul Johnston (eds), *Hobbes's Science of Natural Justice*, 257–276. Dordrecht: Martinus Nijhoff.

Mautner, Thomas. 2005. 'Grotius and the Skeptics', *Journal of the History of Ideas* 66, no. 4: 577–601.

Mautner, Thomas. 2013. 'Natural Law and Natural Rights' in Peter R. Anstey (ed), *The Oxford Handbook of British Philosophy in the Seventeenth Century*, 472–497. Oxford: Oxford University Press.

May, Larry. 1980. 'Hobbes's Contract Theory', *Journal of the History of Philosophy* 18, no. 2: 195–207.

May, Larry. 1987. 'Hobbes on Equity and Justice' in Craig Walton and Paul Johnston (eds), *Hobbes's Science of Natural Justice*, 241–252. Dordrecht: Martinus Nijhoff.

May, Larry. 2013. 'A Hobbesian Approach to Cruelty and the Rules of War', *Leiden Journal of International Law* 26, no. 2: 293–313.

May, Larry. 2013. *Limiting Leviathan: Hobbes on Law and International Affairs*. Oxford: Oxford University Press.

May, Larry. 2014. 'Limiting Leviathan: Reply to My Critics', *Hobbes Studies* 27, no. 2: 199–206.

May, Simon Căbulea. 2010. 'Moral Status and the Direction of Duties', *Ethics* 123, no. 1: 113–128.

May, Simon Căbulea. 2015. 'Directed Duties', *Philosophy Compass* 10, no. 8: 523–532.

McArthur, Neil. 2013. '"Thrown amongst Many": Hobbes on Taxation and Fiscal Policy' in S.A. Lloyd (ed), *Hobbes Today: Insights for the 21st Century*, 178–189. Cambridge: Cambridge University Press.

McMahan, Jeff. 2013. 'Hobbesian Defenses of Orthodox Just War Theory' in S.A. Lloyd (ed), *Hobbes Today: Insights for the 21st Century*, 304–319. Cambridge: Cambridge University Press.

McQueen, Alison. 2020. 'Hobbes's Strategy of Convergence', *Hobbes Studies* 33, no. 2: 135–152.

Mercer, Christia. 2019. 'The Contextualist Revolution in Early Modern Philosophy', *Journal of the History of Philosophy* 57, no. 3: 529–548.

Miller, David. 2012. 'Territorial Rights: Concept and Justification', *Political Studies* 60, no. 2: 252–268.

Milton, John. 1991. *Political Writings*, ed. Martin Dzelzainis. Cambridge: Cambridge University Press.

Missner, Marshall. 1983. 'Skepticism and Hobbes's Political Philosophy', *Journal of the History of Ideas* 44, no. 3: 407–427.

Morauta, James. 2004. 'Three Separation Theses', *Law and Philosophy* 23, no. 2: 111–135.

More, Henry. 1987 [1659]. *The Immortality of the Soul*, ed. Alexander Jacob. Dordrecht: Martinus Nijhoff.

Morgenthau, H.J. 1952. *American Foreign Policy: A Critical Examination*. London: Methuen.

Murphy, James Bernard. 2005. *The Philosophy of Positive Law: Foundations of Jurisprudence*. New Haven: Yale University Press.

Murphy, Mark. 1994. 'Hobbes on Tacit Covenants', *Hobbes Studies* 7, no. 1: 69–94.

Murphy, Mark. 1994. 'Deviant Uses of "Obligation" in Hobbes' *Leviathan*', *History of Philosophy Quarterly* 11, no. 3: 281–294.

282 BIBLIOGRAPHY

Murphy, Mark. 1995. 'Was Hobbes a Legal Positivist?', *Ethics* 105, no. 4: 846–873.

Murphy, Mark. 2016. 'Hobbes (and Austin, and Aquinas) on Law as Command of the Sovereign' in A.P. Martinich and Kinch Hoekstra (eds), *The Oxford Handbook of Hobbes*, 339–358. Oxford: Oxford University Press.

Nagel, Thomas. 1959. 'Hobbes's Concept of Obligation', *The Philosophical Review* 68, no. 1: 68–83.

Nagel, Thomas. 2005. 'The Problem of Global Justice', *Philosophy and Public Affairs* 33, no. 2: 113–147.

Nauta, Lodi. 2002. 'Hobbes on Religion and the Church between *The Elements of Law* and *Leviathan*: A Dramatic Change of Direction?', *Journal of the History of Ideas* 63, no. 4: 577–598.

Neff, Stephen C. 2005. *War and the Law of Nations: A General History*. Cambridge: Cambridge University Press.

Nelson, Eric. 2004. *The Greek Tradition in Republican Thought*. Cambridge: Cambridge University Press.

Nozick, Robert. 1974. *Anarchy, State and Utopia*. Oxford: Basic Books.

Odzuck, Eva. 2017. 'The Concept of Trust in Hobbes's Political Philosophy' in Laszlo Kontler and Mark Somos (eds), *Trust and Happiness in the History of European Political Thought*, 118–141. Leiden: Brill.

Olivecrona, Karl. 2010. 'The Two Levels in Natural Law Thinking', ed. Thomas Mautner, *Jurisprudence* 1, no. 2: 197–224.

Olsthoorn, Johan. 2013. 'Hobbes's Account of Distributive Justice as Equity', *British Journal for the History of Philosophy* 21, no. 1: 13–33.

Olsthoorn, Johan. 2014. 'Forfeiting Citizenship: Hobbes on Traitors, Rebels, and Enemies' in Paschalis M. Kitromilides (ed), *Athenian Legacies: European Debates on Citizenship*, 237–252. Firenze: Olschki.

Olsthoorn, Johan. 2015. 'Hobbes on Justice, Property Rights, and Self-Ownership', *History of Political Thought* 36, no. 3: 471–498.

Olsthoorn, Johan. 2015. 'Why Justice and Injustice Have no Place outside the Hobbesian State', *European Journal of Political Theory* 14, no. 1: 19–36.

Olsthoorn, Johan. 2016. 'Spinoza on Human and Divine Justice', *History of Philosophy Quarterly* 33, no. 1: 21–41.

Olsthoorn, Johan. 2018. 'Grotius and the Early Modern Tradition' in Larry May (ed), *The Cambridge Handbook of the Just War*, 33–56. Cambridge: Cambridge University Press.

Olsthoorn, Johan. 2018. 'Two Ways of Theorizing Collective Ownership of the Earth' in James Penner and Michael Otsuka (eds), *Property Theory: Legal and Political Perspectives*, 187–213. Cambridge: Cambridge University Press.

Olsthoorn, Johan. 2020. 'Francisco Suárez and Hugo Grotius on Distributive Justice and Imperfect Rights', *History of Political Thought* 41, no. 1: 96–119.

Olsthoorn, Johan. 2020. 'On the Absence of Moral Goodness in Hobbes's Ethics', *The Journal of Ethics* 24, no. 2: 241–266.

Olsthoorn, Johan. 2021. 'Hobbes on International Ethics' in Marcus Adams (ed), *A Companion to Hobbes*, 252–267. Malden, MA: Blackwell-Wiley.

Olsthoorn, Johan. 2021. '*Leviathan* Inc.: Hobbes on the Nature and Person of the Commonwealth', *History of European Ideas* 47, no. 1: 17–32.

Olsthoorn, Johan. 2024. 'Between Starvation and Spoilage: Conceptual Foundations of Locke's Theory of Original Appropriation', *Archiv für Geschichte der Philosophie* 106, no. 2: 236–266.

Orr, D. Alan. 2002. *Treason and the State: Law, Politics, and Ideology in the English Civil War*. Cambridge: Cambridge University Press.

Parkin, John. 2007. *Taming the Leviathan: The Reception of the Political and Religious Ideas of Thomas Hobbes in England, 1640–1700*. Cambridge: Cambridge University Press.

Pasqualucci, Paolo. 1990. 'Hobbes and the Myth of "Final War"', *Journal of the History of Ideas* 51, no. 4: 647–657.

Pasquino, Pasquale. 1998. 'Locke on King's Prerogative', *Political Theory* 26, no. 2: 198–208.

Pateman, Carole. 1988. *The Sexual Contract*. Cambridge: Polity.

Peacock, Mark. 2010. 'Obligation and Advantage in Hobbes' *Leviathan*', *Canadian Journal of Philosophy* 40, no. 3: 433–458.

Peters, Richard S. 1967 [1956]. *Hobbes*, second edition. Harmondsworth: Penguin.

Pettit, Philip. 2008. *Made with Words: Hobbes on Language, Mind, and Politics*. Princeton: Princeton University Press.

Pierson, Christopher. 2013. *Just Property: A History in the Latin West, Vol. I: Wealth, Virtue and the Law*. Oxford: Oxford University Press.

Piirimäe, Pärtel. 2010. 'Alberico Gentili's Doctrine of Defensive War and Its Impact on Seventeenth-Century Normative Views' in Benedict Kingsbury and Benjamin Straumann (eds), *The Roman Foundations of the Law of Nations: Alberico Gentili and the Justice of Empire*, 187–209. Oxford: Oxford University Press.

Pink, Thomas. 2011. 'Thomas Hobbes and the Ethics of Freedom', *Inquiry* 54, no. 5: 541–563.

Pino, Giorgio. 2014. 'Positivism, Legal Validity, and the Separation of Law and Morals', *Ratio Juris* 27, no. 2: 190–217.

Plato. 1997. *Complete Works*, ed. J.M. Cooper. Indianapolis: Hackett.

Poole, Thomas. 2012. 'Hobbes on Law and Prerogative' in David Dyzenhaus and Thomas Poole (eds), *Hobbes and the Law*, 68–96. Cambridge: Cambridge University Press.

Poole, Thomas. 2015. *Reason of State: Law, Prerogative and Empire*. Cambridge: Cambridge University Press.

Prall, Stuart E. 1964. 'The Development of Equity in Tudor England', *American Journal of Legal History* 8, no. 1: 1–19.

Pufendorf, Samuel. 1729 [1672]. *Of the Law of Nature and Nations*, transl. Basil Kennett. London: printed for J. Walthoe et al.

Pufendorf, Samuel. 2003 [1673]. *The Whole Duty of Man, According to the Law of Nature*, ed. Ian Hunter and David Saunders. Indianapolis: Liberty Fund.

Pufendorf, Samuel. 1990 [1675]. *On the Natural State of Men*, ed. and transl. Michael Seidler. Lewiston, NY: Mellen Press.

Pufendorf, Samuel. 2014. *The Pufendorf Lectures*, ed. Bo Lindberg. Stockholm: KVHAA.

Rachel, Samuel. 1916 [1676]. *Dissertations on the Law of Nature and of Nations*, ed. Ludwig von Bar. Washington: Carnegie Institution.

Ramelet, Laetitia. 2022. 'Hobbes and the Indirect Workings of Political Consent', *Hobbes Studies* 35, no. 2: 155–175.

Raphael, D.D. 1988. 'Hobbes on Justice' in G.A.J. Rogers and Alan Ryan (eds), *Perspectives on Thomas Hobbes*, 153–170. Oxford: Clarendon Press.

Raphael, D.D. 2001. *Concepts of Justice*. Oxford: Clarendon Press.

Rawleigh, Walter. 1650. *A Discourse of the Originall and Fundamentall Cause of Naturall, Customary, Arbitrary, Voluntary and Necessary Warre*. London: printed by T.W. for Humphrey Moseley.

Rawls, John. 2007. *Lectures on the History of Political Philosophy*, ed. Samuel Freeman. Cambridge, MA: Harvard University Press.

Raz, Joseph. 1979. *The Authority of Law: Essays on Law and Morality*. Oxford: Clarendon Press.

Reichberg, Gregory M. 2007. 'Preventive War in Classical Just War Theory', *Journal of the History of International Law* 9, no. 1: 5–34.

Reichberg, Gregory M. 2008. 'Just War and Regular War: Competing Paradigms' in David Rodin and Henry Shue (eds), *Just and Unjust Warriors: The Moral and Legal Status of Soldiers*, 193–213. Oxford: Oxford University Press.

Reichberg, Gregory M. 2017. *Thomas Aquinas on War and Peace*. Cambridge: Cambridge University Press.

Reichberg, Gregory M., Henrik Syse, and Endre Begby (eds). 2006. *The Ethics of War: Classic and Contemporary Readings*. Malden, MA: Blackwell.

Reid, Thomas. 2007. *On Practical Ethics*, ed. Knud Haakonssen. Edinburgh: Edinburgh University Press.

Reinhardt, Nicole. 2016. *Voices of Conscience: Royal Confessors and Political Counsel in Seventeenth-Century Spain and France*. Oxford: Oxford University Press.

BIBLIOGRAPHY

Rhodes, Rosamond. 2009. 'Hobbes's Fifth Law of Nature and Its Implications', *Hobbes Studies* 22, no. 2: 144–159.

Risse, Mathias. 2020. *On Justice: Philosophy, History, Foundations*. Cambridge: Cambridge University Press.

Robison, Meghan. 2023. 'Mother Lords: Original Maternal Dominion and the Practice of Preservation in Hobbes', *Hypatia* 38, no. 1: 65–85.

Robson, Gregory J. 2015. 'Two Psychological Defenses of Hobbes's Claim against the "Fool"', *Hobbes Studies* 28, no. 2: 132–148.

Rodin, David. 2002. *War and Self-Defense*. Oxford: Clarendon Press.

Rosen, Michael. 2011. 'The History of Ideas as Philosophy and History', *History of Political Thought* 32, no. 4: 691–720.

Rosler, Andrés. 2011. 'Odi et Amo? Hobbes on the State of Nature', *Hobbes Studies* 24, no. 1: 91–111.

Rousseau, J.J. 1987 [1762]. 'On the Social Contract' in *Jean-Jacques Rousseau: The Basic Political Writings*, ed. D.A. Cress, 141–227. Indianapolis: Hackett.

Rousseau, J.J. 2005. 'The State of War' in *The Collected Writings of Rousseau*, vol. 11, ed. Christopher Kelly, 61–73. Hanover: University Press of New England.

Russell, Frederick H. 1975. *The Just War in the Middle Ages*. Cambridge: Cambridge University Press.

Rutherford, Samuel. 1644. *Lex, Rex: The Law and the Prince. A Dispute for the Just Prerogative of King and People*. London: printed for John Field.

Ryan, Alan. 1996. 'Hobbes's Political Philosophy' in Tom Sorell (ed), *The Cambridge Companion to Hobbes*, 208–245. Cambridge: Cambridge University Press.

Saastamoinen, Kari. 2002. 'Hobbes and Pufendorf on Natural Equality and Civil Sovereignty' in Ian Hunter and David Saunders (eds), *Natural Law and Civil Sovereignty*, 189–203. New York: Palgrave MacMillan.

Sachs, David. 1995. 'Notes on Unfairly Gaining More: Pleonexia' in Rosalind Hursthouse, Gavin Lawrence, and Warren Quinn (eds), *Virtues and Reasons: Philippa Foot and Moral Theory*, 176–183. Oxford: Oxford University Press.

Salter, John. 2005. 'Grotius and Pufendorf on the Right of Necessity', *History of Political Thought* 26, no. 2: 284–302.

Scaltsas, Theodore. 1995. 'Reciprocal Justice in Aristotle's *Nicomachean Ethics*', *Archiv für Geschichte der Philosophie* 77, no. 3: 248–262.

Schmitt, Carl. 1996 [1938]. *The Leviathan in the State Theory of Thomas Hobbes: Meaning and Failure of a Political Symbol*, transl. George Schwab. Westport, CT: Greenwood Press.

Schmitt, Carl. 2007 [1932]. *The Concept of the Political*, expanded edition, ed. George Schwab. Chicago: The University of Chicago Press.

Schneewind, J.B. 2010. *Essays on the History of Moral Philosophy*. Oxford: Oxford University Press.

Schröder, Peter. 2017. *Trust in Early Modern International Political Thought, 1598–1713*. Cambridge: Cambridge University Press.

Schwartz, Daniel. 2012. 'Suárez on Distributive Justice' in idem (ed), *Interpreting Suárez: Critical Essays*, 163–184. Cambridge: Cambridge University Press.

Schwartz, Daniel. 2018. 'Late Scholastic Just War Theory' in Seth Lazar and Helen Frowe (eds), *The Oxford Handbook of Ethics of War*, 122–144. Oxford: Oxford University Press.

Schwartz, Daniel. 2018. 'Thomas Aquinas and Antonio de Córdoba on Self-Defence: Saving Yourself as a Private End', *British Journal for the History of Philosophy* 26, no. 6: 1045–1063.

Seneca. 2011. *On Benefits*, ed. Miriam Griffin and Brad Inwood. Chicago: The University of Chicago Press.

Sexby, Edward. 1986 [1657]. 'Killing Noe Murder' in David Wootton (ed), *Divine Right and Democracy: An Anthology of Political Writing in Stuart England*, 360–388. Harmondsworth: Middlesex.

Shakespeare, William. 2008. *The Norton Shakespeare*, second edition, ed. Stephen Greenblatt et al. New York: W.W. Norton.

BIBLIOGRAPHY   285

Shaver, Robert. 1996. 'Grotius on Scepticism and Self-Interest', *Archiv für Geschichte der Philosophie* 78, no. 1: 27–47.

Sheridan, Patricia. 2011 'Resisting the Scaffold: Self-Preservation and Limits of Obligation in Hobbes's *Leviathan*', *Hobbes Studies* 24, no. 2: 137–157.

Shue, Henry and David Rodin (eds). 2007. *Preemption: Military Action and Moral Justification.* Oxford: Oxford University Press.

Sidney, Algernon. 1996 [1698]. *Discourses Concerning Government*, ed. Thomas G. West. Indianapolis: Liberty Fund.

Skidelsky, Edward. 2019. 'What Moral Philosophers Can Learn from the History of Moral Concepts', *History of European Ideas* 45, no. 3: 311–321.

Skinner, Quentin. 1978. *The Foundations of Modern Political Thought, Vol. 2: The Age of Reformation.* Cambridge: Cambridge University Press.

Skinner, Quentin. 1981. *Machiavelli: A Very Short Introduction.* Oxford: Oxford University Press.

Skinner, Quentin. 1988. 'A Reply to My Critics' in James Tully (ed), *Meaning and Context: Quentin Skinner and His Critics*, 231–288. Cambridge: Cambridge University Press.

Skinner, Quentin. 1996. *Reason and Rhetoric in the Philosophy of Hobbes.* Cambridge: Cambridge University Press.

Skinner, Quentin. 2002. *Visions of Politics, Vol. I: Regarding Method.* Cambridge: Cambridge University Press.

Skinner, Quentin. 2003. 'States and the Freedom of Citizens' in Quentin Skinner and Bo Stråth (eds), *States and Citizens: History, Theory, Prospects*, 11–27. Cambridge: Cambridge University Press.

Skinner, Quentin. 2008. *Hobbes and Republican Liberty.* Cambridge: Cambridge University Press.

Skinner, Quentin. 2018. *From Humanism to Hobbes: Studies in Rhetoric and Politics.* Cambridge: Cambridge University Press.

Slomp, Gabriella. 2007. 'Kant against Hobbes: Reasoning and Rhetoric', *Journal of Moral Philosophy* 4, no. 2: 207–222.

Slomp, Gabriella. 2022. *Hobbes against Friendship: The Modern Marginalisation of an Ancient Political Concept.* Cham: Palgrave Macmillan.

Smith, David Chan. 2014. *Sir Edward Coke and the Reformation of the Laws: Religion, Politics and Jurisprudence, 1578–1616.* Cambridge: Cambridge University Press.

Sommerville, J.P. 1992. *Thomas Hobbes: Political Ideas in Historical Context.* London: Macmillan Press.

Sommerville, J.P. 1996. 'Lofty Science and Local Politics' in Tom Sorell (ed), *The Cambridge Companion to Hobbes*, 246–273. Cambridge: Cambridge University Press.

Sommerville, J.P. 2014 [1986]. *Royalists and Patriots: Politics and Ideology in England, 1603–1640*, second edition. London: Routledge.

Sommerville, J.P. 2016. 'Hobbes and Absolutism' in A.P. Martinich and Kinch Hoekstra (eds), *The Oxford Handbook of Hobbes*, 378–396. Oxford: Oxford University Press.

Sorabji, Richard. 2014. *Moral Conscience through the Ages: Fifth Century BCE to the Present.* Oxford: Oxford University Press.

Sorell, Tom. 2001. 'Hobbes and the Morality beyond Justice', *Pacific Philosophical Quarterly* 82, no. 3–4: 227–242.

Sorell, Tom. 2016. 'Law and Equity in Hobbes', *Critical Review of International Social and Political Philosophy* 19, no. 1: 29–46.

Spinoza, Benedictus de. 2016. *The Collected Works of Spinoza*, vol. 2, ed. and transl. Edwin Curley. Princeton: Princeton University Press.

Springborg, Patricia. 2009. '*Behemoth* and Hobbes's Science of Just and Unjust' in Tomaž Mastnak (ed), *Hobbes's Behemoth: Religion and Democracy*, 148–169. Exeter: Imprint Academic.

Springborg, Patricia. 2011. 'Hobbes's Fool the *Insipiens*, and the Tyrant-King', *Political Theory* 39, no. 1: 85–111.

Springborg, Patricia. 2015. 'Hobbes, Donne and the Virginia Company: *Terra Nullius* and "The Bulimia of Dominium"', *History of Political Thought* 36, no. 1: 113–164.

286 BIBLIOGRAPHY

Sreedhar, Susanne. 2010. *Hobbes on Resistance: Defying the Leviathan*. Cambridge: Cambridge University Press.

Sreedhar, Susanne. 2020. 'The Right of Nature and Political Obedience' in Robin Douglass and Johan Olsthoorn (eds), *Hobbes's On the Citizen: A Critical Guide*, 71–88. Cambridge: Cambridge University Press.

Sreedhar, Susanne. [forthcoming]. *Hobbes on Sex*. Oxford: Oxford University Press.

Sreenivasan, Gopal. 2010. 'Duties and Their Direction', *Ethics* 120, no. 3: 464–494.

Stephen, Leslie. 2012 [1904]. *Hobbes*. Cambridge: Cambridge University Press.

Stilz, Anna. 2019. *Territorial Sovereignty: A Philosophical Exploration*. Oxford: Oxford University Press.

Straumann, Benjamin. 2015. *Roman Law in the State of Nature: The Classical Foundations of Hugo Grotius' Natural Law*, transl. Belinda Cooper. Cambridge: Cambridge University Press.

Straumann, Benjamin. 2021. 'Thucydides, Hobbes, and the Melian Dialogue' in Mark Somos and Anne Peters (eds), *The State of Nature: Histories of an Idea*, 6–27. Leiden: Brill.

Strauss, Leo. 1952 [1936]. *The Political Philosophy of Hobbes: Its Basis and Its Genesis*, transl. E.M. Sinclair. Chicago: University of Chicago Press.

Strauss, Leo. 1953. *Natural Right and History*. Chicago: The University of Chicago Press.

Suárez, Francisco. 2015. *Selections from Three Works*, ed. Thomas Pink. Indianapolis: Liberty Fund.

Swanson, S.G. 1997. 'The Medieval Foundations of John Locke's Theory of Natural Rights: Rights of Subsistence and the Principle of Extreme Necessity', *History of Political Thought* 18, no. 3: 399–458.

Szabó, Kinga Tibori. 2011. *Anticipatory Action in Self-Defence: Essence and Limits under International Law*. The Hague: Springer.

Tarlton, Charles D. 2002. 'The Despotical Doctrine of Hobbes, Part 1: The Liberalization of Leviathan', *History of Political Thought* 22, no. 4: 587–618.

Taylor, A.E. 1938. 'The Ethical Doctrine of Hobbes', *Philosophy* 13, no. 52: 406–424.

Thivet, Delphine. 2008. 'Thomas Hobbes: A Philosopher of War or Peace?', *British Journal for the History of Philosophy* 16, no. 4: 701–721.

Thomasius, Christian. 2011 [1688/1705]. *Institutes of Divine Jurisprudence, with Selections from Foundations of the Law of Nature and Nations*, ed. Thomas Ahnert. Indianapolis: Liberty Fund.

Thompson, Martyn P. 1986. 'The History of Fundamental Law in Political Thought from the French Wars of Religion to the American Revolution', *American Historical Review* 91, no. 5: 1103–1128.

Thompson, Michael. 2004. 'What Is It to Wrong Someone? A Puzzle about Justice' in R. Jay Wallace, Philip Pettit, Samuel Scheffler, and Michael Smith (eds), *Reason and Value: Themes from the Philosophy of Joseph Raz*, 333–384. Oxford: Oxford University Press.

Thucydides. 1998. *The Peloponnesian War*, ed. and transl. Steven Lattimore. Indianapolis: Hackett.

Tuck, Richard. 1983. 'Grotius, Carneades and Hobbes', *Grotiana* 4, no. 1: 43–62.

Tuck, Richard. 1987. 'The "Modern" Theory of Natural Law' in Anthony Pagden (ed), *The Languages of Political Theory in Early-Modern Europe*, 99–120. Cambridge: Cambridge University Press.

Tuck, Richard. 1989. *Hobbes: A Very Short Introduction*. Oxford: Oxford University Press.

Tuck, Richard. 1993. *Philosophy and Government, 1572–1651*. Cambridge: Cambridge University Press.

Tuck, Richard. 1996. 'Hobbes's Moral Philosophy' in Tom Sorell (ed), *The Cambridge Companion to Hobbes*, 175–207. Cambridge: Cambridge University Press.

Tuck, Richard. 1999. *The Rights of War and Peace: Political Thought and the International Order from Grotius to Kant*. Oxford: Oxford University Press.

Tuck, Richard. 2013. 'Grotius, Hobbes, and Pufendorf on Humanitarian Intervention' in Stefano Recchia and J.M. Welsh (eds), *Just and Unjust Military Intervention: European Thinkers from Vitoria to Mill*, 96–112. Cambridge: Cambridge University Press.

Tully, James. 1980. *A Discourse on Property: John Locke and His Adversaries*. Cambridge: Cambridge University Press.

BIBLIOGRAPHY   287

[Tyrrell, James]. 1681. *Patriarcha non Monarcha: The Patriarch Unmonarch'd*. London: Richard Janeway.

[Tyrrell, James]. 1692. *A Brief Disquisition of the Law of Nature*. London: Richard Baldwin.

Undersrud, David. 2014. 'On Natural Law and Civil Law in the Political Philosophy of Hobbes', *History of Political Thought* 35, no. 4: 683–716.

Uniacke, Suzanne. 1994. *Permissible Killing: The Self-Defence Justification of Homicide*. Cambridge: Cambridge University Press.

Van Apeldoorn, Laurens. 2019. 'Hobbes on Evil' in Thomas Nys and Stephen de Wijze (eds), *The Routledge Handbook of the Philosophy of Evil*, 70–82. London: Routledge.

Van Apeldoorn, Laurens. 2020. 'On the Person and Office of the Sovereign in Hobbes' *Leviathan*', *British Journal for the History of Philosophy* 28, no. 1: 49–68.

Van Apeldoorn, Laurens. 2020. 'Property and Despotic Sovereignty' in Robin Douglass and Johan Olsthoorn (eds), *Hobbes's On the Citizen: A Critical Guide*, 108–125. Cambridge: Cambridge University Press.

Van Apeldoorn, Laurens. 2021. 'Hobbes on Property: Between Legal Certainty and Sovereign Discretion', *Hobbes Studies* 34, no. 1: 58–79.

Van Apeldoorn, Laurens. 2023. 'Hobbes on Treason and Fundamental Law', *Intellectual History Review* 33, no. 2: 183–203.

Van Duffel, Siegfried and Dennis Yap. 2011. 'Distributive Justice before the Eighteenth Century: The Right of Necessity', *History of Political Thought* 32, no. 3: 449–464.

Vattel, Emer de. 2008 [1758]. *The Law of Nations*, ed. Béla Kapossy and Richard Whatmore. Indianapolis: Liberty Fund.

Vaughan, Geoffrey M. 2002. *Behemoth Teaches Leviathan: Thomas Hobbes on Political Education*. Lanham: Lexington.

Velthuysen, Lambert van. 2013 [1649]. *A Letter on the Principles of Justness and Decency, Containing a Defence of the Treatise De Cive of the Learned Mr Hobbes* , ed. Malcolm de Mowbray. Leiden: Brill.

Venezia, Luciano. 2014. 'Hobbes' Two Accounts of Law and the Structure of Reasons for Political Obedience', *European Journal of Political Theory* 13, no. 3: 282–298.

Venezia, Luciano. 2015. *Hobbes on Legal Authority and Political Obligation*. New York: Palgrave Macmillan.

Vitoria, Francisco de. 1991. *Political Writings*, ed. Anthony Pagden and Jeremy Lawrance. Cambridge: Cambridge University Press.

Vollerthun, Ursula. 2017. *The Idea of International Society: Erasmus, Vitoria, Gentili and Grotius*, ed. James L. Richardson. Cambridge: Cambridge University Press.

Waldron, Jeremy. 1988. *The Right to Private Property*. Oxford: Clarendon Press.

Waldron, Jeremy. 2001. 'Hobbes and the Principle of Publicity', *Pacific Philosophical Quarterly* 82, no. 3–4: 447–474.

Wallis, John. 1662. *Hobbius Heauton-timorumenos, or a Consideration of Mr Hobbes His Dialogues*. Oxford: printed by A. & L. Lichfield.

Walzer, Michael. 2015 [1977]. *Just and Unjust Wars: A Moral Argument with Historical Illustrations*, fifth edition. New York: Basic Books.

Ward, Lee. 2020. 'Equity and Political Economy in Thomas Hobbes', *American Journal of Political Science* 64, no. 4: 823–835.

Warrender, Howard. 1957. *The Political Philosophy of Hobbes: His Theory of Obligation*. Oxford: Oxford University Press.

Warrender, Howard. 1962. 'Obligations and Rights in Hobbes', *Philosophy* 37, no. 142: 352–357.

Watkins, J.W.N. 1973 [1965]. *Hobbes's System of Ideas: A Study in the Political Significance of Philosophical Theories*. London: Hutchison and Co.

Watson, Alan (ed). 1985. *The Digest of Justinian*, 4 vols. Philadelphia: University of Pennsylvania Press.

Weithman, Paul. 2019. 'Hobbes on Persons and Authorization' in S.A. Lloyd (ed), *Interpreting Hobbes's Political Philosophy*, 173–190. Cambridge: Cambridge University Press.

288 BIBLIOGRAPHY

Whelan, F.G. 1981. 'Language and Its Abuses in Hobbes' Political Philosophy', *American Political Science Review* 75, no. 1: 59–75.

White, Michael J. 2019. 'How *Ius* (Right) Became Distinguished from *Lex* (Law): Two Early Episodes in the Story', *History of Political Thought* 40, no. 4: 583–606.

Williams, Bernard. 2005. *In the Beginning Was the Deed: Realism and Moralism in Political Argument*, ed. Geoffrey Hawthorn. Princeton: Princeton University Press.

Wilson, Catherine. 2008. *Epicureanism at the Origins of Modernity*. Oxford: Clarendon Press.

Wohlforth, William C. 2008. 'Realism' in Christian Reus-Smit and Duncan Snidal (eds), *The Oxford Handbook of International Relations*, 131–149. Oxford: Oxford University Press.

Wolff, Christian. 1934 [1749]. *Jus Gentium Methodo Scientifica Pertractatum*, 2 vols, ed. Joseph H. Drake. Oxford: Clarendon Press.

Wolin, Sheldon S. 2004 [1960]. *Politics and Vision: Continuity and Innovation in Western Political Thought*, expanded edition. Princeton: Princeton University Press.

Wright, George. 2004. 'Authority and Theodicy in Hobbes's *Leviathan*', *Rivista di Storia della Filosofia* 59, no. 1: 175–204.

Yates, Arthur. 2013. 'A Hohfeldian Analysis of Hobbesian Rights', *Law and Philosophy* 32, no. 4: 405–434.

Yates, Arthur. 2014. 'The Right to Punish in Thomas Hobbes's *Leviathan*', *Journal of the History of Philosophy* 52, no. 2: 233–254.

Young, Eileen. 1964. 'The Development of the Law of Diplomatic Relations', *British Yearbook of International Law* 40: 141–182.

Zagorin, Perez. 2000. 'Hobbes without Grotius', *History of Political Thought* 21, no. 1: 16–40.

Zagorin, Perez. 2007. 'Hobbes as a Theorist of Natural Law', *Intellectual History Review* 17, no. 3: 239–255.

Zagorin, Perez. 2009. *Hobbes and the Law of Nature*. Princeton: Princeton University Press.

Zaitchik, A. 1982. 'Hobbes's Reply to the Fool: The Problem of Consent and Obligation', *Political Theory* 10, no. 2: 245–266.

Zarka, Y.C. 1992. 'La Propriété chez Hobbes', *Archives de Philosophie* 55, no. 4: 587–605.

Zarka, Y.C. 2004. 'The Political Subject' in Tom Sorell and Luc Foisneau (eds), *Leviathan after 350 Years*, 167–182. Oxford: Clarendon Press.

Zouche, Richard. 1911 [1650]. *An Exposition of Fecial Law and Procedure, or of Law between Nations*, ed. J.L. Brierly. Washington: Carnegie Institution.

Index

For the benefit of digital users, indexed terms that span two pages (e.g., 52–53) may, on occasion, appear on only one of those pages.

Tables are indicated by an italic *t* following the page number.

absolutism, political 8, 14, 113–14, 145
action without right *see* injury
All Laws Just 145–46, 157–61
Allotment Argument 117–18, 127–31, 137–39, 267–68
ambassadors of peace 162, 196–97, 228–29
Aquinas, Thomas
  on justice and merit 91–93, 98–99, 106–7
  on war and self-defence 203–4, 207
argumentative overdetermination 24–25, 165–66, 171–72, 267–68
Aristotle 84, 150–51
  on justice 56–57, 90–93, 97, 110
  on natural inequality 99, 104
Assimilation Argument 224, 230–33, 235
Augustine 173, 206, 262
authorization 103, 152–53, 169–72, 254, 267–68
Authorization Argument 12, 24, 103, 146, 167–74, 267–68
Ayala, Balthazar 219–20, 247–48

Bacon, Francis 211, 215–16, 218, 237–38, 241
Bayle, Pierre 269
Bible 76–78
blame, moral 61–62, 65–66, 72–74
Bodin, Jean 4, 116, 137
Bramhall, John 6, 72, 158–60, 168, 251–52

charity 101, 214–15
children 249–50
  filial obligations of 50–55
Cicero 122–23n.28, 262
  on faith with pirates 219–20
  on war and self-defence 203–4, 205–6
citizen 248–50
Citizenship Forfeiture 242–43, 247–58, 261–62
Coke, Edward 158, 162, 164–65, 247–48, 260–61
Coke, Roger 39–40
Collective Victimhood 46–49
commonwealth
  as a corporate person 167, 197, 235, 249–50
  by acquisition 29–30, 51–52, 129–31

dissolution of 258, 262
  by institution 29–30, 43–44, 131
conceptual engineering 7–8, 268
conquest 53, 129–31, 202–3, 226–27, 229–30
consent 167–69
  attributed 31–32, 50–55
Consent Argument 24, 165, 167–70, 172–74, 267–68
contextualism 18–20
corpus juris civilis 32–33, 45, 127–28, 206 *see also* justice, *suum cuique tribuere*
corruption 56, 98–99, 100 *see also prosopolepsia*
covenant
  of mutual trust 183–84
  of peace 42, 48–49, 80–81, 141–42, 171–72, 187, 268–69
  of single trust 30, 183–84
  of subjection 42–43, 48–49, 51–54, 80–81, 187, 268–69
  validating conditions 182–85, 187–88
Covenant Argument 180–84
Creation Argument 117–18, 131, 135–40, 143–44, 192–94
crime 46–49, 62–63, 79–82, 157, 244–47, 260
  and legal excuses 112, 142–43, 151–52
cruelty 60–61, 200–1, 213
Cudworth, Ralph 6, 56n.3
Cumberland, Richard 33–34, 250

definitional convergence 25–26, 82
despotism 17, 51–52, 128–31, 139, 150–51
distrust 217–19 *see also* trust
dominium 128–31 *see also* property

education 9–10n.30
enmity, natural 198, 217–21, 246
Epicureanism 6
equality
  material 101, 111
  natural 50–51, 67–68, 71–74, 79, 201–2, 221
  of power 10, 42–43, 133, 226
  of worth 99–101, 106, 107–8

290   INDEX

equity 89–103, 109–15, 136–37, 162, 194–95
  broad 26, 94–96, 111
  narrow 26, 95–96, 101, 111–12, 136
  as procedural justice 110–15

fear *see* just fear
first seizure 111, 136–37 *see also* lot
fool 70–71, 245
  reply to the 258–61
freedom 149–50, 269–70
  absolute natural 50–51, 77–78, 231
free gift 106–7, 185–86

Gentili, Alberico 205, 210–11, 215–16, 218–21,
    237–38, 242–43, 247–48, 256
God
  judging conscience 68–70, 85, 184, 232
  as legislator 71, 74–78, 228, 265–66
  the mortal *see* sovereign
  see also theodicy, divine
gratitude 46, 218–19, 224–25, 234–36
Grotius, Hugo 8–9, 220–21
  on justice and rights 32–33, 38–39, 91–93,
    104–6, 110
  on property 119–21, 142–43
  on war and self-defence 203–4, 207–11, 214–
    15, 216–17, 223, 246–47

injury
  as action without right 25, 31–40, 64,
    79, 208–9
  directionality of 40–49, 79–81
  against God 71
  vs. loss 44–49
  as unjust action 25, 36–39, 64
  by violating natural law 63, 80–81
innocence
  legal 111–13
  in war 198, 207–9, 237

Jesus Christ 77, 112–13
jus ad bellum 203–5, 237–38
jus gentium see law of nations
just fear 182–85, 210–11, 215–17, 238–39
justice
  of arbitrators 9, 98–99, 100–1, 109–10, 135–
    37, 193–95
  commutative 12–14, 90–94, 97, 105–6, 126,
    136, 194–95
  of contractors 92–94, 126
  conventionalist reading of 5–8, 156–57
  criminal 92–93, 98–99, 111–14
  distributive 12–14, 90–92, 104–8, 143–44
    changing account of 96–101, 102–3

as duty of subjects 9, 136, 194–95
as equity 89–90, 98–103, 109–15, 136–37,
  160–61, 193–95
Leviathan's redefinition of 31–32, 36–38, 49,
  159–60, 189–90
suum cuique tribuere 16, 91, 103, 108–10, 115,
  136, 160–61, 193–94
universal 12–14, 90–91
virtue of 83–85, 194–95, 269–70

Kant, Immanuel 4, 12–13
King James VI & I 12, 97n.39, 165–66

labour 139–40
law
  agrarian 135n.75
  civil 149–53
  common 94–96, 164–65 *see also* equity, broad
  distributive 89–90, 131–44, 152, 160–
    61, 192–96
  divine positive 75–78 *see also* Bible
  fundamental 245–46
  of nations 199–200, 222–24, 227–40
  of nature *see* natural law
  penal 131–34, 152, 161
legal positivism 21–22, 145–49, 152, 172–75
    see also Separability Thesis;
    Sources Thesis
Leibniz, Gottfried Wilhelm 7–8, 10, 221
Liberality Argument 90, 96–97, 102–4, 108
liberty *see* freedom
Locke, John 38, 74, 200, 246–47
  on property 120–21
lot, distribution by 101, 111, 136–37

Machiavelli, Niccolò 3n.2, 16–17, 199, 241
merit 90, 103–10, 136–37, 160–61, 193–94
Merit-Grace Argument 90, 103, 107–8
morality *see* natural law
Mutual Containment Thesis 163–65

natural law 66–67
  binding in conscience 67, 69, 232–33
  as civil law 76–82, 163–65, 228
  as dictates of right reason 11, 74–76
  dispensation clause of 66–68, 120–21, 184–
    88, 200–1, 214–16, 225–26
  as distinct from justice of actions 11–12, 56–
    65, 78–82, 86, 180
  as divine law 74–78, 265–66
  as imposing directed duties 63, 79–81
  silent in war 63, 200–1, 225–26, 257–58
natural rights
  to enslave 198, 211–12, 226–27, 229–30

inalienable 37–38, 124, 142–43, 151–52, 184–85, 190, 209, 220–21
  laying down 40–43
  see also right of nature; resistance
No Accusation Without Law 65, 71–74, 78–79, 186
No Law Unjust 145–46, 165–76
No Pact Argument 13–14, 29–31, 45, 101–2, 159, 165–67
No Wicked Laws 162–65

obedience
  passive 4, 14
  simple 6–7, 42–43, 150–51
obligation
  directed vs. nondirected 11, 43, 50, 57–63, 79–81, 266–67
  of justice 11, 50, 57–60, 266–67
  self-assumed 50–55
  see also political obligation
ownership *see* dominium; property

pact *see* covenant
pardon 48, 257–58
passions 269–70 *see also* just fear; vain-glory
patrimonial kingdom *see* commonwealth by acquisition
peculium 127–31 *see also* property
personation *see* representation
pirates 184, 219–21, 247–48, 256
pleonexia 96, 97–100, 142
political legitimacy 239–40, 265
political obligation
  and citizenship 242–43, 256, 261–62
  double 44, 46
  release from 52–53, 242–43, 250–51, 258
power 212
  irresistible 10, 53n.63, 133n.68
Precision Argument 117, 124–27, 137–38, 143–44, 192
primogeniture 111, 136–37 *see also* lot
property 108–10, 116–44, 191–96
  citizens as *see* slavery
  not excluding the sovereign 16, 117–18, 126–31, 137–39, 143–44
  in oneself 121, 139–42
  prelegal claims to 121–22, 126, 140–44
prophecy 77
Propriety Argument 181, 191–97
prosopolepsia 96, 97–101, 111
Pufendorf, Samuel
  critic of Hobbes 30–31, 33–34, 46, 94, 129–30, 192, 196–97
  on property 119–21
  on war and self-defence 203–4, 217

punishment *see also* justice, criminal
  authorized 152–53, 254–55
  vs. hostility 254
  threats of 83, 85, 188, 260–61, 269–70
  and war 203–5

realism
  about international relations 16–17, 179–80, 199n.2, 224–25, 240–41
  political 269
  about war 199, 268–69
reason
  right 72–76
  of state 8–9, 16–17, 241
rebellion 3–4, 45, 145, 239–40, 242–62, 265, 269–70
  not punishable 252–56
reconstructionism 20–23
representation, of the people 166–67, 235–36
resistance, rights of 14, 24, 37–38, 151–53, 160, 175–76, 190, 254, 257
Revised Covenant Argument 180–81, 184–89, 191, 194–97
right intention 68, 185–86, 195, 213–15, 221, 238–40
right of nature 65–68, 208–9
  as blameless liberty 65–66, 73–74
  relational reading of 68, 73–74, 187, 266
  as subjective right 67–68, 73, 185, 201–2
  see also natural rights; right to everything
right to everything 49–50, 198
  as precluding property 118–19, 121, 132, 191–92, 197
  as right to rule 42–43, 229–30, 251
  as right to sin 64–65, 68, 186
  as right of war 66, 141, 198, 201–3, 229–30, 236–37
rights, types of
  claim-rights 21–22, 38–39, 47n.49
  liberties 35–36, 38–39, 133–34
  naked vs. vested 35–36, 41–42, 65–66, 118–19, 141
  of necessity 119–20, 142–43
  perfect vs. imperfect 12–13, 91–92, 104–6, 110
  territorial 197

scarcity 193n.26
Scripture *see* Bible
Security Argument 122–27, 137–38, 143–44, 192
self-defence, rights of 14, 65–66, 73–74, 201–9, 257–58 *see also* right of nature
Separability Thesis 16, 145–49, 172–75 *see also* legal positivism
serial composition 23

292 INDEX

sin 61–63, 69
Sinning with Right 63–65, 70–72, 186, 266–67
slavery 53n.63, 126–31, 151–52, 190
  citizenship equated with 128–31, 248–49
social contract
  of government 42–43, 268–69
  of property 119–21
  see also covenant
Sole Measure 145–46, 153–58, 165, 168, 175–76
Sources Thesis 16, 145–52, 175–76 *see also* legal
    positivism
sovereign
  accountable to God alone 86, 116, 136–37,
    173–74, 233–36, 240, 266–67
  duties of the 233–36
  moral wrongdoing 10–12, 56–59, 86, 112–13,
    116–17, 161–62
  prerogative 113–14, 138–39, 152–53, 255
  two bodies of the 174–75, 256–57
  vindicating the 4–5, 9–14, 54, 56–57, 86, 101–
    3, 116–17, 145–46, 159–60, 174–76, 196,
    240, 265–70
sovereignty
  absolute 8, 128–29, 168
  by acquisition 29–30, 51–54, 129–31
  arbitrary 8
  despotic *see* despotism
  by institution 29–30, 129–31
state *see* commonwealth
state of nature 50–54, 256–58 *see also* war
  absence of property in *see Statism about*
    Property
  covenants in 180–88, 215–16, 238–39
  disagreement in 72–74, 114–15, 120–
    21, 153–54
  exiting the 80–81, 182–83
  interpersonal vs. international 204–5, 223–
    27, 230–31
  no justice and injustice in *see Statism about*
    Justice
Statism about Justice 35–36n.21, 179–97,
    258

Statism about Property 117–18, 125–27, 135–37,
    192–97, 204–5
Suárez, Francisco
  on justice 32–33, 91–92, 100–1, 107
  on law and equity 94–95, 147, 227–28
  on war and self-defence 207–9, 223
subject *see* citizen

taxation 100–1, 102–3, 126–27, 137–39
theodicy
  civil 10, 265
  divine 10
Thucydides 221, 241
treason 243–47, 252–56
treaties, international 16–17, 196–97,
    235, 238–39
truce *see* covenant of peace
trust 198, 217–19 *see also* distrust
Tyrrell, James 33–34, 186, 216n.90

Untraceable Intentions 64–71, 73–74, 79, 86,
    186, 215–17, 221

vain-glory 213–14, 234
Vattel, Emer de 219–20, 226n.9, 232, 247–48
virtue
  of justice 83–85, 194–95, 269–70
  moral vs. personal 75–76
Vitoria, Francisco de 200, 207–8, 223

war
  of all against all 203, 212, 217, 226
  civil 239–40
  defensive 198, 207, 210–12, 221, 237–38, 241
  international 218, 224–27
  laws of 219–20, 247–48, 256
  preventive 202–3, 205–6, 210–12, 215–18,
    226–27, 237–38
  see also state of nature
Wolff, Christian 232, 247–48
worth 104–8
wrong *see* injury